Application of Artificial Intelligence in Production and Services

Edited by

Pancham Singh
Department of Computer Science
Engineering and Information Technology
Ajay Kumar Garg Engineering College
Ghaziabad, Uttar Pradesh
India

Avinash Kumar Sharma
Department of Computer Science & Engineering (CSE)
Sharda School of Computing Science & Engineering (SSCSE)
Sharda University
Greater Noida, Uttar Pradesh
India

Mrignainy Kansal
Department of Computer Science and Engineering
Netaji Subhas University of Technology (NSUT)
New Delhi, India

&

Amarjeet Prajapati
Department of Computer Science
Engineering and Information Technology
Jaypee Institute of Information Technology
Noida, Uttar Pradesh
India

Application of Artificial Intelligence in Production and Services

Editors: Pancham Singh, Avinash Kumar Sharma, Mrignainy Kansal and Amarjeet Prajapati

ISBN (Online): 979-8-89881-417-5

ISBN (Print): 979-8-89881-418-2

ISBN (Paperback): 979-8-89881-419-9

Published by Bentham Science Publishers Pte. Ltd. Singapore, in collaboration with
Eureka Conferences, USA.

First published in 2026.

Bentham Science Publishers Pte. Ltd.
No. 9 Raffles Place
Office No. 26-01
Singapore 048619
Singapore
Email: subscriptions@benthamscience.net

BENTHAM SCIENCE

CONTENTS

FOREWORD

In the rapidly evolving landscape of technology, few fields have captured the imagination and potential of industries and societies alike as profoundly as Artificial Intelligence (AI). The transformative power of AI lies not only in its ability to revolutionize processes and create new opportunities but also in its capacity to redefine what is possible across a multitude of sectors. It is with great enthusiasm that I introduce Application of Artificial Intelligence in Industry and Services, a timely and comprehensive resource that addresses the growing need for accessible, practical knowledge in this critical field.

As someone who has dedicated a significant part of my career to exploring and advancing the frontiers of AI, I am particularly impressed by the scope and depth of this book. The editors, Pancham Singh, Mrignainy Kansal, Dr. Avinash Kumar Sharma, Dr. Ritu Sibal, and Dr. Amarjeet Prajapati have brought together a collection of insights that not only demystify AI but also highlight its real-world applications across various industries. This is a book that speaks to both the novice and the expert, offering clear explanations of complex concepts while simultaneously pushing the boundaries of what we understand about AI's role in modern industry and services.

One of the standout aspects of this book is its focus on practical applications. In a real world where AI is increasingly integrated into everyday processes from healthcare and agriculture to manufacturing and digital marketing, it is crucial that we understand not just the theory behind AI, but also how it is being utilized to drive innovation and efficiency. This book succeeds in bridging the gap between abstract concepts and tangible outcomes, providing readers with a roadmap for how AI can be leveraged to meet real-world challenges. Moreover, the editors have wisely included discussions on some of the most cutting-edge and forward-thinking areas of AI research, such as quantum computing and sustainable AI practices. These fields represent the next wave of technological advancement and are critical for anyone looking to stay ahead of the curve. The inclusion of these topics underscores the book's relevance and its importance as a resource for those who are serious about understanding the future of AI. In addition to its technical and practical insights, this book also addresses the broader ethical and societal implications of AI. As AI continues to permeate more aspects of our lives, it is imperative that we consider the impact of this technology on individuals, communities, and the environment. The discussions in this book encourage readers to think critically about these issues, fostering a more holistic understanding of AI's role in society.

It is my belief that the *Application of Artificial Intelligence in Industry and Services* will become an essential reference for anyone involved in AI, whether they are students, researchers, or industry professionals. The knowledge contained within these pages is not just valuable, it is necessary for anyone looking to navigate the complex and ever-changing landscape of AI. I commend the editors and contributors for their outstanding work in creating a book that is both informative and inspiring. It is a privilege to write this foreword and to endorse a book that I am confident will have a lasting impact on the field of Artificial Intelligence.

Girija Chetty
Head of School of IT and Systems
University of Canberra
Australia

PREFACE

In an era where technology is rapidly evolving and integrating into every facet of our lives, Artificial Intelligence (AI) stands out as one of the most transformative and influential fields. The journey of AI, from its inception to its current state, has been marked by ground breaking discoveries, innovative applications, and profound societal impacts. This book, titled Application of Artificial Intelligence in Industry and Services, seeks to illuminate the latest developments in AI, offering a comprehensive guide that bridges the gap between theoretical knowledge and practical applications.

The primary aim of this book is to demystify the complexities of AI, making it accessible to a broad audience, including students, professionals, and experts who are keen to explore the frontiers of AI research. We have endeavoured to present AI concepts in a clear, straightforward manner, ensuring that readers of varying expertise levels can grasp the fundamental and advanced concepts in the subject.

One of the key features of this book is its focus on practical applications. Each chapter delves into how AI is revolutionizing different industries, from healthcare and robotics to environmental science and sustainable development. By showcasing real-world examples, we hope to demonstrate the tangible benefits and challenges of AI, emphasizing its relevance in today's global landscape.

Moreover, this book explores emerging trends that are shaping the future of AI, such as the intersection of quantum computing and AI, as well as the rise of sustainable AI practices. These discussions are not just technical; they also touch upon the ethical implications of AI, prompting readers to consider the broader impact of this powerful technology on society.

As we look ahead, the potential of AI appears boundless. This book concludes with speculative discussions on where AI might be headed, aiming to spark the imagination of our readers and encourage forward-thinking dialogue.

We believe this book will serve as a valuable resource for anyone interested in understanding and leveraging AI in their respective fields. Whether you are an academic, a practitioner, or simply someone curious about AI, we hope this book will inspire you to engage with AI in meaningful and impactful ways.

We are grateful to the contributors and experts who have shared their knowledge and insights, making this book a comprehensive and authoritative guide to the world of AI. We hope that as you turn the pages, you find the clarity, inspiration, and depth that you seek in your journey through the fascinating realm of Artificial Intelligence.

Pancham Singh
Department of Computer Science
Engineering and Information Technology
Ajay Kumar Garg Engineering College
Ghaziabad, Uttar Pradesh
India

Avinash Kumar Sharma
Department of Computer Science & Engineering (CSE)
Sharda School of Computing Science & Engineering (SSCSE)
Sharda University
Greater Noida, Uttar Pradesh
India

Mrignainy Kansal
Department of Computer Science and Engineering
Netaji Subhas University of Technology (NSUT)
New Delhi, India

&

Amarjeet Prajapati
Department of Computer Science
Engineering and Information Technology
Jaypee Institute of Information Technology
Noida, Uttar Pradesh
India

List of Contributors

Ajay Bahadur	Department of Commerce & Management, GNIOT Institute of Professional Studies, Greater Noida, Uttar Pradesh, India
Ajeet Kumar Sharma	Department of Computer Science & Engineering (CSE), Sharda School of Computing Science & Engineering (SSCSE), Sharda University, Greater Noida, Uttar Pradesh, India
Anju Saha	Department of CSE, USICT, GGS Indraprastha University, Delhi, India
Anasuya Patil	Department of Pharmacy, KLE College of Pharmacy, KLE University- 590010, Bengaluru, Karnataka, India
Anurag Sati	Department of CSE & IT, Jaypee Institute of Information Technology (JIIT), Noida, India
Arpit Saxena	Department of Commerce & Management, GNIOT Institute of Professional Studies, Greater Noida, Uttar Pradesh, India
Ashi Agarwal	Department of Computer Science, ABES Engineering College, Ghaziabad, Uttar Pradesh, India
Asheesh Tiwari	Department of Computer Science & Applications, GLA University, Mathura, India
Asmita Yadav	Department of CSE & IT, Jaypee Institute of Information Technology (JIIT), Noida, India
Atul Sharma	Department of CSE &IT, Jaypee Institute of Information Technology (JIIT), Noida, India
Avinash Kumar Sharma	Department of Computer Science & Engineering (CSE), Sharda School of Computing Science & Engineering (SSCSE), Sharda University, Greater Noida, Uttar Pradesh, India
Ayushi Bhatnagar	School of Life and Basic Sciences, Jaipur National University, Jaipur, India
Bharti Chugh	Department of CSE, Krishna Institute of Engineering & Technology (KIET), Ghaziabad, Uttar Pradesh, India
C. Chellaswamy	Department of Electronics and Communication Engineering, SRM TRP Engineering College, Tiruchirappalli 621105, Tamil Nadu, India
C. Reginamary	Department of Electronics and Communication Engineering, MRK Institute of Technology, Kattumannarkoil 608301, Tamil Nadu, India
Deepika Yadav	Department of Computer Science, Bharati Vidyapeeth's College of Engineering, New Delhi, India
G. Gandhimathi	Department of Electronics and Communication Engineering, SRM TRP Engineering College, Tiruchirappalli 621105, Tamil Nadu, India
Gagan Tyagi	Department of Development, Technical Architect, Tech Mahindra, Noida, Uttar Pradesh, India
Jaishree Jain	Department of Computer Science and Engineering, Ajay Kumar Garg Engineering College, Ghaziabad, Uttar Pradesh, India
Jayasankar Narayanan	Department of Pharmacy, SRM Institute of Science and Technology, Potheri, Tamil Nadu, India

Juhi Sharma	School of Life and Basic Sciences, Jaipur National University, Jaipur, India
Kranthi Kumar K.	Department of Pharmaceutics, Lloyd Institute of Management and Technology, Greater Noida, Uttar Pradesh, India
Kratika Pathak	School of Life and Basic Sciences, Jaipur National University, Jaipur, India
Laxmi Pandey	Department of PGDM, Institute of Management Studies (IMS), Ghaziabad, Uttar Pradesh, India
Mradul Kumar Jain	Department of Computer Science and Engineering, Ajay Kumar Garg Engineering College, Ghaziabad, Uttar Pradesh, India
Mrignainy Kansal	Department of Computer Science and Engineering, Netaji Subhas University of Technology (NSUT), New Delhi, India
Mufti Mohammad Usman	Department of CSE & IT, Jaypee Institute of Information Technology (JIIT), Noida, India
Pancham Singh	Department of Computer Science, Engineering and Information Technology, Ajay Kumar Garg Engineering College, Ghaziabad, Uttar Pradesh, India
Pankaj Bhatt	Department of Pharmaceutics, Lloyd Institute of Management and Technology, Greater Noida, Uttar Pradesh, India
Pawan Kumar	Department of Computer Science and Engineering, Ajay Kumar Garg Engineering College, Ghaziabad, Uttar Pradesh, India
Preeti Garg	Department of CSE, KIET Group of Institutions, Ghaziabad, Uttar Pradesh, India
Preeti Jain	Department of Management, Ajay Kumar Garg Institute of Management, Ghaziabad, Uttar Pradesh, India
Princy Tyagi	Department of Computer Science & Engineering, Swami Rama Himalayan University, Dehradun, Uttarakhand, India
R. Venkatesh	Department of Physics, PSNA College of Engineering and Technology (Autonomous), Dindigul 624622, Tamil Nadu, India
Rakesh Kumar	Department of Computer Science & Applications, GLA University, Mathura, India
Rashi Singhal	Department of PGDM, Institute of Management Studies (IMS), Ghaziabad, Uttar Pradesh, India
Ruchira Goel	Department of Applied Science, Ajay Kumar Garg Engineering College, Ghaziabad, Uttar Pradesh, India
Saurabh Singhal	Department of Computer Science & Engineering (CSE), Sharda School of Computing Science & Engineering (SSCSE), Sharda University, Greater Noida, Uttar Pradesh, India
Shivani Jain	Department of CSE, SCSET, Bennett University, Greater Noida, Uttar Pradesh, India
Shweta Ran	Department of CSE & IT, Jaypee Institute of Information Technology, Noida, Uttar Pradesh, India
Sidham Jain	Department of CSE & IT, Jaypee Institute of Information Technology (JIIT), Noida, India
Sonika Niraj Motan	School of Allied Health Sciences, Jaipur National University, Jaipur, India

Tushar Gupta	Department of CSE &IT, Jaypee Institute of Information Technology (JIIT), Noida, India
Uma Maheshwari K.	Department of Electronics and Communication Engineering, SRM TRP Engineering College, Tiruchirappalli 621105, Tamil Nadu, India
Updesh Kumar Jaiswal	Department of Computer Science and Engineering, Ajay Kumar Garg Engineering College, Ghaziabad, Uttar Pradesh, India
Vema Kiran	School of Pharmaceutical Sciences, Mohan Babu University (MBU), Tirupati, Andhra Pradesh, India
Vinay Choudhary	Department of Ophthalmology, JNU Institute of Medical Sciences and Research Center, Jaipur, India
Vinesh	Department of Commerce & Management, GNIOT Institute of Professional Studies, Greater Noida, Uttar Pradesh, India
Yash Singh	Department of CSE &IT, Jaypee Institute of Information Technology (JIIT), Noida, India

CHAPTER 1

A Journey Through the Evolution of Code Smell Detection Tools and Techniques

Shivani Jain[1] and **Anju Saha**[2,*]

[1] *Department of CSE, SCSET, Bennett University, Greater Noida, Uttar Pradesh, India*

[2] *Department of CSE, USICT, GGS Indraprastha University, Delhi, India*

Abstract: Code smells are prevalent indicators of suboptimal design implementation within source code. Detecting and refactoring these smells can significantly improve code quality and maintenance ease, while neglecting them can amplify technical debt and render systems obsolete. In recent years, researchers have contributed diverse techniques and tools to facilitate the identification of code smells. This article comprehensively reviews the current state-of-the-art strategies for code smell detection. It scrutinizes findings from fifty-eight studies spanning the period from 2004 to 2024. The article provides an inventory of available code smell detection tools, delving deeply into their principal features, detection strategies, and prospects of availability. The study identifies promising avenues for improving code-smell detection tools and proposes directions for future research. The insights and recommendations presented in this chapter serve as a compass for developers and researchers, guiding them in creating and adopting code-smell detection tools, ultimately advancing the quality and maintainability of software systems.

Keywords: Code smell detection, Literature review, Machine learning, Software maintainability, Tool evaluation.

INTRODUCTION

Software systems are embedded in our day-to-day lives, and their importance continues to grow as technology advances. Developing and maintaining them requires lots of time, capital, and effort. Unfortunately, they become obsolete over time; one reason is the ignorance of code smells. A code smell is a structural flaw in source code that violates fundamental design principles [1]. The presence of code smells can reduce maintainability, readability, and reusability, degrade system performance, prevent changes, and increase technical debt. Code smells should always be addressed, as they can result in future errors, defects, and faults.

* **Corresponding author Anju Saha:** Department of CSE, USICT, GGS Indraprastha University, Delhi, India; E-mails: anju@ipu.ac.in

Pancham Singh, Avinash Kumar Sharma, Mrignainy Kansal, & Amarjeet Prajapati (Eds.)

Unlike syntax errors, which are easily detectable by compilers, smells are difficult to spot but are a necessary component of the maintenance phase [2]. A complete list of code smells and their categorization is presented in Table 1.

Table 1. Definition and categorization of code smells.

Code Smell	Definition and Examples
Bloaters	Gigantic classes or methods that become difficult to understand and manage. *e.g.* - Long Method **(LM)**, Large Class **(LC)**, Primitive Obsession **(PO)**, Long Parameter List **(LPL)**, Data Clumps **(DCL)**.
Object-Oriented Abusers	Incomplete or incorrect employment of object-oriented programming principles. *e.g.* - Alternative Classes with Different Interfaces **(ACDI)**, Refused Bequest **(RB)**, Switch Statements **(SS)**, Temporary Field **(TF)**.
Change Preventers	To introduce change, one has to change other modules. *e.g.* - Divergent Change **(DIC)**, Parallel Inheritance Hierarchies **(PIH)**, Shotgun Surgery **(SHS)**.
Dispensable	Superfluous code, like dead or duplicated code. *e.g.* - Comments, Duplicate Code **(DUC)**, Data Class **(DC)**, Dead Code **(DEC)**, Lazy Class **(LAC)**, Speculative Generality **(SG)**.
Couplers	Significantly interdependent classes and methods that share too many objects and data. *e.g.* - Feature Envy **(FE)**, Inappropriate Intimacy **(II)**, Incomplete Library Class **(ILC)**, Message Chains **(MC)**, Middle Man **(MM)**.

Code smell can occur for various reasons, such as poorly structured or poorly designed code that results in complex or redundant code, making it difficult to maintain and update. Overly complex logic, a lack of abstraction and testing, and quick fixes and short-term solutions are other reasons that contribute to the problem. Code written by developers with different coding styles and practices can lead to code smells, as it can be challenging to maintain consistent coding standards.

Detecting code smells in software systems can be a challenging task due to several factors, including:

- **Code complexity:** As software systems grow in size and complexity, it becomes more difficult to detect code smells because they can be hidden in convoluted code structures.
- **Contextual knowledge:** Code smells can be highly contextual, meaning that they may not be easily detected by automated tools without an understanding of the code's intended functionality and design.
- **False positives and false negatives:** Smell detection tools may produce false positives (*i.e.*, identifying code smells that are not actually present) or false negatives (*i.e.*, missing code smells that are actually present), leading to incorrect or incomplete assessments of the code quality.

- **Lack of standardization:** Code smells are not standardized, and different experts may use varying definitions and criteria for identifying them, leading to inconsistent detection.
- **Tool limitations:** Some smell-detection tools may be limited in their ability to detect certain types of code smells or may not support all programming languages, making them challenging to use across different software development contexts.

Addressing these challenges requires a multifaceted approach that combines automated smell-detection tools with manual code reviews by experts with a deep understanding of the code's design and intended functionality. It also requires continuous learning and improvement of the code smell detection tools to increase their accuracy and reduce false positives and negatives.

Code refactoring can be done to address smells and improve the code base [3]. Refactoring is a quick, small strategic change to code to eliminate code smells. It modifies the internal structure without changing the exterior functionality. It can be done during code reviews, fixing or troubleshooting errors, and incorporating new features. As a result, the system's internal structure becomes more robust, readable, efficient, maintainable, and less complex. It improves overall performance, scalability, and security, and reduces entropy, coupling, and rigidity in the system. It can be done manually or with the aid of tools. There are risks involved in refactoring [4]. It may require significant changes to existing code, which can disrupt ongoing development activities. It can introduce new bugs or break existing functionality, especially if the refactoring is not thoroughly tested. It can be time-consuming and require significant resources like development time, testing, and code review. It can sometimes lead to code that is more complex and harder to maintain, rather than improving the quality of the code [5]. Without clear goals, refactoring can lead to wasted effort or, even worse, introduce bugs. In conclusion, while refactoring can lead to significant benefits, weighing each risk and approaching it carefully, with a clear goal and a solid testing plan to avoid potential issues, is crucial.

RELATED WORK

There is a wide variety of literature reviews that pointed out current gaps in research, pros and cons of code smell detection tools, most widely analyzed smells, refactoring practices, and the impact of smells on quality attributes. Some of the related studies are presented below.

Mens [6] presented a comprehensive overview of research on software refactoring and restructuring. The classification was based on five criteria: supported refactoring activities, techniques, artifact types, tool development considerations, and impact on the development process. Key open challenges were identified. The need for formalisms, methods, and tools to enhance consistency, scalability, and flexibility in refactoring emerged. Despite increasing commercial tools, ongoing research is vital to uncover and address tool limitations in software refactoring.

Fontana *et al.* [7] conducted an experiment involving five code smell detection tools and highlighted their shortcomings. They observed challenges in tool usability and noted insufficient documentation. The deduction rules employed and the metric thresholds were not immediately apparent. Additionally, the tools used anonymous inner classes that lacked customization to suit specific scenarios.

Hamid *et al.* [8] conducted a comparative study of the code-detection capabilities of JDeodrant and InCode. Detection of code smells, such as God Class and Feature Envy, was tested on two versions of the XtremeMP software project. The tools disagreed with each other due to their different approaches [9, 10].

Fernandes *et al.* [11] did a comparative study of code smell detection tools. They found 84 tools in the literature, and twenty-nine were available online. They employed six detection techniques to detect sixty-one code smells in C, C++, C#, and Java. Tools like infusion [12], PMD [13], and JSpIRIT [14] provided redundant detection results for the same code smell and had prevalent usability issues.

Dallal and Abdin *et al.* [15] empirically evaluated the impact of Object-Oriented refactoring techniques on several internal and external quality attributes. The findings revealed that diverse refactoring scenarios can produce contrasting effects on various quality attributes. Hence, the notion that refactoring universally enhances all facets of software quality must be revised. While the vote-counting study effectively illuminated the influence of specific refactoring scenarios on internal quality factors such as cohesion, coupling, complexity, inheritance, and size [16]. It fell short in assessing impacts on external and additional internal quality attributes due to limited data.

Palomba *et al.* [17] conducted an empirical study to find the lifecycle of code smell co-occurrences. It implied that 59% of smelly classes are affected by multiple code smells, and scheduled refactoring actions eliminate smell co-occurrences. Method-level code smells may be the root cause of introducing class-level smells. It concluded that more research should focus on designing co-occurrence-aware code-smell detectors and refactoring approaches. Finally, code-smell co-occurrences are generally removed together, leading to the deletion of the affected code components and requiring significant restructuring or a scheduled refactoring action.

Hozano *et al.* [18] conducted a large-scale empirical study with 75 developers to examine the interpretation of 15 code smells and their detection strategies. The study revealed that developers have very different perspectives on detecting code smells, and the specific heuristics they employ consistently influence agreement. Factors such as their educational background and industry experience did not consistently influence the agreement among the developers.

Sobrinho *et al.* [19] presented an extensive systematic review focusing on the 5 W's of code smells - Which smells are the most studied? When was there a boom in research? What are the most common research topics and problems explored? Who are the most famous researchers, and where is most research happening? Duplicated Code, Large Class, Feature Envy, Long Method, and Data Class are the most studied smells in the literature. Researchers have proposed alternative interpretations and synonyms for existing code smells, showcasing a fractured definition landscape. This divergence stems from a lack of a systematic or formal taxonomy for classifying code anomalies. Notably, this study area has grown in popularity, garnering increased recognition within the scientific community. Smell detection and impact is the most researched area, and prevention is the least. The study identified various tools employed in experiments for addressing smells, yet many lack accessible implementations, hindering their usability and impeding reproducibility. Interestingly, publicly available tools can effectively detect most smells.

Sabir *et al.* [20] conducted a systematic literature review to explore pivotal techniques for detecting smells across diverse software engineering paradigms, spanning from object-oriented (OO) to service-oriented (SO). The study identified two primary methods:

1. Static source code analysis, encompassing variants like behavioural, empirical, algorithm-based, methodology-based, and linguistic analysis, and
2. Dynamic source code analysis employing dynamic threshold adaptation, often employing genetic algorithms to replace fixed thresholds. Noteworthy detection techniques, transcending domains, include those relying on (a) Source code metrics, (b) SVN or CVS-based source code mining, (c) Domain-Specific Language, (d) Genetic Algorithms, and (e) Parallel Evolutionary Algorithm.

Azeem *et al.* [21] presented a meta-analysis of machine learning-based code smell detection techniques. The analysis revealed a prominent emphasis on code smells like God Class, Long Method, Functional Decomposition, and Spaghetti Code in the literature. Machine learning primarily leans on Decision Trees and Support Vector Machines. JRip and Random Forest emerge as standout classifiers in terms of performance. Successful models leverage numerous independent variables.

Moreover, these findings highlight existing challenges that demand further research.

Aljedaani *et al.* [22] conducted an exhaustive literature review to curate a repository of twenty-two tools. Subsequently, they undertake a comparative examination to delineate the range of smell types detected by each tool. They highlight significant attributes, including programming language compatibility, testing framework support, detection methodology, and adoption trends. Their investigation unveils that tools are proficient in identifying test smells within Java, Scala, Smalltalk, and C++ test suites, with Java enjoying the most widespread backing. These tools manifest as command-line utilities and IDE plugins. The analysis underscores notable overlap among tools in detecting specific smell types, such as General Fixtures.

Reis *et al.* [23] presented a systematic literature review on tools and techniques for code smell detection and visualization. Detecting code smells remains challenging. They highlighted the need to minimize subjectivity in defining and identifying smells. Expand the range of detected smells and supported languages. Create and share datasets to facilitate replicable validation of detection and visualization techniques. The dominant methods for identifying code smells include search-based and metric-based approaches. Most studies opt for open-source software, predominantly using Java. God Class, Feature Envy, and Long Method are the most analyzed smells. In many studies, machine learning is utilized, often employing Genetic Programming, Decision Trees, SVM, and Association Rules. Visualization-based approaches vary, using methods like city metaphors, 3D visualization, interactive ambient visualization, polymetric views, and graph models.

CODE SMELL DETECTION TECHNIQUES

This segment delineates the methodology employed to conduct the review while mitigating the potential influence of researcher bias. The method encompasses several vital steps, including identifying research questions, formulating a comprehensive search strategy, establishing criteria for study selection, and executing the associated data extraction and analytical procedures.

Search Strategy

There has been substantial research over the years on techniques for detecting code smells. The search process of a literature review is a critical step to ensure the comprehensive and unbiased identification of relevant research papers [24]. The objective was to unveil all the applicable techniques to detect smells. A comprehensive and relevant search string was developed that captured the main concepts related to the research questions. The search string that was formed using the search terms is given below: *(CodeSmell OR DesignSmell OR AntiPattern OR BadSmell) AND (Tool OR Technique OR Method OR Procedure) AND (Detection OR Prediction OR Identification)*

Academic databases were searched, including IEEE Xplore, ACM Digital Library, Scopus, Springer Link, Science Direct, Web of Science, Google Scholar, and conference proceedings. A preliminary search using the search string is conducted to assess its effectiveness and relevance. Out of 365 articles, suitable studies were selected based on publication date, study design, target population, and language. This step ensures that the search focuses on the most relevant studies [25]. The titles and abstracts of the retrieved papers were reviewed to determine their relevance to the research objective. Papers that did not meet the requirements were eliminated.

The full-text versions of the selected documents were obtained and read after the screening. Manual searches in crucial journals, conference proceedings, and other relevant sources were conducted to identify additional studies that might have been missed in the database search. Relevant data from the selected studies, including study characteristics, methodology, findings, and conclusions, were extracted. The quality and validity of the included studies were checked. This step ensures that the selected studies meet the required standards of evidence. The findings from the selected studies are synthesized and presented. The literature review below is comprehensive, reliable, and follows a rigorous and transparent methodology. Sixty-nine studies were selected from the year 2004 to 2024. The techniques are presented in chronological order and can be divided into the following categories:

Metric-Based Detection Techniques

Methodologies that use software metrics for smell identification fall under this category. This may include evaluating optimized threshold values for differentiating smelly from non-smelly code components. The following are the studies implementing metric-based strategies.

Marinescu *et al.* [26] devised metrics-based rules to identify ten code smells, including Shotgun Surgery, Refused Bequest, God Class, *etc.* He created a methodology for converting an informal design rule into a detection strategy and validated this approach through experimental verification across various extensive case studies. To find threshold values, he reviewed literature studies, used a tuning machine, and analyzed historical versions of the system.

Munro *et al.* [27] introduced a novel metric-driven detection method wherein they defined code smells using a template comprising three principal components: a name for the code smell, a textual depiction detailing its characteristics, and heuristics for its identification. This technique successfully identified two object-oriented code smells, Lazy Class and Temporary Field. He employed software metrics and threshold values on two Java-based systems for validation.

Researchers [28] have proposed definitions of various metrics and threshold values for detecting bad smells related to Aspect-Oriented Programming. A total of eight code smells, including Borrowed Cutpoint, Identical Role, and Junk Material, among others, underwent testing and validation across multiple methods within telecom software.

Bertran *et al.* [29] introduced a group of architecturally relevant code smells and demonstrated their association with architectural deterioration. They put forth a collection of metrics and techniques for the early detection of these smells, aiming to forestall the emergence of errors and bugs.

An Eclipse plug-in named Bad Smell Detection Tool (BSDT) [30] was developed to detect code smells in Java systems. Smells, such as Large Class, Long Method, Long Parameter List, Switch Statements, Parallel Inheritance Hierarchies, Data Class, and Lazy Class, can be detected. It uses a pre-defined threshold value of software metrics for detection purposes.

JSNOSE *et al.* [31] developed a metric-based code smell detection tool for JavaScript smells. Thirteen specific code smells in JavaScript, including Closure Smells, Excessive Global Variables, Nested Callbacks, *etc.*, were introduced and defined. The tool employs static and dynamic client-side code analyses to identify these smells. The tool's ability to detect smells was evaluated across 11 web applications, yielding JSNOSE precision of 93% and recall of 98%.

Fontana *et al.* [32] proposed a data-driven technique to determine optimal threshold values for code metrics to help detect code smells. They have investigated five code smells: God Class, Data Class, Brain Method, Dispersed Coupling, and Shotgun Surgery, as well as Message Chain. The technique relied on the statistical distribution of metrics to select threshold values, and it applied a nonparametric procedure to eliminate the portion of the distribution that was not useful for thresholding. The thresholds were customized for each code smell by filtering the dataset for that code smell.

Chen *et al.* [33] introduced ten Python-based code smells and proposed a metric-based detection method. Some smells are Long Message Chains, Long Base Class Lists, Long Lambda Functions, Long Ternary Conditional Expressions, Complex

Container Comprehension, and Multiply-Nested Containers. Three different strategies to specify metric thresholds were used and compared: Experience-Based Strategy [34] (requires experienced technicians), Statistics-Based Strategy (uses statistical measurements), and Tuning Machine Strategy [35]. The tuning machine strategy establishes an example repository to adjust threshold values that ideally align with the results of manual inspection, and it achieved the highest accuracy when tested on 106 projects. The crucial observation was that Long Parameter Lists and Long Methods are more prevalent than other smells.

Singh *et al.* [36] established criteria for detecting two method-level code smells based on the functional and semantic characteristics of the method. Measures such as size, cyclomatic complexity, cohesion factor, and semantic relatedness were considered for identifying the Long Method. Detection of a Long Parameter List involves assessing both the size of the parameter list and the complexity of the data types within it. This technique demonstrated superior performance in empirical testing across six open-source systems when compared to contemporary methodologies [37].

Mayvan *et al.* [38] introduced an innovative metric-based approach for detecting code smells and identifying refactoring opportunities. Their methodology began with an extensive literature review to compile metric rules for various code smells. A comprehensive investigation was conducted on Duplicate Code, Request Bequest, Parallel Inheritance Hierarchy, Message Chain, Shotgun Surgery, Primitive Obsession, Divergent Change, *etc.* Subsequently, the most prevalent metrics were identified, and optimal threshold values were determined. Detected code smells were then subjected to the suggested refactoring. The efficacy of this approach was evaluated on three open-source systems and compared against Rasool *et al.* [39], CheckStyle [40], and PMD [41].

Semi-Automatic Techniques

Semi-automatic techniques for code smell detection combine automated tools with human intervention to identify and analyze potential code smells. These techniques leverage the strengths of both automated algorithms and developers' cognitive abilities to enhance the accuracy and relevance of the detection process. The following are the studies that follow a semi-automatic approach.

NosePrints *et al.* [42] developed a visualization tool to visually inspect defect warnings, allowing developers to filter out false positives quickly. A catalog of lightweight and coherent visualizations for Statement, Class, Method, and Collaboration code smells was introduced. It is a Visual Studio [43] plug-in that scans source or byte code to identify and visually present potential code smells.

They tested the scalability and feasibility of the tool on three industrial projects and two open-source projects.

Moha *et al.* [44] introduced the DEtection & CORrection (DECOR) methodology designed to elucidate four anti-patterns and fifteen code smells. They used rule cards formulated with a Domain-Specified Language (DSL) for each code smell. This approach is instantiated by DETection EXpert (DETEX), an automated component that facilitates the generation of detection algorithms. The DECOR method comprises five sequential steps: description analysis, specification, processing, detection, and validation. Its validation encompassed examination across eleven open-source systems, with precision and recall as performance metrics.

Carneiro *et al.* [45] created a tool to gauge how much multiple views contribute to visualizing code smells. The tool, SourceMiner, is an Eclipse plug-in designed to assist in evaluating concern views within Java source code. The tool is not limited to representing modular structures such as packages, classes, and methods; it also supports multiple concern views. They established and implemented four sets of views to illustrate the source code and the associated concerns affecting it: (i) The concern's package-class-method structure (size and complexity), (ii) The concern's inheritance-wise structure (size and inheritance), (iii) Concern dependency (coupling), and (iv) Concern dependency weight (coupling). The tool can visualize code smells like Divergent Change, God Class, and Feature Envy. Precision and recall values indicate that the multiple-view approach substantially supports code-smell identification.

Khomh *et al.* [46] used a Goal-Question-Metric (GQM)- based approach to build Bayesian Belief Networks (BBNs) for detecting anti-patterns, known as Bayesian DeTection EXpert (BDTEX). BBN was based on metrics and the properties of the anti-pattern for its development. Calibration was done automatically using Bayes' theorem. The validity of BDTEX was tested on two systems, Gantt Project v1.10.2 and Xerces v2.7.0. Three anti-patterns: Blob, Functional Decomposition, and Spaghetti Code were studied. It outperformed DECOR in terms of precision, recall, and utility for quality analysts.

The authors proposed an approach [47] for generating feedback based on anti-patterns that affect the performance of software systems, focusing on their representation and detection. They introduced a concept of modeling anti-patterns as logical predicates. They demonstrated the use of an engine to detect these anti-patterns in an XML representation of the software system. The validity of the approach was tested on the Electronic Commerce System (ECS) as a case study.

Palomba *et al.* [48] recommended a new technique to detect smells that cannot be identified by competitive approaches or solely by manual code analysis. Historical Information for Smell Detection (HIST) exploited change history to detect instances of five code smells: Divergent Change, Shotgun Surgery, Parallel Inheritance, Blob, and Feature Envy. The precision of HIST ranges between 72% and 86%, and its recall ranges between 58% and 100% when tested on twenty open source projects.

Hecht *et al.* [49] developed a PAPRIKA tool to detect four object-oriented and four Android code smells from binary code. The tool was tested on fifteen popular apps downloaded from the Google App Store. They discovered that anti-patterns implemented in the source code can be detected at the bytecode level. Both types of anti-patterns were found in all analyzed applications. Object-oriented anti-patterns are as present in Android applications as in non-mobile applications, except for the Swiss Army Knife anti-pattern. They discovered that Android-specific anti-patterns were more frequent than object-oriented anti-patterns.

Using the information retrieval method, researchers coined a novel technique called Textual Analysis for Code Smell Detection (TACO) [50]. It successfully detected five code smells, *i.e.*, Long Method, Feature Envy, Blob, Promiscuous Package, and Misplaced Class. It analyzed the properly decomposed textual blocks that compose a code component to apply information retrieval methods and measured the probability that a given smell affects the component. TACO's precision ranges from 67% to 77%, its recall from 72% to 84%, and it performed better than DECOR and Jdeodorant.

Palomba *et al.* [51] introduced ADOCTOR (AnDrOidCodesmell detecTOR), a novel code smell detector that identifies 15 Android-specific code smells. Code Smells were selected from the catalog proposed by Reimann *et al.* [52]. Some of them were Durable Wakelock, Inefficient Data Structure Public Data, Slow Loop, *etc.* The tool was validated on 18 Android applications. It was revealed that the tool reaches, on average, 98% of precision and 98% of recall.

Arcan [53] was developed for detecting Java architectural smells by evaluating several architectural dependency issues. Arcan can detect three architectural smells, *i.e.*, Cycle Dependency, Unstable Depen- dency, and Hub-Like Dependency. The detection techniques exploited graph database technology, allowing for high scalability in smell detection and better management of large amounts of dependencies of multiple kinds.

Android apps need specific permissions to function, but not all developers follow the guidelines for using them safely. This can lead to privacy and security risks for users. A tool called P-Lint [54] was developed to help catch these issues. It identified suspicious permission use in Android code, such as improper use of custom permissions, requesting permissions when intents could be used, improper usage of functionality, and inconsistent or confusing rationales. The tool was validated on 40 applications and yielded promising results.

Liu and Zhang *et al.* [55] developed a smell Detection Tool (DT) to detect code snippets affected by Duplicate Code and Feature Envy. The tool used a dynamic programming algorithm (DP) to determine similarities between code snippets or redundancy. To detect Feature Envy, an Abstract Syntax Tree (AST) is used, a tree structure that represents the grammatical structure of the source code. DT scored higher accuracy than detection tools like CheckStyle, PMD, iPlasma [56], and JDeodrant.

An extension tool for Arcan [57] was developed to detect five architectural smells- Unstable Dependency, Hub-Like Dependency, Cyclic Dependency, Multiple Architectural Smells, and Specification- Implementation Violation present in C and C++. The tool was built with four components: a) System Reconstructor, which traverses the project and extracts dependencies; b) Graph Manager, which builds the dependency graph; c) Metrics Engine, which computes the software metrics; and d) Architectural Smell Engine, which detects the architectural smells. The tool was validated using six open-source projects and performed well.

Palomba *et al.* [58] developed TASTE (Textual Analysis for Test Smell Detection) [58] that can detect three types of test smells in test cases- General Fixture, Eager Test, and Lack of Cohesion of Methods. The tool is a text-based tool that uses information retrieval techniques to identify smells. It can be elaborated into three main steps to detect test smell instances, *i.e.*, (i) Extraction of textual components from test cases, (ii) Text normalization, and (iii) Detection rule application. This technique performed better than two code-metrics-based strategies and was 44% more effective than structural-based techniques when tested on 12 Java systems [59, 60].

Gadient *et al.* [61] developed a static analysis tool that analyzes Android Inter-Component Communication (ICC) to detect security vulnerabilities and their corresponding smells. It was built on top of Android Lint. It implements the UastScanner and XmlScanner interfaces to check the presence of security code smells. Identification and feedback on 12 security code smells pertinent to ICC are provided within the IDE, and the tool was validated across 700 open-source apps. Some of the smells addressed are Persistent Dynamic Permission, Broken Service Permission, Custom Scheme Channel, Insecure Path Permission, Incorrect Protection Level, Broken Path Permission Precedence, *etc.*

Rahman *et al.* [62] developed a static analysis tool called Security Linter for Infrastructure as Code scripts (SLIC) that uses a rule-based approach. It identifies seven security smells in configuration scripts, such as empty passwords, the use of HTTP without TLS, invalid IP address bindings, and the use of weak cryptographic algorithms. They validated 1726 IaC scripts collected from 293 open-source repositories to identify security smells.

Li *et al.* [63] developed a static analysis tool called DLFinder to detect duplicate logging code smells, indicating a poor understanding of developers' dynamic view of the system. There are five patterns by which problematic duplicate logging manifests itself. They are as follows: detecting inadequate information in catch blocks, detecting inconsistent error-diagnostic information, detecting log message mismatch, detecting inconsistent log level, and detecting duplicate logs in polymorphism. The tool was tested on six systems: Hadoop, CloudStack, ElasticSearch, Cassandra, Camel, and Wicket. DLFinder successfully detected 72 out of the 82 instances when tested.

Another extension of the Arcan tool was also developed to address the issue of microservice smells [64]. Smells like Cyclic Dependencies, Hard-Coded Endpoints, and Shared Persistence were detected to reduce architectural debt. It used a static code analysis approach for detection and was validated across five open-source projects with a microservices architecture.

Kumara *et al.* [65] employed a semantic approach to detect smells related to deployment in cloud applications. They designed semantic models, called ontologies, to formally describe a deployment model using the Description and Situation (DnS) pattern. This ontology was based on TOSCA (Topology and Orchestration Specification for Cloud Applications) [66], which provides standardized descriptions of heterogeneous, distributed applications. SPARQL-based rules were used to define rules and detect smells in deployment models. Three case studies solidify the feasibility of the approach.

Borrelli *et al.* developed Unity Linter [67], a Static Code Analysis Tool (SCAT), to detect smells in Unity video games. Seven smells were selected after surveying 68 developers. Such smells covered various aspects of video game development, including performance issues (*e.g.*, allocating and destroying GameObjects in updates, heavyweight Update methods), maintainability issues (*e.g.*, lack of separation of concerns, coupling objects through the IDE inspector), and behavioral issues (animation speed depends on the frame rate). The tool was validated on 100 open-source projects, with precision ranging from 86% to 100% and recall ranging from 50% to 100%. Sources of imprecision and limited recall were due to the approximate data-flow analysis and other heuristics used in a lightweight analysis.

The MSANose tool [68] was developed to detect 11 microservice-specific code smells in distributed applications. Code smells such as Wrong Cuts, ESB Usage, Hard-Coded Endpoints, Shared Persistency, Cyclic Dependency, *etc.*, were analyzed. They validated the tool on two robust benchmark microservice applications and verified its accuracy. The results showed that smells can be detected within microservice applications using bytecode and/or source code analysis throughout the development process, and even before deployment to production.

Fatima *et al.* [69] developed an extension of Android Lint (AL) that can detect and correct twelve code smells and energy bugs to resolve quality and energy drain issues. Novel smells like No Low Memory Resolver, Public Data, Lifetime Containment, Long Wait State, *etc.*, and energy bugs such as Resource Leak, Vacuous Background Services, and Immortality Bug can be detected and corrected. The tool was validated across nine open-source applications; it detected smells and energy bugs with average precision, recall, and F-measure of 93%, 96%, and 94%, respectively. It accurately corrected 84% of selected code smells and energy bugs. The tool was compared with Android Lint [70], PMD, and SonarLint [71] in terms of coverage and with Paprika [49] in terms of performance.

Zhu *et al.* proposed a novel approach, DSIR (Design Smell Detection *via* Inter-class Relation) [72], which tackles the limitations of token-based [73] and Abstract Syntax Tree (AST)-based design smell detection methodologies. The source code was parsed for transformation into AST [74]. Preorder traversal was implemented to obtain a sequence of node tokens. A class-level semantic graph is generated for each target class from the UML class diagram. Then, BiLSTM (Bidirectional Long-Short Term Memory network with attention mechanism) [75] and R-GCN (Relational Graph Convolution Network) were applied separately, and the output of both models was combined by weight. 500 Java projects were selected from GitHub to build a new dataset with class-relation information to conduct experimentation [76]. DSIR outperformed Random Forest, ASTNN, and LSTM [77] by 31% in terms of F-measure.

Ferreira and Valente proposed a catalog of twelve code smells for React-based JavaScript applications and a ReactSniffer tool [78] to detect them. The smells were identified by conducting a grey literature review by analyzing 52 documents and interviewing six professional software developers. Some React smells included Large Component, Inheritance instead of Composition, Prop Drilling,

Force Update, Low Cohesion, *etc.* The tool had two components. First was a parser that generated an AST from the front-end file. The second was a smell-detection component that traversed the AST using a preorder algorithm to search for and inspect smelly React elements. The effectiveness of the tool was validated on ten GitHub projects. They discovered that the most commonly occurring React smells and removal rates range from 0.9% to 50.5%.

UnityLint [79] was developed to detect eighteen code smells in Unity video games. Smells related to animation, physics, rendering, design, and game life were addressed. The tool had two components. First was Fact Extractor, an analyzer that extracted facts from video game source code and metadata. The second was the Smell Detector, which leveraged detection rules to find smells on top of the extracted attributes. UnityLint was tested across 70 Unity open-source projects and achieved precision of 92% and recall of 85%.

Automatic Detection Techniques

Automatic techniques use tools and algorithms to identify patterns, structures, or characteristics in source code that may indicate code smells. These techniques aim to automate code-smell detection. Automatic techniques offer efficiency and scalability, allowing developers to identify and address code quality issues more systematically. The following are studies that are automatic in nature.

Ballis *et al.* [80] proposed a technique to detect smelly instances and anti-patterns in UML diagrams. UML represents the design structure of code, and early detection of anti-patterns can save effort and help build more robust systems. The visual representation was achieved by incorporating minimal graphical elements into UML to convey patterns and anti-patterns. The proposed notation is intended for integration into a tool's GUI front end. This tool demonstrated the capability to identify patterns and anti-patterns in design models.

Llano and Pooley *et al.* [81] focused on detecting and correcting Object-Oriented anti-patterns, such as God Class and Poltergeist. They proposed a language-independent approach and defined a UML-based specification for anti-patterns. They established design transformations for correction based on local and structural refactoring. It contributes to the future automation of code-smell detection and correction using a language-independent approach.

Nguyen *et al.* [82] developed WebScent to detect embedded code smells in dynamic web applications. These smells concern modularity and separation of concerns, resulting in more maintenance effort. A dynamic mapping method was employed, utilizing a PHP interpreter to execute server code and record the mapping of all fragments in the resulting client-side code to their original positions in the server code. Then, code smells were identified in the generated client-side code by analyzing both the client-side code and the corresponding positions of its elements in the server code. Finally, the tool located the embedded code smells within the corresponding positions in the server code based on the detected client-side code smells.

Arendt and Taentzer *et al.* [83] developed a tool to ensure the quality of model-based systems on the Eclipse Modeling Framework. It can evaluate system metrics and, based on that, detect code smells and refactor them. Its functionality can be set according to domain-specific and project-specific needs. Two custom QA plugins, called the specification module and the application modules, were developed. A set of 10 UML2 metrics was calculated on model instances with 100 to 1,00,000 elements to validate the metrics calculation module. Similarly, a set of seven selected smells and complex refactoring were analyzed for the smell detection and refactoring module.

Ligu *et al.* [84] proposed a technique to identify Refused Bequests developed by improper use of inheritance in Object-Oriented systems. It occurs when a subclass does not use inherited behavior and can be corrected by refactoring 'Replacement by Delegation'. To determine whether clients use inherited methods, the system's functionality is tested with appropriate unit tests to assess the essence of inheritance. An indicator of smell strength on a "thermometer" was derived from the outcomes of this approach and other structural data. The suggested method has been put into practice as an Eclipse plugin.

Kim *et al.* [85] proposed a methodology that defined code smells using OCL (Object Constraint Language). They first transformed Java source code into JavaAST (Java Abstract Syntax Tree) and then into JavaEAST (Java Extended AST) meta-model based on XML. They then detected a code smell using the specified OCL and refactored. The JavaEAST-based document is then again transformed into Java source code by reverse engineering. This method can detect six code smells, like Feature Envy, Refused Bequest, Switch Statements, Message Chains, *etc.*

Chaudron *et al.* [86] developed a PoSDef tool that identifies and prioritizes code smells in UML class diagrams. They compared its performance with two existing tools, SDMetrics and MetricView. The tool was validated using two open-source systems and one sizable industrial system. Users can decide which regions require prioritization and set objectives such as reducing coupling and increasing flexibility. The tool can then identify and prioritize smells, which can be addressed manually or with a refactoring tool.

Kumar and Chabra *et al.* [87] proposed a two-level dynamic analysis approach to detect Feature Envy, a method-level code smell. At the first level, they separate all methods suspected of being feature-envious by eliminating methods closely bound to their classes. At the second level, they identify the actual culprits by thoroughly analyzing their behavior during execution. The tool has fewer false negatives than the tools in Code and JDeodorant when applied to two Java open-source systems.

Vidal *et al.* [88] developed a tool called SpIRIT: Smart Identification of Refactoring opportunITies that detects ten types of smells in code and prioritizes them as well. It uses three criteria for prioritization: if the smelly component has undergone several changes over time, the developer's choice of smell to be treated, and smells that make modification difficult. Smells like Brain Class, Brain Method, Data Class, Disperse Coupling, Feature Envy, and Tradition Breaker are detected. Two case studies validated the efficiency of the tool.

Peruma *et al.* [89] developed TSDETECT, an automated test smell detection tool for Java software systems, whichuses a set of predefined detection rules to identify 19 types of test smells in test suites. Default Test, Duplicate Assert, Eager Test, Empty Test, Ignored Test, Lazy Test, Magic Number Test, Mystery Guest, *etc.* are some of the test smells addressed. The tool's effectiveness was tested on a benchmark of 65 unit test files containing instances of 19 test smell types and achieved an average precision score of 96% and an average recall score of 97%.

Machine and Deep Learning Based Detection Techniques

Machine Learning (ML) and Deep Learning (DL) techniques for code smell detection leverage the power of artificial intelligence to identify patterns and structures indicative of suboptimal coding practices automatically. Both techniques often depend on the quality and representativeness of the training data. The following are the machine and deep learning inspired studies.

Hassaine *et al.* [90] proposed IDS (Immune-based Detection Strategy), a machine-learning technique inspired by the human immune system, which draws parallels from AIS (Artificial Immune Systems), a classification algorithm, emulating the immune system's defense mechanisms. This approach established an analogy between human biology and system design. By utilizing metrics as features to identify "smelly" classes analogous to pathogens, IDS compared metric values of classes to those of detected smelly classes. The study revealed IDS's versatility beyond specific design smells, even identifying Large Class and Long Method smells. IDS surpassed DECO and BBN in precision and computation time while mitigating the bias inherent.

Bryton [91] used the Binary Logistic Regression (BLR) to derive the probability of the method being a long method. Long Method tries to centralize the intelligence of the class and is hard to modify and understand. This approach benefited from experts' knowledge and used statistical techniques to calibrate coefficients. It also ranked the instances of the Long Method by probability, and developer can prioritize their refactoring. True Positive Rate achieved by BLR was 86%, and True Negative Rate was 99%.

Maneerat and Muenchaisri *et al.* [92] proposed preemptive detection of design smells before implementation, enhancing software quality. Extracting twenty-seven software metrics from seven systems using Magic- Draw 9.5 SP1.1, a reverse engineering tool was developed, providing UML models and source code metrics. Machine learning models were trained to detect Lazy Class, Feature Envy, Middle Man, Message Chains, Long Method, *etc.* While Naive Bayes, VFI, and J48 fell short with prediction rates below 90%, Logistic Regression, IB1, IBk, and Random Forest exceeded 90%. Conclusively, no single machine learning algorithm could consistently forecast all targeted bad smells precisely.

Maiga *et al.* [93] introduced SMURF, a Support Vector Machine approach incorporating practitioners' feedback to detect Blob, Spaghetti Code, Functional Decomposition, and Swiss Army Knife. SMURF's accuracy, precision, and recall were superior to those of DETEX and BDTEX across three systems. Experimental results demonstrated SMURF's incremental nature, allowing for training set expansion. Unlike DETEX, SMURF offers applicability across subset, intra-system, and inter-system configurations. Moreover, practitioner feedback enhanced SMURF's accuracy, accentuating its effectiveness.

Peiris *et al.* [94] presented a machine-learning approach, called the Non-intrusive Performance Anti-pattern Detector (NiPAD), to classify anti-patterns that directly affect software performance. NiPAD implements Logistic Regression, Naive Bayes, Fisher's Linear Discriminant, and Support Vector Machines with Linear and RBF kernels. It can predict the presence of the 'One Lane Bridge' code smell with 94% accuracy.

Fontana *et al.* [95] implemented 32 variations of machine learning classifiers to detect four code smells, *i.e.*, Data Class, Feature Envy, Long Method, and God Class. They developed four datasets for each code smell by extracting object-oriented and quality metrics from 74 Java systems. They used existing detection tools (Advisors) to estimate the values of the dependent variables. A team of trained MSc students manually validated all datasets. J48 and JRIp algorithms were used to extract detection rules and to select the threshold values for the metrics. They claimed that 100 training examples are sufficient to achieve 95% accuracy, and that accuracy ranged from 85% to 99% across all algorithms.

Hadj-Kacem and Bouassida *et al.* [96] used a hybrid deep learning methodology to detect the four most common code smells - God Class, Data Class, Long Method, and Feature Envy. First, a deep auto-encoder is employed to reduce dimensionality, and then an Artificial Neural Network (ANN) is implemented as a classifier. The ANN consists of input, hidden, and output layers, in which neurons are connected, and each connection has a weight. Since it is a binary classification, the output neuron will determine whether it is a code smell. Precision, recall, and F-measure were above ninety percent for all cases.

Liu *et al.* [97] used deep neural networks and advanced deep learning techniques to automatically select features from source code to detect Feature Envy. These techniques can automatically build a complex mapping between features and predictions. A labeled training dataset was also generated without human intervention for the neural network-based classifier. This technique outperformed JDeodrant and JMove across seven open-source systems.

Mhawish and Gupta *et al.* [98] analyzed multiple feature selection techniques and machine learning classification algorithms for binary-label and multi-label datasets for code smell detection. The Min-Max technique was used to normalize the datasets, and to further improve accuracy, a genetic algorithm-based Naive Bayes and correlation-based feature selection were employed. Kernel-based algorithms, such as SVM with an RBF kernel function, and network-based algorithms were also applied [99]. Deep Neural Network, Multilayer Perceptron Algorithms (MLP); Tree-based algorithms - Decision Tree, Random Forest, and Gradient Boosted Trees were optimized using grid search. The tree-based algorithms achieved the best accuracy values.

Lin *et al.* [100] used a deep learning convolutional network to detect eight smells in source code. The code was transferred to an XML file so that convolutional networks could process it. Then, the code segment proposal leveraged the heuristic search to generate inputs. A high F-measure was recorded to detect Speculative Generality, Refused Bequest, Duplicate Code, Contrived complexity, Shotgun surgery, *etc.*

Sharma *et al.* [101] inspected the feasibility of deep learning methods for code smell detection. They used Convolution Neural Networks and Recurrent Neural Networks as their principal hidden layers and autoencoder models. Four smells-Complex Method, Complex Conditional, Feature Envy, and Multifaceted Abstraction were detected and tested on the 1, 072 C# and 100 Java repositories.

Results showed that transfer learning is feasible for implementation smells with performance comparable to direct learning.

Ho *et al.* [102] proposed a fusion of deep learning techniques, DEEPSMELLS, to detect Complex Methods, Complex Conditional, Feature Envy, and Multifaceted Abstraction. A deep Convolutional Neural Network (CNN) was employed to learn the complex hierarchical representations of the code fragments. Then, the Long Short-Term Memory (LSTM) recurrent neural network was applied serially to improve the quality of the context encoding and preserve semantic information. Deep neural networks classify with a weighted loss function to reduce the impact of skewed data distribution. This approach outperformed AE-Dense, AE-CNN, and AE-LSTM.

Search-Based Detection Techniques

Search-based techniques for code smell detection involve using optimization algorithms to find optimal threshold values and detection rules, and to tune the hyperparameters of supervised machine learning algorithms, *etc.* Some of the studies employing search-based techniques are as follows.

Kessentini *et al.* [103] developed detection rules using a Genetic Algorithm (GA) to detect Blob, Spaghetti Code, and Functional Decomposition. They validated their approach on two open-source systems, GanttPro ject and Xerces. GA performed 75% better than Harmony Search, Particle Swarm Optimization, and Simulated Annealing in evaluating optimal detection rules.

Ouni *et al.* [104] used search-based techniques to detect and correct three code smells: Blob, Spaghetti Code, and Functional Decomposition. Genetic Programming was used to generate detection rules to identify code smells, and NSGA-II (Non-dominated Sorting Genetic Algorithm) was implemented to select refactoring techniques that reduce correction effort. Moreover, the approach was validated on six open-source Java projects and outperformed DÉCOR.

Boussa *et al.* proposed a novel strategy, the Competitive CoEvolutionary Algorithm (CCEA) [105], for detecting Blob, Spaghetti Code, and Functional Decomposition. It combined the generation of code-smell examples with the production of detection rules based on quality metrics. Two populations were evolved simultaneously, with the first generating a set of detection rules that maximized the coverage of a set of code smell examples. The second one maximized the number of "artificial" code smells generated that were not covered by solutions from the first population. When tested across four open-source systems, the CCEA approach performed much better (at the 99% confidence level) than existing single-population approaches, Genetic Programming, and Artificial Immune Systems.

A search-based technique called cooperative Parallel Evolutionary Algorithms (CPEA) with random search was presented by Kessentini *et al.* [106], in which two populations evolved in parallel. The first population generated a set of detection rules using genetic programming. Simultaneously, a second population attempted to detect code smells by comparing code against examples of well-designed code. Both populations were evaluated on the same system, and the solutions were penalized based on the consensus, *i.e.*, the intersection of the detection results of both populations. The CPEA is more effective than DECOR and Jdeodorant, based on a benchmark of nine sizeable open-source systems, where more than 85% precision and recall were achieved across eight code smells.

Ouni *et al.* [107] introduced a multi-objective search-based tool MORE based on the Nondominated Sorting Genetic Algorithm (NSGA-III). It detected seven code smells (God Class, Feature Envy, Data Class, Spaghetti Code, Shotgun Surgery, Lazy Class, and Long Parameter List) and introduced four patterns (Visitor, Factory Method, Singleton, and Strategy) into the source code, thereby improving overall quality. The efficacy of MORE was evaluated using a benchmark of 7 medium and large-scale open-source systems.

It was compared with two multi-objective search algorithms and random search. Software quality improved by fixing 84% of code smells and introducing an average of 6 design patterns [108, 109]. Developers considered the suggested refactoring to be relevant and meaningful (an average of 69%).

Saranya *et al.* [110] used EGAPSO (Euclidean distance-based Genetic Algorithm and Particle Swarm Optimization) to identify code smells present in models, specifically class diagrams. Blob, Functional Decomposition, Spaghetti Code, Data Class, and Feature Envy were the smells under scrutiny. Instead of relying on a threshold value, this approach detected all code smells based on the similarity between the system under study and the set of defect examples, where the former is the initial model, and the latter is the base example. The approach was tested on three open-source projects and outperformed the Genetic Algorithm, DECOR, Multi-Objective Genetic Programming (MOGP), and Parallel Evolutionary Algorithm (PEA).

Kaur *et al.* [111] developed the Sandpiper Optimization Algorithm (SOA), a novel nature-inspired algorithm for solving real-life engineering problems. The swarm-based meta-heuristic algorithm was inspired by the migration and attacking behavior of sandpipers. The SOA algorithm was used to optimize the hyperparameter values of the decision tree, a machine-learning algorithm for accurately detecting code smells. The ranking of code smells was also done to prioritize them for refactoring.

In another work, Kaur *et al.* [112] used the Sandpiper Optimization Algorithm to optimize the hyperparameters of B-J48 to achieve the best performance in code smell detection. The detection approach of code smells was tested on three open-source Java systems. It outperformed the Genetic Algorithm, Multi-Objective Genetic Programming (MOGP), and Parallel Evolutionary Algorithm (PEA) in terms of precision, recall, Average Number of Detected Defects (ANDD), and F-measure.

Draz *et al.* [113] used the Whale Optimization Algorithm as a classifier to find ideal code smell detection rules. It focused on nine code smells, including Feature Envy, Spaghetti Code, Data Class, Lazy Class, and Functional Decomposition. The approach was tested on five open-source systems. It achieved an average precision of 94.24% and recall of 93.4%. Its performance was compared with Multi-Objective Genetic Programming (MOGP), MOAIS, Genetic Programming (GP), Genetic Algorithm (GA), and Competitive CoEvolutionary Algorithm (CCEA).

Boutaib *et al.* [114] introduced ADIODE, an evolutionary algorithm that evolves a population of detectors encoded as ODTs (Oblique Decision Trees) using the F-measure as a fitness function. ADIODE efficiently approximates globally optimal detectors using effective oblique splitting hyperplanes and metric thresholds. The approach was validated on six open-source software systems and outperformed Genetic Programming (GP), Multi-Objective Genetic Programming (MOGP), BLOB, and DECOR. The F-measure of ADIODE ranges from 91.23% to 95.24%, and its AUC lies between 0.9273 and 0.9573.

ANALYSIS OF CODE SMELL DETECTION TOOLS

Code-smell detection tools are crucial for maintaining large, complex, and evolving software systems. They are essential for improving software quality and reducing maintenance costs. Using tools can increase productivity and save time by automating the process. This allows developers to focus on other aspects of the code, such as improving functionality, rather than spending time manually detecting code smells. Tools can facilitate code reviews by highlighting potential issues [115]. This makes it easier for developers to identify and address issues before merging code into the main codebase. Tools can be educational for developers, as they highlight common anti-patterns and encourage writing better code. Over time, developers become more conscious of avoiding these smells, leading to improved coding practices. For legacy projects or code bases inherited from other teams, these tools can help quickly identify areas for improvement and prioritize refactoring efforts. Finally, manually detecting smells can be an error-prone process, so taking the support of automatic and semi-automatic tools and techniques will really help the situation. There are many tools available for code smell detection. A list of such tools available online is presented in Table **2**.

Table 2. List of code smell detection tools available online.

Year Updated	Tool Name	Developed In	Detected Bad Smells	Detection Language	Detection Technique	Available for Free	Plug-in	GUI
2023	CodeBeat	Ruby on Rails	DUC, LC, LM, GC, *etc.*	Swift, Objective-C, Go, Ruby, Python, Java	AST	Both	Yes	Yes
2023	Code Climate	Ruby on Rails	DEC, DUC, LM, LC, MC, FE, DCL, SS, LPL, RB	Ruby, JavaScript, Python, Java, PHP, and Go	Static analysis	No	Yes	Yes
2023	IntelliJ IDEA	NA	DCL, FE, LC, DUC, DEC, *etc.*	Kotlin, Groovy, Scala, Python, JavaScript	NA	Both	Yes	Yes
2022	JArchitect	Java	DEC, LM, LPL, FE, LM, DC, RB, *etc.*	Java, C#, and Python	Metrics	No	Yes	Yes
2022	SonarQube	Java	DUC, LM, LC, and LPL	Java (including Android), C#, C, C++	Static analysis	No	Yes	Yes
2021	JSpIRIT	Java	LC, LM, DC, FE, GC, RB	C++, Java, Smalltalk	Metrics	Yes	Both	Yes
2021	SDMetrics	Java	LC	UML diagrams	NA	Yes	No	Yes
2021	Clone Digger	Python	DUC	Java, Python, C#, C/C++, Ruby	Tree	Yes	Yes	Yes
2021	PMD	Java	DUC, LC, LM, and LPL	C, C#, C++, Java, PHP, JavaScript	NA	Yes	Yes	Yes

(Table 2) cont.....

Year Updated	Tool Name	Developed In	Detected Bad Smells	Detection Language	Detection Technique	Available for Free	Plug-in	GUI
2021	Gendarme	C#	DUC, LC, LM, LPL, MC, SG	.NET, Mono	Rules	Yes	Yes	Yes
2021	CCFinderX	C++	DUC	C, C++, Java, and C#	Token	Yes	Yes	Yes
2021	Checkstyle	Java	DUC, LC, LM, LPL	Java, C++, C#, and PHP	NA	Yes	Yes	Yes
2020	FindBugs	Java	SS, DUC, DEC, MC	Java	Static analysis	Yes	Yes	Yes
2020	Java Clone Detector	C++	DUC	Java	Tree	Yes	No	No
2019	JDeodorant	Java	FE, GC, LM, SS	Java	Metrics, AST	Yes	Yes	Yes
2017	iPlasma	Java	DUC, GC, FE, RB	C++, Java	Textual analysis	Yes	No	Yes
2015	ConQAT	Java	DUC	ABAP, ADA, C++, C#, Java	Metrics	No	Both	Yes
2013	Borland Together	Java	DUC	C#, C++, Java	Metrics	No	Yes	Yes
2013	inCode Helium	Java	GC, DC, DUC, LM, RB, SHS	C, C++, Java	Metrics	Both	Both	Yes
2012	SYMake	NA	Cyclic Dependency, Duplicated Prerequisites	C and Java	NA	Yes	No	Yes
2012	inFusion Hydrogen	NA	DUC, DC, DCL, FE, LC	C, C++, Java	NA	No	Yes	Yes
2011	NiCad	C	DUC	C, C#, Java, etc	Textual analysis	Yes	Yes	Yes
2011	TrueRefactor	Java	LC, LM, DUC, LPL	Java	Graph	Yes	No	Yes
2010	StenchBlossom	Java	Comments, DCL, GC	Java	Metrics	Yes	Yes	Yes
2010	Wrangler	Erlang	DUC	Erlang	Textual analysis	Yes	Yes	Yes
2008	NosePrints	NA	FE, II, LC, TF, PIH	NA	NA	No	Both	Yes

(Table 2) cont.....

Year Updated	Tool Name	Developed In	Detected Bad Smells	Detection Language	Detection Technique	Available for Free	Plug-in	GUI
2007	DECKARD	C	DUC	Java	AST	Yes	No	No
2005	Duplication Detector (DuDe)	Java	DUC	Language independent	Textual analysis	Yes	No	Yes
2002	jCosmo	NA	Instance of, SS, Typecast	Java	Tree	NA	No	Yes

DISCUSSION

This section reports the findings of the literature review and answers the targeted research questions. The literature review delves into the techniques and methodologies used in various software systems to detect code smells. These methods span different categories, including metric-based, semi-automatic, automatic, machine- and deep-learning-based, and search-based techniques. These methods collectively contribute to a diverse toolbox for detecting and addressing code smells in software systems.

What are the Limitations in Detecting Code Smells Through Current Tools and Techniques in Software Systems that Researchers Need to Address?

The field of code smell detection is continually progressing, with researchers and developers actively addressing various challenges. Key concerns include the lack of standardized definitions and detection thresholds for code smells, leading to inconsistent results across tools, and the difficulty in achieving high accuracy due to code smells' subjective nature and diverse contexts. Scalability issues arise when identifying, analyzing, and resolving code smells in large-scale software systems, leading to resource-intensive processes and potential usability concerns.

Furthermore, some tools have limited coverage in detecting code smells, and there's a lack of empirical evaluations of refactoring techniques, making it challenging to determine effective methods for different code smells. Code smell detection tools may struggle with context awareness and multilingual support, occasionally flagging code patterns incorrectly. Additionally, detecting architectural smells and encouraging tool adoption pose unique challenges. Maintaining rule sets, addressing domain-specific code smells, handling legacy code, and integrating tools seamlessly into development workflows also present hurdles. Despite these challenges, the field is advancing with machine learning and static analysis techniques, aiming to effectively balance automation and human judgment to enhance code quality and maintainability.

What Opportunities can help Developers and Researchers Build more Extensible and Robust Tools?

Code smell detection tools are crucial for identifying suboptimal design, complexity, and maintainability issues in software code. These tools must possess several key attributes to serve their purpose effectively. First, they must automatically pinpoint a wide range of code smells, including long methods, god classes, and duplicated code, ensuring comprehensive detection without introducing false positives. Visualization capabilities are essential for helping users grasp the severity of detected issues, enabling informed decision-making.

Furthermore, these tools should exhibit proficiency across various programming languages to accommodate diverse software projects. They should detect code smells, propose and automate refactoring actions, and ensure behavior preservation throughout the refactoring process. Additionally, the ability to assess the associated costs, time commitments, and benefits of refactoring activities, and to prioritize resolution efforts, is crucial. Adaptability to project-specific requirements, including configurable threshold values, is essential. Integration with popular development environments, workflows, build and version control systems, and Continuous Integration pipelines streamlines code-smell detection. The tool should provide comprehensive reports with precise details on identified code smells, including their location and severity. Scalability, extensibility, open-source nature, active user communities, and ongoing developer support are vital for the tool's efficiency, collaborative development, and continual improvement.

CONCLUSION

In conclusion, this article has comprehensively examined the landscape of code smell detection tools and techniques, offering valuable insights into their current state, challenges, and prospects. Through an extensive review of 69 studies spanning nearly 2 decades, we have gained a holistic understanding of the evolution and challenges of code-smell detection strategies.

Standardizing concepts is vital for consistent smell detection. Defining uniform threshold values remains unsettled, leading to disparities among technique outcomes. Aligning smell-detection approaches to achieve more consistent results is a goal. Smells in the design deteriorate, impacting attributes like maintainability and understandability. The lack of benchmark systems for smell-detection tools warrants attention. Early-stage smell detection cuts maintenance costs. Current devices detect a few smells and support a single language, limiting versatility. Exploring co-occurrences, such as cause-and-effect relationships and interconnected smells, is promising. The connection between code smells and refactoring can be complicated. There needs to be more research and practical identification of refactoring opportunities. Auto-mated refactoring is challenging due to behavior preservation issues. Although refactoring only improves some quality aspects uniformly, it is vital for tackling technical debt. Architectural refactoring poses risks, estimation challenges, and priority dilemmas. Unlimited refactoring options defy the need for custom solutions for all user needs. Industry and academia collaboration is essential to validate tool results in detecting false positives and negatives.

The inventory of twenty-nine used code smell detection tools presented in this chapter offers a detailed analysis of their strengths, limitations, and potential availability, enabling practitioners and researchers to make informed choices. The discussion on challenges and constraints these tools face has highlighted critical aspects. By recognizing these challenges, the software development community can direct its efforts towards developing more effective and practical solutions. The proposed directions for future research serve as a roadmap for advancing code smell detection tools. The integration of machine learning techniques holds immense promise in augmenting the accuracy and efficiency of detection. Furthermore, enhancing the flexibility and scalability of tools aligns with the dynamic nature of modern software development paradigms. Creating automated tools that empower developers to identify code smells efficiently is a step towards improving software quality and maintainability.

The insights and recommendations offered herein are intended to guide developers, researchers, and practitioners in creating and adopting sophisticated code-smell detection tools. As the software landscape evolves, these tools will be integral in pursuing robust, maintainable, high-quality software systems. By leveraging the knowledge shared in this article, we envision a future where software engineering is enriched by advanced tools that improve code quality, streamline maintenance processes, and, ultimately, lead to more resilient software systems.

REFERENCES

[1] N. Yoshida, T. Saika, E. Choi, A. Ouni, and K. Inoue, "Revisiting the relationship between code smells and refactoring", *IEEE 24th International Conference on Program Comprehension (ICPC),* pp. 1-4, 2016.
[http://dx.doi.org/10.1109/ICPC.2016.7503738]

[2] M. Tufano, F. Palomba, G. Bavota, R. Oliveto, M. Di Penta, A. De Lucia, and D. Poshyvanyk, "When and why your code starts to smell bad", *IEEE/ACM 37th IEEE International Conference on Software Engineering,* vol. 1, pp. 403-414, 2015.
[http://dx.doi.org/10.1109/ICSE.2015.59]

[3] M. Kim, T. Zimmermann, and N. Nagappan, "A field study of refactoring challenges and benefits", *Proceedings of the ACM SIGSOFT 20th International Symposium on the Foundations of Software Engineering,* pp. 1-11, 2012.
[http://dx.doi.org/10.1145/2393596.2393655]

[4] A. Kaur, "A systematic literature review on empirical analysis of the relationship between code smells and software quality attributes", *Arch. Comput. Methods Eng.*, vol. 27, no. 4, pp. 1267-1296, 2020. [http://dx.doi.org/10.1007/s11831-019-09348-6]

[5] T. Mens, and T. Tourwe´, "A survey of software refactoring", *IEEE Trans. Softw. Eng.*, vol. 30, no. 2, pp. 126-139, 2004. [http://dx.doi.org/10.1109/TSE.2004.1265817]

[6] F.A. Fontana, E. Mariani, A. Mornioli, R. Sormani, and A. Tonello, "An experience report on using code smells detection tools", *IEEE Fourth International Conference On Software Testing. Verification And Validation Workshops,* pp. 450-457, 2011. [http://dx.doi.org/10.1109/ICSTW.2011.12]

[7] A. Hamid, M. Ilyas, M. Hummayun, and A. Nawaz, "A comparative study on code smell detection tools", *International Journal of Advanced Science and Technology,* vol. 60, pp. 25-32, 2013. [http://dx.doi.org/10.14257/ijast.2013.60.03]

[8] M. Fokaefs, N. Tsantalis, and A. Chatzigeorgiou, "Jdeodorant: Identification and removal of feature envy bad smells", *Ieee International Conference On Software Maintenance.,* pp. 519-520, 2007.

[9] R. Marinescu, G. Ganea, and I. Verebi, "Incode: Continuous quality assessment and improvement", *14th European Conference on Software Maintenance and Reengineering,* pp. 274-275, 2010. [http://dx.doi.org/10.1109/CSMR.2010.44]

[10] E. Fernandes, J. Oliveira, G. Vale, T. Paiva, and E. Figueiredo, "A review-based comparative study of bad smell detection tools", *Proceedings of the 20th International Conference on Evaluation and Assessment in Software Engineering,* pp. 1-12, 2016. [http://dx.doi.org/10.1145/2915970.2915984]

[11] X. Liu, and C. Zhang, "The detection of code smell on software development: a mapping study", *5th International Conference on Machinery, Materials and Computing Technology (ICMMCT 2017),* pp. 560-575, 2017. [http://dx.doi.org/10.2991/icmmct-17.2017.120]

[12] A. Rani, and J.K. Chhabra, "Evolution of code smells over multiple versions of softwares: An empirical investigation", *2nd International Conference for Convergence in Technology (I2CT),* pp. 1093-1098, 2017. [http://dx.doi.org/10.1109/I2CT.2017.8226297]

[13] S. Vidal, H. Vazquez, J.A. Diaz-Pace, C. Marcos, A. Garcia, and W. Oizumi, "Jspirit: a flexible tool for the analysis of code smells", *34th International Conference of the Chilean Computer Science Society (SCCC),* pp. 1-6, 2015. [http://dx.doi.org/10.1109/SCCC.2015.7416572]

[14] J. Al Dallal, and A. Abdin, "Empirical evaluation of the impact of object-oriented code refactoring on quality attributes: A systematic literature review", *IEEE Trans. Softw. Eng*, vol. 44, no. 1, pp. 44-69, 2018. [http://dx.doi.org/10.1109/TSE.2017.2658573]

[15] J.A.M. Santos, J.B. Rocha-Junior, L.C.L. Prates, R.S. Nascimento, M.F. Freitas, and M.G. Mendonça, "A systematic review on the code smell effect", *J. Syst. Softw.,* vol. 144, pp. 450-477, 2018. [http://dx.doi.org/10.1016/j.jss.2018.07.035]

[16] F. Palomba, G. Bavota, M. Di Penta, F. Fasano, R. Oliveto, and A. De Lucia, "A large-scale empirical study on the lifecycle of code smell co-occurrences", *Inf. Softw. Technol.,* vol. 99, pp. 1-10, 2018. [http://dx.doi.org/10.1016/j.infsof.2018.02.004]

[17] M. Hozano, A. Garcia, B. Fonseca, and E. Costa, "Are you smelling it? Investigating how similar developers detect code smells", *Inf. Softw. Technol.,* vol. 93, pp. 130-146, 2018. [http://dx.doi.org/10.1016/j.infsof.2017.09.002]

[18] E.V.P. Sobrinho, A. De Lucia, and M.A. Maia, "A systematic literature review on bad smells–5 w's:

which, when, what, who, where", *IEEE Trans. Softw. Eng.,* vol. 47, no. 1, pp. 17-66, 2021. [http://dx.doi.org/10.1109/TSE.2018.2880977]

[19] F. Sabir, F. Palma, G. Rasool, Y.G. Guéhéneuc, and N. Moha, "A systematic literature review on the detection of smells and their evolution in object-oriented and service-oriented systems", *Softw. Pract. Exper.,* vol. 49, no. 1, pp. 3-39, 2019. [http://dx.doi.org/10.1002/spe.2639]

[20] M.I. Azeem, F. Palomba, L. Shi, and Q. Wang, "Machine learning techniques for code smell detection: A systematic literature review and meta-analysis", *Inf. Softw. Technol.,* vol. 108, pp. 115-138, 2019. [http://dx.doi.org/10.1016/j.infsof.2018.12.009]

[21] W. Aljedaani, A. Peruma, A. Aljohani, M. Alotaibi, M.W. Mkaouer, A. Ouni, C.D. Newman, A. Ghallab, and S. Ludi, *Test smell detection tools: A systematic mapping study.* Evaluation and Assessment in Software Engineering, 2021, pp. 170-180.

[22] J. Pereira dos Reis, F. Brito e Abreu, G. de Figueiredo Carneiro, and C. Anslow, "Code smells detection and visualization: a systematic literature review", *Arch. Comput. Methods Eng.,* vol. 29, no. 1, pp. 47-94, 2022. [http://dx.doi.org/10.1007/s11831-021-09566-x]

[23] B. Barn, S. Barat, and T. Clark, "Conducting systematic literature reviews and systematic mapping studies", *Proceedings of the 10th Innovations in Software Engineering Conference,* pp. 212-213, 2017. [http://dx.doi.org/10.1145/3021460.3021489]

[24] D. Budgen, and P. Brereton, "Performing systematic literature reviews in software engineering", *Proceedings of the 28th international conference on Software engineering,* pp. 1051-1052, 2006. [http://dx.doi.org/10.1145/1134285.1134500]

[25] R. Marinescu, "Detection strategies: Metrics-based rules for detecting design flaws", *IEEE International Conference on Software Maintenance,* pp. 350-359, 2004. [http://dx.doi.org/10.1109/ICSM.2004.1357820]

[26] M.J. Munro, "Product metrics for automatic identification of" bad smell" design problems in java source-code", *11th IEEE International Software Metrics Symposium (METRICS'05),* IEEE, pp. 15-15, 2005. [http://dx.doi.org/10.1109/METRICS.2005.38]

[27] K. Srivisut, and P. Muenchaisri, "Bad-smell metrics for aspect-oriented software", *6th IEEE/ACIS International Conference on Computer and Information Science (ICIS 2007),* IEEE, pp. 1060-1065, 2007.

[28] I.M. Bertran, "Detecting architecturally-relevant code smells in evolving software systems", *Proceedings of the 33rd International Conference on Software Engineering,* pp. 1090-1093, 2011. [http://dx.doi.org/10.1145/1985793.1986003]

[29] P. Danphitsanuphan, and T. Suwantada, *"Code smell detecting tool and code smell-structure bug relationship," in 2012 Spring Congress on Engineering and Technology.* IEEE, 2012, pp. 1-5.

[30] A.M. Fard, and A. Mesbah, "Jsnose: Detecting javascript code smells", *13th international working conference on Source Code Analysis and Manipulation (SCAM),* pp. 116-125, 2013. [http://dx.doi.org/10.1109/SCAM.2013.6648192]

[31] F.A. Fontana, V. Ferme, M. Zanoni, and A. Yamashita, "Automatic metric thresholds derivation for code smell detection", *2015 IEEE/ACM 6th International Workshop on Emerging Trends in Software Metrics,* pp. 44-53, 2015.

[32] Z. Chen, L. Chen, W. Ma, X. Zhou, Y. Zhou, and B. Xu, "Understanding metric-based detectable smells in Python software: A comparative study", *Inf. Softw. Technol.,* vol. 94, pp. 14-29, 2018. [http://dx.doi.org/10.1016/j.infsof.2017.09.011]

[33] R. Marinescu, "Metrics-based rules for detecting design flaws", *Proceedings of the 20th IEEE International Conference on Software Maintenance,* 2004.

[http://dx.doi.org/10.1109/ICSM.2004.1357820]

[34] P.F. Mihancea, and R. Marinescu, "Towards the optimization of automatic detection of design flaws in object-oriented software systems", *Ninth European conference on software maintenance and reengineering,* IEEE, pp. 92-101, 2005. [http://dx.doi.org/10.1109/CSMR.2005.53]

[35] R. Singh, A. Bindal, and A. Kumar, "Long method and long parameter list code smells detection using functional and semantic characteristics", *International Journal of Recent Technology and Engineering (IJRTE),* vol. 8, no. 6, pp. 2223-2232, 2020. [http://dx.doi.org/10.35940/ijrte.E5888.038620]

[36] X. Zhang, S. Sun, and K. Zhang, "A novel comprehensive approach for estimating concept semantic similarity in wordnet", 1703.01726

[37] B. Bafandeh Mayvan, A. Rasoolzadegan, and A. Javan Jafari, "Bad smell detection using quality metrics and refactoring opportunities", *J. Softw. (Malden),* vol. 32, no. 8, p. e2255, 2020. [http://dx.doi.org/10.1002/smr.2255]

[38] G. Rasool, and Z. Arshad, "A lightweight approach for detection of code smells", *Arab. J. Sci. Eng.,* vol. 42, no. 2, pp. 483-506, 2017. [http://dx.doi.org/10.1007/s13369-016-2238-8]

[39] S. Ma¨kela¨, and V. Leppa¨nen, "Japroch: A tool for checking programming style", *Kolin Kolistelut—Koli Calling,* p. 151, 2004.

[40] T. Paiva, A. Damasceno, J. Padilha, E. Figueiredo, and C. Sant'Anna, *Experimental evaluation of code smell detection tools.* Software Visualization, Evolution, and Maintenance, 2015.

[41] C. Parnin, C. Go¨rg, and O. Nnadi, "A catalogue of lightweight visualizations to support code smell inspection", *Proceedings of the 4th ACM Symposium on Software Visualization,* pp. 77-86, 2008. [http://dx.doi.org/10.1145/1409720.1409733]

[42] S. Amann, S. Proksch, S. Nadi, and M. Mezini, "A study of visual studio usage in practice", *23rd International Conference on Software Analysis, Evolution, and Reengineering (SANER),* vol. 1, pp. 124-134, 2016. [http://dx.doi.org/10.1109/SANER.2016.39]

[43] N. Moha, Y.G. Gueheneuc, L. Duchien, and A.F. Le Meur, "Decor: A method for the specification and detection of code and design smells", *IEEE Trans. Softw. Eng.,* vol. 36, no. 1, pp. 20-36, 2010. [http://dx.doi.org/10.1109/TSE.2009.50]

[44] G.F. Carneiro, M. Silva, L. Mara, E. Figueiredo, C. Sant'Anna, A. Garcia, and M. Mendonc¸a, "Identifying code smells with multiple concern views", *Brazilian Symposium on Software Engineering,* IEEE, pp. 128-137, 2010. [http://dx.doi.org/10.1109/SBES.2010.21]

[45] F. Khomh, S. Vaucher, Y.G. Guéhéneuc, and H. Sahraoui, "BDTEX: A GQM-based Bayesian approach for the detection of antipatterns", *J. Syst. Softw.,* vol. 84, no. 4, pp. 559-572, 2011. [http://dx.doi.org/10.1016/j.jss.2010.11.921]

[46] V. Cortellessa, A. Di Marco, and C. Trubiani, "An approach for modeling and detecting software performance antipatterns based on first-order logics", *Soft. Syst. Model.,* vol. 13, no. 1, pp. 391-432, 2014. [http://dx.doi.org/10.1007/s10270-012-0246-z]

[47] F. Palomba, G. Bavota, M.D. Penta, R. Oliveto, D. Poshyvanyk, and A. De Lucia, "Mining version histories for detecting code smells", *IEEE Trans. Softw. Eng.,* vol. 41, no. 5, pp. 462-489, 2015. [http://dx.doi.org/10.1109/TSE.2014.2372760]

[48] G. Hecht, R. Rouvoy, N. Moha, and L. Duchien, "Detecting antipatterns in android apps", *2nd ACM international conference on mobile software engineering and systems,* pp. 148-149, 2015. [http://dx.doi.org/10.1109/MobileSoft.2015.38]

[49] F. Palomba, A. Panichella, A. De Lucia, R. Oliveto, and A. Zaidman, "A textual-based technique for smell detection", *24th international conference on program comprehension (ICPC).* , pp. 1-10, 2016. [http://dx.doi.org/10.1109/ICPC.2016.7503704]

[50] F. Palomba, D. Di Nucci, A. Panichella, A. Zaidman, and A. De Lucia, "Lightweight detection of android-specific code smells: The adoctor project", *24th international conference on software analysis, evolution and reengineering (SANER),* pp. 487-491, 2017. [http://dx.doi.org/10.1109/SANER.2017.7884659]

[51] J. Reimann, M. Brylski, and U. Aßmann, *A tool-supported quality smell catalogue for android developers.* vol. Vol. 34. Softwaretechnik-Trends, 2014.

[52] F.A. Fontana, I. Pigazzini, R. Roveda, D. Tamburri, M. Zanoni, and E. Di Nitto, "Arcan: A tool for architectural smells detection", *IEEE International Conference on Software Architecture Workshops (ICSAW),* IEEE, pp. 282-285, 2017. [http://dx.doi.org/10.1109/ICSAW.2017.16]

[53] S. Kalhor, M. R. Keyvanpour, and A. Salajegheh, "Experimental evaluation and comparison of anti-pattern detection tools by the gold standard", In: *2022 12th International Conference on Computer and Knowledge Engineering (ICCKE)* IEEE, 2022, pp. 361-366. [http://dx.doi.org/10.1109/ICCKE57176.2022.9960137]

[54] A. Biaggi, F. A. Fontana, and R. Roveda, "An architectural smells detection tool for c and c++ projects", In: *2018 44th Euromicro Conference on Software Engineering and Advanced Applications (SEAA)* IEEE, 2018, pp. 417-420. [http://dx.doi.org/10.1109/SEAA.2018.00074]

[55] F. Palomba, A. Zaidman, and A. De Lucia, "Automatic test smell detection using information retrieval techniques", *IEEE International Conference on Software Maintenance and Evolution (ICSME),* IEEE, pp. 311-322, 2018. [http://dx.doi.org/10.1109/ICSME.2018.00040]

[56] B. Van Rompaey, B. Du Bois, S. Demeyer, and M. Rieger, "On the detection of test smells: A metrics-based approach for general fixture and eager test", *IEEE Trans. Softw. Eng.,* vol. 33, no. 12, pp. 800-817, 2007. [http://dx.doi.org/10.1109/TSE.2007.70745]

[57] A.K. Sharma, N. Chanderwal, A. Prajapati, P. Singh, M. Kansal, Ed., *Advancing Software Engineering Through AI, Federated Learning, and Large Language Models.* IGI Global, 2024. [http://dx.doi.org/10.4018/979-8-3693-3502-4]

[58] P. Gadient, M. Ghafari, P. Frischknecht, and O. Nierstrasz, "Security code smells in Android ICC", *Empir. Softw. Eng.,* vol. 24, no. 5, pp. 3046-3076, 2019. [http://dx.doi.org/10.1007/s10664-018-9673-y]

[59] A. Rahman, C. Parnin, and L. Williams, "The seven sins: Security smells in infrastructure as code scripts", In: *2019 IEEE/ACM 41st International Conference on Software Engineering (ICSE)* IEEE, 2019, pp. 164-175. [http://dx.doi.org/10.1109/ICSE.2019.00033]

[60] Z. Li, T.-H. Chen, J. Yang, and W. Shang, "Dlfinder: characterizing and detecting duplicate logging code smells", In: *2019 IEEE/ACM 41st International Conference on Software Engineering (ICSE)* IEEE, 2019, pp. 152-163. [http://dx.doi.org/10.1109/ICSE.2019.00032]

[61] I. Pigazzini, F.A. Fontana, V. Lenarduzzi, and D. Taibi, "Towards microservice smells detection", *Proceedings of the 3rd International Conference on Technical Debt,* pp. 92-97, 2020. [http://dx.doi.org/10.1145/3387906.3388625]

[62] I. Kumara, Z. Vasileiou, G. Meditskos, D.A. Tamburri, W-J. Van Den Heuvel, A. Karakostas, S. Vrochidis, and I. Kompatsiaris, "Towards semantic detection of smells in cloud infrastructure code",

Proceedings of the 10th International Conference on Web Intelligence, Mining and Semantics, pp. 63-67, 2020.
[http://dx.doi.org/10.1145/3405962.3405979]

[63] T. Binz, U. Breitenbu¨cher, F. Haupt, O. Kopp, F. Leymann, A. Nowak, and S. Wagner, "Opentosca–a runtime for tosca-based cloud applications", *11th International Conference, ICSOC 2013,* pp. 692-695, .Berlin, Germany

[64] A. Borrelli, V. Nardone, G.A. Di Lucca, G. Canfora, and M. Di Penta, "Detecting video game-specific bad smells in unity projects", *Proceedings of the 17th international conference on mining software repositories,* pp. 198-208, 2020.
[http://dx.doi.org/10.1145/3379597.3387454]

[65] A. Walker, D. Das, and T. Cerny, "Automated code-smell detection in microservices through static analysis: A case study", *Appl. Sci. (Basel),* vol. 10, no. 21, p. 7800, 2020.
[http://dx.doi.org/10.3390/app10217800]

[66] I. Fatima, H. Anwar, D. Pfahl, and U. Qamar, Detection and correction of android-specific code smells and energy bugs: An android lint extension.

[67] P. Singh, M. Kansal, M.K. Singh, S. Kumar, and A. Dwivedi, Crop disease prediction using deep learning algorithms.*Convergence of cloud computing, AI, and agricultural science.* IGI Global, 2023, pp. 290-305.
[http://dx.doi.org/10.4018/979-8-3693-0200-2.ch015]

[68] P.H. de Andrade Gomes, R.E. Garcia, G. Spadon, D.M. Eler, C. Olivete, and R.C.M. Correia, Teaching software quality via source code inspection tool
[http://dx.doi.org/10.1109/FIE.2017.8190658]

[69] H. Zhu, Y. Li, J. Li, and X. Zhang, *"An efficient design smell detection approach with inter-class relation," 2023 Software Engineeringa nd Knowledge Engineering* SEKE, 2023.

[70] W. Xu, and X. Zhang, "Multi-granularity code smell detection using deep learning method based on abstract syntax tree", *Proc. 33rd Int. Conf. Software Engineering and Knowledge Engineering,* pp. 503-509, 2021.
[http://dx.doi.org/10.18293/SEKE2021-014]

[71] H. Liu, J. Jin, Z. Xu, Y. Zou, Y. Bu, and L. Zhang, "Deep learning based code smell detection", *IEEE Trans. Softw. Eng.,* vol. 47, no. 9, pp. 1811-1837, 2019.

[72] M. Kansal, P. Singh, P. Srivastava, R. Singhal, N. Deep, and A. Singh, Mental health monitoring in the digital age: a comprehensive analysis.*Future of AI in Medical Imaging.* IGI Global, 2024, pp. 168-183.
[http://dx.doi.org/10.4018/979-8-3693-2359-5.ch011]

[73] A. Tian, C. Zhang, M. Rang, X. Yang, and Z. Zhan, "Ra-gcn: Relational aggregation graph convolutional network for knowledge graph completion", *Proceedings of the 2020 12th international conference on machine learning and computing,* pp. 580-586, 2020.
[http://dx.doi.org/10.1145/3383972.3384067]

[74] Y. Li, A. Liu, L. Zhao, and X. Zhang, *Hybrid model with multi-level code representation for multi-label code smell detection,* .
[http://dx.doi.org/10.1142/S0218194022500723]

[75] F. Ferreira, and M.T. Valente, "Detecting code smells in React-based Web apps", *Inf. Softw. Technol.,* vol. 155, p. 107111, 2023.
[http://dx.doi.org/10.1016/j.infsof.2022.107111]

[76] M. Bosco, P. Cavoto, A. Ungolo, B.A. Muse, F. Khomh, V. Nardone, and M. Di Penta, "Unitylint: A bad smell detector for unity",
[http://dx.doi.org/10.1109/ICPC58990.2023.00033]

[77] D. Ballis, A. Baruzzo, and M. Comini, "A minimalist visual notation for design patterns and

antipatterns", *Fifth International Conference on Information Technology: New Generations (itng 2008),* IEEE, pp. 51-56, 2008.
[http://dx.doi.org/10.1109/ITNG.2008.227]

[78] P. Singh, M. Kansal, S. Lahiri, H. Vishnoi, and L. Mittal, A Transparency System for ICU Using Machine Learning and AI.*Enhancing Medical Imaging with Emerging Technologies.* IGI Global, 2024, pp. 51-69.
[http://dx.doi.org/10.4018/979-8-3693-5261-8.ch004]

[79] H.V. Nguyen, H.A. Nguyen, T.T. Nguyen, A.T. Nguyen, and T.N. Nguyen, "Detection of embedded code smells in dynamic web applications", *Proceedings of the 27th IEEE/ACM International Conference on Automated Software Engineering,* pp. 282-285, 2012.
[http://dx.doi.org/10.1145/2351676.2351724]

[80] T. Arendt, and G. Taentzer, "A tool environment for quality assurance based on the Eclipse Modeling Framework", *Autom. Softw. Eng.,* vol. 20, no. 2, pp. 141-184, 2013.
[http://dx.doi.org/10.1007/s10515-012-0114-7]

[81] E. Ligu, A. Chatzigeorgiou, T. Chaikalis, and N. Ygeionomakis, "Identification of refused bequest code smells", *IEEE International Conference on Software Maintenance,* IEEE, pp. 392-395, 2013.
[http://dx.doi.org/10.1109/ICSM.2013.55]

[82] P. Singh, U.K. Jaiswal, E. Jain, N. Kuamr, and V. Mishra, "A Novel Methodology Utilizing Modern CCTV Cameras and Software as a Service Model for Crime Detection and Prediction", *Int. J. Perform. Eng.,* vol. 21, no. 2, 2025.

[83] M.R. Chaudron, B. Katumba, and X. Ran, "Automated prioritization of metrics-based design flaws in uml class diagrams",
[http://dx.doi.org/10.1109/SEAA.2014.82]

[84] S. Kumar, and J.K. Chhabra, "Two level dynamic approach for feature envy detection", *International conference on computer and communication technology (ICCCT),* IEEE, pp. 41-46, 2014.
[http://dx.doi.org/10.1109/ICCCT.2014.7001467]

[85] S.A. Vidal, C. Marcos, and J.A. Díaz-Pace, "An approach to prioritize code smells for refactoring", *Autom. Softw. Eng.,* vol. 23, no. 3, pp. 501-532, 2016.
[http://dx.doi.org/10.1007/s10515-014-0175-x]

[86] A. Peruma, K. Almalki, C.D. Newman, M.W. Mkaouer, A. Ouni, and F. Palomba, "Tsdetect: An open source test smells detection tool", *Proceedings of the 28th ACM joint meeting on european software engineering conference and symposium on the foundations of software engineering,* pp. 1650-1654, 2020.
[http://dx.doi.org/10.1145/3368089.3417921]

[87] S. Hassaine, F. Khomh, Y. Gue'he'neuc, and S. Hamel, "Ids: An immune-inspired approach for the detection of software design smells", *Seventh International Conference on the Quality of Information and Communications Technology,* IEEE, pp. 343-348, 2010.
[http://dx.doi.org/10.1109/QUATIC.2010.61]

[88] P. Singh, M. Kansal, P. Panwar, M. Mishra, K. Patel, and A.K. Sharma, "An AI and ML-Enhanced Approach with IoT for Pothole Detection to Ensure Pedestrian Safety During Flooding", *International Conference on Advances and Applications of Artificial Intelligence and Machine Learning,* pp. 203-216, 2023.Singapore

[89] N. Maneerat, and P. Muenchaisri, "Bad-smell prediction from software design model using machine learning techniques",
[http://dx.doi.org/10.1109/JCSSE.2011.5930143]

[90] A. Maiga, N. Ali, N. Bhattacharya, A. Sabane′, Y. Gue'he'neuc, and E. Aimeur, "Smurf: A svm-based incremental anti-pattern detection approach",
[http://dx.doi.org/10.1109/WCRE.2012.56]

[91] M. Peiris, and J.H. Hill, "Towards detecting software performance anti-patterns using classification techniques", *Softw. Eng. Notes,* vol. 39, no. 1, pp. 1-4, 2014. [http://dx.doi.org/10.1145/2557833.2560586]

[92] P. Singh, and M. Kansal, An online platform for timely access to medical care with the help of real-time data analysis.*Wellness Management Powered by AI Technologies,* pp. 103-131, 2025.

[93] M. Hadj-Kacem, and N. Bouassida, A hybrid approach to detect code smells using deep learning. [http://dx.doi.org/10.5220/0006709801370146]

[94] H. Liu, Z. Xu, and Y. Zou, "Deep learning based feature envy detection", *Proceedings of the 33rd ACM/IEEE international conference on automated software engineering,* pp. 385-396, 2018. [http://dx.doi.org/10.1145/3238147.3238166]

[95] M.Y. Mhawish, and M. Gupta, "Predicting code smells and analysis of predictions: Using machine learning techniques and software metrics", *J. Comput. Sci. Technol.,* vol. 35, no. 6, pp. 1428-1445, 2020. [http://dx.doi.org/10.1007/s11390-020-0323-7]

[96] A. Gupta, B. Suri, and V. Bhat, "Android smells detection using ml algorithms with static code metrics", *5th International Conference on Recent Developments in Science, Engineering and Technology,* Springer, pp. 64-79, 2020. [http://dx.doi.org/10.1007/978-981-15-5827-6_6]

[97] T. Lin, X. Fu, F. Chen, and L. Li, "A novel approach for code smells detection based on deep leaning", *Proceedings 1,* pp. 171-174, .

[98] T. Sharma, V. Efstathiou, P. Louridas, and D. Spinellis, "Code smell detection by deep direct-learning and transfer-learning", *J. Syst. Softw.,* vol. 176, p. 110936, 2021. [http://dx.doi.org/10.1016/j.jss.2021.110936]

[99] A. Ho, A.M. Bui, P.T. Nguyen, and A. Di Salle, "Fusion of deep convolutional and lstm recurrent neural networks for automated detection of code smells", *Proceedings of the 27th International Conference on Evaluation and Assessment in Software Engineering,* pp. 229-234, 2023. [http://dx.doi.org/10.1145/3593434.3593476]

[100] M. Kessentini, H. Sahraoui, M. Boukadoum, and M. Wimmer, "Search-based design defects detection by example", *Proceedings 14,* pp. 401-415, 2011.

[101] A. Ouni, M. Kessentini, H. Sahraoui, and M. Boukadoum, "Maintainability defects detection and correction: a multi-objective approach", *Autom. Softw. Eng.,* vol. 20, no. 1, pp. 47-79, 2013. [http://dx.doi.org/10.1007/s10515-011-0098-8]

[102] M. Boussaa, W. Kessentini, M. Kessentini, S. Bechikh, and S. Ben Chikha, "Competitive coevolutionary code-smells detection", *5th International Symposium, SSBSE 2013,* pp. 50-65, .St. Petersburg, Russia

[103] W. Kessentini, M. Kessentini, H. Sahraoui, S. Bechikh, and A. Ouni, "A cooperative parallel search-based software engineering approach for code-smells detection", *IEEE Trans. Softw. Eng.,* vol. 40, no. 9, pp. 841-861, 2014. [http://dx.doi.org/10.1109/TSE.2014.2331057]

[104] A. Ouni, M. Kessentini, M. Ó Cinnéide, H. Sahraoui, K. Deb, and K. Inoue, "MORE: A multi-objective refactoring recommendation approach to introducing design patterns and fixing code smells", *J. Softw. (Malden),* vol. 29, no. 5, p. e1843, 2017. [http://dx.doi.org/10.1002/smr.1843]

[105] Hui Li, and Qingfu Zhang, "Multiobjective optimization problems with complicated pareto sets, moea/d and nsga-ii", *IEEE Trans. Evol. Comput.,* vol. 13, no. 2, pp. 284-302, 2009. [http://dx.doi.org/10.1109/TEVC.2008.925798]

[106] K. Deb, A. Pratap, S. Agarwal, and T. Meyarivan, "A fast and elitist multiobjective genetic algorithm:

NSGA-II", *IEEE Trans. Evol. Comput.,* vol. 6, no. 2, pp. 182-197, 2002. [http://dx.doi.org/10.1109/4235.996017]

[107] P. Singh, N. Pahuja, M. Kansal, S. Gurung, U. Shukla, and S. Gupta, "Enhancing Tourism Experiences and Preserving Cultural Heritage with AR and VR", In: *2024 2nd International Conference on Disruptive Technologies (ICDT)* IEEE, Mar 2024, pp. 225-231. [http://dx.doi.org/10.1109/ICDT61202.2024.10489490]

[108] A. Kaur, S. Jain, and S. Goel, "Sandpiper optimization algorithm: a novel approach for solving real-life engineering problems", *Appl. Intell.,* vol. 50, no. 2, pp. 582-619, 2020. [http://dx.doi.org/10.1007/s10489-019-01507-3]

[109] A. Kaur, S. Jain, and S. Goel, "SP-J48: a novel optimization and machine-learning-based approach for solving complex problems: special application in software engineering for detecting code smells", *Neural Comput. Appl.,* vol. 32, no. 11, pp. 7009-7027, 2020. [http://dx.doi.org/10.1007/s00521-019-04175-z]

[110] M.M. Draz, M.S. Farhan, S.N. Abdulkader, and M. Gafar, "Code smell detection using whale optimization algorithm", *Comput. Mater. Continua,* vol. 68, no. 2, pp. 1919-1935, 2021. [http://dx.doi.org/10.32604/cmc.2021.015586]

[111] M. Gong, L. Jiao, H. Du, and L. Bo, "Multiobjective immune algorithm with nondominated neighbor-based selection", *Evol. Comput.,* vol. 16, no. 2, pp. 225-255, 2008. [http://dx.doi.org/10.1162/evco.2008.16.2.225] [PMID: 18554101]

[112] S. Boutaib, S. Bechikh, F. Palomba, M. Elarbi, M. Makhlouf, and L.B. Said, "Code smell detection and identification in imbalanced environments", *Expert Syst. Appl.,* vol. 166, p. 114076, 2021. [http://dx.doi.org/10.1016/j.eswa.2020.114076]

[113] D. Sahin, M. Kessentini, S. Bechikh, and K. Deb, "Code-smell detection as a bilevel problem", *ACM Trans. Softw. Eng. Methodol.,* vol. 24, no. 1, pp. 1-44, 2014. [TOSEM]. [http://dx.doi.org/10.1145/2675067]

[114] G. Lacerda, F. Petrillo, M. Pimenta, and Y.G. Guéhéneuc, "Code smells and refactoring: A tertiary systematic review of challenges and observations", *J. Syst. Softw.,* vol. 167, p. 110610, 2020. [http://dx.doi.org/10.1016/j.jss.2020.110610]

[115] M. Kaya, S. Conley, Z. S. Othman, and A. Varol, "Effective software refactoring process", In: *2018 6th International Symposium on Digital Forensic and Security (ISDFS)* IEEE, 2018, pp. 1-6. [http://dx.doi.org/10.1109/ISDFS.2018.8355350]

CHAPTER 2

A Novel Extraction of Features for a Speech Recognition System in a Noisy Environment using Machine Learning

Princy Tyagi[1,*] and **Preeti Jain**[2]

[1] *Department of Computer Science & Engineering, Swami Rama Himalayan University, Dehradun, Uttarakhand, India*

[2] *Department of Management, Ajay Kumar Garg Institute of Management, Ghaziabad, Uttar Pradesh, India*

Abstract: Speech has played a significant role in human communication from the dawn of civilization. Emotions should be naturally conveyed in spoken communication. The use of voice to determine human emotions in automated technologies is unreliable. To comprehend human thought processes, a machine must first grasp the aural capacities of the human ear. The processing of emotions enhances the authenticity and importance of contemporary speech technologies. Spectral properties play a crucial role in classifying audio signals. This study focuses on extracting spectral information from speech, specifically pitch and Mel-frequency components. Cepstral coefficients, also known as Mel-frequency cepstral coefficients (MFCCs) and Linear Prediction Cepstral Coefficients (LPCCs). The LPCC coefficients are utilized to achieve emotion categorization. Prior to choosing CAT Boost as the classifier, we compared and analyzed other techniques. A speech emotion database, consisting of over 100 individuals exhibiting a wide range of emotions, is used for training and testing. A supplementary voice database derived from a multitude of movie snippets is used to enhance the authenticity of the vocal output.

Keywords: Artificial intelligence, Authentication, CAT Boost, LPCC, MFCC, Spectral features.

INTRODUCTION

Speaking is a means of interpersonal interaction. Each word that is spoken is formed by phonetically combining a set number of vowels and syllable speech sound elements. Human languages come in tens of thousands of variants, many of which are mutually unintelligible due to differences in vocabulary, grammatical

* **Corresponding author Princy Tyagi:** Department of Computer Science & Engineering, Swami Rama Himalayan University, Dehradun, Uttarakhand, India; E-mail: princy04sharma@gmail.com

Pancham Singh, Avinash Kumar Sharma, Mrignainy Kansal, & Amarjeet Prajapati (Eds.)

organization, and the collection of speech sounds [1]. The majority of polyglots, or speakers of several human languages, are able to converse in two or more of them. Humans can sing because they possess the same vocal skills that allow them to speak.

In many cultures, the language of writing originated from speech, which frequently differs from a similar spoken language with respect to grammar, spelling, and phonetics. This phenomenon is referred to as diglossia. According to certain experts in psychology, speaking functions as a conversation within the neural network to enhance and structure understanding [2]. While also serving as a medium of communication. Speech is most commonly utilized in interactions, or the process of transmitting messages. Both the total amount of knowledge included in the communication, expressed as an ensemble of discrete characters and the rate at which knowledge is communicated can be expressed in words and bits per second (bps). Speech recognition systems have significantly evolved over the past few decades, becoming an integral part of modern technology. Features include artificial intelligence, mechanized customer service, and hands-free control systems. The ability to accurately recognize and process human speech in real time has opened numerous opportunities for enhanced user experiences and improved accessibility. However, one of the most persistent challenges faced by speech recognition systems is their performance in noisy environments [3]. Background noise can significantly degrade speech recognition accuracy, making it difficult for these systems to distinguish the desired speech signal from surrounding noise. It is shown in Fig. (**1**).

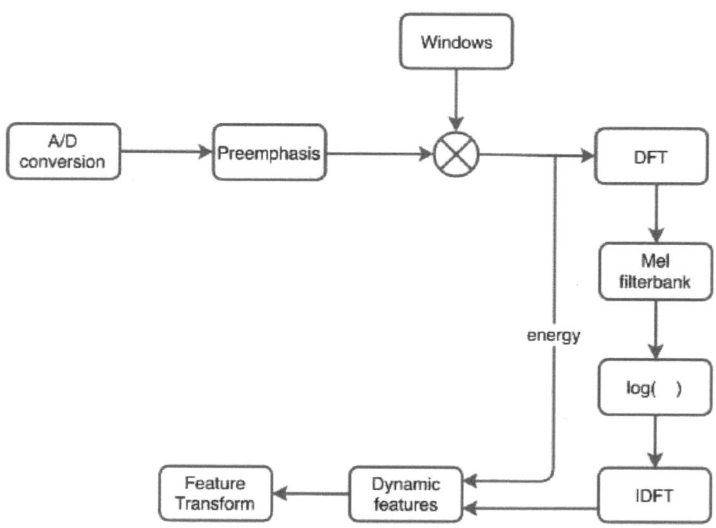

Fig. (1). Signal Processing Flow for Speech Feature extraction.

The process of identifying human emotions is known as emotion recognition. The accuracy with which individuals can gauge the emotions of others varies greatly. The application of technology to assist with emotional identification is a relatively recent field of research. The strategy often works best when it is used in a setting with a variety of modality options. The most focus has been on physiologic mechanisms, as assessed by devices worn, spoken expressions, handwritten responses to text, and gestures in cinematography. Traditional approaches to speech recognition often struggle in noisy conditions due to their reliance on handcrafted features and conventional noise reduction techniques, which may not generalize well across different types of noise and varying acoustic environments. This limitation has driven the exploration of advanced methods that can robustly extract significant characteristics from noisy voice streams to enhance classification performance. Machine learning, particularly deep learning, has emerged as a powerful tool for feature extraction and pattern recognition in complex and noisy data. By leveraging vast amounts of data and the computational power of modern processors, machine learning algorithms can learn to identify intricate patterns and features that are difficult to capture with traditional methods. This has led to significant improvements in speech recognition system performance, especially in challenging acoustic environments.

This chapter delves into the novel extraction of features for a speech recognition system operating in noisy environments, using machine learning. The focus is on identifying and designing prominent features that can enhance the robustness and accuracy of speech recognition systems in the presence of various types and levels of noise. Key goals include developing feature-extraction methods that are not only effective at isolating the speech signal but also computationally efficient and scalable for real-world applications.

Speech recognition in noisy environments remains a significant challenge, as background noise often obscures critical speech features, leading to recognition errors. However, recent advancements in deep learning have introduced powerful methods for overcoming such challenges. One such method, **UIU-Net**, originally designed for infrared small-object detection, has demonstrated remarkable feature-extraction capabilities under difficult conditions [4]. By leveraging advanced Artificial neural networks for language signal interpretation, we can enhance the efficiency of speech recognition systems in noisy settings. These techniques proficiently separate and emphasize the essential characteristics of speech, even amongst considerable activity, thereby enhancing ultimate efficacy in use. During this study, researchers investigated the most effective method for detecting the emotional content of voice signals using a variety of AI architectures. After extensive testing, we advised using this method for speech recognition of emotions, as it produces high-quality results with a higher accuracy rate.

LITERATURE SURVEY

Mutual sharing of information as well as exchange go hand in hand. A normal discourse between two individuals starts with a shared acquaintance and culminates with a reciprocal reliance. Before transmitting human emotions to robots, it is critical that we understand how people perceive emotions. Over the years, significant work has been devoted to extracting and recognizing speech constituents [5]. Innovation has enabled devices, software, and algorithms to understand and comprehend conversations and orders. Voice questions are resolved by popular digital assistants such as Google Assistant, Siri, and Echo. Although these applications are fluent in two languages and adept at following verbal commands, they are incapable of recognizing emotions. Should you enter "I am in pain" in one of these applications, they will return movies, music, *etc.*

(NLP) and (AI) both assist businesses as well as industry in developing marketing strategies by detecting emotions. Rather than text messages, many individuals share audio on social networking platforms. While it first converts the voice into written form before using NLP, conventional NLP techniques do not perform well when audio discussions take the place of literature [6]. Voice emotion detection is used in medical technologies, Virtual Reality for Education, Entrepreneurship, and the entertainment industry [7]. While we can extract the essential voice characteristics, we need to clean linguistic data by removing noise [8]. After transforming the speech amplitude into a parameterized representation, we can extract features for later evaluation and processing at a slower data-collection rate. Excellent craftsmanship; extraction of features simplifies information categorization [9].

The technology should simulate human harmonics to retrieve speech elements that are most similar to the sound heard by humans [10]. Various methods, including MFCC, LPC, LPCC, LSF, and PLP, provide fundamental features of hearing and speech. To keep the alphabetically significant parts of the spoken word stream, MFCC filters pitch continuously at low frequencies and monotonically at the highest frequencies [11]. Whereas LSF uses the geometry of the nostrils and oral channels to forecast the picture's pharmacological significance, LPC helps locate forming agents and the peaks in the range of colours [12].

In speech recognition, Mel-Frequency Cepstral Coefficients (MFCC) and Linear Predictive Coding (LPC) are two traditional feature extraction techniques that have been widely used [13]. MFCCs capture the spectral characteristics of speech by analyzing its frequency content, which is mapped onto a Mel-scale that simulates human hearing. This makes MFCC particularly effective in capturing the perceived frequency bands for speech recognition tasks. LPC, on the other hand, is based on the idea that speech signals can be approximated by a linear model of their past values, providing a representation of the vocal tract's shape and the speech signal's formants [14]. In comparison to newer methods like deep learning-based feature extractors, Convolutional Neural Networks (CNNs), or Recurrent Neural Networks (RNNs), MFCC and LPC are more simplistic and do not automatically learn complex patterns in data [15]. While deep learning methods can extract features from raw waveform data, learning hierarchical features that capture intricate patterns, MFCC and LPC rely on predefined signal processing techniques. Newer methods offer more flexibility and adaptability to noisy environments, improving performance by automatically adapting to variations in speech signals across different conditions [16]. The overview of key topics and references in speech recognition and feature extraction is shown in Table **1**.

Table 1. Overview of key topics and references in speech recognition and feature extraction.

Reference	Topic	Details
[1 - 4]	Extraction and recognition of speech constituents	Significant work has been done in extracting and recognizing appropriate speech constituents over the years.
[5]	Limitations of digital assistants	Digital assistants like Google Assistant, Siri, and Echo can understand commands but cannot recognize emotions.
[6]	Challenges in NLP for audio messages	Traditional NLP methods do not work well with audio messages on social networking systems.
[7]	Applications of voice emotion detection	Used in medical technologies, virtual reality for education, entrepreneurship, and the entertainment industry.
[8]	Noise removal in speech data	Importance of cleaning linguistic data by removing noise for better feature extraction.
[9]	Feature extraction for speech processing	Transforming speech amplitude to a parameterized representation for feature extraction and processing.
[10]	Human-like speech element retrieval	Technology should simulate human harmonics to retrieve speech elements similar to human perception.
[11]	Methods for fundamental feature extraction	MFCC, LPC, LPCC, LSF, and PLP methods provide fundamental features for hearing and speech.
[12]	Details of feature extraction methods	-**MFCC**: Filters pitches at low frequencies and monotonically at high frequencies. -**LSF**: Uses nostril and oral channel geometry to predict pharmacological significance. -**LPC**: Locates formants and peaks in the color range.

METHODOLOGY

CatBoost (Categorical Boosting) is a gradient boosting algorithm specifically designed to efficiently handle categorical data, making it especially well-suited for tasks like speech recognition, where features often contain categorical or non-numeric representations. One of the key advantages of using CatBoost in speech recognition systems is its ability to automatically process categorical features without requiring extensive preprocessing, unlike other machine learning algorithms that typically need manual encoding of categorical variables. This reduces the complexity of the feature engineering process and enhances the overall system's efficiency [17].

CatBoost also incorporates advanced techniques such as ***ordered boosting***, which helps reduce overfitting and improve model generalization. This feature is particularly valuable when dealing with noisy environments, where speech signals may be distorted by background noise or other interferences. By applying CatBoost, we can achieve higher classification accuracy, especially when managing complex, noisy, and non-linear relationships in the data. These challenges are common in speech signal processing tasks, and CatBoost's ability to adapt to such complexities makes it an ideal choice for improving the robustness and performance of speech recognition systems.

Method Formulation

Multilingual Indian sounds aim to express emotions. An experimental research configuration. The hardware and the data set are divided into different groups.

Processor: 2.5 gigahertz, the generation Intel Core I7

System of functioning: Windows 10, the operating system

Bandwidth and Storage conditions: NV visuals with sixteen gigabytes of DDR4 random access memory.

Space required: 1 Tera Byte of storage.

A dataset with reasonably natural expressions was created. In order to practice and evaluate emotion recognition methods, the UTU, which is partly based on the Naturalistic Emotional Speech Catalog (UTU-SNESC), was developed. A collection of some material covers lines of dialogue by well-known Indian actors as well as actresses. The multilingual Indian sounds are intended to express sentiments. The UTU-SNESC dataset is shown in Table **2**.

Table 2. UTU-SNESC dataset.

Feelings	Sound Clips	Contribution
Impartial	145	15.35%
Panic	157	143.27%
Temper	99	23.51%
Anguish	190	10.18%
Cheerfulness	110	20.43%
Surprise	150	14.27%

Model

The program reads each voice file and then filters them by removing silent ones. Following that, MFCC and LPC characteristics are extracted. Pitching is then determined. A method retains only the most vital elements [18]. The test dataset is constructed by saving the retained MFCC and LPC features, pitch, and tone for each speech file as vector representations. The work of art is clearly shown in Fig. (2).

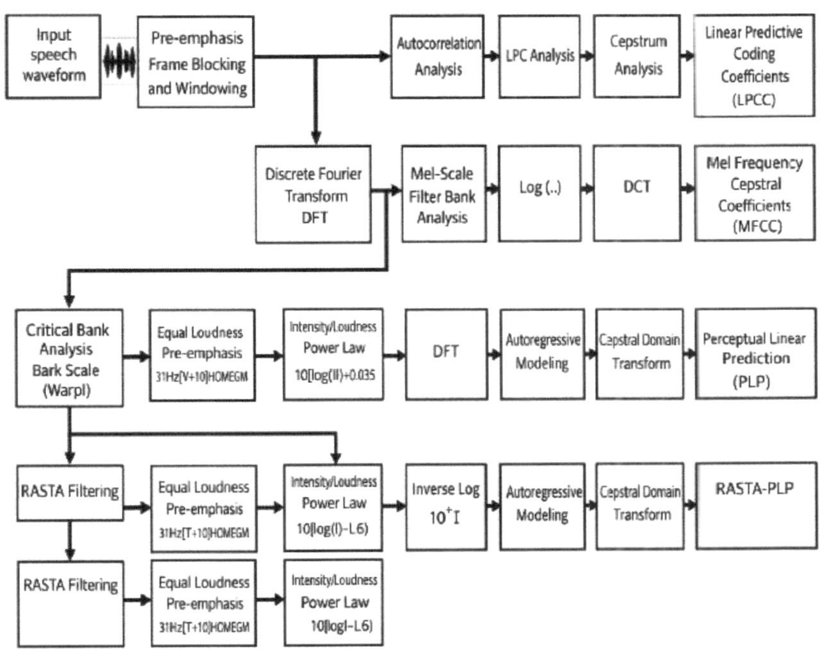

Fig. (2). Hybrid Model of Speech Recognitions.

Fig. (**1**) shows a pictorial illustration of the framework. The framework for forecasting, as shown in Fig. (**3**), uses classification output to predict feelings in the fresh voice. The stages below illustrate exactly how the algorithm's structure acts in all its aspects:

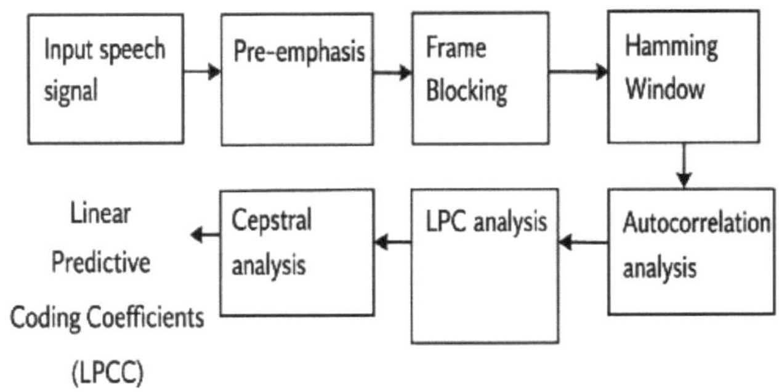

Fig. (3). Predictive based model.

Step 1 involves reading the file with different types of responses and linguistics.

Step 2: Speech filtration minimizes silences.

Step3. Removal of MFCC and LPC facilities. Pitch calculation.

Step 4: Properties that fulfil unspecified quality are protected.

Step 5: Identify characteristics according to the attitude of the voice.

Step 6: Prepare cat boost modelling with the required features.

Step 7: Develop models with attributes and labelling.

Step 8: Infer emotion.

Use an alternative voice for delivery. Repetition of steps 2–4 To predict sentiment, run profiles with modified features.

Objective Purpose

The primary objective of this study is to develop the forecasting of sentiment utilizing many Indian languages that are spoken across different regions. The function may be quantitatively stated as follows:

Voice Filtration

1. A data-dependent investigation was conducted in a recording studio environment. Here, the following calculation is applied to remove specific silent regions from the recording:

$$V_f = \begin{Bmatrix} 0, V_I \text{ is not speech} \\ 1, V_I \text{ is speech} \end{Bmatrix} \quad \textbf{(1)}$$

Using Equation (1), the code loops through the speech stream and removes any zeros. The value of Vf includes modulated noise.*MFCC feature Extraction*

$$V_{MF} = MFCC(V_f) \ldots\ldots\ldots\ldots fn(2) \quad \textbf{(2)}$$

To identify spatial properties of the message, function fn (2) calculates the initial and second components of the cepstral variable shown in Eq. (2). The initial part of the algorithms explains how it works:

Algorithm 1: *deployment of MFCC.*

Install: Initialize required variables.

The FFT size is 2048, and the hop size is 10 ms.

Sampling Rate: 44100 (44.1 KZ) Minimum Frequency=0

max_ freq=sampling_ rate/2 num _of_ mel_ filters=10

DCT filter=20 Fr=12

Steps:

Here is a possible reconstruction of the algorithm:

1. Divide the audio stream into parts of a predetermined duration and use a Hann window on every part.
2. Utilize the fast Fourier transform to determine the strength of the spectrum for every frame.
3. Apply triangular filters to translate the power spectral to Mel scales.
4. Apply a discrete cosine transform with the mel-scaled power spectrum in order to calculate the mel frequency cepstral coefficient.
5. Compute the initial and secondary periodic variations of the MFCC in order to comprehend the temporal progression of the audio signal.

The pseudocode for the revised technique

The user provides an audio signal x(n) as information, with an appropriate sampling rate of fs. The frame duration is n, the hop duration is h, and the desired number of MFCCs is m. Additionally, the user specifies the needed filter classes.

Output of MFCCs: c (1), c (2) ..., c (M) and MFCC

1. Apply a filter called a high-pass filter on x(n) using a minimum threshold frequency of 100 Hz in order to attenuate the low-frequency interference. Calculate the initial-order Modification in the audio data to amplify a frequently occurring component.
2. Separate the pre-amplified signal into overlapping frames with length n and hop length h. To limit spectral leakage, apply a windowing function to each frame (*e.g.*, a Hamming window).
3. Power spectra. a. Using a Fourier transform, calculate the magnitude of the spectra for each frame. b. Squaring the magnitude spectra yields power spectra.
4. Mail Frequency Filter Bank. Define F triangular filter banks that are uniformly distributed over the Mel frequency scale. Apply each filter branch to the power spectrum to compute the energy of the filter branch. Apply the logarithm function to the energy of each filter branch to reduce the range of values.
5. Apply a Discrete Cosine Transform to the log-filter-bank values to obtain a set of M Mel-frequency cepstral coefficients (MFCCs). Remove the first MFCC (which represents the mean of the signal) and retain the following M-1 coefficients.
6. Coefficient of Lift: Apply a lifting operation to the Mel-Frequency Cepstral Coefficients (MFCCs) to emphasize the higher-order components. The lifter method is a cosine formula with an input value of Q. It can be expressed as: lifter[i]= 1 + Q/2 * sin (pi * i / Q), where i ranges from 1 to M-1. Utilize a lifter to carry out element-wise augmentation on Mel-frequency cepstral coefficients (MFCCs).
7. Output MFCC for each frame.

Linear Predictive Filter (LPC)

A linear predictive filter (LPC) utilizes past data to anticipate future values. The LPC algorithm generates distinct waveforms from the salivary glands in the vocal tract, which change based on the level and pitch of the voice being produced. LPC analyses messages by recognizing the power source substances, mitigating the impact they have on the information's magnitude, and subsequently assessing the magnitude and robustness of the residual evidence. The procedure for eliminating compounds is referred to as inversion sorting [19]. The term "residual" commonly denotes an indication that persists with the elimination of other elements.

Yule-Walker Equations

The Yule-Walker equations are fundamental equations in the context of Autoregressive (AR) modelling, which is closely related to Linear Predictive Coding (LPC) [20]. The Yule–Walker formulas provide a connection between the autocorrelation coefficient of a time interval and the variables in a self-correcting model.

For a stationary time series x(n), the Yule-Walker equations are given by:

$$r(k) = \sum_{m=1}^{p} \left[a(m)r(k-m) + \partial^{2}\delta(k) \right] \tag{3}$$

The Yule-Walker eq. (3) can be solved to find the AR coefficients $a(m)$ given the autocorrelation function $r(k)$. This is typically done using techniques like the Levinson-Durbin recursion or matrix inversion methods.

Algorithm 2

LPC Processing for Feature Extraction

Generate and set the appropriate settings.

Step 1: Create a framework for the audio file.

Step 2: Create a wind that forcefully strikes the frame.

Step 3: Calculate the self-correlation coefficient of the computer by performing the Fast Fourier Transform (FFT) on the squared power of the atmospheric signal. The exponent used in the FFT should be the next higher power of 2 than the size of the wind signal multiplied by 2, minus 1. The result of the FFT should be squared and stored in variable A. The size of the air signal should be stored in variables m and n.

Step 4: Resolve the distorted correlation (r/m).

Step 5: Solve the linear predictive coding LPC (r, N).

Here, the variable N denotes the order of anything.

We have computed the Linear Predictive Coding (LPC) up to the 10th order. The procedure will output 10 prominent characteristics.

Calculate Pitch

After filtering the speech, its autocorrelation is used to determine its pitch. Equation 3 demonstrates the calculations required for this approach [21].

Pitch = (*sampling frequency*)/(*max+index*)

max is the maximum lag

Index is the maximum peak
Algorithm 3: Pitching Computation
Setup: Declare and assign appropriate parameters.
1: Start with MF and data. Retrieve Bandwidth and statistics extracted from a recording track.
2: $\frac{MF}{(MF\times0.052)}$= Minimum
3: $\frac{MF}{2}$= Maximum
4: Generate a graph illustrating the self-correlation between the lowest and greatest intervals.
5 Take: FS the first shoot of the plot.
6: $\frac{FS}{2}$ =X
7: Move X from minimum to maximum.
8: High_p determines maximum peak X.
9: [F== High_p] index
10: $\frac{MF}{(High+index)}$= Pitch using Equation (3).

RESULTS AND DISCUSSION

The methods of statistical analysis employed to produce the conclusions are provided in conjunction with the results, which are shown in Figs. (**2** and **3**).

Fig. (**2**) shows the frequency curve of a single speaker. In the Bollywood movie, the graph was drawn without any filtering. Fig. (**3**) shows the output of the second algorithm overlaid on top of the underlying voice.

The effect of Eq. (1) is shown in Fig. (**4**), where the sound estimation plot of the recorded spoken material has very few gaps at the beginning or end. During the intervals between quiet periods, the original signal is removed. Fig. (**5**) shows the pitch of the filtered sound. The frequency shift has a pronounced effect on the pitch of the filtered sound, and noise persists during filtering. For illustration, only the accelerated section of the video is shown.

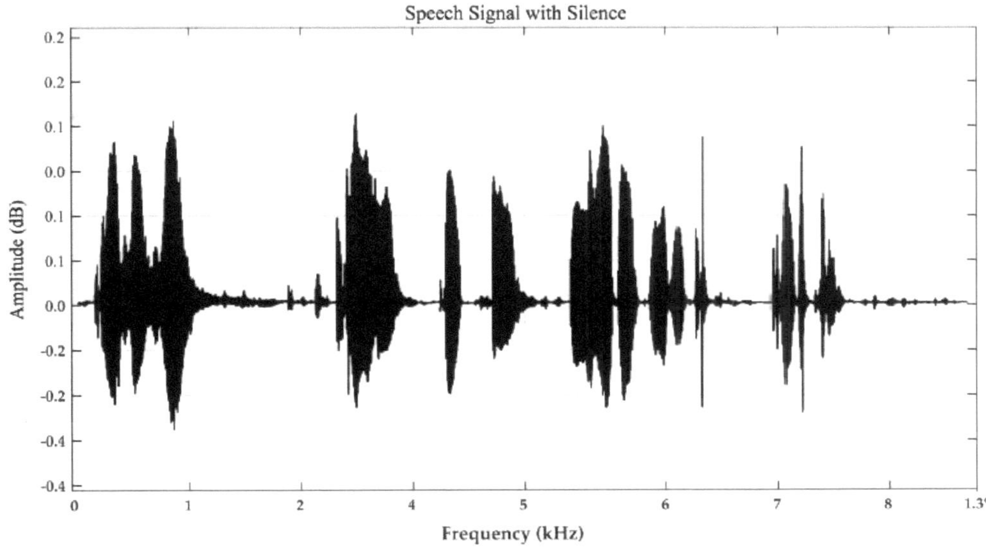

Fig. (4). Initial Voice.

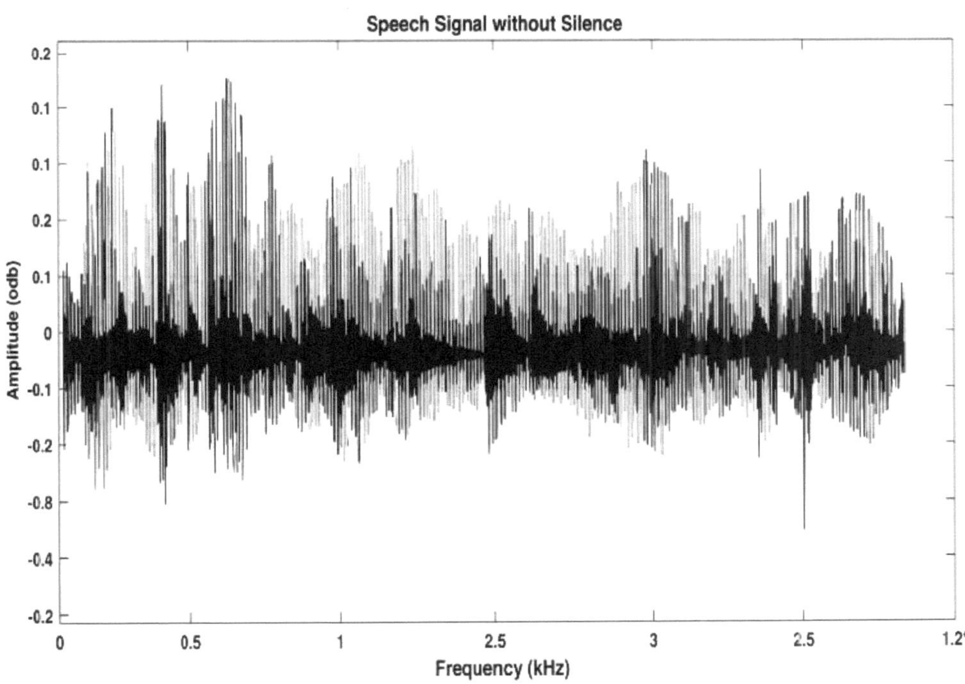

Fig. (5). Clarified Voice.

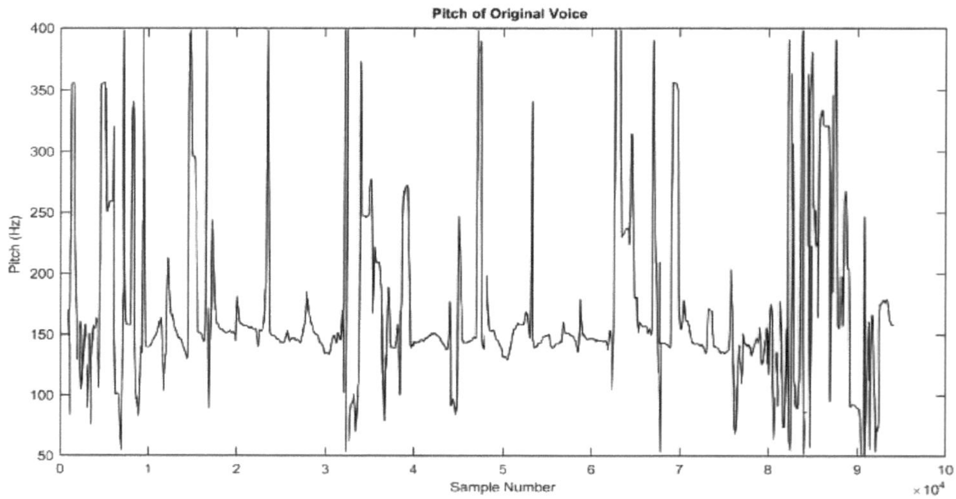

Fig. (6). Sound Estimation Plot.

As shown in Table **3**, the findings corroborated our decision to employ CatBoost for both forecasting and categorization. CatBoost uses data analysis techniques to identify data characteristics.

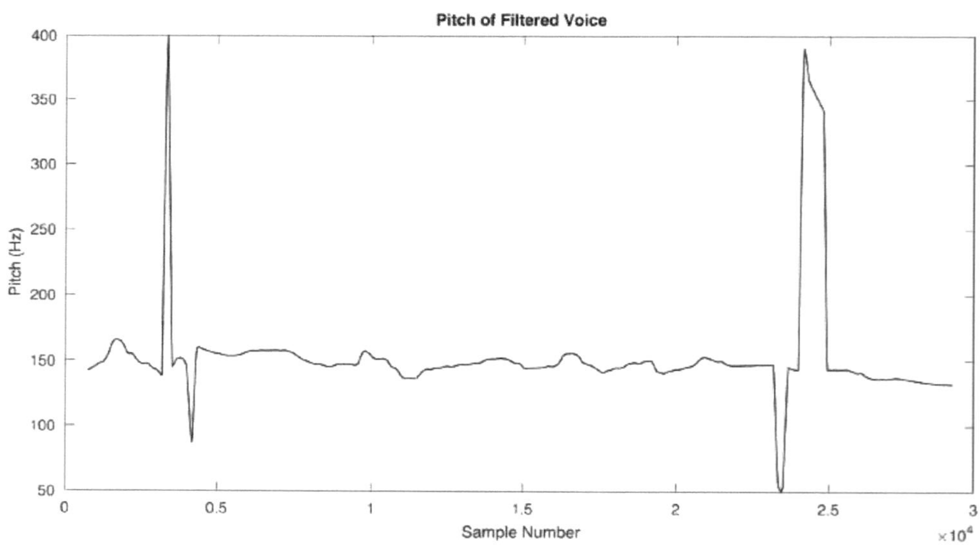

Fig. (7). Shows the Pitch of the Filtering Sound.

Table 3. Evaluation of anguish using algorithms.

Procedure	Precise	Call Rate	Accrete
CNN	0.83	1	0.88
LSTM	0.85	1	0.90
Boost	0.87	1	0.91
Light GBM	0.85	1	0.89
Cat Boost	0.93	1	0.94

The CatBoost algorithm is used in Table **2** for both training and forecasting purposes. Verification and testing used 20% of the data, while the remaining 80% was allocated for training. Tables **2** and **3** demonstrate the rationale for selecting CatBoost. The findings corroborate our choice of employing CatBoost for both forecasting and classification. CatBoost utilizes data analysis techniques to ascertain the characteristics of the data [22]. Table **4** explains the evaluation of cheerfulness using the algorithm. Upon conducting a thorough comparison of all classification algorithms, it was determined that CatBoost exhibited the highest level of accuracy. CatBoost has a focus on Indian languages. The offered data was limited due to the small number of participants, making training and classification on a small dataset challenging. CatBoost can extract and recognize voices even in noisy environments, such as a cocktail party [23]. With Indian languages and smaller datasets, the estimated accuracy rate of 95.05% is quite promising. CatBoost could be utilized to develop an Indian-language speech bot. Even in the presence of significant vibration, it continues to function effectively. Native language speakers will find it easier to interact with computers due to CatBoost. Businesses may benefit from its capabilities in recognizing the speaker's emotions and responding appropriately.

Table 4. Evaluation of cheerfulness using the algorithm.

procedure	Precise	Call rate	Accrete
CNN	0.80	1	0.90
LSTM	0.82	1	0.92
Boost	0.84	1	0.93
Light GBM	0.81	1	0.92
Cat Boost	0.89	1	0.96

Hybrid models, which combine traditional feature extraction techniques like MFCC and LPC with machine learning algorithms such as CatBoost, provide a powerful approach to speech recognition. These models capitalize on the strengths of both classical and modern methods, offering a balanced solution for improving performance. While MFCC and LPC are well-established methods for extracting features in noisy environments, machine learning algorithms like CatBoost bring robust classification capabilities that can adapt to complex and non-linear patterns within the data. This combination of feature extraction and advanced classification enhances the overall system's ability to process and recognize speech effectively, even in challenging conditions [24].

The integration of these two approaches allows for more accurate and efficient operation of speech recognition applications in real-world scenarios, such as virtual assistants, transcription services, or emotion recognition systems. In practical AI-based systems, hybrid models ensure that speech recognition remains reliable and precise, even when background noise interferes with signal clarity. Additionally, hybrid models are particularly advantageous in applications that require real-time processing, as they combine the computational efficiency of traditional methods with the predictive power of machine learning algorithms. This makes them well-suited for embedded systems, mobile applications, and other environments with limited computational resources, ensuring that performance stays optimal without sacrificing speed or accuracy.

We intend to integrate additional languages and voices in the future. In a strange situation, we would like to see many natural speakers speaking at the same time. We need to evaluate the performance of wavelets and FFT in transforming the signal to frequency [25]. Although there is some overlap, the subsequent models ought to have the capability to comprehend a greater number of Indian languages. This might facilitate the development of technologies that can accurately perceive and interpret the emotional states of patients. Medical personnel may use emotion identification for the betterment of patients.

MOTIVATION

Speech recognition in noisy environments continues to pose significant challenges, as background interference often degrades the accuracy of conventional systems. With the rise of AI applications in real-world scenarios, there is an increasing need to address these issues and improve the performance of speech recognition systems under such conditions. This research leverages state-of-the-art techniques, such as UIU-Net and Decoupled-and-Coupled Networks, which have shown remarkable results in domains like small object detection and hyperspectral image super-resolution. By adapting these advanced methods to speech recognition, particularly for emotion detection, this study introduces a novel approach to feature extraction in noisy environments. The novelty lies in applying these cutting-edge techniques to emotional speech recognition, enhancing both the accuracy and robustness of speech recognition systems in diverse, real-world settings.

CONCLUSION

Cat Boost has demonstrated superior performance in speech recognition tasks, particularly for Indian languages, despite the challenges posed by limited data and noisy environments. Its robustness and high accuracy make it an ideal choice for developing advanced speech recognition systems that can understand and interact with users in their native languages. As the technology continues to evolve, integrating more languages, handling multiple speakers, and improving emotional recognition capabilities will further enhance the applicability and effectiveness of speech recognition systems across various industries. By focusing on these future directions, we can develop more inclusive, accurate, and emotionally intelligent speech recognition technologies that meet the diverse needs of users worldwide.

REFERENCES

[1] 1. Feature Extraction for a Speech Recognition System in Noisy Environment A Study, 2010 Second International Conference on Computer Engineering and Applications, Bali, Indonesia, pp. 358-361, Available from: https://jonathan-hui.medium.com/speech-recognition-feature-extraction-mfc-plp-5455f5a69dd9
[http://dx.doi.org/10.1109/ICCEA.2010.76]

[2] Modification of the speech feature extraction module for the enhancement of the system for automated lectures transcription, Proceedings *ELMAR-2012*, Zadar, Croatia, pp. 223-226, 2012.

[3] Optimal feature extraction and selection strategies for voice processing: A review, *International Conference on Communication and Signal Processing (ICCSP)*, Melmaruvathur, India, 2016, pp. 1669–1673
[http://dx.doi.org/10.1109/ICCSP.2016.7754447]

[4] L.B. Letaifa, M.I. Torres, and R. Justo, "Adding dimensional characteristics for emotion identification on speech", *5th International Conference on Advanced Technologies for Signal and Image Processing (ATSIP),* pp. 1-6, 2020.Sousse, Tunisia
[http://dx.doi.org/10.1109/ATSIP49331.2020.9231766]

[5] P. Singh, A. Asthana, B. Solanki, S. Tomar, M. Kansal, and G. Tyagi, "A comprehensive analysis and sensitivity model for emotion detection in text", In: *Applications of Artificial Intelligence in 5G and Internet of Things.* CRC Press, 2025, pp. 332-337.
[http://dx.doi.org/10.1201/9781003532521-63]

[6] E. Lakomkin, M. A. Zamani, C. Weber, S. Magg, and S. Wermter. Incorporating End-to-End Speech Recognition Models for Sentiment Analysis, *International Conference on Robotics and Automation (ICRA),* Montreal, QC, Canada, pp. 7976–7982.

[7] M.S. Mustaqeem, M. Sajjad, and S. Kwon, "Clustering-Based Speech Emotion Recognition by Incorporating Learned Features and Deep BiLSTM", *IEEE Access,* vol. 8, no. 8, pp. 79861-79875, 2020.
[http://dx.doi.org/10.1109/ACCESS.2020.2990405]

[8] K. Garg, and G. Jain, "A Comparative Study of Noise Reduction Techniques for Automatic Speech Recognition Systems", *International Conference on Advances in Computing, Communications and Informatics (ICACCI),* pp. 2098-2103, 2016.Jaipur, India
[http://dx.doi.org/10.1109/ICACCI.2016.7732361]

[9] Comparison of feature extraction approaches for speech identification in noise-free and in traffic noise environment, *6th Conference on Speech Technology and Human-Computer Dialogue (SpeD)*, Brasov, Romania, pp. 1-8
[http://dx.doi.org/10.1109/SPED.2011.5940729]

[10] P. Singh, M. Kansal, M. Srivastava, and M. Gupta, "Smart agriculture resource allocation and cost optimization using ML in cloud computing environment", *Convergence of Cloud Computing, AI, and Agricultural Science* , pp. 152-163, 2023.
[http://dx.doi.org/10.4018/979-8-3693-0200-2.ch008]

[11] A review of feature extraction methods for voice processing, by Gill AS. 2016's 5(10):18551–18556 for the *International Journal of Engineering and Computer Science*

[12] Line spectrum representation of linear predictor coefficients of speech signals, Itakura F. 57(S1): S35-S35, 1975, *The Journal of the Acoustical Society of America.*

[13] D. O'Shaughnessy, *Speech Communication: Human and Machine.* 2nd ed. Addison-Wesley: Reading, MA, USA, 2000.

[14] J. Makhoul, "Linear prediction: A tutorial review", *Proc. IEEE,* vol. 63, no. 4, pp. 561-580, 1975.
[http://dx.doi.org/10.1109/PROC.1975.9792]

[15] P. Singh, A. Asthana, B. Solanki, S. Tomar, M. Kansal, and G. Tyagi, "A comprehensive analysis and sensitivity model for emotion detection in text", In: *Applications of Artificial Intelligence in 5G and Internet of Things.* CRC Press, 2025, pp. 332-337.
[http://dx.doi.org/10.1201/9781003532521-63]

[16] A. Graves, S. Fernández, and J. Schmidhuber, "Bidirectional LSTM networks for improved phoneme classification and recognition", *Proc. of the International Conference on Artificial Neural Networks,* 2005.
[http://dx.doi.org/10.1007/11550907_126]

[17] L. Prokhorenkova, G. Gusev, A. Vorobev, A.V. Dorogush, and A. Gulin, "CatBoost: unbiased boosting with categorical features", *Adv. Neural Inf. Process. Syst.,* p. 31, 2018.

[18] V.Z. Këpuska, and H.A. Elharati, "Robust Speech Recognition System Using Conventional and Hybrid Features of MFCC, LPCC, PLP, RASTA-PLP and Hidden Markov Model Classifier in Noisy Conditions", *Journal of Computer and Communications,* vol. 3, no. 6, pp. 1-9, 2015.
[http://dx.doi.org/10.4236/jcc.2015.36001]

[19] "Spoken Indian language identification: a survey of characteristics and databases, by B", *Aarti and S. K. Kopparapu Sdhan,* vol. 43, no. 4, p. 53, 2018.
[http://dx.doi.org/10.1007/s12046-018-0841-y]

[20] P. Singh, M. Kansal, S. Lahiri, H. Vishnoi, and L. Mittal, "A Transparency System for ICU Using Machine Learning and AI", In: *Enhancing Medical Imaging with Emerging Technologies.* IGI Global, 2024, pp. 51-69.
[http://dx.doi.org/10.4018/979-8-3693-5261-8.ch004]

[21] Speech Enhancement Using Generative Adversarial Network by Distilling Knowledge from Statistical Method, *Appl. Sci. (Basel),* vol. 9, no. 16, p. 3396, 2019.
[http://dx.doi.org/10.3390/app9163396]

[22] A.J. Oxenham, "Pitch Perception", *J. Neurosci.,* vol. 32, no. 39, pp. 13335-13338, 2012.
[http://dx.doi.org/10.1523/JNEUROSCI.3815-12.2012] [PMID: 23015422]

[23] M. Kansal, P. Singh, S. Shukla, and S. Srivastava, "A comparative study of machine learning models for house price prediction and analysis in smart cities", *International Conference on Electronic Governance with Emerging Technologies,* pp. 168-184, 2023.Cham
[http://dx.doi.org/10.1007/978-3-031-43940-7_14]

[24] D. Matrouf, and M. Mohammad Amini, "Data augmentation *vs.* noise correction for x-vector speaker

identification systems in noisy contexts", *28th European Signal Processing Conference (EUSIPCO),* pp. 1-5, 2021.Amsterdam, Netherlands

[25] Z. Zhang, J. Geiger, J. Pohjalainen, A.E.D. Mousa, W. Jin, and B. Schuller, "Deep learning for environmentally robust speech recognition: An overview of recent developments", *ACM Trans. Intell. Syst. Technol.,* vol. 9, no. 5, pp. 1-28, 2018. [http://dx.doi.org/10.1145/3178115]

CHAPTER 3

AI for Social Goods: Applications in Environment Sciences and Sustainability

Juhi Sharma[1,*], **Kratika Pathak**[1], **Ayushi Bhatnagar**[1], **Vinay Choudhary**[2] and **Sonika Niraj Motan**[3]

[1] *School of Life and Basic Sciences, Jaipur National University, Jaipur, India*

[2] *Department of Ophthalmology, JNU Institute of Medical Sciences and Research Center, Jaipur, India*

[3] *School of Allied Health Sciences, Jaipur National University, Jaipur, India*

Abstract: The evolution of humanity increasingly relies on the natural environment, yet its future vitality may face constraints due to environmental decline caused by various factors such as population growth, industrialization, and urbanization. This century has seen unprecedented environmental degradation, posing ongoing challenges to life itself. Concurrently, globalization transitioning into digitization has ushered in the era of the Fourth Industrial Revolution, where Artificial Intelligence (AI) plays a crucial role. AI and other advanced technologies are pivotal in enhancing efficiency, speed, and accuracy across various industries and developments. Moreover, AI's integration is crucial for achieving the United Nations Sustainable Development Goals, aiming to improve the quality of life, bolster climate resilience, enhance environmental health, and promote global equity. By 2030, AI is expected to drive environmental intelligence, underpinning efforts towards sustainability. In this context, the focus is on exploring how AI can support environmental sustainability for a brighter future. A critical aspect involves understanding AI's potential in transitioning businesses to a Circular Economy model, particularly in energy management. Through a detailed multi-case analysis spanning different sectors, it is evident that AI positively impacts efficiency and emissions management. This technological intervention aids in mitigating occupational risks associated with hazardous agents, although challenges remain in terms of employee acceptance. These insights are crucial for stakeholders navigating the integration of AI into corporate strategies, highlighting the transformative potential of AI in fostering sustainable practices and outcomes

Keywords: AI tools, Environmental intelligence, Interventions, Machine learning, Sustainability goal.

* **Corresponding author Juhi Sharma:** School of Life and Basic Sciences, Jaipur National University, Jaipur, India; E-mail: juhivv5360@gmail.com

Pancham Singh, Avinash Kumar Sharma, Mrignainy Kansal, & Amarjeet Prajapati (Eds.)

INTRODUCTION

Human-induced climate change and environmental degradation are pressing global issues. Advanced technologies, particularly Artificial Intelligence (AI), offer promising solutions to these challenges. AI, with its ability to learn and perform tasks similar to humans, has the potential to lessen our reliance on natural resources and improve environmental governance, thereby supporting more sustainable lifestyles [1]. This study examines AI's potential to address major socio-environmental problems through two case studies. The first case study illustrates how AI can help design and implement strategies to promote pro-environmental behavior in communities. The second case study explores AI-driven methods for efficiently managing wildfires and optimizing renewable energy production. The findings highlight AI's capacity to significantly advance global sustainability efforts significantly, suggesting data-driven interventions and leadership strategies to accelerate progress in mitigating climate change [2].

Humanity is currently facing an unprecedented crisis in the form of climate change, which threatens not only the planet's biodiversity but also the well-being and survival of its inhabitants. This emergency, intensified by decades of unsustainable industrial and economic practices, necessitates urgent and innovative action across all sectors of society, including sustainable economic practices in health and the use of clean resources. Industry 4.0 (I4.0) has introduced a range of innovative tools that could drive the shift towards more sustainable business practices [3].

Artificial Intelligence (AI) is particularly noted for its ability to streamline processes, reduce resource consumption, and enhance decision-making. Despite these advantages, there remains a significant knowledge gap at the business level regarding the concrete and measurable benefits of AI for improving energy efficiency and lowering emissions. This gap is especially notable when considering key strategic factors for businesses, such as product cost, quality, lead time, risk management, and stakeholder satisfaction [4].

Understanding the implications of AI on these variables is crucial for informed decision-making regarding energy efficiency and emission reduction in industrial operations. Efforts to enhance energy efficiency are directly influenced by energy allocations and environmental regulations, which are pivotal in advancing towards a low-carbon energy transition. AI is increasingly recognized as a pivotal tool in addressing the climate crisis. Its potential applications span a wide spectrum: optimizing resource consumption, improving transportation efficiency, enhancing urban planning effectiveness, fostering sustainable energy systems, and even facilitating breakthroughs in materials research. However, the environmental impact of AI systems must also be considered critically [5].

The production and operation of AI systems necessitate significant resources. From the mining of rare earths required for hardware components to energy consumption at data centers and the eventual disposal of electronic waste, the lifecycle of AI systems can generate substantial environmental footprints. Improper disposal can further pose risks of chemical releases, undermining environmental sustainability goals [6]. Therefore, while AI holds promise in advancing sustainability efforts, its overall environmental impact must be carefully managed to ensure that its benefits outweigh its resource consumption and emissions, thereby truly contributing to global environmental goals.

Renewable Energy & Clean Fuels

Artificial Intelligence (AI) holds the potential to revolutionize the management of renewable energy through predictive capabilities and intelligent grid systems. By leveraging AI, renewable energy production can be made more efficient and cost-effective. For instance, AI can enhance the accuracy of rainfall predictions, thereby reducing costs and minimizing carbon emissions. Furthermore, AI technologies can optimize energy storage, improve delivery operations, and enhance the reliability and integration of renewable energy sources. These advancements enable dynamic pricing and trading mechanisms that respond effectively to fluctuations in energy demand [7].

An example of AI's impact is IBM's use of AI to enhance rainfall prediction accuracy, resulting in a significant 30% improvement in forecasts. This improvement has led to more efficient operation of their facilities, increased renewable energy production, and reduced carbon emissions [8].

AI for Energy Preservation and Renewable Energy

As the reliability of energy systems and cost management become increasingly critical, optimizing power generation, planning energy storage, and forecasting demand have grown more complex. This challenge is largely due to the rising variability in production and distribution systems, despite the global increase in renewable energy adoption.

Integrating agile supply and demand management is crucial for maintaining stability and efficiency throughout the energy value chain. As electrical grid operations evolve into the digital era, they generate vast amounts of data on energy production and consumption. Effectively analyzing these large data sets enables managers to make quick and informed decisions [9]. Machine Learning

(ML) algorithms, such as adaptive neuro-fuzzy systems, neural networks, and pattern recognition, are widely used to develop predictive models for wind power generation across various time scales.

Due to the stochastic and intermittent nature of wind patterns and turbine power generation, wind power prediction is divided into four time scales: very short-term, short-term, medium-term, and long-term. Choosing the appropriate technique for each time scale is essential, considering the operational constraints of wind turbines for optimization, control, and modeling purposes. Accurate energy generation predictions are vital for effective power system management, enabling better turbine control for load tracking and energy trading, and improving the monitoring of energy systems.

AI and Climate Change Modeling and Prediction

Climate change has become one of the most critical global challenges, impacting ecosystems, societies, and economies worldwide. Scientific consensus attributes a significant portion of this change to human activities, particularly the release of greenhouse gases that contribute to the warming of the Earth's climate. The advent of Artificial Intelligence (AI) and Machine Learning (ML) has introduced transformative capabilities to climate change research. These technologies have revolutionized our ability to predict future climate scenarios and assess the environmental impacts of human actions [10]. A list of various tools and applications is shown in Fig. (**1**).

AI and ML have revolutionized climate change research through advanced data analysis, pattern recognition, and predictive modeling. These tools excel in handling vast and complex datasets, uncovering nuanced patterns and relationships that traditional methods might overlook. In the realm of climate prediction, AI and ML techniques enable more precise modeling of complex climate systems [11]. This enhances our ability to forecast extreme weather events, changes in precipitation patterns, and shifts in temperature more accurately than before. AI and ML algorithms are distinguished by their proficiency in managing vast and varied datasets, a capability particularly beneficial for climate change research. This field relies on diverse data sources such as atmospheric measurements, satellite observations, oceanic data, and historical climate records. AI and ML excel in integrating and analyzing these datasets, revealing intricate patterns and correlations that traditional methods may overlook [12].

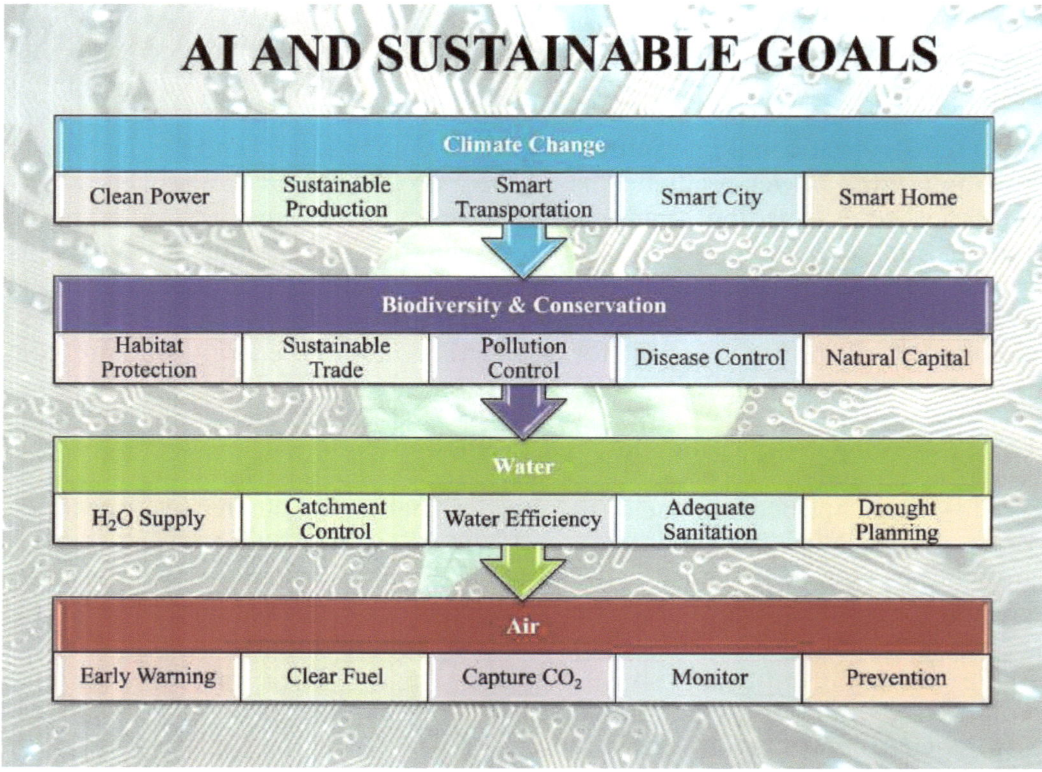

Fig. (1). List of various AI tools and their applications.

In predictive modeling, AI and ML algorithms have emerged as robust tools, harnessing the richness of diverse datasets to enhance accuracy. Whether forecasting extreme weather events or projecting sea-level rise, these technologies facilitate a deeper exploration and more refined understanding of climate patterns [13]. Furthermore, AI and ML have advanced the field of environmental impact assessment by providing deeper insights into deforestation rates, biodiversity loss, and the dynamics of carbon sequestration. Leveraging these technologies' analytical capabilities enables researchers to evaluate environmental consequences with unprecedented accuracy, informing targeted conservation and mitigation strategies [14].

The agricultural sector faces numerous challenges, including crop diseases, pest outbreaks, water scarcity, and weed proliferation. These issues not only lead to substantial crop losses and financial impacts but also pose significant environmental risks associated with conventional farming practices. Precision agriculture has emerged as a transformative approach in modern farming, focusing on optimizing resource use, increasing crop yields, and reducing environmental footprints. The integration of Artificial Intelligence (AI) and robotics has significantly bolstered the capabilities of precision agriculture systems [15].

AI processes diverse datasets, offering insights into soil health, weather patterns, and crop conditions, significantly enhancing decision-making precision. This synergy of AI with Robotics translates these insights into automated actions, effectively managing tasks like planting, irrigation, and harvesting with exceptional accuracy. Utilizing GPS technology, farmers can precisely locate positions within their fields, facilitating targeted input applications based on performance metrics and previous treatments [16].

A Geographic Information System (GIS) integrates computer hardware, software, and methodologies to process and visualize spatial data, effectively digitizing map information. GIS capabilities include receiving, organizing, statistically analyzing, and visually presenting various spatial data categories aligned to a unified coordinate system. Each dataset can be classified and overlaid, combining new information layers to inform subsequent decisions on resource allocation [17]. Being early adopters of AI and other emerging technologies grants farmers a significant advantage. These advancements promise increased farm productivity, improved profitability, and crucially, enable the realization of Precision Agriculture and sustainable farming practices, benefiting society as a whole.

For instance, AI algorithms are being developed to create data-driven models that predict crop yields by analyzing joint dependencies of soil and climate features. Enhancing soil conditions through practices like composting, using manure, and adopting alternative tillage systems can improve soil porosity and aggregation, mitigating physical degradation and reducing factors such as soil-borne pathogens and pollutants. AI also plays a role in creating soil maps that illustrate soil and landscape relationships, offering insights into underground layers and soil compositions [18]. Weeds pose a significant challenge by competing with crops for resources like water, nutrients, and sunlight, some of which can be toxic and pose health risks.

While traditional spraying methods are commonly used to control weeds, they can have adverse effects on public health and the environment through excessive use. AI-driven weed detection systems have been developed in laboratories to precisely calculate the amount of spray needed and accurately target application, reducing costs and minimizing the risk of crop damage [19]. In urban waste management, AI technologies are increasingly applied to optimize waste collection and disposal processes, improving efficiency and environmental sustainability.

The integration of artificial intelligence and robotics into urban waste treatment facilities represents a transformative approach to solid waste management, enhancing operational efficiency and promoting sustainability. AI-driven systems enable municipalities to reduce costs, enhance safety, and minimize environmental impacts associated with waste handling. Intelligent garbage bins are pivotal in this evolution, focusing on automating waste sorting and monitoring processes. Data collected from these bins can be transmitted for further analysis and processing, supporting informed decision-making in waste management practices. IoT-based smart bins, such as those initiated under programs like Swachh Bharat, aim to optimize garbage collection efficiency, mitigate disease transmission, and improve overall urban hygiene.

The widespread adoption of smart garbage bins is currently limited by their high implementation costs. However, alongside smart bins, waste sorting robots equipped with technologies such as Simultaneous Localization and Mapping (SLAM) and instance segmentation can handle diverse field conditions. These robots automate the sorting of construction and demolition waste, enhancing the efficiency of waste management processes [20].

Sensor-based waste monitoring, using Wireless Sensor Networks (WSNs), provides a method for tracking waste generation, identifying its sources, and evaluating waste management strategies within a specific area. These networks consist of self-organizing wireless sensors that monitor physical and environmental parameters. Additionally, Artificial Intelligence (AI) is increasingly seen as a transformative force in urban development. With its capabilities for learning, predicting outcomes, and potentially operating autonomously, AI offers significant opportunities to advance and manage smart cities. Its applications include predictive maintenance, improved citizen services, and enhanced sustainability initiatives [21].

The convergence of AI and 5G technologies has opened extensive possibilities for ubiquitous applications in smart cities, including automated vehicles, healthcare, and smart homes. Continuous environmental monitoring is crucial to maintaining the quality of life in urban areas. A chatbot application utilizing Artificial Neural Networks (ANNs) facilitates communication between governments and citizens, leveraging regression techniques to guide decision-making in building smart cities through innovative social involvement.

Smart Manufacturing

Artificial Intelligence (AI) finds extensive application in manufacturing to improve both product quality and quantity. In the realm of 3D printing, AI is employed in developing predictive models for surface roughness and lead time estimation [22].

In ophthalmology, AI primarily targets prevalent conditions such as diabetic retinopathy, age-related macular degeneration, glaucoma, as well as other issues like retinopathy of prematurity, cataracts (both age-related and congenital), and retinal vein occlusion (NLM). The field of AI-assisted medical screening and diagnosis, especially through image analysis, is progressing swiftly. For example, computer algorithms can now diagnose skin cancers such as melanoma using macro images taken with standard cameras. Similarly, in ophthalmology, AI aids in medical imaging identification and provides auxiliary diagnoses for sight-threatening conditions [23].

Two primary deep learning models utilized in these applications are Convolutional Neural Networks (CNNs) and Massively Trained Artificial Neural Networks (MTANNs). CNNs conduct convolution operations within the network architecture, whereas MTANNs perform these operations externally. After iterative processes, CNNs typically culminate with a convolution layer connected to the entire network. CNNs require a substantial volume of training images compared to MTANNs. CNNs have demonstrated successful applications in various fields such as large-scale image classification and scene labeling [24].

Recent studies have introduced preliminary algorithms for various ophthalmic conditions such as DR, ROP, AMD, RVO, glaucoma, and cataracts. However, despite numerous advancements, achieving 100% accuracy and sensitivity remains rare. This limitation underscores the influence of both computer techniques and the quality of input images. Factors contributing to poor image quality in posterior or anterior segment imaging include patient movement, undilated pupils, frequent blinking, opaque refractive media, and inadequate fixation. Moreover, the accuracy of annotations by experts is crucial as it forms the basis for computer learning, necessitating standardized training for annotators [25]

AI has gained significant traction in ophthalmological image processing, particularly with fundus photographs, achieving accuracy levels that rival those of clinical experts. Its integration into ophthalmology has significantly advanced the field, improving diagnostic precision, patient care, and treatment outcomes. Deep learning frameworks are crucial for detecting and quantifying ophthalmic features from imaging data, enhancing image analysis, facilitating tissue segmentation, and enabling predictive analytics [26].

In healthcare education, AI is transforming training and simulation by providing personalized and adaptive learning experiences. AI applications also extend to treatment planning, using imaging technologies such as Optical Coherence Tomography (OCT) and OCT Angiography (OCTA) to detect subtle structural changes in ocular tissues. These systems assist in predicting surgical outcomes and monitoring potential complications from systemic medications [27].

In meibography analysis, which is vital for diagnosing and monitoring meibomian gland dysfunction, AI plays a pivotal role. AI's predictive analytics can forecast disease progression, enabling the development of personalized prevention strategies and treatment plans. It also improves patient triage by evaluating the severity and urgency of conditions, ensuring appropriate levels of care. On the other hand, unsupervised learning analyzes unlabeled data to identify underlying patterns or structures without prior knowledge of potential outcomes. Reinforcement learning (RL), a machine learning technique, trains algorithms through a trial-and-error process, rewarding or penalizing actions to promote optimal decision-making [28].

Reinforcement learning helps algorithms learn through experimentation, with feedback guiding them to achieve the best results. In ophthalmology, RL is applied to various areas such as managing chronic eye conditions, refining surgical techniques, and improving image segmentation. Convolutional Neural Networks (CNNs) have shown remarkable success in ophthalmic imaging. The development and validation of AI-powered tools for prioritizing retinal diseases highlight this progress. The integration of CNNs with imaging modalities like Fundus Autofluorescence (FAF), Optical Coherence Tomography (OCT), and color fundus photographs has significantly improved diagnostic accuracy for conditions such as glaucoma, corneal ulcers, and macular edema [29].

In OCTA technology, advancements in Deep Learning (DL) have led to substantial improvements in image clarity and quality. An innovative algorithm utilizing the U-net architecture for DL, known as Intelligent Denoise, has been introduced to reduce noise in enface OCTA images. This technique effectively enhances image quality by minimizing background noise and improving the continuity of vascular structures. AI's impact on pharmacology encompasses drug discovery, clinical trials, personalized medicine, pharmacogenomics, pharmacovigilance, and clinical toxicology. Given AI's rapid progress in healthcare, clinical pharmacologists must grasp its implications and applications in clinical practice. Digital technology advancements and innovative approaches in drug research and development have led to the rising adoption of machine learning and data-driven algorithms in crucial pharmaceutical domains. These include supporting new drug discovery, drug repurposing, and drug supervision. Artificial Intelligence (AI) represents a multidisciplinary approach that has garnered significant success in recent years, particularly through advancements in Machine Learning (ML) and Deep Learning (DL).

AI/ML in Pharmacology

AI and Machine Learning (ML) play a pivotal role in pharmacological sciences, enhancing analytical techniques such as Magnetic Resonance Imaging (MRI), X-ray imaging, Electrocardiogram (ECG), and histopathology. These technologies deliver more precise results through advanced sensor and data acquisition systems compared to traditional methods. AI also enhances healthcare data by analyzing inputs and stored data, enabling more accurate detection of retinal and dermal responses. Additionally, AI contributes to healthcare services related to animal research by analyzing animal behavior, movement patterns, and physiological and pathological changes. It also aids in selecting appropriate drugs for specific conditions in animal models [30]. The list of various tools and applications are shown in Table **1**.

Table 1. Different application fields of AI.

S. No.	Field/ Area	AI Tools	Applications	Refs.
1.	Ophthalmology	Deep Learning	AI system had taught itself to accurately detect Diabetic Retinopathy (DR) and diabetic macular edema in fundus photographs.	Gulshan V *et al.*, 2016
		IDX-DR (IDX)	DR- Screening	Abràmoff *et al.*,2018
		EyeArt System	Fundus Screening	Ipp *et al.*,2021
		AEYES-DS	ETDRS Screening	Dvey etal.,2021
		i-ROP DL	For ROP Screening	Brown *et al.*,2018
		Retmarker DR	For Retinopathy	Nita *et al.*, 2024.
		Eye Nuk	Identification of macular edema, or moderate NPDR changes	Nita *et al.*, 2024.
		ResNet	Identifying referable cataracts	Nita *et al.*, 2024.
		CC-Cruiser	Demonstrated high accuracy for identifying the region, density, and degree of congenital cataract formation based on slit-lamp photographs.	Liu *et al.*,2017

(Table 1) cont.....

S. No.	Field/ Area	AI Tools	Applications	Refs.
2	Pharmacology	MYCIN	It was an expert system-based AI that was able to recommend appropriate antibiotics using a knowledge base composed of a large number of rules in the form of if-then statements.	Ursula *et al.*,2018
		ChemMapper	Predicting drug-target interactions.	Lounkine *et al.*, 2012
		Hit Dexter	ML technique to predict molecules that might respond to biochemical assays.	Debleena *et al.*,2021
		DeepChem	MLP model that uses a Python-based AI system to find a suitable candidate in drug discovery.	Zhu H, 2020
		DeltaVina	A scoring function for rescoring drug–ligand binding affinity.	Debleena *et al.*,2021
		DeepNeuralNetQSAR	Python-based system driven by computational tools that aid in the detection of the molecular activity of compounds.	Chan *et al.*,2019
		TargeTox and PrOCTOR	Toxicity prediction	Debleena *et al.*,2021
3	Climate Change	The European Centre for Medium-Range Weather Forecasts (ECMWF)	The ECMWF uses Machine learning to improve weather forecasts, including predicting the tracks of hurricanes and cyclones more accurately.	Kishan *et al.*,2023
4	Biodiversity & Conservation	Global Fishing Watch	Build networks of biodiversity driver monitoring sensors, and mandate data openness for supply chains that are high-risk drivers of biodiversity loss.	Nicolas *et al.*, 2022
5	Water	FNN	Pattern recognition, regression, classification	Gulzar *et al.*, 2021
6	Air	Smart PLS Version 4.0 GFS	AIR Protection System Global Forecast System	Hardini *et al.*, 2023 Patel *et al.*, 2023

AI in Medical Diagnosis

Natural Language Processing (NLP) serves as a valuable tool, enabling doctors to efficiently study descriptors from chest X-rays and aiding in the treatment of infectious diseases.

AI in Drug Discovery and Progress

Typically, it takes about 13.5 years for a molecule to receive approval, with Research and Development (R&D) costs estimated at around $2.6 billion. However, AI has markedly impacted drug discovery and development by speeding up timelines and lowering costs associated with lengthy processes, thanks to more efficient resource utilization.

Role of AI in Adverse Drug Reactions

Pharmacovigilance encompasses the monitoring, detection, and prevention of adverse reactions associated with newly developed or developing drugs. These concerns extend beyond initial testing to post-marketing surveillance, where the focus is on identifying unwanted effects from normal drug doses in the population. A plethora of databases are utilized to report and analyze adverse drug reactions, with developing countries often employing systematic collection methods involving Marketing Authorization Holders (MAHs) and adverse drug reaction monitoring centers [31, 32].

The comprehensive processes involved include detecting adverse drug events, assessing their severity, maintaining technical databases, reporting drug interactions, and generating safety reports. These protocols are labor-intensive and prone to human errors due to their reliance on manual intervention. Managing the vast global dataset requires ongoing technological advancements to ensure effective tracking and analysis [33].

Economic sustainability broadens the scope of economic activities beyond immediate needs to ensure future generations' requirements are also met. This shift is critical amidst pressing global challenges such as climate change, biodiversity loss, and resource scarcity. As societies undergo socio-ecological transformations, questions of fairness arise concerning the distribution of natural resources and their impact on the quality of life [35].

Economic sustainability places the economy within boundaries defined by social and environmental considerations. In this context, the implications of AI systems must be carefully assessed. These systems can profoundly influence wealth distribution through decisions on social benefits, loans, housing, and economic structures. Therefore, their deployment requires responsible management to align with sustainable economic practices [34].

CONCLUSION

Artificial Intelligence (AI) driven by Machine Learning (ML), particularly Deep Learning (DL), has significantly advanced tasks previously deemed challenging for AI. However, these ML methods are often resource-intensive, consuming substantial compute power and energy, leading to significant carbon emissions that contribute to climate change. Moreover, the platforms supporting ML systems also impose environmental impacts beyond carbon emissions. Efforts to enhance the environmental sustainability of ML have predominantly focused on improving efficiency in computing and energy consumption. However, we argue that solely improving efficiency is insufficient to achieve true environmental sustainability for ML. We highlight three key discrepancies that illustrate the complex interactions and variables involved in assessing the environmental impacts of ML. These discrepancies span technical and non-technical factors, demonstrating why efficiency alone cannot fully mitigate ML's environmental footprint.

RECOMMENDATIONS

To address these challenges comprehensively, we advocate for a systems thinking approach. This holistic perspective considers the broader ecosystem of ML development and deployment, aiming to integrate environmental sustainability considerations at every stage. By embracing systems thinking, we propose a more viable pathway to enhance the environmental sustainability of ML technologies.

REFERENCES

[1] L. Lu, "In-depth analysis of artificial intelligence for climate change mitigation", *Applied and Computational Engineering,* vol. 64, pp. 152-158, 2024. [http://dx.doi.org/10.20944/preprints202402.0022.v1]

[2] F. Taghikhah, E. Erfani, I. Bakhshayeshi, S. Tayari, A. Karatopouzis, and B. Hanna, "Artificial intelligence and sustainability: solutions to social and environmental challenges", In: *Artificial intelligence and data science in environmental sensing.* Academic Press, 2022, pp. 93-108. [http://dx.doi.org/10.1016/B978-0-323-90508-4.00006-X]

[3] S. Tong, H. Bambrick, P.J. Beggs, L. Chen, Y. Hu, W. Ma, W. Steffen, and J. Tan, "Current and future threats to human health in the Anthropocene", *Environ. Int.,* vol. 158, p. 106892, 2022. [http://dx.doi.org/10.1016/j.envint.2021.106892] [PMID: 34583096]

[4] J. Achan, A.O. Talisuna, A. Erhart, A. Yeka, J.K. Tibenderana, F.N. Baliraine, P.J. Rosenthal, and U. D'Alessandro, "Quinine, an old anti-malarial drug in a modern world: role in the treatment of malaria", *Malar. J.,* vol. 10, no. 1, p. 144, 2011. [http://dx.doi.org/10.1186/1475-2875-10-144] [PMID: 21609473]

[5] M. Kansal, P. Singh, S. Kumar, and R. Sibal, "Predicting stock market price over the years by utilizing machine learning algorithms. In Artificial Intelligence, Blockchain", *Comput. Secur.,* vol. 1, pp. 72-78,

2023.

[6] W.R.L. Anderegg, J.T. Abatzoglou, L.D.L. Anderegg, L. Bielory, P.L Kinney, and L. Ziska, "Anthropogenic climate change is worsening North American pollen seasons", *Proc. Natl. Acad. Sci. USA,* vol. 118, no. 7, p. e2013284118, 2021. [http://dx.doi.org/10.1073/pnas.2013284118] [PMID: 33558232]

[7] E.K. Austin, T. Handley, A.S. Kiem, J.L. Rich, T.J. Lewin, H.H. Askland, S.S. Askarimarnani, D.A. Perkins, and B.J. Kelly, "Drought-related stress among farmers: findings from the Australian Rural Mental Health Study", *Med. J. Aust.,* vol. 209, no. 4, pp. 159-165, 2018. [http://dx.doi.org/10.5694/mja17.01200] [PMID: 30041594]

[8] R.P. Bird, and N.A.M. Eskin, "The emerging role of phosphorus in human health", *Adv. Food Nutr. Res.,* vol. 96, pp. 27-88, 2021. [http://dx.doi.org/10.1016/bs.afnr.2021.02.001] [PMID: 34112356]

[9] S. Jeble, S. Kumari, and Y. Patil, "Role of big data in decision making", *Operations and Supply Chain Management: An International Journal,* vol. 11, no. 1, pp. 36-44, 2017.

[10] M. Kansal, P. Singh, S. Shukla, and S. Srivastava, "A comparative study of machine learning models for house price prediction and analysis in smart cities", *International Conference on Electronic Governance with Emerging Technologies,* pp. 168-184, 2023. [http://dx.doi.org/10.1007/978-3-031-43940-7_14]

[11] X. Liu, J. Jiang, K. Zhang, E. Long, J. Cui, M. Zhu, Y. An, J. Zhang, Z. Liu, Z. Lin, X. Li, J. Chen, Q. Cao, J. Li, X. Wu, D. Wang, and H. Lin, "Localization and diagnosis framework for pediatric cataracts based on slit-lamp images using deep features of a convolutional neural network", *PLoS One,* vol. 12, no. 3, p. e0168606, 2017. [http://dx.doi.org/10.1371/journal.pone.0168606] [PMID: 28306716]

[12] S. Bresciani, F. Ciampi, F. Meli, and A. Ferraris, "Using big data for co-innovation processes: Mapping the field of data-driven innovation, proposing theoretical developments and providing a research agenda", *Int. J. Inf. Manage.,* vol. 60, p. 102347, 2021. [http://dx.doi.org/10.1016/j.ijinfomgt.2021.102347]

[13] A.A. Nazarenko, J. Sarraipa, L.M. Camarinha-Matos, C. Grunewald, M. Dorchain, and R. Jardim-Goncalves, "Analysis of relevant standards for industrial systems to support zero defects manufacturing process", *J. Ind. Inf. Integr.,* vol. 23, p. 100214, 2021. [http://dx.doi.org/10.1016/j.jii.2021.100214]

[14] R.H. Hamilton, and W.A. Sodeman, "The questions we ask: Opportunities and challenges for using big data analytics to strategically manage human capital resources", *Bus. Horiz.,* vol. 63, no. 1, pp. 85-95, 2020. [http://dx.doi.org/10.1016/j.bushor.2019.10.001]

[15] A. K. Sharma, N. Chanderwal, A. Prajapati, P. Singh, M. Kansal, Ed., *Advancing Software Engineering Through AI, Federated Learning, and Large Language Models.* IGI Global: Hershey, PA, USA, 2024. [http://dx.doi.org/10.4018/979-8-3693-3502-4]

[16] D.S. Char, M.D. Abràmoff, and C. Feudtner, "Identifying ethical considerations for machine learning healthcare applications", *Am. J. Bioeth.,* vol. 20, no. 11, pp. 7-17, 2020. [http://dx.doi.org/10.1080/15265161.2020.1819469] [PMID: 33103967]

[17] A. Tucker, Z. Wang, Y. Rotalinti, and P. Myles, "Generating high-fidelity synthetic patient data for assessing machine learning healthcare software", *NPJ Digit. Med.,* vol. 3, no. 1, p. 147, 2020. [http://dx.doi.org/10.1038/s41746-020-00353-9] [PMID: 33299100]

[18] S. Siddique, and J.C.L. Chow, "Machine learning in healthcare communication", *Encyclopedia,* vol. 1, no. 1, pp. 220-239, 2021. [http://dx.doi.org/10.3390/encyclopedia1010021]

[19] J.A. Roth, M. Battegay, F. Juchler, J.E. Vogt, and A.F. Widmer, "Introduction to machine learning in digital healthcare epidemiology", *Infect. Control Hosp. Epidemiol.,* vol. 39, no. 12, pp. 1457-1462, 2018.
[http://dx.doi.org/10.1017/ice.2018.265] [PMID: 30394238]

[20] M. Kansal, P. Singh, U. Agarwal, K. Singhal, K. Arora, and M. Dixit, "Enhancing Real Estate Price Prediction in Smart Cities: A Comparative Analysis of Machine Learning Techniques", *International Conference on Advances in Distributed Computing and Machine Learning,* pp. 71-84, 2024.Singapore
[http://dx.doi.org/10.1007/978-981-97-3523-5_6]

[21] Z. Ahmed, K. Mohamed, S. Zeeshan, and X. Dong, "Artificial intelligence with multi-functional machine learning platform development for better healthcare and precision medicine", *Database (Oxford),* vol. 2020, p. baaa010, 2020.
[http://dx.doi.org/10.1093/database/baaa010] [PMID: 32185396]

[22] T. Han, N. Stone-Weiss, J. Huang, A. Goel, and A. Kumar, "Machine learning as a tool to design glasses with controlled dissolution for healthcare applications", *Acta Biomater.,* vol. 107, pp. 286-298, 2020.
[http://dx.doi.org/10.1016/j.actbio.2020.02.037] [PMID: 32114183]

[23] S. Jadhav, R. Kasar, N. Lade, M. Patil, and S. Kolte, "Disease prediction by machine learning from healthcare communities", *Int. J. Sci. Res. Sci. Technol.,* vol. 5, pp. 29-35, 2019.
[http://dx.doi.org/10.32628/IJSRST19633]

[24] S. Ardabili, A. Mosavi, P. Ghamisi, F. Ferdinand, A. Varkonyi-Koczy, U. Reuter, T. Rabczuk, and P. Atkinson, "Covid-19 outbreak prediction with machine learning", *Algorithms,* vol. 13, no. 10, p. 249, 2020.
[http://dx.doi.org/10.3390/a13100249]

[25] Kansal, M., Singh, P., Chaurasia, P., Dwivedi, A., & Ali, S. (2024, March). Blockchain-Powered Food Supply Chain Tracking: A Paradigm Shift for Transparency, Accountability, and Quality Assurance Through BlockTrackers. In 2024 *2nd International Conference on Disruptive Technologies (ICDT)* (pp. 194-200). IEEE.

[26] Rayed, M. E., Islam, S. S., Niha, S. I., Jim, J. R., Kabir, M. M., Mridha, M. F. (2024). Deep learning for medical image segmentation: State-of-the-art advancements and challenges. Informatics in Medicine Unlocked, 101504.

[27] S. Kadomoto, A. Uji, Y. Muraoka, T. Akagi, and A. Tsujikawa, "Enhanced visualization of retinal microvasculature in optical coherence tomography angiography imaging via deep learning", *J. Clin. Med.,* vol. 9, no. 5, p. 1322, 2020.
[http://dx.doi.org/10.3390/jcm9051322] [PMID: 32370282]

[28] L. Dong, W. He, R. Zhang, Z. Ge, Y.X. Wang, J. Zhou, J. Xu, L. Shao, Q. Wang, Y. Yan, Y. Xie, L. Fang, H. Wang, Y. Wang, X. Zhu, J. Wang, C. Zhang, H. Wang, Y. Wang, R. Chen, Q. Wan, J. Yang, W. Zhou, H. Li, X. Yao, Z. Yang, J. Xiong, X. Wang, Y. Huang, Y. Chen, Z. Wang, C. Rong, J. Gao, H. Zhang, S. Wu, J.B. Jonas, and W.B. Wei, "Artificial intelligence for screening of multiple retinal and optic nerve diseases", *JAMA Netw. Open,* vol. 5, no. 5, pp. e229960-e229960, 2022.
[http://dx.doi.org/10.1001/jamanetworkopen.2022.9960] [PMID: 35503220]

[29] A. Choudhary, S. Ahlawat, S. Urooj, N. Pathak, A. Lay-Ekuakille, and N. Sharma, "A deep learning-based framework for retinal disease classification", *Healthcare,* vol. 11, no. 2, p. 212, 2023.
[http://dx.doi.org/10.3390/healthcare11020212]

[30] M. Kansal, P. Singh, M. Srivastava, and P. Chaurasia, "Empowering agriculture with conversational AI: an application for farmer advisory and communication", *Convergence of Cloud Computing, AI, and Agricultural Science,* pp. 210-227, 2023.
[http://dx.doi.org/10.4018/979-8-3693-0200-2.ch011]

[31] H. Siala, and Y. Wang, "SHIFTing artificial intelligence to be responsible in healthcare: A systematic review", *Soc. Sci. Med.,* vol. 296, p. 114782, 2022.

[http://dx.doi.org/10.1016/j.socscimed.2022.114782] [PMID: 35152047]

[32] T. Davenport, and R. Kalakota, "The potential for artificial intelligence in healthcare", *Future Healthc. J.,* vol. 6, no. 2, pp. 94-98, 2019.
[http://dx.doi.org/10.7861/futurehosp.6-2-94] [PMID: 31363513]

[33] G.W. Lee, H. Shin, and M.C. Chang, "Deep learning algorithm to evaluate cervical spondylotic myelopathy using lateral cervical spine radiograph", *BMC Neurol.,* vol. 22, no. 1, p. 147, 2022.
[http://dx.doi.org/10.1186/s12883-022-02670-w] [PMID: 35443618]

[34] S. Gerke, T. Minssen, and G. Cohen, "Ethical and legal challenges of artificial intelligence-driven healthcare", In: *Artificial intelligence in healthcare.* Academic Press, 2020, pp. 295-336.
[http://dx.doi.org/10.1016/B978-0-12-818438-7.00012-5]

[35] V.O.K. Li, J.C.K. Lam, and J. Cui, "AI for social good: AI and big data approaches for environmental decision-making", *Environ. Sci. Policy,* vol. 125, pp. 241-246, 2021.
[http://dx.doi.org/10.1016/j.envsci.2021.09.001]

CHAPTER 4

Android Application for Blind People

Asmita Yadav[1,*], **Yash Singh**[1], **Tushar Gupta**[1] and **Atul Sharma**[1]

[1] *Department of CSE &IT, Jaypee Institute of Information Technology (JIIT), Noida, India*

Abstract: The visually impaired are people who face many difficulties and are disadvantaged in our society, especially those who live independently without being dependent on others. Technology is shaping the future and changing the way people live. Technology can help people overcome some of these problems. With the voice-based mobile application, where users can tell it to do certain tasks without seeing the application, their lives can be made easier. The project will include two main areas: machine learning research and Android application development. It will include machine learning, data collection, prioritization, model selection, training, evaluation, and deployment. Android application development components will include user interface design, image capture, preprocessing, object detection, post-processing, user interactions, persistent rendering, and integration with other technologies. By combining these two things, we will create an application that can improve the daily life of visually impaired people and make them independent and safe. This project aims to design and develop a mobile application for the visually impaired to help them do the most necessary tasks in daily life demands like scanning any text using the device's camera to read (textbook, newspaper, documents, street address, *etc.*), reading the current location, weather detection, phone battery status, and time and date, *etc.*

Keywords: Assistive technology, Android development, Independent living, Image capture, Machine learning, Object detection, User interface design, Voice-based mobile application, Visually impaired.

INTRODUCTION

The visually impaired are people who face many difficulties and are disadvantaged in our society, especially those who live independently without being dependent on others. This project aims to develop an Android application for object detection that can assist visually impaired individuals in navigating their surroundings. The application will use machine learning algorithms, specifically YOLO (You Only Look Once), to detect objects in real-time from the

* **Corresponding author Asmita Yadav:** Department of CSE &IT, Jaypee Institute of Information Technology (JIIT), Noida, India; E-mail: asmita.yadav85@gmail.com

Pancham Singh, Avinash Kumar Sharma, Mrignainy Kansal, & Amarjeet Prajapati (Eds.)

camera feed of a mobile device. The detected objects will be communicated to the user through audio feedback. The project will involve two main components: object detection using machine learning and Android application development [1]. The machine learning component will include data collection, preprocessing, model selection, training, evaluation, and deployment.

Technology is shaping the future and changing the way people live. Technology can help people overcome some of these problems. With the voice-based mobile application, where users can tell it to do certain tasks without seeing the application, their lives can be made easier. This app is for the visually impaired to scan text (books, magazines, documents, addresses, *etc.*) using a camera, read the current location, explore weather, phone battery status, time, and date, and more. The Android application we created for the visually impaired has great potential to be developed and expanded in the future. The visually impaired are people who face many difficulties and are disadvantaged in our society, especially those who live independently without being dependent on others. Technology is shaping the future and changing the way people live. Technology can help people overcome some of these problems [2]. With the voice-based mobile application, where users can tell it to do certain tasks without seeing the application, their lives can be made easier. This project is for the visually impaired to scan text (books, magazines, documents, addresses, *etc.*) using a camera, read the current location, explore weather, phone battery status, time, and date, and more.

Our mobile phone Android app is designed to serve not only blind people, but also older people with vision problems. This kind of help for the visually impaired already exists, but differently,*i.e* Make My Eyes. Make My Eyes is a free mobile application with one goal: to make the world accessible to the blind and visually impaired [3]. The app connects blind and visually impaired people with volunteers and companies from around the world through live calls. Since its inception in January 2015, 5,969,805 volunteers have signed up to help blind and visually impaired users [4, 5]. Be My Eyes users can request help in over 180 languages, making the app the largest online community for the blind and low vision and one of the largest organizations in the world. Volunteers enter Make My Eyes to lend their eyes to the blind and see some to work together and solve problems [6]. The story of Be My Eyes began in 2012 with Hans Jorgen Wiberg, a Danish furniture engineer who is also visually impaired. Through her work with the "Danish Association for the Blind," she realized that blind or visually impaired people often need some help with their daily work. However, it was not until a blind friend told him that he could use the phone to communicate with family and friends who could help him with these tasks. The idea for Be My Eyes belonged to Hans Jorgen [7]. Rather than relying on friends and family, using a network of people who can help, he believes telephone technology can be used to help people who are blind or visually impaired.

Objectives

The main objectives are that we focus on various areas of this application, including the creation of Smart Calculator, Smart Reader, Text-to-Speech, and Smart Voice Assistant as follows:

- **OCR Reader:** The purpose of OCR is to successfully edit or convert any type of text or text to written. Documents containing text, such as printed or scanned text, are converted to digital text, which can be modified for deepening and further processing.
- **Calculator:** The purpose of the calculator is to get the result and convey it to a blind person *via* text-to-speech so that the user does not need to do any business touches.
- **Weather:** The purpose of the weather function is to show the user current weather information by taking the user's location name.

Second Goal: This project also aims to provide a good GUI for humans, which includes different functions such as reading the current user's battery percentage, reading Weather content, reading history, and a voice-based calculator to calculate simple numbers. It is done by the user, making the user interaction as easy, interactive, and efficient as possible to make the project a good client [8]. The project also looks forward to making a difference in society by making small donations to make a big difference and help those in need.

Purpose and Scope

There are more than 253 million blind or low-vision people in the world. To make the world more accessible to them, we need to create tools that can adapt to the situation that surrounds us. The project was designed with the daily struggles of blind and visually impaired people, such as reading, current location, weather detection, phone battery status, time, and date [9]. This application contains Google Voice input. Blind users need to speak some words to open special functions to help people. This application can also be used for people who are always there. Many visually impaired people make their lives easier thanks to these applications. Thanks to these applications, the lives of many visually impaired people have become easier. Being able to read something that is only in the field of vision is a task that may require a blind person to seek help from others. In the Google Voice Typing app, visually impaired users say a few words to activate special features.

The app has a simple function where users swipe right or left on the screen to open the voice assistant and talk to it. A text-to-speech approach to listening app functionality and usage. It is designed to help deaf people communicate more easily with others. This application allows visually impaired users to perform some daily tasks such as reading, calculator, weather, location, time, and date to know the phone battery with the help of touching the phone screen. Also, the most important thing is that the user uses a voice command to turn it on, say read to turn on the special function. In this application, most of the difficulties of the blind are handled and solved one by one. The first need is made more dependent, which allows us to include non-mortgage files, home files, or other library modules in our Android project. Then the UI of the application is created in the XML file [10]. In the Main Function, all methods are created in Java language that will help users open various functions with a simple voice. Use the floating touch event so users can swipe left and right. The user will read the function or operation of the application by swiping the left side of the screen. When you swipe right on the screen, the Google Voice device will start. After the user gives the voice command, it will automatically switch to the corresponding function. Let's say if the user says "read", it automatically turns on reading. This allows users to tap the screen, take a photo, and have the text read aloud.

Methods Used:

Text-to-Speech (TTS):

Text-to-Speech is a way to convert text into spoken audio messages [11]. Text-to-Speech is an essential tool for speech output to provide feedback to users. It is used in software applications that require audio output features. When the user enters a voice command, Speech-to-Text converts the speech into text, and TTS then outputs the corresponding response as audio.

Speech-to-Text (STT):

Android has a built-in Speech-to-Text feature that allows users to provide voice feedback to the software. In the background, the audio input will be converted to text and used as input for the application's processing.

LITERATURE SURVEY

The paper [12] describes the development of a new Android application that is designed to assist blind and visually impaired people in their daily lives. The application provides a variety of features that are intended to improve accessibility and convenience for these users. The authors describe the various features of the application, which include voice recognition and text-to-speech capabilities, as well as a variety of tools for navigating and exploring the environment [13]. For example, the application includes a GPS that can be used to provide directions and guidance to the user, as well as an object recognition feature that can identify objects in the user's environment and provide information about them [14]. The authors also describe a series of tests that were conducted to evaluate the effectiveness of the application in assisting blind and visually impaired users. The results of these tests showed that the application was effective in improving accessibility and convenience for these users. Overall, this research paper presents an interesting application of mobile technology in the context of improving accessibility and convenience for blind and visually impaired individuals [15]. The development of such applications has the potential to improve the quality of life for these individuals greatly and help to bridge the gap between them and the rest of society.

This research paper [16] describes the development of a mobile application designed to assist visually impaired individuals in their daily lives. The application provides features such as voice recognition and text-to-speech capabilities, as well as a variety of tools for navigating and exploring the environment. The paper outlines the various features of the EyeMate application, which include object detection and recognition, barcode scanning, and facial recognition. These features allow visually impaired users to identify objects in their environment and obtain information about them, as well as navigate unfamiliar areas and recognize individuals. The paper also discusses the blind tracker feature, which is designed to help users locate and identify nearby individuals [17]. The feature uses Bluetooth technology to detect nearby devices and provides audio alerts to the user when someone is within a certain distance. The effectiveness of the EyeMate application was evaluated through a series of experiments, which showed that it was able to successfully identify objects and provide accurate information about them [18]. Additionally, the blind tracker feature was found to be effective in helping users locate nearby individuals. Overall, the EyeMate application presented in this research paper represents an important development in the field of assistive technology, providing visually impaired individuals with a range of useful features to help them navigate and explore their environment more easily.

The research paper titled "Substitute Eyes for the Blind with Navigator Using Android" [19] presents the development of a mobile application that assists visually impaired individuals in their daily activities. The application is designed to act as a substitute for the eyes of a visually impaired person by using the smartphone's camera to capture images of the surroundings and provide audio feedback to the user [20]. The paper outlines the various features of the application, which include object detection, facial recognition, and navigation.

The application can detect objects in the user's surroundings and provide audio feedback describing the object's location, shape, and color. The facial recognition feature can identify individuals and provide audio feedback to the user, enabling them to recognize people in their environment. Additionally, the navigation feature provides turn-by-turn audio directions to help the user navigate unfamiliar environments [21]. The paper describes the algorithms used in the application to perform object detection, facial recognition, and navigation. The effectiveness of the application was evaluated through a series of experiments, which showed that it was able to successfully identify objects, recognize faces, and provide accurate navigation instructions. Overall, the "Substitute Eyes for the Blind with Navigator Using Android" research paper demonstrates an important development in the field of assistive technology, providing visually impaired individuals with a range of features to help them navigate and explore their environment more easily.

The research paper titled "Android-based voice assistant for blind people" presents the development of a mobile application designed to assist visually impaired individuals in their daily lives. The application is designed to act as a voice assistant for visually impaired users, providing them with audio feedback to help them navigate and perform various tasks. Additionally, the application provides a variety of tools to help visually impaired users navigate their environment, including a GPS navigation system [22], an obstacle detection system, and a location reminder system. These features help users move around safely and efficiently, and also help them to remember important locations. The paper discusses the effectiveness of the application, which was evaluated through a series of user tests. The results showed that the application was able to successfully assist visually impaired users in their daily lives, providing them with important information and helping them navigate their environment more easily [23]. Overall, the research paper demonstrates an important development in the field of assistive technology, providing visually impaired individuals with a range of useful features to help them navigate and explore their environment more easily [24].

The research paper titled "Accessibility of Android-Based Mobile Devices: A Prototype to Investigate Interaction with Blind Users" presents the development of a prototype Android-based mobile device designed to investigate the accessibility of mobile technology for visually impaired individuals. The paper discusses the challenges that visually impaired users face when using mobile devices, such as the lack of tactile feedback and difficulty in navigating touchscreens. The prototype device was designed to address these challenges by incorporating a variety of accessibility features, such as a touchpad with tactile feedback and an audio interface. The paper outlines the features of the prototype device, including a built-in screen reader, voice recognition, and haptic feedback

[25]. The device was evaluated through a series of user tests, which showed that visually impaired users were able to successfully interact with the device and perform a variety of tasks, including making phone calls and sending text messages. The paper concludes that the prototype device is a promising development in the field of assistive technology for visually impaired users, and highlights the importance of designing accessible mobile devices to ensure that all users can benefit from the advantages of mobile technology. In another paper, the authors propose a general framework for object detection in images [26]. The framework consists of three main stages: a feature extraction stage, a learning stage, and a detection stage.

The feature extraction stage involves selecting a set of features that are relevant to the objects to be detected [27]. The learning stage involves training a classifier using a set of positive and negative examples. Finally, the detection stage involves applying the classifier to the features extracted from a new image to detect objects. The authors apply this framework to the problem of face detection and demonstrate that it outperforms previous methods. They also suggest [28] that the framework could be applied to other object detection problems, such as detecting vehicles or buildings, by simply changing the features used and the training data.

In another paper, the authors propose a real-time object detection system called YOLOv3, which stands for You Only Look Once version 3 [29]. The system uses a deep neural network to detect objects in images and videos in real-time. The YOLOv3 model is faster and more accurate than previous versions of YOLO, and it achieves state-of-the-art performance on several object detection benchmarks. The authors also introduce several improvements to the YOLOv3 model, including the use of residual connections and multi-scale predictions. The residual connections allow the model to learn features at multiple levels of abstraction, while the multi-scale predictions enable the model to detect objects of different sizes [30]. Overall, the YOLOv3 model represents a significant advance in the field of object detection and has many potential applications in fields such as surveillance, robotics, and autonomous vehicles.

The research paper "Real-Time Object Detection for Visually Challenged People" [31] discusses the development of a real-time object detection system designed to assist visually challenged individuals. The proposed system utilizes the YOLOv3 algorithm, along with an Android application, to detect and identify objects in real-time through a smartphone camera. The system is designed to provide an audio output, in addition to text output, to aid visually challenged individuals in identifying objects in their environment [32]. The proposed system was tested on a dataset of various objects and showed promising results in terms of accuracy and real-time detection speed [33]. The authors suggest that the proposed system could be a valuable tool for visually challenged individuals in daily life. The research paper presents an Android-based object detection system for visually impaired individuals.

The proposed system uses the YOLO (You Only Look Once) algorithm to detect objects in real-time using a smartphone camera. The system converts the visual information into speech output, which is communicated to the user through earphones. The paper discusses the design and implementation of the system, along with the various challenges faced in its development [34]. The system is evaluated through user testing, and the results indicate that the proposed solution can help visually impaired individuals detect objects in their surroundings with high accuracy. Overall, the paper highlights the potential of using smartphone technology to develop assistive solutions for individuals with visual impairments. The paper presents an Android application for object recognition that can help visually impaired individuals. The app uses the smartphone's camera to capture images and then processes them using the TensorFlow object detection API [35]. The app can recognize several objects, including everyday items and text. Once the object is detected, the app provides an audio message to the user, identifying the object. The paper concludes that the app can be useful for the visually impaired community, as it provides them with a simple and efficient method for object recognition.

REQUIREMENT ANALYSIS AND SOLUTION APPROACH

This project's problem statement is to create an application that can sense and recognise the user's speech, convert it to text, and then analyse this text to perform reading operations for reading text from images by the text-to-speech method, and then read this text to the user. It also detects the object with the help of TensorFlow to know what object it is, which is done through the camera. For this, it needs the user's permission and a smart reminder that sets the task by reminder [36]. Voice-based calculator, GPS for tracking the user's location, weather data to learn about the local climate, battery % activity to determine whether the phone needs to be charged or not, and other features. Text-to-speech (TTS) systems frequently simply aren't aware of how to pronounce a word (consider how challenging this can be, especially for unusual words spelt in peculiar ways or for words that have two possible homographs that are pronounced differently, like “put” the very common verb and “put” the less frequently pronounced verb that has to do with golf). Modern TTS systems have good audio quality, but they have trouble pronouncing words that aren't common. Perhaps the biggest issue they have is unnatural.

Object Detection: Perspective change for object detection, objects viewed from different angles will look completely different. Take a simple glass as an example. Consider the top view of the black coffee cup, which looks different from one side, and the top view of the cappuccino cup, and the third side view of the mug [37]. This is one of the problems with object detection because most tools learn to use images only from certain perspectives.

Smart Reminder: The user will not be able to receive reminders because information has not been entered in the reminder function of this application. Users must provide complete information to enable timely notification.

Location: To access the current location of the user, this user must grant location permission from their smartphone. Also, this requires a good internet connection to find the current location of the user; otherwise, the user will not be able to get the correct location.

Calculator: The role of the calculator is to solve simple calculations for customers in daily life. This value is given by the user, but sometimes errors can occur if the user does not assign these functions to the correct value. Users must submit the correct code to get a response.

The project also looks forward to making a difference in society by making small donations to make a big difference and help those in need. Today, almost everyone suffers from blindness, speech impairment, or some other physical disability [38]. In such cases, speech-to-text and text-to-speech will be their best services. With this awareness, the program has been designed and created to meet the needs of individuals with special abilities. This work is a small effort to make their life easier.

CONCEPTUAL MODELS

System Flowchart

A system flowchart is a graphical representation of the information flow in a system in software engineering. The diagram has several steps that determine where inputs enter the system and where outputs leave the system. With the help of diagrams, you can control the decision about the situation and how information flows into the system. So the flowchart is the representation of the flow of information in order, without counting the small ones, and in order of the size of the system [39]. A system flowchart has individual steps in a sequential manner and a diagram with many symbols that help to see and understand the process and data flow in the system. An image or the whole process begins with an oval symbol denoting the beginning of the process. It is basically drawn from the top of the page and continues to the bottom using various symbols [40].

Fig. (**1**) explains the system design of the app It is an important phase of software development that involves creating a detailed design for the system. It defines the architecture, data structure, algorithms, and techniques used to ensure that the system meets the requirements. The design of the system should consider scalability and reliability. Applications must be designed to handle large amounts of data and provide reliable and timely product discovery.

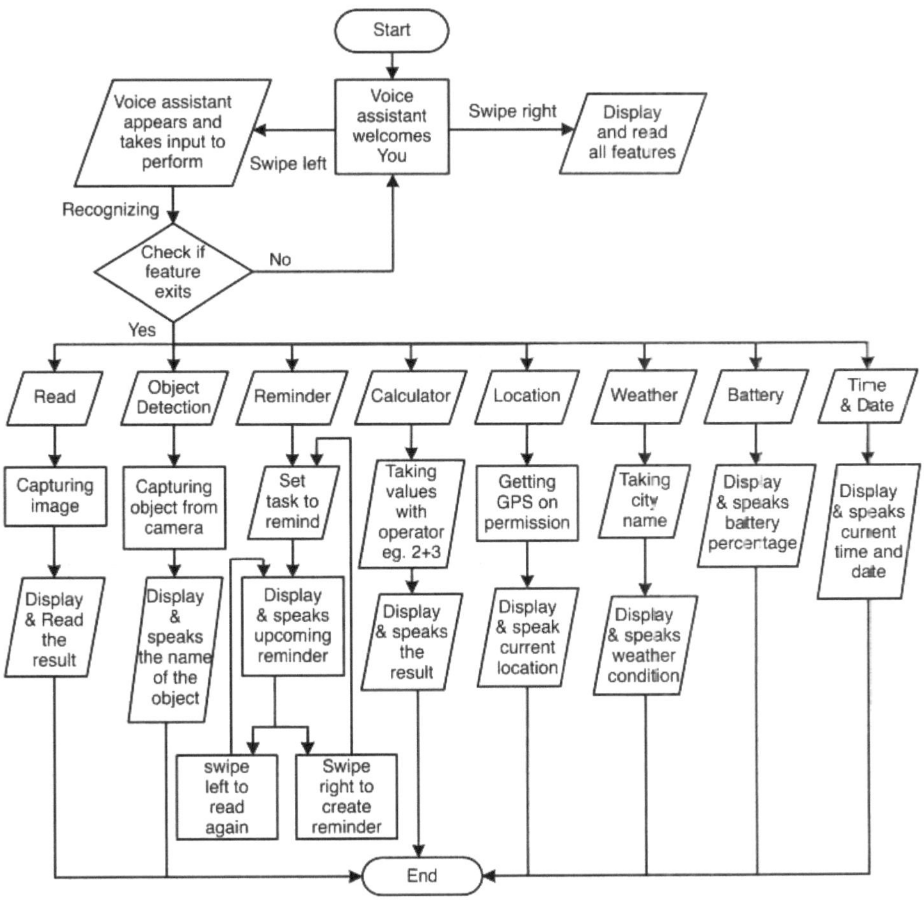

Fig. (1). System flow diagram.

Use Case Diagram

There are two actors in this reference image: the visually impaired user and the camera. An Android app is represented as a system rather than an actor, as it is not a separate entity from the development process. Users show the different functions the system can perform, including controlling objects in the camera view, annotating objects for the user, guiding the customer, and setting reminders for future products. This reference file represents the main function of the blind application. Fig. (**2**) explains the use case diagram of the same.

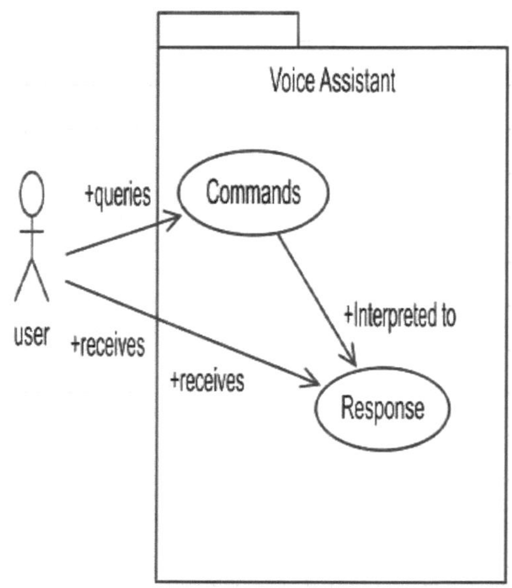

Fig. (2). Use case diagram.

Class Diagram

Fig. (**3**) shows that the object detection class uses the camera class to capture and store images, and the object identification class uses the object detection class to get the list of detected objects. Both the navigation system and the notification class use the object detection class to get the list of detected objects and the object description class to provide the user with a description of the object.

Security Issues

Data security and privacy concerns are one of the most common and sensitive issues in software. User information must be kept confidential at all times. The project aims to ensure that users' confidential information does not fall into the hands of unauthorized persons and remains safe.

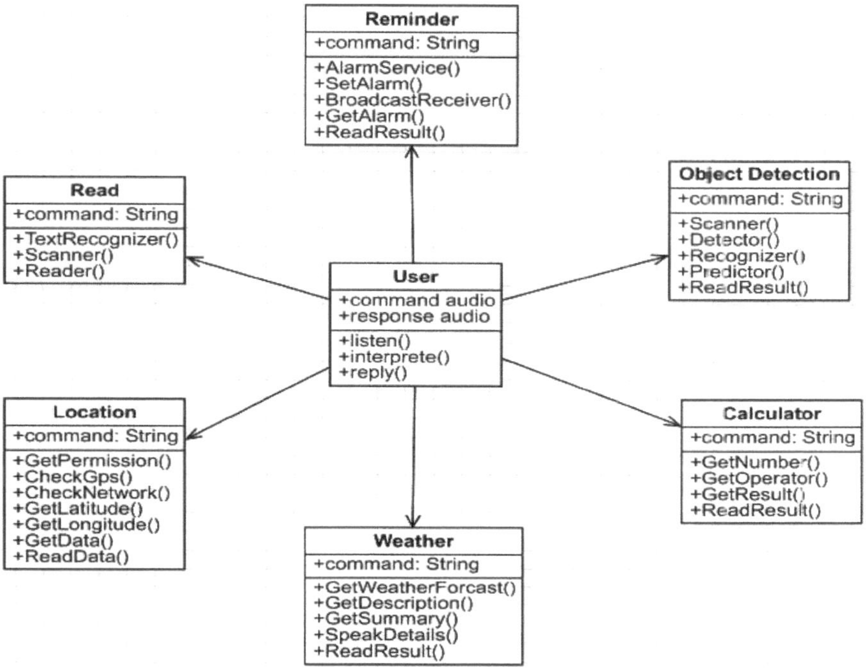

Fig. (3). Class diagram.

STEPS TO PREPARE A RISK POLICY APPLICATION.

Step 1: Risk Identification

Identify current risks and predict future risks. This is an important task for the team. All policies and construction procedures will be based on this result.

Step 2: Use in business

It's important to learn from others to understand their strengths and weaknesses. Such information will help you use them to your advantage. Safety procedures should be followed regularly so that evidence will help find the best on the market.

Step 3: Information about its scope

The security policy created should be clearly stated. He will know about everything he covers. Accurate segmentation of all this avoids confusion and makes it easy to retrieve specific information and complete any task.

Step 4: Policy

Clarify the rules created for each department in the policy. Provide details that will help the team accomplish all planned tasks. Putting these one step ahead will make the whole process go more smoothly.

Step 5: Review and Update

It is important to review and update your security application. This is necessary not only when attacked by external threats, but also for assessing and predicting future risks in order to plan better. In addition, security systems should always use the best tools for their purpose.

RESULTS AND DISCUSSION

YOLOv5 implementation: In Fig. (**4**) YOLOv5 shows a decent accuracy, and it trains the data in a much shorter period of time for more classes than YOLOv3 [40]. Also, YOLOv3 is compatible with darknet, so the custom weights are much easier to use with different libraries like openCV, but YOLOv5 is not compatible, as it generates PyTorch files.

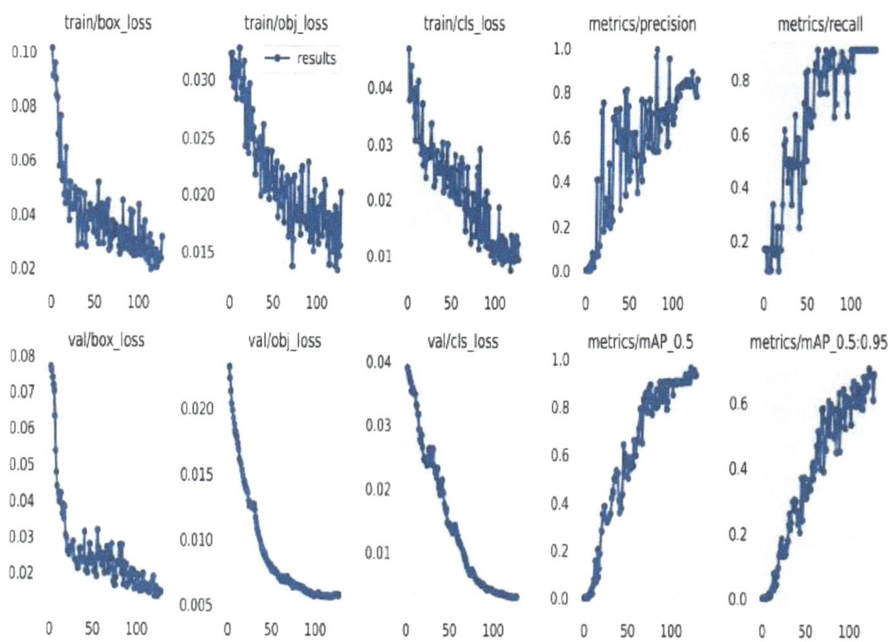

Fig. (4). Precision metric curve.

CONCLUSION AND FUTURE WORK

The Android application we created for the visually impaired has great potential to be developed and expanded in the future. Here are some future possibilities for this project with respect to its integration with wearable devices:

1. The app can be integrated with devices such as smart glasses to provide hands-free guidance to the visually impaired
2. Multilingual Support: The app can be developed to support multiple languages, allowing it to reach a wide range of users.
3. Real-Time Obstacle Avoidance: The application can be extended to include obstacle avoidance, and the user gets real-time feedback on how to track objects.
4. Improved accuracy and speed: Using deeper learning models and more advanced editing techniques, the application can be further enhanced to identify objects with greater accuracy and speed.
5. Crowdsourced Object Detection Dataset: Creating a crowdsourced object detection dataset allows the application to recognize unique objects and better serve the needs of the visually impaired.
6. Integration with other technologies: Integration with other technologies, such as speech recognition, natural language processing, and machine translation, can improve the application and provide a better user experience.

The future of this work includes the integration of wearables, support for multiple languages, avoidance of time constraints, improved accuracy and speed, crowdsourced data generation for product discovery, and integration with other technologies. The development and integration of these features will make the application more accessible and useful for visually impaired people.

REFERENCES

[1] M.S.R. Tanveer, M.M.A. Hashem, and M.K. Hossain, "Android assistant EyeMate for blind and blind tracker", *18th International Conference on Computer and Information Technology (ICCIT),* pp. 266-271, 2015.
[http://dx.doi.org/10.1109/ICCITechn.2015.7488080]

[2] S. Bharambe, R. Thakker, H. Patil, and K. M. Bhurchandi, "Substitute Eyes for Blind with Navigator Using Android", *Texas Instruments India Educators' Conference,* pp. 38-43, 2013.
[http://dx.doi.org/10.1109/TIIEC.2013.14]

[3] M. Barata, A. Galih Salman, I. Faahakhododo, and B. Kanigoro, "Android based voice assistant for blind people", *Libr. Hi Tech News,* vol. 35, no. 6, pp. 9-11, 2018.
[http://dx.doi.org/10.1108/LHTN-11-2017-0083]

[4] N.B. Arifin, R. Johari, S.M. Sapuan, S.S.S. Rashid, and R.A. Hamzah, "Accessibility of Android-Based Mobile Devices: A Prototype to Investigate Interaction with Blind Users", *Procedia Comput. Sci.,* vol. 59, pp. 133-140, 2015.
[http://dx.doi.org/10.1016/j.procs.2015.07.380]

[5] M. Kansal, P. Singh, P. Chaurasia, A. Dwivedi, and S. Ali, "Blockchain-Powered Food Supply Chain Tracking: A Paradigm Shift for Transparency, Accountability, and Quality Assurance Through BlockTrackers", *2nd International Conference on Disruptive Technologies (ICDT),* pp. 194-200, 2024. [http://dx.doi.org/10.1109/ICDT61202.2024.10489045]

[6] C.P. Papageorgiou, M. Oren, and T. Poggio, "A general framework for object detection", *Sixth International Conference on Computer Vision (IEEE Cat. No.98CH36271),* pp. 555-562, 1998.Bombay, India [http://dx.doi.org/10.1109/ICCV.1998.710772]

[7] J. Redmon, A. Farhadi (2018), "Real Time Object Detection Using YOLOv3," arXiv preprint arXiv:1804.02767, Available at: https://arxiv.org/abs/1804.02767

[8] S. Vaidya, N. Shah, N. Shah, and R. Shankarmani, "Real-Time Object Detection for Visually Challenged People", *4th International Conference on Intelligent Computing and Control Systems (ICICCS),* pp. 311-316, 2020. [http://dx.doi.org/10.1109/ICICCS48265.2020.9121085]

[9] A. Badave, R. Jagtap, R. Kaovasia, S. Rahatwad, and S. Kulkarni, "Android Based Object Detection System for Visually Impaired", *International Conference on Industry 4.0 Technology (I4Tech), Pune, India,* pp. 34-38, 2020. [http://dx.doi.org/10.1109/I4Tech48345.2020.9102694]

[10] M. Kansal, P. Singh, P. Srivastava, R. Singhal, N. Deep, and A. Singh, "Mental health monitoring in the digital age: a comprehensive analysis", In: *Future of AI in Medical Imaging.* IGI Global, 2024, pp. 168-183. [http://dx.doi.org/10.4018/979-8-3693-2359-5.ch011]

[11] S.A. Jakhete, P. Bagmar, A. Dorle, A. Rajurkar, and P. Pimplikar, "Object Recognition App for Visually Impaired", *IEEE Pune Section International Conference (PuneCon),* pp. 1-4, 2019.Pune, India

[12] J. Redmon, and A. Farhadi, "YOLOv3: An Incremental Improvement", *arXiv preprint arXiv:1804.02767,* 2018.

[13] S.S. Khan, and S.F. Tahir, "A review of vision-based systems for outdoor navigation of visually impaired", *J. Ambient Intell. Humaniz. Comput.,* vol. 8, no. 5, pp. 661-680, 2017.

[14] S. Majumdar, and J. Mukherjee, "A Survey on Computer Vision-based Techniques for Assistive Technology", *Proceedings of the International Conference on Information Technology and Computer Communications,* Springer., pp. 273-282, 2019.

[15] P. Singh, A. Asthana, B. Solanki, S. Tomar, M. Kansal, and G. Tyagi, "A comprehensive analysis and sensitivity model for emotion detection in text", In: *Applications of Artificial Intelligence in 5G and Internet of Things.* CRC Press, 2025, pp. 332-337. [http://dx.doi.org/10.1201/9781003532521-63]

[16] T. Kurata, and M. Kikuchi, "Development of an Object Detection Device for the Blind Based on Thermal Imaging", *15th International Workshop on Advanced Motion Control (AMC),* pp. 319-324, 2018.

[17] R.L. Manduchi, and A. Kurniawati, "Blind navigation with a depth camera", *IEEE Trans. Cybern.,* vol. 45, no. 12, pp. 2723-2733, 2015. [http://dx.doi.org/10.1109/TCYB.2015.2389336]

[18] C. Xiao, Y. Cao, and Y. Liu, "An Intelligent Object Detection System for Visually Impaired People", *5th International Conference on Cloud Computing and Intelligence Systems (CCIS),* pp. 324-328, 2018.

[19] S.S. Khan, and S.F. Tahir, "A review of vision-based systems for outdoor navigation of visually impaired", *J. Ambient Intell. Humaniz. Comput.,* vol. 8, no. 5, pp. 661-680, 2017. [http://dx.doi.org/10.1007/s12652-016-0388-7]

[20] P. Singh, and M. Kansal, "An Online Platform for Timely Access to Medical Care with the Help of Real-Time Data Analysis", *Wellness Management Powered by AI Technologies,* pp. 103-131, 2025.

[21] A. El Saddik, H. Tawfik, T. Stafylakis, and J.N. Carter, "Assistive technology for visually impaired and blind people: A review and a methodology", *J. Ambient Intell. Humaniz. Comput.,* vol. 10, no. 7, pp. 2623-2647, 2019.
[http://dx.doi.org/10.1007/s12652-019-01318-7]

[22] P. Singh, N. Pahuja, M. Kansal, S. Gurung, U. Shukla, and S. Gupta, "Enhancing Tourism Experiences and Preserving Cultural Heritage with AR and VR", *2nd International Conference on Disruptive Technologies (ICDT),* pp. 225-231, 2024.
[http://dx.doi.org/10.1109/ICDT61202.2024.10489490]

[23] P. Kardyś, *A. Dą browski, M. Iwanowski and D. Huderek, "A new Android application for blind and visually impaired people," 2016 Signal Processing: Algorithms, Architectures, Arrangements, and Applications.* SPA: Poznan, Poland, 2016, pp. 152-155.
[http://dx.doi.org/10.1109/SPA.2016.7763604]

[24] T.A. Qureshi, M. Rajbhar, Y. Pisat, and V. Bhosale, "AI based app for blind people", *International Research Journal of Engineering and Technology,* vol. 8, no. 3, pp. 2883-2887, 2021.

[25] A.K. Sharma, N. Chanderwal, A. Prajapati, P. Singh, M. Kansal, Ed., *Advancing Software Engineering Through AI, Federated Learning, and Large Language Models.* IGI Global, 2024.
[http://dx.doi.org/10.4018/979-8-3693-3502-4]

[26] A. Khan, and S. Khusro, "An insight into smartphone-based assistive solutions for visually impaired and blind people: issues, challenges and opportunities", *Univers. Access Inf. Soc.,* vol. 20, no. 2, pp. 265-298, 2021.
[http://dx.doi.org/10.1007/s10209-020-00733-8]

[27] S. Mahdy, I. Yousri, M. Hamady, M. Ashraf, A. Morad, and Y.A. Elshrief, "Smart Blind Stick using Mobile Application and Bluetooth Module", *International Journal of Industry and Sustainable Development,* vol. 6, no. 1, pp. 43-53, 2025.
[http://dx.doi.org/10.21608/ijisd.2024.307950.1079]

[28] A. Alayed, "Are Saudi Arabian banks' mobile applications accessible for blind or partially sighted users?: a customers' perspective and evaluation", *Univers. Access Inf. Soc.,* vol. 24, no. 1, pp. 585-606, 2025.
[http://dx.doi.org/10.1007/s10209-023-01082-y]

[29] H. Garg, S. Jhunthra, M. Kindra, V. Dixit, and V. Gupta, "A deep learning-based integrated voice assistance system for partially disabled people", In: *Uncertainty in Computational Intelligence-Based Decision Making.* Academic Press, 2025, pp. 293-310.
[http://dx.doi.org/10.1016/B978-0-443-21475-2.00010-2]

[30] P. Singh, U.K. Jaiswal, E. Jain, N. Kuamr, and V. Mishra, "A Novel Methodology Utilizing Modern CCTV Cameras and Software as a Service Model for Crime Detection and Prediction", *Int. J. Perform. Eng.,* vol. 21, no. 2, 2025.

[31] G. Shyamala, G.B. Pallavi, N.R. Latha, H.S. Shreesha, and V.B. Sushanth, "Blindaid: Assisting The Visually Impaired In Object Detection And Tracking Using Slam", *Int. J. Environ. Sci.,* vol. 11, no. 3s, pp. 647-658, 2025.

[32] K. Mane, S. Rane, K. Mane, and S. Patinge, Android Application Camera for Text and Product Labelling for Unsighted People. *Grenze International Journal of Engineering & Technology (GIJET),* 10, 2024.

[33] M. Awad, J. El Haddad, E. Khneisser, T. Mahmoud, E. Yaacoub, and M. Malli, "Intelligent eye: A mobile application for assisting blind people", In: *2018 IEEE Middle East and North Africa Communications Conference (MENACOMM)*, 2018, pp. 1-6.
[http://dx.doi.org/10.1109/MENACOMM.2018.8371005]

[34] R. Goel, U.K. Jaiswal, P. Singh, S.P. Yadav, and P. Upadhyay, "Deep Learning for Early Brain Tumor Detection: A Keras-Based Approach Using MRI and CT Imaging", In: *Demystifying the Role of Natural Language Processing (NLP) in Mental Health*, 2025, pp. 145-180. [http://dx.doi.org/10.4018/979-8-3693-4203-9.ch009]

[35] R. Neto, and N. Fonseca, "Camera reading for blind people", *Procedia Technol.,* vol. 16, pp. 1200-1209, 2014. [http://dx.doi.org/10.1016/j.protcy.2014.10.135]

[36] M.C. Rodriguez-Sanchez, M.A. Moreno-Alvarez, E. Martín, S. Borromeo, and J.A. Hernandez-Tamames, "Accessible smartphones for blind users: A case study for a wayfinding system", *Expert Syst. Appl.,* vol. 41, no. 16, pp. 7210-7222, 2014. [http://dx.doi.org/10.1016/j.eswa.2014.05.031]

[37] M. Barata, A. Galih Salman, I. Faahakhododo, and B. Kanigoro, "Android based voice assistant for blind people", *Libr. Hi Tech News,* vol. 35, no. 6, pp. 9-11, 2018. [http://dx.doi.org/10.1108/LHTN-11-2017-0083]

[38] A.S. Shaik, G. Hossain, and M. Yeasin, "Design, development and performance evaluation of reconfigured mobile Android phone for people who are blind or visually impaired", *Proceedings of the 28th ACM International Conference on Design of Communication,* pp. 159-166, 2010. [http://dx.doi.org/10.1145/1878450.1878478]

[39] A. Rodrigues, H. Nicolau, K. Montague, J. Guerreiro, and T. Guerreiro, "Open challenges of blind people using smartphones", *Int. J. Hum. Comput. Interact.,* vol. 36, no. 17, pp. 1605-1622, 2020. [http://dx.doi.org/10.1080/10447318.2020.1768672]

[40] A. Khan, and S. Khusro, "A mechanism for blind-friendly user interface adaptation of mobile apps: a case study for improving the user experience of the blind people", *J. Ambient Intell. Humaniz. Comput.,* vol. 13, no. 5, pp. 2841-2871, 2022. [http://dx.doi.org/10.1007/s12652-021-03393-5]

CHAPTER 5

Application of AI in the Education Sector with special Reference to India and the USA

Arpit Saxena[1,*], **Ashi Agarwal**[2], **Ajay Bahadur**[1], **Laxmi Pandey**[3], **Vinesh**[1] and **Rashi Singhal**[3]

[1] *Department of Commerce & Management, GNIOT Institute of Professional Studies, Greater Noida, Uttar Pradesh, India*

[2] *Department of Computer Science, ABES Engineering College, Ghaziabad, Uttar Pradesh, India*

[3] *Department of PGDM, Institute of Management Studies (IMS), Ghaziabad, Uttar Pradesh, India*

Abstract: Artificial Intelligence (AI) is reinventing student learning and instructor instruction, and quickly changing the education sector. This study examines the various applications, challenges, and future directions in the Education Sector, with special reference to India and the USA. AI-driven platforms enable customized tutoring, tests, and feedback in adaptive learning settings that address the needs of each individual learner. Furthermore, by automating repetitive tasks such as scheduling and grading, AI improves administrative efficiency and frees up teachers' time to focus on student engagement and innovative teaching methods. This paper outlines the current state of artificial intelligence in the education sector, along with the opportunities and challenges that lie ahead for its application and advancement.

Keywords: Artificial Intelligence (AI), Adaptive learning environments, Education, Education sector, Learning.

INTRODUCTION

Artificial Intelligence (AI) has become a key technological development with significant effects across education and many other fields. AI-driven innovations have begun transforming traditional educational processes over the last few years, opening new possibilities for pedagogical insights, administrative efficiency, and individualized learning. Artificial Intelligence (AI) technologies are multifaceted, ranging from large-scale dataset analysis to interactive natural language processing systems and machine learning algorithms [1]. Adaptive learning environments that accommodate the unique requirements and preferences of each student are made possible by utilizing these skills in education. Based on real-time

* **Corresponding author Arpit Saxena:** Department of Commerce & Management, GNIOT Institute of Professional Studies, Greater Noida, Uttar Pradesh, India; E-mail: arpitanasaxena@gmail.com

Pancham Singh, Avinash Kumar Sharma, Mrignainy Kansal, & Amarjeet Prajapati (Eds.)

evaluations of students' performance, AI-driven tutoring systems can offer individualized feedback and customize learning paths.

Furthermore, by automating repetitive tasks such as monitoring student records, scheduling, and assessment grading, AI improves administrative efficiency. Researchers [2] found that automation frees up more time for educators to focus on instructional design and student interaction while also lessening their administrative workload. Even with these developments, there are still obstacles and moral dilemmas with using AI in the classroom. A study in [3] suggested that thoughtful deliberation is necessary regarding matters such as data privacy, algorithmic bias, and the fair allocation of AI resources to educational institutions and students.

Globally, Artificial Intelligence (AI) is transforming the education industry, with profound effects on both industrialized countries like the US and developing ones like India. AI is increasingly used in the US to improve administrative efficiency and individualized learning experiences. Personalized learning environments and the ways students engage with instructional materials are being transformed by initiatives such as AI-powered tutoring systems and adaptive learning platforms [4]. According to Artificial Intelligence (AI), technologies facilitate administrative processes by automating tasks such as scheduling, grading, and data management. This allows educators to concentrate more on teaching and student growth. In an educational system as diversified and resource-rich as the US one, this efficiency is essential [5].

On the other hand, India, with its enormous and varied educational landscape, is also adopting AI to solve issues with scale, quality, and accessibility. According to [6], AI-driven projects in India include tailored learning platforms that address a range of learning demands and regional languages. Furthermore, AI is changing Indian educational assessments so they are more responsive to student learning outcomes and adaptive [7]. However, when it comes to ensuring equitable access to AI-powered educational materials, responsibly employing AI, and addressing concerns about computational bias and data privacy, both countries face comparable challenges [8].

REVIEW OF AI IN EDUCATION

The field of education has a revolutionary opportunity in the realm of Artificial Intelligence (AI). Both India and the USA are investigating AI tools and technologies for the purposes of individualized learning, increased administrative effectiveness, and better educational results. This review highlights the parallels and discrepancies between these two nations' approaches to the integration of AI in education.

For both India and the USA, determining the unique demands of respective educational institutions is an essential first step. Personalized learning opportunities, administrative task simplification, student support, and instructor empowerment are a few examples of these needs [9]. Institutions need to identify their AI integration goals and objectives before setting any. Another crucial factor to consider is the availability of resources (money, technology, and teacher preparation) [10]. According to studies, schools in the USA prioritize individualized learning platforms and AI-powered tools to support educators, whereas schools in India appear particularly interested in bridging the access divide through online platforms [11, 12]. The analysis of related documents per year is shown in Fig. (**1**).

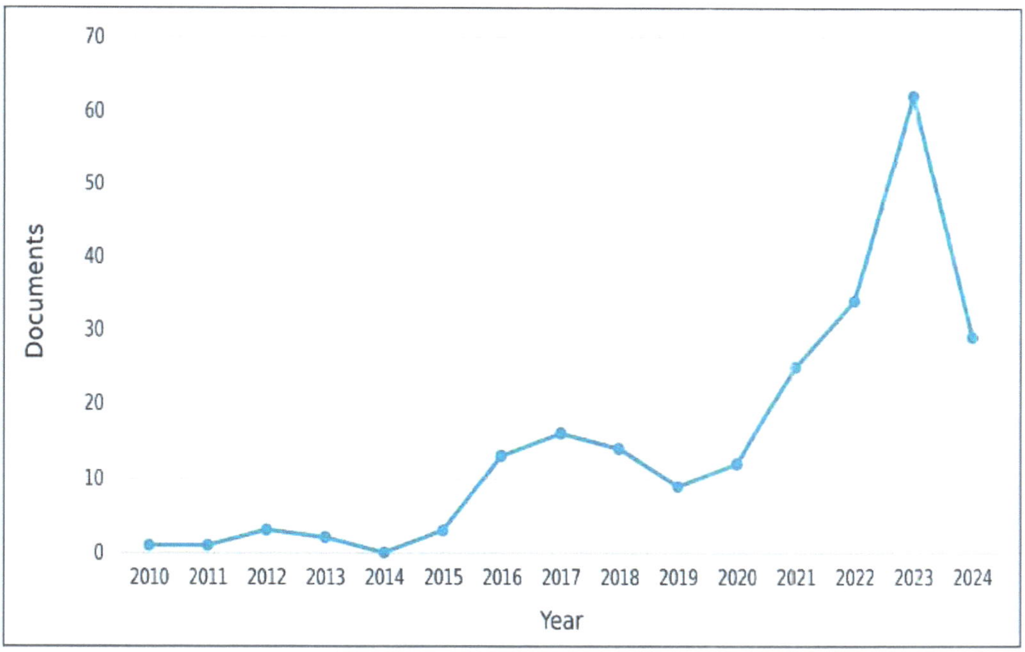

Fig. (1). Analysis of related documents per year.

Figs. (**1 and 2**) show that most of the research articles have been published in 2023 from 2010 to 2024. The USA had the highest number of documents during that time, and after that, India ranked 2 in research publications. From these total publications, some reference papers are discussed below:

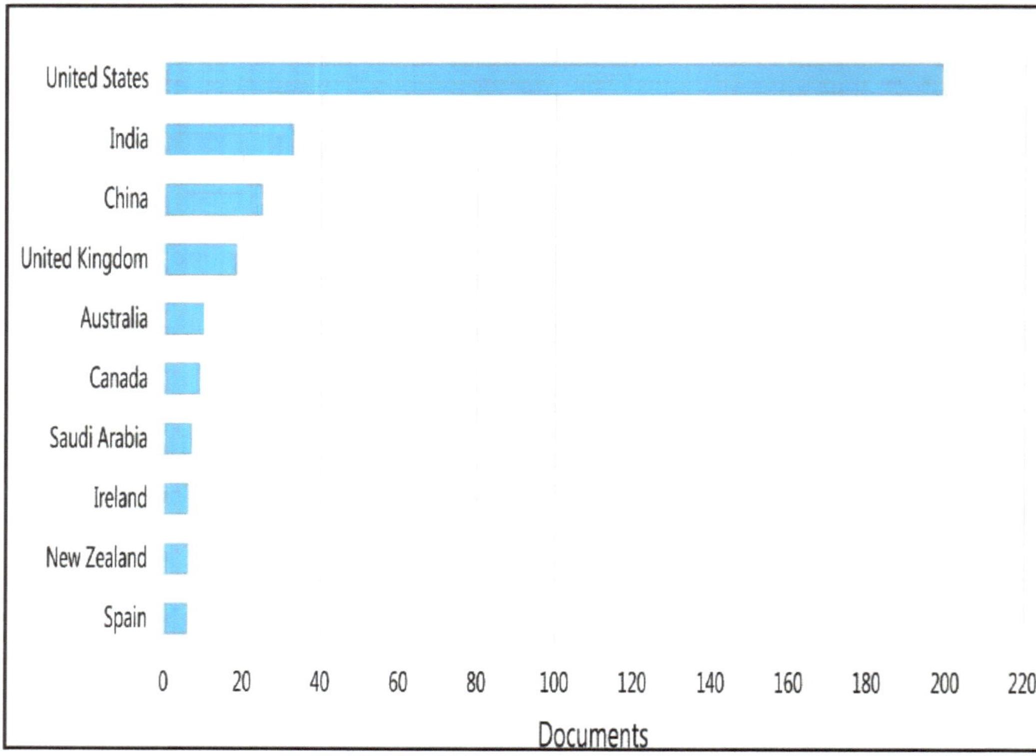

Fig. (2). Analysis of documents by countries.

The researchers in a study [13] reviewed existing AI systems in education, their pedagogic assumptions, and potential roadblocks. It provides a typology of AIED systems, discusses various ways of using AI in education, and explores different interpretations of AI and education, addressing misunderstandings and gaps in knowledge.

Traditional teaching methods have undergone a change with the introduction of Artificial Intelligence (AI) in education. This review [14] emphasizes the potential of instructional technology and personalized learning to meet individual requirements, improve student engagement, and maximize learning results. Real-time feedback, intelligent tutoring systems, and adaptable content distribution are all components of AI-driven personalized learning. It also examines how AI might be used to create content, develop curricula, and enhance evaluation methods. Nevertheless, the assessment also addresses issues such as algorithmic bias, privacy concerns, and the digital divide. The evaluation urges cooperation in the development of moral standards and fair distribution of AI-enhanced learning materials.

The researchers in a study [15] investigated how university teachers feel about generative AI-based tools and AI language models in higher education. The study investigates adoption-related sentiment, awareness, and variables that influence attitude. The findings indicate that while teachers have a generally good attitude toward AI tools, there is no relationship between attitude and method of instruction. CS educators are less confident in their ability to recognize work generated by AI, despite having greater confidence in their technical knowledge.

The researchers in the article "Future Possibilities and Challenges of AI in Education" [16] examine the transformative potential and obstacles of AI in education. While acknowledging the challenges of transforming fundamental education paradigms, the chapter imagines a future in which customized learning, AI-enhanced creativity, seamless assessment, global collaboration, and ethical education flourish.

The researchers emphasized the drawbacks of statistical modeling in the classroom, the possibility that AI could exacerbate the social injustices faced by pupils from underrepresented groups, the costs associated with machine-readable curricula, and the environmental and ecological consequences of data-intensive AI. It demands that conversations on AI and education be reevaluated with an emphasis on equity, resistance, and power [17].

A review of existing literature revealed a lack of research on AI application in education. The researcher sought to fill this gap by studying the application of AI in the education sector, with special reference to India and the USA.

Objectives of AI in the Education Sector: Context of India and the USA

In the education sector, Artificial Intelligence (AI) seeks to accomplish several major goals that are suited to the unique requirements and difficulties that nations like the US and India face.

a. Customized Learning: AI technologies allow for the customization of educational procedures and content to meet the requirements, interests, and learning styles of each individual student.
b. Enhanced Teaching and Learning: AI enables teachers to deliver high-quality instruction by automating grading, facilitating data-driven instructional decisions, and offering real-time feedback.
c. Increasing Inclusivity and Accessibility: AI can address educational disparities by providing high-quality education to all students, regardless of location or socioeconomic background. The Government of India has launched efforts such as the National Education Policy 2020 [18], which highlights the use of

technology, especially Artificial Intelligence (AI), to improve equity and inclusivity in education.

d. Effective Administrative Operations: AI simplifies administrative tasks such as scheduling, student enrollment, and resource distribution, reducing administrative constraints and freeing up teachers to focus more on instruction.

e. Assistance for Instructors: Artificial Intelligence (AI) provides tools to enhance professional growth and provide insights into student achievement and educational patterns that shape pedagogical approaches [19]. AI is being included in teacher preparation programs in the USA and India to improve pedagogical approaches and promote ongoing development [20].

f. Ethics in AI Education: Transparency in decision-making procedures, algorithmic bias, and data privacy are all ethical issues that must be addressed if trust and equity are to be upheld. According to the Government of India and the US Department of Education, both nations are actively developing frameworks and guidelines to govern the ethical use of AI in educational contexts [21].

APPLICATION OF AI IN THE EDUCATION SECTOR

Although it may be difficult to provide a year-by-year analysis with exact details, the following table summarizes the historical evolution and current uses of AI in education for both India and the United States of America. A Historical Look at the Context of India and the USA is shown in Table **1**.

Table 1. A historical look in the context of india and USA.

	Feature	India	USA
1	Early 2010s (Focus)	Technology integration in education (remote learning)	Exploration of AI for intelligent tutoring systems and automated grading.
	Examples	Initiatives like e-learning platforms and satellite-based education.	Early versions of AI-powered tutors like Knewton.
	Challenges	Infrastructure limitations, lack of awareness about AI.	Cost of implementation.
2.	Mid-2010s (Focus)	Emergence of EdTech startups offering basic adaptive learning platforms.	Universities offer AI and machine learning programs. The rise of adaptive learning platforms like Khan Academy.
	Examples	Byju's, Meritnation.	Khan Academy, Knewton (more advanced features).
	Challenges	Teacher training, data privacy concerns.	Equitable access to technology

(Table 1) cont.....

Feature		India	USA
3	Late 2010s - Present (Focus)	Personalized learning, bridging access gaps, and teacher support.	Personalized learning, adaptive learning, and skill development for future jobs.
	Examples	CBSE introducing AI as a subject, and the government initiatives for online learning in remote areas.	AI-powered tutoring systems and learning platforms (*e.g.*, Khan Academy with personalized feedback), and universities offering AI and machine learning programs.
	Challenges	Infrastructure limitations, teacher training, and data privacy concerns.	Cost of implementation, equitable access to technology.
	Emerging Applications (2024 and beyond)	AI-powered career guidance, VR/AR integration, AI-driven content creation.	AI-powered career guidance, VR/AR integration, AI-driven content creation, and exploration of AI for administrative tasks.
	Focus of AI application	Personalized learning, bridging access gaps, and teacher support.	Personalized learning, adaptive learning, skill development for future jobs.
	Challenges	Infrastructure limitations, teacher training, and data privacy concerns.	Cost of implementation, equitable access to technology.
	Examples	• CBSE introducing AI as a subject • EdTech companies offering adaptive learning platforms • Government initiatives for online learning in remote areas	• AI-powered tutoring systems and learning platforms (*e.g.*, Khan Academy, Knewton) • Universities offering AI and machine learning programs • Use of AI for personalized feedback and assessments

Table **1** highlights current trends and potential opportunities while offering a historical perspective. Both nations have a steady trend of putting more emphasis on AI in education, albeit at differing levels of priority depending on their requirements. Though the USA concentrates on enhanced learning experiences and preparing students for the workforce, India prioritizes overcoming infrastructure obstacles and increasing access to education. Both countries have difficulties with fair access and data privacy. Personalized content production, VR/AR immersive learning, and AI integration for career assistance all present interesting prospects for the future. The challenges and solutions of AI in the education sector are shown in Table **2**.

Table 2. Challenges and solution of AI in education sector.

AI in the Education Sector	India	USA
Challenges	• Infrastructure Limitations, • Teacher Training, • Data Privacy Concerns	• Cost of Implementations, • Equitable access to Technology, • Teacher Bias
Solution	• Government Initiatives, • Focus on open-source AI Tools, • Develop Data Privacy Regulations	• Public-Private Partnerships, • Focus on Teachers Training, • Develop Bias Mitigation Strategies

Table **3** summarizes that the major challenges in India, a barrier to the widespread deployment of AI tools, are the unreliability of internet connectivity and the scarcity of devices in rural locations. To properly integrate AI tools and comprehend their limitations, educators must receive training. It is necessary to address data on, storage, and security procedures for student data used by AI systems. While in the USA, creating and implementing reliable AI-powered learning resources can be costly for educational institutions [22]. Low-income kids may not have access to the gadgets and internet required for artificial intelligence tools, hence perpetuating the digital divide. If AI algorithms are not properly created and overseen, they may reinforce current prejudices in education.

Table 3. Policies and initiatives.

-	**Policies & Initiatives**
India	National Education Policy, 2020: • Technology integration, especially Artificial Intelligence (AI), is emphasized in the NEP. • It promotes the creation of AI-powered technologies for individualized education. • Applications of AI are in line with a focus on skill development and vocational education.
	Atal Innovation Mission: • AIM encourages entrepreneurship and innovation in educational institutions. • It promotes AI-related initiatives and contests.
	AI Research Institutes & Centres: • AI in education is the subject of research at institutions like IITs and IISc. • Adoption of AI is fueled by partnerships with academics and industry.
	AI in School Education Program: • The Ministry of Education launched this program with the goal of incorporating AI into the curriculum. • AI-enabled content production and instructor training are included.
USA	Every Student Succeeds Act: • States are encouraged by ESSA to investigate cutting-edge methods, such as artificial intelligence, to enhance education. • There are funding options available for AI-driven initiatives.
	AI in Education Research and Development Act: • Laws to support AI research in education have been proposed. • Aims to use AI to improve instruction, learning, and evaluation.
	Future Ready Schools: • A national campaign encouraging technology integration and digital learning. • The topic of education that is prepared for the future includes AI.

The ethical and responsible application of AI in education must be prioritized, with a focus on student welfare and data protection, by both India and the USA. To guarantee that AI technologies are efficient, flexible, and meet the unique requirements of any educational system, ongoing research and development are essential.

India should bridge the digital divide and spend money developing infrastructure, especially in rural regions. To assist schools in implementing AI tools, offer grants or training courses. To make open-source AI tools more accessible to schools, promote their development and use [23]. Provide precise guidelines for AI platforms on the gathering, storage, and application of data in the classroom.

In the USA, the government should work together with tech firms to give low-income schools discounted access to AI tools and should include AI training in programs for teacher education and offer possibilities for continued professional development. The Government should use methods to find and fix any possible biases in the AI systems that are utilized in education.

Obstacles in Integrating AI into Education?

While incorporating Artificial Intelligence (AI) into education has enormous potential, there are drawbacks and moral dilemmas to be aware of.

- **Accessibility Concerns:** It is imperative to guarantee fair and equal access to AI-powered resources for educators and students alike. A digital divide may result from differences in digital skills and technology infrastructure.
- **Sustained Training and Assistance:** To utilize AI tools in the classroom successfully, teachers require ongoing professional development.
- **Ethical Use in Assessment:** There are ethical concerns when using AI to evaluate student performance. To prevent unfair outcomes, processes must be responsible and transparent [24].
- **Potential Biases in AI Algorithms:** According to a study [25], AI algorithms have the potential to propagate inequality or biases if they are not used wisely. Ethical oversight is needed to prevent inadvertent discrimination.
- **Data Security and Privacy:** Educational establishments gather and examine a lot of student information. When using AI, protecting sensitive data and maintaining privacy are vital considerations [26 - 28].
- **Potential Loss of Human Touch:** Although AI increases productivity, human interaction should still be a part of it. Automation and individualized instruction must coexist.

Applying AI in Education: Initiatives in India and the USA

The following are the policies and programs pertaining to AI in education in both the USA and India:

The successful integration of AI in education requires continuous effort, as policies and projects evolve over time.

Integrating AI in Education: A Comparative Look at India and the USA.

There are significant contextual variations to consider, even though the fundamental steps for integrating AI in education in India and the USA are the same. Fig. (**3**) shows the process of integrating AI in the education sector of India and the USA.

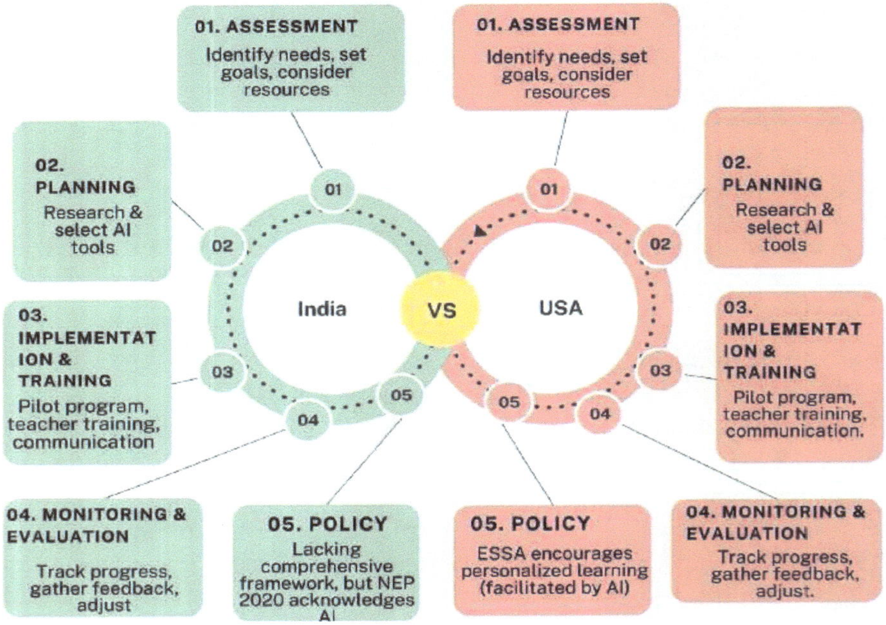

Fig. (3). Process of integrating AI in the education sector of India and the USA.

Comparability's

- **Assessment and Planning:** Prior to implementation, both nations place a strong emphasis on determining needs (administrative duties, customized learning, *etc.*), establishing goals, and taking resources (budget, technology, training, *etc.*) into account [29].
- **Implementation and Training:** Both entail teacher training on AI tools and data privacy, parent and student communication, and trial initiatives.
- **Monitoring & Evaluation:** In both situations, keeping tabs on developments, getting input, and modifying strategies are essential.

Variations

Policy Landscape

- USA: AI-enabled individualized learning experiences are encouraged by the Every Student Succeeds Act (ESSA).
- India: The National Education Policy 2020 recognizes the promise of AI, but lacks a comprehensive AI policy framework.

Target Areas

- India: Personalized learning and closing the access gap through AI-powered online platforms are top priorities.
- USA: There is much attention paid to personalized learning platforms and AI-powered tutoring systems that support educators.

Resources and Infrastructure

- USA: Compared to India, it generally possesses a more advanced technology infrastructure. This could have an impact on how quickly and widely AI is adopted in classrooms.

How can Instructors Get Ready for a World Powered by AI?

There are some tactics that instructors in the USA and India might use to get ready for an AI-driven future [30 - 33]:

- Promote AI Literacy: Teachers and students should be aware of AI's advantages and disadvantages, as well as how it operates. They can navigate the effects of AI on education with this fundamental understanding.
- Prioritize Problem-Solving and Critical Thinking: Since AI can automate repetitive tasks, educators should focus on helping students acquire skills that AI cannot simply replicate. Problem-solving, creativity, and critical thinking are crucial.
- Engage together with Industry and Government officials: To keep up with AI developments, talk to industry professionals and legislators. To build relevant learning experiences, cultivate partnerships.
- Foster Lifelong Learning: AI is constantly evolving; thus, teachers and students need to be flexible and willing to take on new tasks.
- Integrate AI into the Curriculum: Create curricula that address issues related to artificial intelligence. Inform students about the applicability, biases, and ethical considerations of AI. Promote practical initiatives with AI tools.

Ensuring Fairness and Equity in AI-powered Education

To establish an inclusive and equitable learning environment, fairness and equity must be guaranteed in AI-powered education [34 - 36].

AI Privacy and Ethical Application

- India should enact strict data protection legislation to protect the privacy of students. Legislators and educators ought to prioritize ethical AI practices.
- USA: To secure student data, tighten privacy laws (like FERPA). Promote openness in the AI algorithms that are applied in learning environments.

Fairness and Equity

- India should address the digital divide by granting everyone equal access to technology. Fill in the gaps in the underprivileged and rural communities.
- USA: Pay attention to the fair allocation of AIEd resources. Consider pupils with specific needs, linguistic variety, and socioeconomic factors.
- Both: Keep an eye out for biased and discriminatory outcomes in AI systems. Assess their effects on marginalized populations on a regular basis [37].

Trusted Algorithms

- India should create policies for the certification and auditing of AI algorithms. Make sure that decision-making procedures are transparent.
- USA: Encourage the study of AI models that are understandable. To create reliable systems, promote cooperation between academics, researchers, and business professionals.

Pedagogical Efficacy

- India: Combine AI with pedagogies that are appropriate for the country's culture. Adapt information to regional contexts.
- USA: Examine adaptive learning platforms that address students' diverse needs. Make individualized education a priority [38 - 40]. To develop an AI-powered educational system that supports equity, inclusion, and excellence, stakeholders-educators, legislators, researchers, and students-must work together.

CONCLUSION AND FUTURE SCOPE

The use of AI in education is completely changing how we teach and learn. AI has the enormous potential to enhance educational outcomes for every student by personalizing learning experiences, automating tasks, and encouraging deeper involvement. There are still obstacles to overcome, but there is no denying AI's potential benefits for education. AI has the potential to be a very useful tool for making learning more egalitarian, engaging, and tailored for every student if ethical issues are addressed, accessibility is maintained, and teachers are given the necessary training. The field of education is about to undergo a revolutionary change as AI technology advances.

AI will be able to create tailored learning pathways with dynamic adjustments based on student achievement, going beyond simple content customization to meet individual needs. AI-powered Augmented Reality and Virtual Reality (VR/AR) will make for more dynamic and captivating educational experiences. Consider historical simulations or virtual laboratories. For greater use, especially in rural areas, the development of AI tools that can comprehend and provide instruction in different Indian languages is essential. To provide fair access to technology and AI-powered educational materials, public-private collaborations and government actions are crucial. Additional assistance for students with disabilities and personalization of learning experiences can be achieved through the continued development of AI tools.

REFERENCES

[1] A. Bhutoria, "Personalized education and Artificial Intelligence in the United States, China, and India: A systematic review using a Human-In-The-Loop model", *Computers and Education: Artificial Intelligence,* vol. 3, p. 100068, 2022. [http://dx.doi.org/10.1016/j.caeai.2022.100068]

[2] N. Simhadri, and T.N.V.R. Swamy, "Awareness among teaching on AI and ML applications based on fuzzy in education sector at USA", *Soft Comput.,* pp. 1-9, 2023. [http://dx.doi.org/10.1007/s00500-023-08329-z] [PMID: 37362281]

[3] P. Blikstein, and U. Wilensky, "A new methodology for studying and teaching computational thinking", *Br. J. Educ. Technol.,* vol. 49, no. 5, pp. 855-872, 2018. [http://dx.doi.org/10.1111/bjet.12560]

[4] A. Núñez-Marcos, G. Azkune, and A. Almeida, "AI and education: Current trends and emerging pedagogical challenges", *IEEE-RITA,* vol. 14, no. 1, pp. 4-11, 2019.

[5] A. Kanwar, and K. Balasubramanian, "Artificial intelligence and the future of education", *Journal of Educational Technology,* vol. 17, no. 1, pp. 1-6, 2020.

[6] R.S. Baker, "Stupid tutoring systems, intelligent humans", *Int. J. Artif. Intell. Educ.,* vol. 26, no. 2, pp. 600-614, 2016. [http://dx.doi.org/10.1007/s40593-016-0105-0]

[7] N. Sclater, "Artificial Intelligence in education: Promises and implications for teaching and learning", *Br. J. Educ. Technol.,* vol. 50, no. 2, pp. 619-627, 2019.

[8] N. Vashishtha, "AI and education in India: Challenges and opportunities", *Journal of Educational Technology,* vol. 18, no. 1, pp. 12-19, 2020.

[9] A. Agarwal, "Artificial Intelligence in Indian Education System", *Int. J. Eng. Manag. Res.,* vol. 9, no. 3, pp. 67-70, 2019.

[10] K. Sharma, and K. Verbert, "Ethical considerations in AI-based education: A systematic review", *IEEE Trans. Learn. Technol.,* vol. 14, no. 1, pp. 43-54, 2021.

[11] Artificial intelligence in education: challenges and opportunities for sustainable development Available from: https://www.unesco.org/en/articles/challenges-and-opportunities-artific-

al-intelligence-education

[12] Singh, P., Pahuja, N., Kansal, M., Gurung, S., Shukla, U., & Gupta, S. (2024, March). Enhancing Tourism Experiences and Preserving Cultural Heritage with AR and VR. In 2024 *2nd International Conference on Disruptive Technologies (ICDT)* (pp. 225-231). IEEE. [http://dx.doi.org/10.1109/ICDT61202.2024.10489490]

[13] EkStep website. (2024, July). Available from: https://aspire-india.org/ek-step-foundation/

[14] DreamBox Learning website. (2024, July). Available from: https://www.dreambox.com/

[15] W. Holmes, and I. Tuomi, "State of the art and practice in AI in education", *Eur. J. Educ.,* vol. 57, no. 4, pp. 542-570, 2022. [http://dx.doi.org/10.1111/ejed.12533]

[16] Blessing Osawaru, N.M. Al Hamad, O.N. Chisom, B. Osawaru, and O.E. Adewusi, "AI in education: A review of personalized learning and educational technology", *GSC Advanced Research and Reviews,* vol. 18, no. 2, pp. 261-271, 2024. [http://dx.doi.org/10.30574/gscarr.2024.18.2.0062]

[17] Kansal, M., Singh, P., Singh, M. K., & Varshney, S. *A systematic study of services and security model in cloud computing: A brief overview. Convergence of Cloud Computing, AI, and Agricultural Science*, 1-16, 2023.

[18] M. Kayyali, "Future possibilities and challenges of AI in education", In: *Transforming education with generative AI: Prompt engineering and synthetic content creation.* IGI Global, 2024, pp. 118-137. [http://dx.doi.org/10.4018/979-8-3693-1351-0.ch006]

[19] Selwyn, N. (2024). On the limits of artificial intelligence (AI) in education. Nordisk tidsskrift for pedagogikk og kritikk, 10(1), 3-14.

[20] P. Singh, M. Srivastava, M. Kansal, A.P. Singh, A. Chauhan, and A. Gaur, "A comparative analysis of modern frontend frameworks for building large-scale web applications", *2023 International Conference on Disruptive Technologies (ICDT),* IEEE., pp. 531-535, 2023. [http://dx.doi.org/10.1109/ICDT57929.2023.10150911]

[21] Government of India. National Education Policy 2021. Available from: https://www.education.gov.in/en/nep-new

[22] US Department of Education. ED Policy and Guidance on AI in education. Available from: https://tech.ed.gov/aipolicy

[23] Abimbola, C., Chisom, O. N., & Adeniyi, I. S. Integrating AI in education: Opportunities, challenges, and ethical considerations. Magna Scientia Advanced Research and Reviews, 10(02), 006–013, 2024

[24] R. Goel, U. K. Jaiswal, P. Singh, S. P. Yadav, and P. Upadhyay, "Deep Learning for Early Brain Tumor Detection: A Keras-Based Approach Using MRI and CT Imaging", In: *Demystifying the Role of Natural Language Processing (NLP) in Mental Health* IGI Global: Hershey (PA), 2025, pp. 145-180. [http://dx.doi.org/10.4018/979-8-3693-4203-9.ch009]

[25] S. Sharma, G. Singh, and C.S. Sharma, *Artificial intelligence in Indian higher education institutions: a quantitative study on adoption and perceptions.* Int J Syst Assur Eng Manag, 2024. [http://dx.doi.org/10.1007/s13198-023-02193-8]

[26] Eden, N. C. A., Chisom, N. O. N., & Adeniyi, N. I. S. Integrating AI in education: Opportunities, challenges, and ethical considerations. Magna Scientia Advanced Research and Reviews, 10(2), 006–013, 2024 [http://dx.doi.org/10.30574/msarr.2024.10.2.0039]

[27] D. Ifenthaler, R. Majumdar, P. Gorissen, M. Judge, S. Mishra, J. Raffaghelli, and A. Shimada, *Artificial Intelligence in Education: Implications for Policymakers, Researchers, and Practitioners.* Technology, Knowledge and Learning, 2024.

[http://dx.doi.org/10.1007/s10758-024-09747-0]

[28] Sadhana, and D. S. Yadav, "Ethical Considerations in AI-Driven Education Balancing Innovation and Responsibility", *International Journal of Innovative Research in Technology,* vol. 10, no. 10, pp. 49-50, 2024.

[29] M. Kansal, P. Singh, S. Shukla, and S. Srivastava, "A comparative study of machine learning models for house price prediction and analysis in smart cities", *International Conference on Electronic Governance with Emerging Technologies,* pp. 168-184, 2023. [http://dx.doi.org/10.1007/978-3-031-43940-7_14]

[30] J. Kengam, "Artificial intelligence in education", *ResearchGate,* 2020. [http://dx.doi.org/10.13140/RG.2.2.16375.65445]

[31] M. Khawrin, and E. Nderego, "Opportunities and Challenges of AI towards Education: A Systematic Literature Review", *International Journal on Language Research and Education Studies.,* vol. 13, pp. 266-271, 2023.

[32] Need for leveraging AI in India's education sector - Hindustan Times. Available from: https://indiaai.gov.in/article/lack-of-ai-policies-in-education-is-a-significant-cha-lenge-for-india-unesco-report

[33] Available from: https://www.hindustantimes.com/ht-insight/future-tech/need-for-leveraging-ai-in-indias-education-sector-101716450004610.html

[34] Preparing for the Future: How AI will Transform Education in 2024 - Eklavvya. Available from: https://www.eklavvya.com/blog/ai-education-2024/

[35] Why do Indian students rush to study AI and machine learning at US schools? - Investing Abroad News | The Financial Express, Available from: https://www.financialexpress.com/business/investing-abroad-record-number-of-indians-applying-to-us-schools-to-study-ai-and-machine-learning-3490087/

[36] M. Kansal, P. Singh, P. Srivastava, R. Singhal, N. Deep, and A. Singh, "Mental health monitoring in the digital age: a comprehensive analysis", In: *Future of AI in Medical Imaging.* IGI Global, 2024, pp. 168-183. [http://dx.doi.org/10.4018/979-8-3693-2359-5.ch011]

[37] M. Kansal, P. Singh, M. K. Singh, and S. Varshney, "A systematic study of services and security model in cloud computing: A brief overview", In: *Convergence of Cloud Computing, AI, and Agricultural Science* John Wiley & Sons, 2023, pp. 1-16.

[38] A. Jaiswal, and C.J. Arun, "Potential of Artificial Intelligence for transformation of the education system in India", *Int. J. Educ. Dev. Using Inf. Commun. Technol.,* vol. 17, no. 1, pp. 142-158, 2021.

[39] R. Shoukat, "Harnessing AI for Educational Transformation: A Comparative Study of China, India and Pakistan", *Strategic Studies,* vol. 44, no. 1, pp. 116-134, 2024.

[40] A. Jaiswal, and C.J. Arun, "Potential of Artificial Intelligence for transformation of the education system in India", *Int. J. Educ. Dev. Using Inf. Commun. Technol.,* vol. 17, no. 1, pp. 142-158, 2021.

CHAPTER 6

Artificial Intelligence (AI) Powered Pedagogy: Transforming Education Through Personalization and Automation

R. Venkatesh[1,*]

[1] *Department of Physics, PSNA College of Engineering and Technology (Autonomous), Dindigul 624622, Tamil Nadu, India*

Abstract: The incorporation of Artificial Intelligence (AI) into educational systems marks a transformative era, promising to reshape both students' learning journeys and educators' teaching methodologies. This chapter embarks on a comprehensive exploration of AI's multifaceted contributions to education, spanning diverse realms. Initially, it delves into the realm of individual learning experiences guided by AI algorithms. These algorithms adapt in real-time to the different needs and preferences of students individually, enhancing learning outcomes and cultivating a more engaging educational experience. Moreover, the chapter delves into the realm of administrative automation facilitated by AI-powered educational tools. These tools streamline cumbersome tasks such as grading assessments, managing administrative workflows, and providing instantaneous feedback. By automating these processes, educators can devote more time and energy to focus on the essential aspects of teaching and mentoring, thereby nurturing a more enriched educational environment. Furthermore, the chapter explores the expansive terrain of AI's role in content creation, curation, and recommendation. AI-driven platforms have the capacity to synthesize and curate vast repositories of educational materials, tailoring the content to match the different styles and preferences for learning. This not only provides an enriched learning experience but also enhances critical thinking skills by presenting students with diverse perspectives and resources. In tandem with these advancements, the chapter meticulously examines the ethical dimensions and complexities involved in incorporating AI into educational settings. Emphasizing principles of transparency, equity, and data privacy, it underscores the imperative of navigating these ethical considerations to ensure that AI-driven educational initiatives remain ethically sound and socially responsible. Finally, the chapter underscores the imperative of collaborative efforts among educators, technologists, policymakers, and other parties to fully leverage AI's potential in education. By fostering robust partnerships and interdisciplinary dialogue, stakeholders can collectively navigate challenges, leverage opportunities, and steer the trajectory of education towards a more innovative and inclusive future for future generations.

* **Corresponding author R. Venkatesh:** Department of Physics, PSNA College of Engineering and Technology (Autonomous), Dindigul 624622, Tamil Nadu, India; E-mail: sukatesh@gmail.com

Pancham Singh, Avinash Kumar Sharma, Mrignainy Kansal, & Amarjeet Prajapati (Eds.)

Keywords: Artificial Intelligence (AI), Adaptive algorithms, Critical thinking skills, Education, Grading, Personalized learning.

INTRODUCTION

Most significantly, Artificial Intelligence in education represents a new product for the process of teaching and learning, which has unleashed innovation and opportunity within the classroom. Modern AI indeed has enormous, transformative potential; one that can change educational practices from personalized learning experiences to even automated administrative tasks. It is through such capabilities in leveraging machine learning algorithms and data analytics that AI can provide educational content best suited to students' individual needs and learning styles, optimize and design the process for content creation and curation, and also reduce administrative loads on teachers [1]. Such an integration not only improves the efficiency and effectiveness of teaching and learning but also opens the door to new pedagogical approaches and opportunities for educational equity and inclusion. As AI continues to evolve and permeate educational systems worldwide, it is essential to explore its multifaceted contributions and navigate the ethical considerations to ensure that AI-driven educational initiatives uphold principles of fairness, transparency, and student well-being [2]. It is in this chapter that the full depth of promises, challenges, and implications is undertaken toward the integration of AI in education, aiming to illuminate the path toward a more innovative, inclusive, and impactful educational future.

Importance of Artificial Intelligence Integration in Education

Incorporating Artificial Intelligence (AI) into education is increasingly recognized as a pivotal step in revolutionizing traditional teaching and learning methods (Fig. 1). Integrating AI into education holds immense importance in shaping the future of learning. AI has the capacity to personalize education, catering to the particular needs and learning preferences of individual students [3]. Through analyzing extensive data, AI can pinpoint areas where students face challenges and offer precise interventions to aid their learning. Additionally, AI-driven tools can streamline administrative duties for educators, enabling them to dedicate more time to teaching and guiding students [4]. AI might also increase accessibility of education by providing resources and aid to learners, independent of geographical location or physical abilities. By adopting AI in education, it will be easy to create learning environments that are inclusive, adaptive, and efficient at helping students succeed in the fast-changing world.

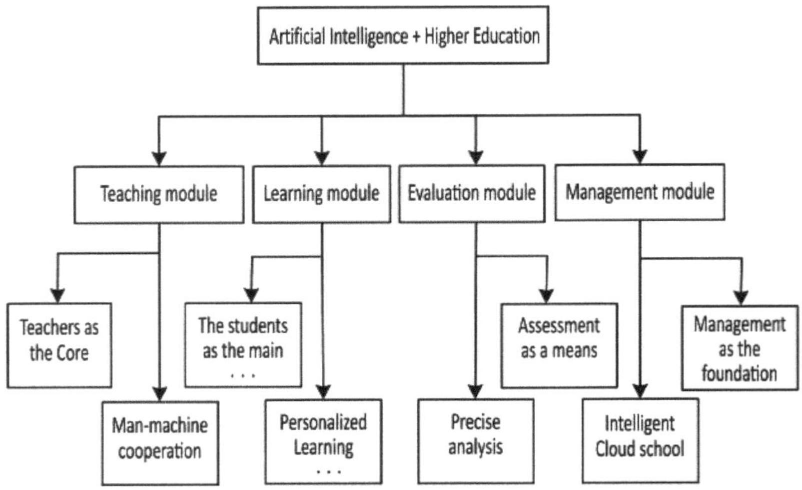

Fig. (1). The integration of artificial intelligence in education.

Personalized Learning: AI enables the creation of customized learning experiences that account for every student's individual needs, preferences, and learning styles. By analyzing student performance and behavior data, AI algorithms can adapt instructional content, pacing, and support mechanisms, thereby optimizing learning outcomes for diverse learners.

Efficiency and Automation: AI streamlines administrative tasks for educators, such as grading assignments, managing workflows, and providing feedback. This automation allows teachers to dedicate more time to higher-value activities, such as personalized instruction, mentoring, and fostering students' critical thinking skills.

Access to Quality Education: AI-powered educational platforms can make high-quality resources and instruction available to everyone, regardless of location or socioeconomic background. By providing personalized, interactive online learning experiences, AI helps bridge gaps in educational access and promotes lifelong learning opportunities for all.

Innovation in Content Creation: AI facilitates the creation, curation, and recommendation of educational content, from adaptive learning modules to interactive simulations. It improves the range and accessibility of educational materials and makes learning more interesting, relevant, and effective for students.

Ethical Considerations and Accountability: AI integration in education demands deliberation on ethical implications: data privacy, algorithmic bias, and transparency. In that respect, stakeholders have to come forward to make sure that the design of the ethical standards and validation rest on the very roots of equity, fairness, and student well-being in AI-led education systems.

Preparation for the Future: AI skills are becoming more important in today's job market. The infusion of AI into education will help learners develop critical digital literacy, computational thinking, and problem-solving skills relevant to succeeding in the economy of the 21st century.

Continuous Improvement and Adaptation: AI enables continuous monitoring and assessment of student progress, allowing educators to identify areas for development and adapt teaching strategies in real-time. This creates the repeated use of the feedback loop in building a culture of continual improvement and innovation in education.

Promise of Revolutionizing Learning and Teaching

The implementation of artificial intelligence in learning and teaching has very high potential to bring a revolution to the area, providing transformational opportunities across many dimensions of education. The aim is to integrate innovative technologies, such as Artificial Intelligence, at the heart of promises to revolutionize learning and teaching. AI can completely transform traditional teaching methodologies in terms of bespoke, adaptive learning experiences designed to help meet the needs of each individual learner [5]. Through the implementation of complex algorithms, AI is able to analyze large amounts of data to find patterns in student performance, letting instructors know when their teaching strategies must be tailored accordingly [6]. Moreover, routine administrative tasks can be automated with AI-powered tools, freeing up more time for educators to engage in meaningful interactions with their students. AI can be used to forge new paths of creativity, collaboration, and critical thinking in education.

Personalized Learning Experiences: AI algorithms analyze a broad range of data on students' performance, their preferences, and learning styles to providie personalized learning experiences. By dynamically adapting content, pacing, and support mechanisms, AI ensures personalized instruction for each student, optimizing their learning outcomes and engagement.

Adaptive Instruction: AI-powered educational platforms can adjust the level of difficulty and sequence of learning activities in real-time based on students'responses and performance. The adaptive instruction ensures that students are appropriately challenged and supported, promoting deeper understanding and mastery of concepts.

Enhanced Feedback Mechanisms: AI makes it possible to give timely and detailed feedback on students' assignments, assessments, and learning progress. Indeed, by freeing educators from tasks such as grading and assessment, AI empowers them to give more personalized and constructive feedback for students' growth and improvement.

Augmented Teaching Practices: AI tools and technologies have a place in enhancing teaching; they can provide educators with important insights into the ways that students learn and the areas in which they struggle. Armed with AI-generated analytics, teachers will be better placed to identify at-risk students earlier, tailor their teaching methods accordingly, and deliver focused interventions that support student success.

Efficient Administrative Support: AI streamlines administrative tasks for educators, such as lesson planning, resource allocation, and student record management. By automating routine tasks, AI enables educators to focus more on instructional design, innovation, and fostering meaningful learning experiences for their students.

Access to High-Quality Educational Resources: AI-driven educational platforms curate and recommend high-quality educational resources tailored to learners' needs and interests. By putting AI to work in content curation and recommendation, educators open an array of multimedia resources, simulations, and interactive learning experiences for students.

Facilitation of Lifelong Learning: AI promotes lifelong learning by providing personalized, adaptive learning activities that meet the evolving requirements of learners throughout their lives. Whether in formal education settings or informal learning environments, AI-powered tools and platforms empower individuals to learn new knowledge and skills at their own pace and convenience.

Innovation in Pedagogy: AI enables the exploration and implementation of innovative pedagogical approaches, such as game-based learning, collaborative learning environments, and immersive simulations. Integrating AI into teaching practices enables educators to develop dynamic, interactive learning experiences that inspire creativity, critical thinking, and collaboration among students.

PERSONALIZED LEARNING WITH AI

Personalized learning with AI (Fig. **2**) signifies a revolutionary approach to education, utilizing artificial intelligence to customize instructional experiences in accordance with the unique needs and preferences of each student. Advanced algorithms and data analytics allow AI to assess learning preferences, strengths, and weaknesses in students, allowing the educator to establish an individualized learning path [7]. These adaptive platforms adjust content, pacing, and support mechanisms in real-time, so that each kid gets a tailored education that really meets their aptitude and interests. By offering tailored feedback, adaptive resources, and engaging activities, AI fosters greater engagement, motivation, and academic success [8]. Moreover, personalized learning with AI promotes inclusivity by accommodating diverse learning needs and providing support for students with disabilities or language barriers. Revolutionary AI learning is continually growing through personalized learning technologies that enable educators to respond to varied student needs and foster lifelong learning.

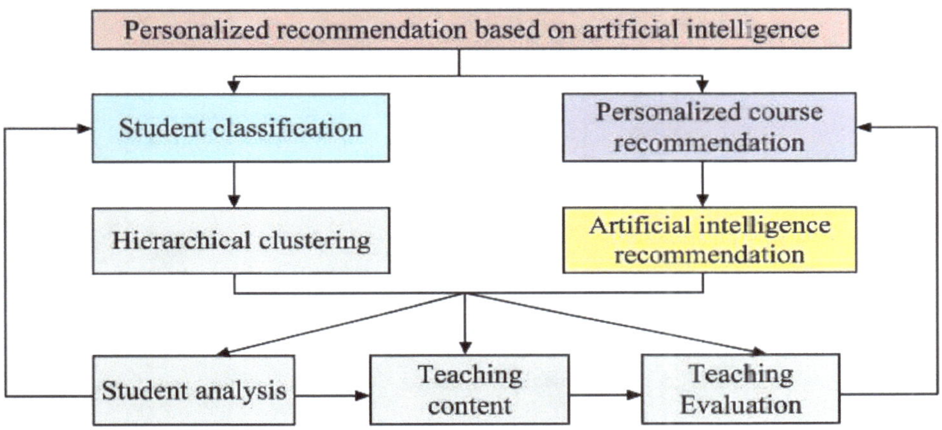

Fig. (2). Personalized learning with AI.

Adaptive Algorithms for Personalized Learning

Adaptive algorithms lie at the heart of personalized learning, offering a dynamic and tailored approach that accommodates the different needs and learning styles of each student (Fig. **3**). These algorithms make use of artificial intelligence and machine learning techniques in analyzing mountains of data created by every student's scores, study preferences, and patterns of behavior [9]. By processing this data, Adaptive algorithms can provide insights into each student's strengths, weaknesses, and areas needing improvement, allowing educators to tailor instruction accordingly. The key feature of adaptive algorithms is their ability to adjust learning paths and content in real-time based on individual student responses and performance. If a student shows a strong understanding of a specific concept, the algorithm can advance them to more challenging material to keep them engaged and stimulated [10]. On the other hand, when a student is struggling with a concept, it can offer additional help, alternative explanations, or even remedial resources to scaffold learning. Furthermore, adaptive algorithms facilitate differentiated instruction, allowing educators to offer customized learning experiences that tend to be in tune with different needs and capabilities of each student [11]. Whether it's adjusting the pace of instruction, adjusting the level of difficulty, or offering targeted interventions, adaptive algorithms empower educators to deliver instruction tailored to the individual needs of their students.

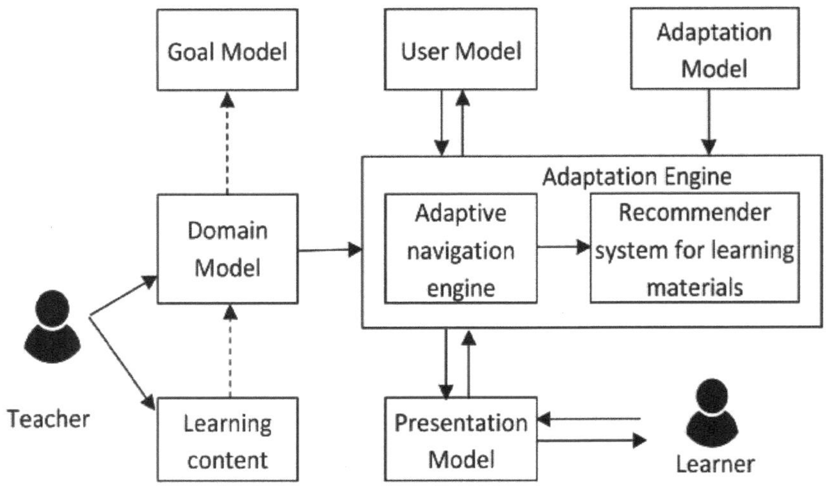

Fig. (3). Adaptive algorithms model for personalized learning.

Moreover, adaptive algorithms promote student agency and autonomy by offering opportunities for choice and self-directed learning. By presenting students with personalized learning paths and adaptive resources, these algorithms foster greater ownership of the learning process, promoting intrinsic motivation and a sense of empowerment [12]. However, while adaptive algorithms hold immense promise for personalized learning, they also raise important concerns about data privacy, algorithmic bias, and ethical use. This will require a collaborative effort by educators, policymakers, and technologists in developing ethical guidelines and safeguards to ensure that adaptive learning systems prioritize equity, transparency, and student well-being.

Customizing Learning Paths to Individual Needs and Preferences

It is a core element of personalized learning, enabled by integrating Artificial Intelligence (AI) technologies into education. With the power of today's advanced algorithms and data analytics, a teacher can truly program an interactive learning experience that can empathize with each student's strengths, weaknesses, interests, and learning style [13]. Central to this approach is adaptive learning, where the instructional path is dynamically adjusted in real-time according to each student's responses and performance.

Artificial intelligence algorithms analyze a wealth of student data with assessment results, behavioral patterns, and engagement metrics, to improve insights into each student's learning profile [14]. With this information, educators can personalize learning paths to address specific learning needs, challenges, and goals. An essential advantage of customizing learning paths is the capability to offer differentiated instruction. Students' progress through content at their own pace, allowing for remediation or acceleration as needed [15]. Furthermore, tailoring learning paths fosters greater engagement and motivation among students. When learning experiences align with their interests and preferences, the students are likely to be more engaged in their learning process. By incorporating interactive elements, multimedia resources, and real-world applications, educators can develop learning experiences that engage each student, capture their attention, and inspire further understanding of the subject. Moreover, tailoring learning paths promotes inclusivity and equity by accommodating diverse learning needs and abilities [16]. In this respect, it is possible to create personalized learning experiences that meet the needs and preferences of students with diverse backgrounds, styles, and learning preferences. This process ensures that every student has the opportunity to succeed and thrive academically. Safeguards must be in place to protect student privacy, mitigate algorithmic bias, and ensure transparency and accountability in decision-making processes [17].

Optimizing Learning Outcomes through Personalization

Personalization has been at the core of education, aiming to optimize learning outcomes by tailoring each instructional experience to learners' unique needs and preferences. By infusing Artificial Intelligence (AI) technologies, educators open a gateway to the use of adaptive algorithms, data analytics, and personalized learning platforms to foster a very dynamic and engaging environment for learning that better prepares students for success [18]. At the core of optimizing learning outcomes through personalization is the ability to deliver tailored instruction that meets learners at their individual level of readiness, interest, and ability. AI algorithms analyze a myriad of data points, including assessment results, learning behaviors, and demographic information, to gain insights into each student's learning profile [19]. By providing customized learning experiences, personalization enhances student engagement and motivation. Whenever learners feel that their learning experiences are relevant and meaningful to their interests, they will become actively involved in the learning process. In addition to that, through personalized learning, there will be a sense of ownership and autonomy that shall further allow learners to take control over their learning journey and, thus, confidently pursue set academic targets. Furthermore, personalization enables educators to target intervention strategies more effectively, providing additional support to students who may be struggling and offering enrichment opportunities for those who are excelling. It will enable educators to tailor instruction appropriately by pointing out areas of strength and weakness and move students toward mastery through scaffolding [20]. Additionally, personalized learning promotes the development of critical thinking, problem-solving, and metacognitive skills. By engaging students in interactive activities, inquiry-based learning tasks, and real-world applications, educators can facilitate deeper levels of understanding and promote higher-order thinking skills. However, to fully optimize learning outcomes through personalization, it is critical to address ethical considerations and provide opportunities for creating personalized learning experiences for all students [21]. It is very important for educators, policymakers, and technologists to develop ethical guidelines that respect students' privacy, reduce algorithmic bias, and promote transparency and accountability in educational institutions.

AUTOMATING ADMINISTRATIVE TASKS

Automating administrative tasks is a strategic approach to improving workflow efficiency and boosting productivity. By pinpointing activities that are repetitive and overtly time-consuming, such as data entry, e-mails management, and scheduling, organizations can use automation tools to streamline these processes [22]. Whether through workflow automation platforms like Zapier or robotic process automation (RPA) tools such as UiPath, automation offers the opportunity to eliminate manual errors, reduce operational costs, and free employees' time for more strategic initiatives [23]. Clearly, careful planning, testing, and refinement must be in place for any automation workflow to fit seamlessly into existing systems and processes. Continuous monitoring and maintenance are required to identify issues and thus optimize performance over time. By embracing automation, businesses can achieve significant gains in productivity and resource allocation while staying competitive in today's fast-paced environment.

AI-Powered Tools for Automating Administrative Duties

AI-powered tools offer a transformative solution for automating administrative duties in education, streamlining processes, and freeing up valuable time for educators and administrators alike [24]. These tools can efficiently handle tasks such as grading assessments, managing student records, scheduling classes, and even providing personalized feedback to students. By leveraging machine learning algorithms, AI systems can analyze data trends to optimize resource allocation, predict future needs, and enhance decision-making processes. On the other hand, Natural Language Processing (NLP) capabilities make AI self-automate communication activities, such as responding to common inquiries or providing updates to stakeholders [25]. Overall, integrating AI-powered tools into education will drive operational efficiency but also allow refocusing by educators on the highest-impact activities that matter to deliver a much better learning experience to students. AI-powered tools for automating administrative duties have become increasingly prevalent across various industries. These tools use artificial intelligence and machine learning algorithms to simplify administrative tasks, enhance efficiency, and minimize human error.

Virtual Assistants: AI-driven virtual assistants like Siri, Google Assistant, and Alexa can schedule appointments, set reminders, send emails, and handle numerous administrative tasks using voice commands or text input.

Chatbots: Chatbots are used on websites and messaging platforms to answer frequent questions, render customer support, and assist with administrative tasks such as scheduling appointments or processing orders.

Document Management Systems: AI-powered document management systems can automatically classify, organize, and retrieve documents, reducing the time spent on manual sorting and searching.

Expense Management: AI tools can analyze expense reports, receipts, and invoices to automatically categorize expenses, detect errors or fraud, and generate expense reports.

Calendar Management: AI-powered calendar management tools can schedule meetings, coordinate availability among team members, and send reminders for upcoming events.

Email Management: AI tools can prioritize emails, categorize them by importance or topic, draft responses based on previous interactions, and even detect and filter spam.

Data Entry Automation: AI algorithms extract data from documents, forms, and images, obviating manual data entry and attendant possible errors.

Workflow Automation: AI-powered workflow automation platforms enable organizations to streamline repetitive tasks, route documents for approval, and integrate with other software systems to automate entire business processes.

HR Management: AI tools are helpful across a range of HR tasks, from resume screening and candidate sourcing to employee induction and performance appraisals.

Project Management: Such AI-driven project management tools could automate task assignment and track the progress of projects, analyze data to identify potential issues, and optimize resource allocation.

Streamlining Grading and Assessment Processes

Streamlining grading and assessment processes using AI-powered tools can significantly improve efficiency, provide more accurate insights, and reduce the burden on educators. AI-powered tools are revolutionizing the grading and assessment processes in education by streamlining tasks and enhancing efficiency [26]. These tools utilize machine learning algorithms to automate the grading of assignments, quizzes, and exams, significantly reducing the time and effort required by educators. By analyzing patterns in student responses, AI can provide instant feedback, enabling students to obtain relevant feedback on their performance and where they need improvement. Not only that, but AI can also provide consistency and, in many cases, fairness in grading, thereby reducing bias or even human error. Additionally, advanced AI algorithms can adapt to different grading criteria and learning objectives, providing personalized assessments tailored to each student's needs [27]. Not only will integrating AI into the grading and assessment processes save educators' time, but it will also improve the quality and effectiveness of feedback, ultimately fostering a more productive learning environment [28].

Automated Grading: AI algorithms can grade multiple-choice, fill-in-the-blank, and other types of objective questions instantly, eliminating the need for manual grading. This saves educators' time and ensures reliability in grading.

Essay and Free-Form Response Evaluation: Natural Language Processing (NLP) algorithms can assess essays and free-form responses by analyzing factors such as grammar, coherence, and relevance to the prompt. While not perfect, these systems can provide valuable output to students and reduce the time instructors spend grading open-ended questions.

Plagiarism Detection: In this regard, AI plagiarism detectors can match student submissions to a large library of academic sources and previously submitted works in establishing instances of plagiarism, thus helping to preserve the integrity of academia and guaranteeing fair assessment among students.

Adaptive Learning Platforms: AI-driven adaptive learning platforms are tailored to each student's strengths, weaknesses, and learning pace. These systems continue to assess student performance and further go on to adjust the content and level of difficulty in assignments.

Data Analytics for Assessment: AI algorithms can use assessment data to identify trends and patterns and pinpoint areas in which students might be struggling. Such insights will help the educator realign teaching methodologies for targeted interventions that will enhance the overall performance of students.

Real-Time Feedback: AI-powered tools can provide immediate feedback to students as they complete assessments, helping them identify mistakes, understand concepts better, and make corrections in real-time.

Peer Assessment Facilitation: AI can facilitate peer assessment by guiding students through the evaluation process, providing rubrics or criteria for assessment, and aggregating peer feedback to generate overall scores.

Voice and Video Analysis: AI technologies can analyze audio and video recordings of presentations, speeches, or language assessments to evaluate factors such as pronunciation, fluency, and delivery.

Proctoring and Exam Integrity: AI-driven proctoring software can identify the students during online exams through their behaviors, like glancing away from the screen or accessing unauthorized resources. This ensures the integrity of exams in remote learning settings.

Delivering immediate feedback to students

It is essential for enhancing learning outcomes and fostering continuous improvement. AI-powered tools can play a important role in delivering timely and personalized feedback across various educational settings [29].

Immediate Grading: AI algorithms can instantly grade objective questions, such as multiple-choice or fill-in-the-blank, offering students immediate feedback on their performance.

Automated Feedback on Assignments: AI-powered systems can analyze student submissions, such as essays or problem-solving tasks, and provide automated feedback on aspects like grammar, structure, content relevance, and accuracy.

Interactive Learning Platforms: AI-driven interactive learning platforms can offer real-time feedback as students engage with educational content. These platforms may include simulations, quizzes, or interactive exercises where feedback is provided instantly based on student responses.

Adaptive Learning Systems: AI-driven adaptive learning systems keep on assessing progress, changing the level of difficulty, and content delivery based on a person's performance in real-time. This provides for personalization so that each student gets feedback that is relevant and timely for them.

Peer Feedback Facilitation: AI tools can facilitate peer feedback by guiding students through the evaluation process, providing criteria or rubrics for assessment, and aggregating peer comments to generate comprehensive feedback for each student.

Language Learning Apps: AI language learning apps have the capabilities to produce immediate feedback on pronunciation, grammar, vocabulary, fluency, *etc*., when students practice speaking or writing in a foreign language.

Coding and Programming Feedback: AI tools can analyze code written by students and provide immediate feedback on syntax errors, logical inconsistencies, and best practices in programming languages.

Virtual Tutoring Systems: Equipped with AI-powered virtual tutoring systems, one can simulate one-to-one tutoring and provide real-time individual feedback on the students' responses, explanations, and strategies for solving problems.

Emotional Feedback and Engagement Monitoring: AI technologies, such as sentiment analysis and facial expression recognition, can gauge students' emotional states and levels of engagement during learning activities, allowing educators to adjust their teaching approach and provide additional support as needed.

ARTIFICIAL INTELLIGENCE IN CONTENT CREATION AND CURATION

The chart delineates the distinctions between content creation and content curation (Table **1**). Content creation involves the genesis of original material, stemming from the creator's ideas, research, or experiences, demanding creative ingenuity and a substantial time investment. Conversely, content curation involves the collection, organization, and dissemination of existing content from diverse sources, requiring adept selection and arrangement skills rather than originality. While creation necessitates subject matter expertise, curation demands proficiency in finding and curating relevant content. Ownership of created content resides with the creator, while curated content remains under the ownership of its original creators. The purpose of creation often spans authority establishment, information dissemination, entertainment, or persuasion, while curation primarily serves to aggregate and present valuable content to a targeted audience. Examples of creation include blog writing, graphic design, and video production, whereas curation entails tasks like compiling lists or creating round-up posts. Creation directly engages the audience with the creator's perspective, while curation engages by offering a collection of valuable resources. Creation fosters creative and critical thinking skills, while curation enhances research, analysis, and organization capabilities. Both creation and curation can positively impact SEO, with original content potentially yielding greater SEO benefits, while curated content contributes to website authority and resourcefulness.

Table 1. The Difference between Content Creation and Content Curation.

Particulars	Content Creation	Content Curation
Definition	The process of generating original content.	The process of gathering, organizing, and sharing existing content.
Source	Originates from the creator's own ideas, research, or experiences.	Gathers content from various sources available on the internet or other media.
Creativity	Requires creative thinking and originality.	Requires selection and arrangement skills rather than originality.
Time Investment	Generally, more time-consuming.	Generally, less time-consuming compared to creation.
Expertise Needed	Requires expertise in the subject matter.	Requires expertise in finding and selecting relevant content.
Ownership	Content is owned by the creator.	Ownership lies with the original creators of the content.
Purpose	Often used to establish authority, inform, entertain, or persuade.	Primarily used to aggregate and present valuable content to a specific audience.
Examples	Writing blog posts, designing graphics, producing videos, *etc.*	Curating articles, compiling lists, creating round-up posts, *etc.*
Engagement	Directly engages the audience with the creator's perspective.	Engages the audience by offering a collection of valuable resources.
Skills Developed	Enhances creative and critical thinking skills.	Enhances research, analysis, and organization skills.
SEO Impact	It may have a greater impact on SEO due to originality and relevance.	It can still impact SEO positively by providing valuable resources and improving website authority.

AI has revolutionized content creation and curation, introducing innovative tools and solutions that streamline processes, enhance quality, and improve relevance across industries. Through natural language generation systems, AI generates written content like articles, reports, and product descriptions efficiently, reducing manual effort [30]. Content personalization algorithms analyze user data to provide customized recommendations, ensuring engagement and satisfaction. Additionally, AI assists in optimizing content strategy by identifying trends and keywords that resonate with the audience, enhancing visibility and reach [31].

Multimedia creation tools powered by AI produce visually appealing images and videos, while transcription and translation capabilities make content accessible globally. Content moderation algorithms filter out harmful content, maintaining a safe online environment. With AI-driven recommendation systems, users receive personalized content feeds, driving engagement and conversion rates. AI also aids in content aggregation, curation, and editing, ensuring consistency and quality [32]. Performance analytics powered by AI provide insights into content effectiveness, guiding future strategies. Overall, AI empowers organizations to deliver impactful, relevant, and engaging content experiences while navigating ethical considerations to ensure transparency and fairness.

AI Algorithms for Generating Educational Content

AI algorithms for generating educational content are revolutionizing the way educational materials are created and distributed, offering scalable and personalized solutions that cater to diverse learning needs [33]. These algorithms, like alternative AI methodologies, are based on NLP and machine learning to produce various educational materials such as textbooks, lecture notes, quizzes, and tutorials [34]. One prominent example is the use of AI-powered Natural Language Generation (NLG) systems to produce educational texts on various topics. These systems can analyze large datasets of educational content, textbooks, and scholarly articles to generate coherent and informative passages that are suitable for different educational levels and learning objectives [35]. Furthermore, AI algorithms can create interactive educational simulations, virtual laboratories, and multimedia presentations that enhance learning experiences and facilitate hands-on learning. AI-driven adaptive learning platforms personalize educational content based on each student's learning style, preferences, and performance metrics, providing customized exercises, explanations, and assessments. Additionally, AI algorithms can assist educators in creating assessment materials, such as quizzes and exams, by generating questions, answer keys, and grading rubrics [36]. The AI algorithms for generating educational content hold immense potential to democratize access to quality education, improve learning outcomes, and support lifelong learning initiatives. However, it's crucial to ensure that AI-generated content aligns with educational standards, promotes critical thinking skills, and addresses ethical considerations related to bias and diversity.

Curating Diverse Learning Materials with AI

AI-based content curation across diverse learning materials will ensure that machine learning algorithms comb through loads of educational content to ultimately give recommendations based on the unique needs and interests of learners. AI-driven content curation platforms make use of advanced algorithms for the analysis of user behavior, preferences, and learning goals in a bid to deliver personalized recommendations drawn from diverse sources such as articles, videos, podcasts, courses, and interactive tutorials. These platforms understand user preferences through techniques such as collaborative filtering, content-based filtering, and hybrid approaches to give relevant suggestions [37]. Taking into account a range of factors from subject matter and difficulty level to format and language, AI algorithms offer a possibility of rich and varied learning materials that are attuned exactly to the particularities of learners' individual learning styles and abilities. In addition, AI-driven content curation strengthens diversity and inclusion by surfacing a great deal of content from many sources and points of view, thereby exposing learners to different perspectives, cultures, and experiences [38]. This not only enriches the learning experience but also fosters empathy, critical thinking, and global awareness. Another thing to be mentioned is that the recommendation algorithms are continuously adaptive and refined according to user feedback and performance data, ensuring that learners receive the most relevant and engaging content over time. AI-powered content curation plays a vital role in democratizing access to education, empowering learners to explore diverse topics, develop new skills, and pursue their learning journey effectively [39]. Moreover, it's essential to address ethical considerations such as algorithmic bias, privacy, and transparency to ensure that AI-driven content curation remains fair, equitable, and accountable.

Recommender Systems for Personalized Content Delivery

AI-driven recommender systems in personalized content delivery create personalized recommendations for users by understanding their preferences, interests, and behaviors. The design of such a system would involve analyzing extensive reams of data emanating from user interactions, content attributes, and contextual information to come up with relevant, personalized recommendations spanning a gamut of applications, entertainment, e-commerce, education, and more. In personalized learning, recommender systems assist learners in finding relevant learning resources, such as articles, videos, courses, and tutorials, taking into account the setting of learning goals, past interactions, and performance metrics [40]. These techniques implement collaborative filtering, content-based filtering, and hybrid approaches to extract the user's preferences and provide accurate recommendations. By considering factors such as subject matter, difficulty level, format, and language, recommender systems ensure that learners receive content that aligns with their individual learning styles and needs [41]. Furthermore, recommender systems adapt and evolve over time, continuously refining their recommendations based on user feedback and behavior data. This iterative process enhances the relevance and effectiveness of personalized content delivery, ultimately improving user satisfaction and engagement. In general, recommender systems play a major role in improving a learner's learning experience by providing him/her with personalized content recommendations to enable exposing himself/herself to new topics, picking up new skills, and thus attaining their objectives of learning more effectively [42]. However, it is essential to address ethical considerations, such as algorithmic bias, transparency, and privacy, to ensure that recommender systems operate in a fair, transparent, and responsible manner.

ETHICAL CONSIDERATIONS AND CHALLENGES

Ethical considerations and challenges surrounding AI are paramount in ensuring the responsible development and deployment of these technologies. Issues such as algorithmic bias, privacy concerns, and transparency gaps highlight the need for robust ethical frameworks. Algorithmic bias, stemming from this, can further lead to biased data or flawed algorithms, leading to discrimination at very critical levels, including hiring and law enforcement. It also raises several privacy concerns since AI systems collect and analyze vast amounts of personal data, hence demanding strict measures in ensuring data protection [43]. Transparency and explainability are crucial for understanding how AI systems arrive at decisions, fostering trust and accountability. Furthermore, concerns about job displacement, autonomy, security risks, and environmental impact underscore the multifaceted ethical landscape of AI. Addressing these challenges requires collaborative efforts across disciplines to develop and implement ethical guidelines, regulations, and accountability mechanisms that uphold fundamental ethical principles while harnessing the transformative potential of AI for societal benefit.

Transparency in AI Algorithms

Transparency in AI algorithms (Fig. **4**) explains why trust must be responsible and transparent and why artificial intelligence must be used ethically. What transparency means is the ability to be understood and explain how AI algorithms work, the data used, and the decisions reached. Achieving transparency in AI algorithms involves several key considerations [44].

Explainability: AI algorithms must be designed in a way that explains their decisions or recommendations, making them transparent and comprehensible to the user. Explainability enables users to comprehend the rationale behind AI outputs, increasing trust and facilitating human oversight.

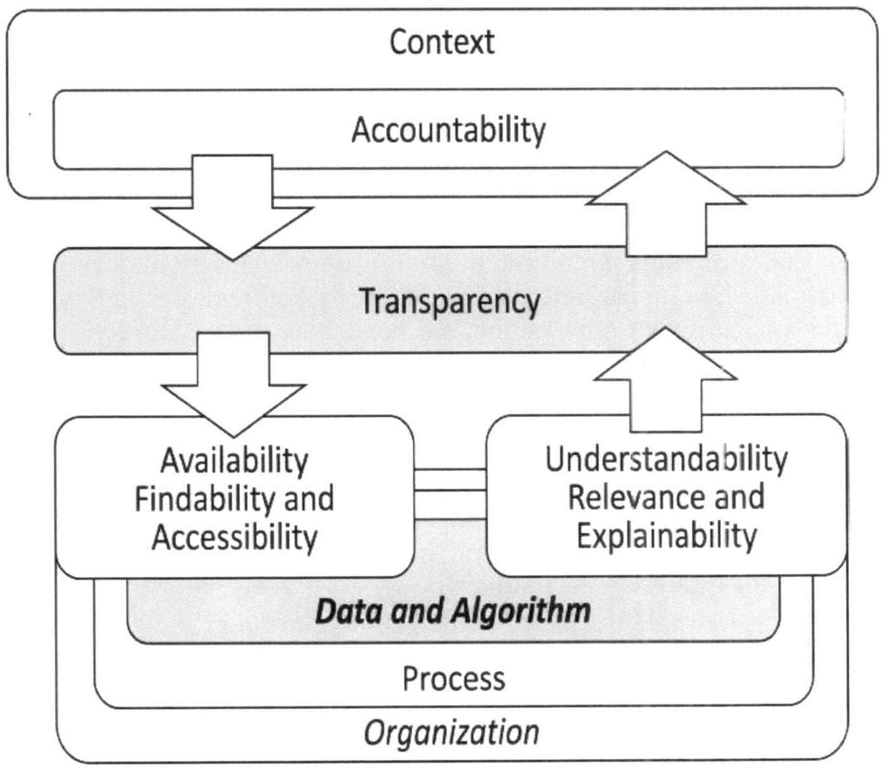

Fig. (4). Flowchart of transparency in AI algorithm.

Model Documentation: Documenting the design, development, and deployment process of AI models is essential for transparency. This includes describing the dataset used for training, the model architecture, hyperparameters, and any preprocessing techniques applied.

Bias Detection and Mitigation: Transparent AI algorithms should identify and mitigate biases present in the data or model. Techniques such as bias detection, fairness assessments, and algorithmic audits help identify and address biases that may lead to discriminatory outcomes.

Openness and Accessibility: Making AI algorithms and datasets publicly accessible promotes transparency and accountability. Open-source AI frameworks, model repositories, and data sharing initiatives enable scrutiny, peer review, and collaboration, fostering transparency and knowledge sharing in the AI community.

User Control and Feedback: Providing users with control over AI algorithms and feedback mechanisms enhances transparency and accountability. Transparency features such as user dashboards, explanations for AI recommendations, and opportunities for feedback empower users to understand and influence AI-driven decisions.

Regulatory Compliance: Adhering to regulatory frameworks and standards, such as GDPR in Europe or the AI Ethics Guidelines by organizations like the IEEE and ACM, promotes transparency and ethical use of AI. Regulatory compliance ensures that AI developers and users adhere to ethical principles and legal requirements concerning transparency, fairness, and accountability.

Education and Awareness: Educating stakeholders about AI algorithms, their capabilities, limitations, and ethical implications is essential for promoting transparency. Increasing awareness about AI technologies empowers users to make informed decisions, ask critical questions, and advocate for transparent and accountable AI systems.

Addressing Equity and Access Concerns

Equity and access issues in relation to AI may be resolved by ensuring that AI technologies are developed, fielded, and used in ways that are forward-looking in terms of fairness, inclusivity, and accessibility to all users of the AI, irrespective of background, identity, or socioeconomic status [45].

Diverse Representation in Data: Ensuring diverse representation in training data used for AI algorithms helps reduce biases and ensures equitable performance of AI systems across diverse demographic groups. Data collection efforts should prioritize inclusivity and diversity to avoid perpetuating existing disparities.

Bias Detection and Mitigation: The mechanisms for the detection and mitigation of biases within AI algorithms need to be created and implemented to support equity. Methods like fairness-aware machine learning and bias mitigation strategies assist in addressing biases that could result in discriminatory outcomes within AI systems.

Accessibility Design: Designing AI technologies with accessibility in mind ensures that individuals with disabilities can access and use these technologies effectively. This includes features such as screen readers, alternative input methods, and compatibility with assistive technologies.

Digital Literacy and Education: Promoting digital literacy and providing education and training on AI technologies ensure that individuals have the knowledge and skills to navigate and benefit from these technologies. Through the provisions of such easily accessible learning materials and programs, the digital divide is bridged, and less advantaged communities are empowered.

Community Engagement and Co-creation: Engaging with the community, in particular, the marginalized and underserved populations, in the design and development of AI technologies, fosters inclusivity and ensures that solutions meet their specific needs and priorities. Co-creation approaches empower communities to participate in decision-making processes and advocate for equitable outcomes.

Policy and Regulation: Enacting policies and regulations that promote equity, fairness, and accessibility in AI is essential for creating a supportive regulatory environment. This includes guidelines for algorithmic transparency, accountability mechanisms, and safeguards against discriminatory practices.

Ethical Considerations and Impact Assessments: Conducting ethical impact assessments and considering the potential social, economic, and ethical implications of AI technologies helps identify and address equity concerns proactively. Ethical guidelines and frameworks provide guidance for developers and policymakers to ensure that AI systems prioritize equity and social justice.

Collaborative Partnerships: Collaborating with stakeholders from government, academia, civil society, and industry fosters collective action to address equity and access concerns in AI. Partnerships among such multi-stakeholders could facilitate sharing knowledge, mobilizing resources, and acting in concert toward a vision of AI ecosystems that are inclusive and equitable.

Securing Data Privacy and Security in AI Deployment

It is paramount to safeguard individuals' rights, protect sensitive information, and maintain trust in AI technologies (Fig. 5). Ensuring data privacy and security in AI implementation within education is paramount to fostering trust and safeguarding sensitive information. Firstly, strict adherence to data protection regulations, such as GDPR or CCPA, should be a foundational principle. This involves obtaining explicit consent for data collection, processing, and storage from students, parents, or guardians [46]. Besides, encrypting the data during its transmission and storage would further decrease the chance of potential risks resulting from unauthorized access. Additionally, multi-factor authentication provides a very strong means of authentication, assuring that only authenticated entities will get access to sensitive information. Regular audits and assessments of AI systems may also help in recognizing and rectifying a vulnerability or breach at the very outset.

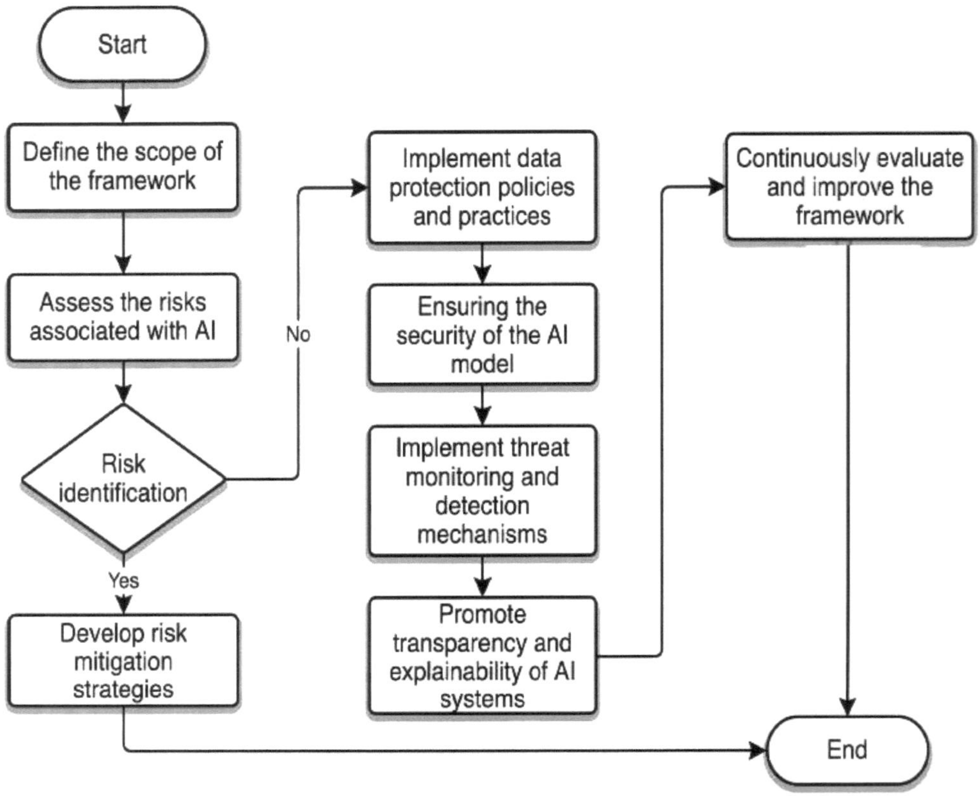

Fig. (5). Flowchart model for data privacy and security in AI.

Data minimization: It is based on the principle that only such data is collected and stored as is absolutely necessary to be processed by AI algorithms for their intended purposes. This means that the risk of unauthorized access, and hence the risks of misuse, are decreased.

Data Encryption: This is the process whereby data, whether in transmission or not, is encrypted against unauthorized interception or access. Strong algorithms of encryption and secure protocols of communication guarantee the confidentiality and security of data throughout its lifecycle.

Access Controls and Authentication: Implementing access controls and authentication mechanisms restricts access to AI systems and data to authorized users only. Role-based access controls, multi-factor authentication, and robust identity management systems help prevent unauthorized access and data breaches.

Anonymization and Pseudonymization: This anonymizes or pseudonymizes Personally Identifiable Information (PII), thereby protecting individuals' privacy through replacing identifying information with non-identifiable data. There is no identifying information for any individual in the data used in AI algorithms; at the same time, analysis and insights are possible.

Privacy by Design and Default: Put the principles of privacy by design and privacy by default into AI systems; thus, at the moment of designing and developing, all requirements concerning privacy will already be taken into account. Proactive measures, such as anonymization, access controls, and transparency mechanisms, in this sense, secure privacy by default.

Data Governance and Compliance: One of the most important parts of implementing AI is setting up robust data governance frameworks, together with compliance functions that help follow relevant privacy regulations in different geographies. Compliance includes impact assessments on privacy, a data protection policy, and a data protection officer.

Secure Development Practices: Security vulnerabilities within AI systems could be noticed and reduced if secure development practices are followed, including security audits, code reviews, and vulnerability assessments. Secure coding practices, coupled with industrial standards and best practices, ensure that AI algorithms are resistant to attacks and breaches.

Monitoring and Incident Response: The organization needs permanent monitoring and incident response procedures in place to quickly identify data privacy and security incidents and respond to them. This would include monitoring of all activities that users make within the system, auditing of system logs, and mechanisms of automated alerting to identify possible suspicious behavior or security threats.

COLLABORATIVE APPROACHES TO AI IN EDUCATION

Collaborative approaches to AI in education involve partnerships between educational institutions, government agencies, industry stakeholders, nonprofit organizations, and research institutions to leverage the transformative potential of AI technologies in teaching and learning. By pooling together expertise, resources, and perspectives from diverse stakeholders, collaborative initiatives aim to develop innovative AI-driven educational solutions that address pressing challenges and meet the needs of learners [47]. These partnerships foster knowledge sharing, resource mobilization, and the co-creation of educational tools and platforms that promote lifelong learning, enhance teaching effectiveness, and improve educational outcomes. In collaborative research, public-private partnerships, industry-academia collaborations, and cross-sectoral initiatives, stakeholders can combine their efforts with the power of AI to create truly inclusive, effective, and equitable learning experiences.

Partnerships Between Educators and Technologists

Partnerships between educators and technologists represent a pivotal collaborative approach in leveraging AI for educational innovation. These partnerships unite the expertise of educators in pedagogy and curriculum design with the technical skills of technologists in AI development and implementation [48]. In this way, educators and technologists can collaborate in exploiting AI's potential to solve educational problems by enhancing teaching practices to improve learning outcomes. Educators provide valuable insights into the needs of learners, the dynamics of the classroom, and the goals of education, while technologists offer technical expertise in AI algorithms, data analysis, and software development. They co-design and co-develop AI-based teaching tools, platforms, and applications that not only respect pedagogical principles but also students' multiple learning styles and students' motivations to engage. Heutagogical partnerships enable AI technologies to be integrated into educational settings, empowering educators to customize learning experiences, enhance instructional strategies, and promote student achievement. In addition, cooperation between educators and technologists would institutionalize a culture of innovation, experimentation, and continuous improvement in education and thus drive further evolution of pedagogies and practices for teaching and learning in the digital age [49]. By fostering collaborative partnerships between educators and technologists, it is in this regard that stakeholders can best leverage AI to alter education for good by empowering learners to thrive in the 21st century.

Policy Frameworks for Responsible AI Use in Education

Policy frames around the ethical, fair, and effective deployment of AI in education are necessary so that responsible use is aligned (Fig. (**6**). These frameworks guide and set principles on how to govern the development, deployment, and evaluation of AI-driven educational tools and practices [50].

Ethical Guidelines: Setting ethical guidelines guarantees that AI technologies in education uphold principles of fairness, transparency, accountability, and privacy. These guidelines cover ethical concerns like algorithmic bias, data privacy, informed consent, and the ethical application of AI in decision-making.

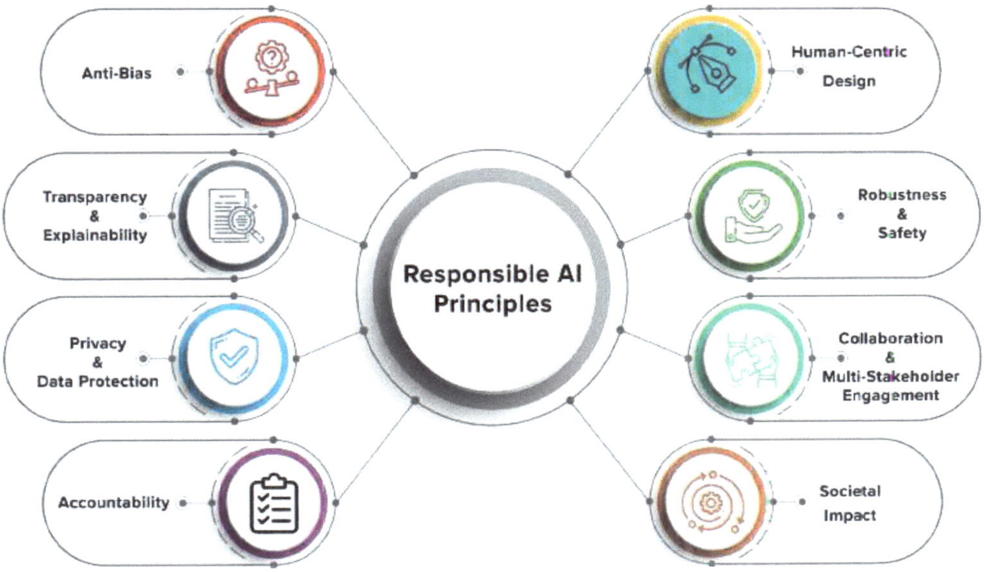

Fig. (6). Responsible AI Principles in Education.

Equity and Inclusion: Policy frameworks prioritize equity and inclusion in AI use by addressing disparities in access to technology, digital literacy, and educational opportunities. Policies promote strategies to mitigate bias, promote diversity, and ensure that AI technologies benefit all learners, including those from underserved and marginalized communities.

Data Privacy and Security: Policies governing data privacy and security in AI use protect students' personal information and sensitive data from unauthorized access, misuse, and breaches. These policies mandate robust data protection measures, encryption protocols, and compliance with relevant privacy regulations, such as GDPR (General Data Protection Regulation) or FERPA (The Family Educational Rights and Privacy Act).

Transparency and Explainability: Policy frameworks emphasize transparency and explainability in AI algorithms and decision-making processes. In that case, educators, students, and relevant stakeholders must know how AI systems work, the data used, and what affects their outputs to guarantee accountability and a relationship built on trust.

Accountability and Governance: Establishing mechanisms for accountability and governance ensures that AI technologies in education are subject to oversight, evaluation, and continuous improvement. Policies define roles and responsibilities, establish reporting mechanisms, and mandate regular audits to monitor compliance with ethical and legal standards.

Education and Training: Policy frameworks promote education and training on responsible AI use for educators, administrators, policymakers, and other stakeholders. Training programs raise awareness about ethical considerations, best practices, and the potential impact of AI on teaching and learning, empowering stakeholders to make informed decisions.

Research and Evaluation: These policies promote research and evaluation initiatives geared toward testing the effectiveness, impact, and ethics of AI technologies in education. The findings from the research inform policy development, help establish trends for emerging issues, and act as guides in the making of evidence-based decisions on integrating AI into educational practice.

International Collaboration: Policy frameworks foster international collaboration and cooperation on responsible AI use in education. Multilateral agreements, standards, and guidelines enable knowledge sharing, capacity building, and harmonization of regulatory approaches across countries and regions.

Engaging Stakeholders for Interdisciplinary Collaboration

Engaging stakeholders for interdisciplinary collaboration is essential for harnessing the full potential of AI in education and addressing complex challenges at the intersection of technology, pedagogy, and policy [51]. Interdisciplinary collaboration involves bringing together diverse stakeholders, including educators, researchers, policymakers, technologists, industry representatives, students, parents, and community members, to collaborate, co-create, and innovate in education.

Identifying Common Goals and Priorities: Establishing common goals and priorities ensures alignment and fosters a shared understanding of the objectives of interdisciplinary collaboration. Stakeholders should articulate their needs, interests, and expectations to identify areas of mutual interest and collaboration.

Creating Collaborative Spaces and Platforms: Creating physical and virtual spaces for collaboration facilitates communication, networking, and knowledge sharing among stakeholders. Collaborative platforms, such as online forums, communities of practice, and professional networks, provide opportunities for stakeholders to connect, exchange ideas, and collaborate on projects.

Promoting Inclusive Participation: Promoting inclusive participation ensures that diverse voices and perspectives are represented in interdisciplinary collaboration efforts. Stakeholders from different backgrounds, disciplines, and expertise areas should have opportunities to contribute, share insights, and co-design solutions.

Facilitating Dialogue and Exchange: Facilitating dialogue and exchange fosters interdisciplinary understanding and collaboration. Workshops, seminars, conferences, and roundtable discussions provide forums for stakeholders to engage in meaningful dialogue, exchange knowledge, and explore interdisciplinary approaches to addressing educational challenges.

Building Capacity and Expertise: The capacity and expertise in interdisciplinarity are endowed by the education of stakeholders in the skills and competencies needed to collaborate across disciplines. Training programs, capacity-building initiatives, and interdisciplinary courses help stakeholders develop collaborative skills, critical thinking abilities, and interdisciplinary perspectives.

Establishing Multi-Stakeholder Partnerships: Establishing multi-stakeholder partnerships enables stakeholders to pool together resources, expertise, and networks to tackle complex challenges collaboratively. Public-private partnerships, academia-industry collaborations, and cross-sectoral initiatives leverage the strengths of different stakeholders to drive innovation and impact in education.

Promoting Trust and Mutual Respect: Promoting trust and mutual respect among stakeholders is essential for fostering effective interdisciplinary collaboration. Building relationships based on trust, transparency, and open communication creates a supportive environment for collaboration and innovation.

Evaluating and Reflecting on Collaborative Efforts: Evaluating and reflecting on collaborative efforts enables stakeholders to assess the impact, effectiveness, and sustainability of interdisciplinary collaboration initiatives. These include feedback mechanisms, evaluation frameworks, and reflective practices that stakeholders may use to learn from their experiences and accordingly adapt their approaches to collaboration.

CONCLUSION

In summary, exploring AI in education has highlighted its transformative potential to reshape teaching and learning methods. While AI provides personalized learning experiences, data-driven insights, and collaborative opportunities, it is essential to address ethical concerns such as bias and privacy to ensure fairness and accountability. Achieving equity and access requires collaborative approaches and policy frameworks that promote inclusivity and address disparities. Educator professional development is essential for effective integration, while interdisciplinary collaboration fosters innovation and holistic solutions. Therefore, there is a clear call for collaboration to fully leverage AI's potential in education. This collaboration is not just a suggestion but a necessity for realizing transformative and inclusive educational practices. Through collaboration across disciplines and sectors, stakeholders can also co-create innovative solutions, identify ethical considerations, promote equity, and above all, empower learners to thrive in the digital age and beyond.

Summary of the Key Insights

The exploration of artificial intelligence in education has unearthed critical insights that underscore its transformative potential in reshaping teaching and learning paradigms. AI offers personalized learning experiences, data-driven decision-making, and opportunities for collaboration, but ethical considerations, including bias and privacy, must be addressed to ensure fairness and accountability. Equity and access are paramount, necessitating collaborative approaches and policy frameworks that promote inclusivity and address disparities. Educator professional development is essential for effective integration, while interdisciplinary collaboration fosters innovation and holistic solutions. In essence, responsible and collaborative implementation of AI in education has the power to revolutionize learning experiences and prepare students for success in the digital era.

Call for Collaboration to Fully Leverage AI's Potential in Education

The potential in education is not just a suggestion but a necessity in our quest for transformative and inclusive educational practices. The integration of AI into education holds immense promise, from personalized learning experiences to data-driven decision-making, but its realization requires concerted efforts from various stakeholders. Educators, policymakers, technologists, researchers, and industry leaders must collaborate across disciplines, institutions, and sectors to harness AI's potential effectively. By fostering collaborative partnerships, it can develop innovative solutions, share good practices, and build capacities in navigating the complexities that come with the implementation of AI in education. Moreover, collaboration enables us to address ethical considerations, such as bias and privacy, while promoting equity and inclusivity in educational practices. By working together, we can make sure to overcome challenges, capitalize on opportunities, and build a future in which AI will strengthen teaching and learning experiences for all kinds of learners, whatever the background or circumstances. Thus, let us respond to the call for collaboration and unite in realizing the complete potential of AI in education, empowering learners to succeed in the digital era and beyond.

REFERENCES

[1] P. Mertala, J. Fagerlund, and O. Calderon, "Finnish 5th and 6th grade students' pre-instructional conceptions of artificial intelligence (AI) and their implications for AI literacy education", *Computers and Education: Artificial Intelligence,* vol. 3, p. 100095, 2022. [http://dx.doi.org/10.1016/j.caeai.2022.100095]

[2] V. Srinivasan, "AI & learning: A preferred future", *Computers and Education: Artificial Intelligence,* vol. 3, p. 100062, 2022. [http://dx.doi.org/10.1016/j.caeai.2022.100062]

[3] J. Su, D.T.K. Ng, and S.K.W. Chu, "Artificial Intelligence (AI) Literacy in Early Childhood Education: The Challenges and Opportunities", *Computers and Education: Artificial Intelligence,* vol. 4, p. 100124, 2023. [http://dx.doi.org/10.1016/j.caeai.2023.100124]

[4] B. Toksha, T. Kulkarni, and P. Gupta, "Impact of AI on Teaching Pedagogy and its Integration for Enhancing Teaching-Learning", *Artificial Intelligence in Higher Education,* pp. 137-152, 2022. [http://dx.doi.org/10.1201/9781003184157-7]

[5] K.E. Matthews, *The Experience of Partnerships in Learning and Teaching. Power of Partnership: Students.* Staff, and Faculty Revolutionizing Higher Education, 2020. [http://dx.doi.org/10.36284/celelon.oa2.7]

[6] M.A. Iroaganachi, "Towards Best Practices in Web-Based Learning and Teaching", *Adv. Educ. Technol. Instr. Des.,* pp. 317-332, 2016. [http://dx.doi.org/10.4018/978-1-4666-9932-8.ch017]

[7] Thimmanna, A.V.N.S.Sharma, Mahesh Sudhakar Naik, S. Radhakrishnan, Aarti Sharma (2023). Personalized Learning Paths: Adapting Education with AI-Driven Curriculum. European Economic Letters. [http://dx.doi.org/10.52783/eel.v14i1.993]

[8] A. Garrido, and E. Onaindia, "Assembling Learning Objects for Personalized Learning: An AI Planning Perspective", *IEEE Intell. Syst.,* vol. 28, no. 2, pp. 64-73, 2013. [http://dx.doi.org/10.1109/MIS.2011.36]

[9] Kinshuk Designing Adaptive and Personalized Learning Environments. Routledge, 2016 [http://dx.doi.org/10.4324/9781315795492]

[10] E. Sangineto, *An Adaptive e-learning Platform for Personalized Course Generation.* Architecture Solutions for E-Learning Systems, 2008. [http://dx.doi.org/10.4018/978-1-59904-633-4.ch014]

[11] Kravčík, M. (2019). 11. Adaptive workplace learning assistance. Personalized Human-Computer Interaction, 283-302. [http://dx.doi.org/10.1515/9783110552485-011]

[12] A. Manoharan, *Diner Rathinasamy Manoharan.* Machine Learning Algorithms for Personalized Learning Paths. International Research Journal of Modernization in Engineering Technology and Science, 2024. [http://dx.doi.org/10.56726/IRJMETS49965]

[13] S. Trapp, L. Thomas, and S. Möbs, "Tailoring Technology-Enhanced Learning Arrangements to

Individual Needs", *International Journal of Advanced Corporate Learning (iJAC),* vol. 2, no. 2, p. 40, 2009.
[http://dx.doi.org/10.3991/ijac.v2i2.833]

[14] M. Kok, E. Kal, C. van Doodewaard, G. Savelsbergh, and J. van der Kamp, "Tailoring explicit and implicit instruction methods to the verbal working memory capacity of students with special needs can benefit motor learning outcomes in physical education", *Learn. Individ. Differ.,* vol. 89, p. 102019, 2021.
[http://dx.doi.org/10.1016/j.lindif.2021.102019]

[15] M. V. Levin, and S. E. Sosenushkin, "E-Learning Resources Requirements Standardization According to Learners' Individual Needs and Preferences", *Open Education,* vol. 1, no. 108, pp. 33-36, 2015.

[16] H. Hills, "Individual Preferences in E-Learning", In: *From Theory to Practice*, 2017, pp. 153-172.
[http://dx.doi.org/10.4324/9781315588391-7]

[17] D. N. Dwivedi, G. Mahanty, and V. N. Dwivedi, "The Role of Predictive Analytics in Personalizing Education", In: *Advances in Educational Technologies and Instructional Design* IGI Global: Hershey (PA), 2024, pp. 44-59.
[http://dx.doi.org/10.4018/979-8-3693-2169-0.ch003]

[18] J. J. Stiegler-Balfour, "Optimizing Teaching Practices and Learning Outcomes Through Pedagogical Research: An ECP Perspective", *PsycEXTRA Dataset,* American Psychological Association, 2014.
[http://dx.doi.org/10.1037/e535272014-001]

[19] L.A. Almusfar, "Optimizing the E-learning experience: The importance of personalization and essential design elements", *E-Learn. Digit. Media,* p. 20427530241239425, 2024.
[http://dx.doi.org/10.1177/20427530241239425]

[20] P. Singh, M. Srivastava, M. Kansal, A.P. Singh, A. Chauhan, and A. Gaur, "A comparative analysis of modern frontend frameworks for building large-scale web applications", *2023 International Conference on Disruptive Technologies (ICDT),* IEEE., pp. 531-535, 2023.
[http://dx.doi.org/10.1109/ICDT57929.2023.10150911]

[21] Q. Gu, and T. Sumner, "Support Personalization in Distributed E-Learning Systems through Learner Modeling", In: *2006 2nd International Conference on Information & Communication Technologies* vol. 1. IEEE, 2006, pp. 610-615.
[http://dx.doi.org/10.1109/ICTTA.2006.1684441]

[22] C. S. Edge, and W. Smith, "Automating Administrative Tasks", In: *Enterprise Mac Administrator's Guide* Apress: Berkeley (CA), 2015, pp. 345-408.
[http://dx.doi.org/10.1007/978-1-4842-1706-1_8]

[23] J. J. Merelo, "Automating System Tasks", In: *Raku Recipes* Apress: Berkeley (CA), 2020, pp. 95-108.
[http://dx.doi.org/10.1007/978-1-4842-6258-0_6]

[24] I. Tzoneva, "Benefits and Challenges in Using AI-Powered Educational Tools", *Education and New Developments,* vol. 1, pp. 297-301, 2023.
[http://dx.doi.org/10.36315/2023v2end079]

[25] P. Singh, A. Asthana, B. Solanki, S. Tomar, M. Kansal, and G. Tyagi, "A comprehensive analysis and sensitivity model for emotion detection in text", In: *Applications of Artificial Intelligence in 5G and Internet of Things.* CRC Press, 2025, pp. 332-337.
[http://dx.doi.org/10.1201/9781003532521-63]

[26] B.E. Walvoord, "The Role of Faculty Grading Processes in Program and General-Education Assessment", *Assess. Eval. High. Educ.,* pp. 573-585, 2017.
[http://dx.doi.org/10.4324/9781315709307-45]

[27] J. Zoul, "Equity in Grading and Assessment", In: *10 Perspectives on Equity in Education* Routledge, 2021, pp. 80-96.
[http://dx.doi.org/10.4324/9781003093145-7]

[28] M. Aram, F. Mödritscher, G. Neumann, and M. Andergassen, "A Grading Data Warehouse Approach to Measuring and Analyzing Learning Performance", *Adv. High. Educ. Prof. Dev.*, pp. 102-126, 2018. [http://dx.doi.org/10.4018/978-1-5225-5936-8.ch005]

[29] A. Shaheen, F. Azam, and K. Irshad, "Anonymous Feedback: A Real-time Feedback to Capture Students' Engagement in Learning Process", *Proceedings of the International Conference on Medical Education (ICME 2021),* 2021. [http://dx.doi.org/10.2991/assehr.k.210930.011]

[30] Singh, P., & Kansal, M. (2025). An Online Platform for Timely Access to Medical Care with the Help of Real-Time Data Analysis. Wellness Management Powered by AI Technologies, 103-131.

[31] I. Kayabas, "Innovative Curriculum Development and Content Creation With Generative AI", *Adv. Educ. Technol. Instr. Des.,* pp. 462-473, 2024. [http://dx.doi.org/10.4018/979-8-3693-1351-0.ch022]

[32] S. Gökoğlu, "Challenges and Limitations of Generative AI in Education", *Adv. Educ. Technol. Instr. Des.,* pp. 158-181, 2024. [http://dx.doi.org/10.4018/979-8-3693-1351-0.ch008]

[33] T. Huber, C. Niklaus, and S. Handschuh, "Enhancing Educational Dialogues: A Reinforcement Learning Approach for Generating AI Teacher Responses", *Proceedings of the 18th Workshop on Innovative Use of NLP for Building Educational Applications (BEA 2023),* 2023. [http://dx.doi.org/10.18653/v1/2023.bea-1.59]

[34] U. Tank, S. Arirangan, A.R. Paduri, and N. Darapaneni, "A Study Towards Building Content Aware Models in NLP using Genetic Algorithms", *EAI Endorsed Transactions on AI and Robotics,* vol. 2, 2023. [http://dx.doi.org/10.4108/airo.4078]

[35] A.K. Sharma, N. Chanderwal, A. Prajapati, P. Singh, M. Kansal, Ed., *Advancing Software Engineering Through AI, Federated Learning, and Large Language Models.* IGI Global, 2024. [http://dx.doi.org/10.4018/979-8-3693-3502-4]

[36] I. Poola, "Why Business Intelligence Needs Artificial Intelligence (AI) and Advanced Natural Language Generation (NLG)", *Journal of Environmental Science, Computer Science and Engineering & Technology,* vol. 6, no. 4, 2017. [http://dx.doi.org/10.24214/jecet.b.6.4.266274]

[37] Y. Liu, "Using AI Technology to Create an Inclusive Environment for Diverse Online Learners", In: *Designing Equitable and Accessible Online Learning Environments* IGI Global: Hershey (PA), 2024, pp. 105-131. [http://dx.doi.org/10.4018/979-8-3693-0268-2.ch006]

[38] P. K. Misra, "Curating Contents for Multidisciplinary Learning", In: *Teaching Competencies for 21st Century Teachers* Routledge, 2023, pp. 55-66. [http://dx.doi.org/10.4324/9781003344452-6]

[39] T. W. Neller, "AI education", *AI Matters,* vol. 3, no. 3, pp. 20-21, 2017. [http://dx.doi.org/10.1145/3137574.3137580]

[40] J. McAuley, "Content and Structure in Recommender Systems", In: *Personalized Machine Learning* Cambridge University Press: Cambridge, 2022, pp. 144-176. [http://dx.doi.org/10.1017/9781009003971.006]

[41] K. M. Pandey, M. Singh, Y. N. Prajapati, S. K. Sonkar, P. Singh, and M. Kumar, "Charitable trust management system to establish connections between charitable trust and the donors/adoptee", *J. Pharm. Negat. Results,* vol. 14, no. 2, 2023.

[42] C. C. Aggarwal, "Content-Based Recommender Systems", In: *Recommender Systems* Springer: Cham, 2016, pp. 139-166. [http://dx.doi.org/10.1007/978-3-319-29659-3_4]

[43] S. Addoura, and F. Al Husseiny, "The rising trend of Metaverse in education: challenges, opportunities, and ethical considerations", *PeerJ Computer Science,* vol. 9, p. e1252, 2023. [http://dx.doi.org/10.7717/peerj-cs.1252]

[44] D. Talia, *Transparency and Accountability of AI Algorithms.* From Algorithms to Thinking Machines, 2023.
[http://dx.doi.org/10.1145/3603178.3603189]

[45] A. Harvey, and J. Stokes, "Education", *Education,* 2019.
[http://dx.doi.org/10.1093/obo/9780199756810-0217]

[46] E. Bertino, M. Kantarcioglu, C.G. Akcora, S. Samtani, S. Mittal, and M. Gupta, "AI for Security and Security for AI", *Proceedings of the Eleventh ACM Conference on Data and Application Security and Privacy,* 2021.
[http://dx.doi.org/10.1145/3422337.3450357]

[47] A. Coroiu, A. Călin, and H-B. Mureşan, "Collaborative Transdisciplinary Educational Approaches in AI", *Proceedings of the 14th International Conference on Computer Supported Education,* 2022. [http://dx.doi.org/10.5220/0011039500003182]

[48] A. Cook-Sather, "Living and learning partnerships in teacher education", In: *Exploring Professional Development Opportunities for Teacher Educators* Routledge, 2021, pp. 1-19.
[http://dx.doi.org/10.4324/9781003160052-1]

[49] C. Day, and L. Smethem, "Partnerships Between Schools and Higher Education", In: *International Encyclopedia of Education* Elsevier, 2010, pp. 757-763.
[http://dx.doi.org/10.1016/B978-0-08-044894-7.00688-6]

[50] M. Ghallab, "Responsible AI: requirements and challenges", *AI Perspectives,* vol. 1, no. 1, p. 3, 2019.
[http://dx.doi.org/10.1186/s42467-019-0003-z]

[51] L. M. Bennett, and H. Gadlin, "Supporting Interdisciplinary Collaboration: The Role of the Institution", In: *Enhancing Communication & Collaboration in Interdisciplinary Research* SAGE Publications: Thousand Oaks (CA), 2014, pp. 356-384.
[http://dx.doi.org/10.4135/9781483352947.n17]

CHAPTER 7

Automated Transcription System for Medical Prescriptions: Merging Technology and Healthcare

Asmita Yadav[1,*], **Mufti Mohammad Usman**[1], **Anurag Sati**[1] and **Sidham Jain**[1]

[1] *Department of CSE & IT, Jaypee Institute of Information Technology (JIIT), Noida, India*

Abstract: The project of machine-generated transcription based on prescriptions centers on the development of an automated transcription system tailored for medical prescriptions using machine learning techniques. By merging technology and healthcare, this initiative aims to streamline and enhance the often laborious and error-prone process of transcribing prescription data into comprehensible and accurate notes. The project's core is encapsulated using libraries such as NumPy, pandas, and Keras. The script carefully preprocesses the prescription data, segregating it into training, testing, and validation sets. The subsequent construction and training of a sequence-t--sequence model, empowered by neural network architectures - Gated Recurrent Unit GRU, enable the system to interpret the complexities of prescription contexts and generate precise transcriptions. Upon model creation and training, the script utilizes an inference mechanism to generate transcriptions from raw prescription texts. The significance of this system lies not only in its automation but also in its potential to significantly reduce transcription errors prevalent in manual processes. It showcases the model's proficiency by displaying machine-generated transcriptions alongside their originals, offering a comprehensive view of its accuracy and efficiency. This project overall serves as an intersection between advanced technology and the healthcare domain, presenting a solution poised to revolutionize medical documentation workflows. The report surrounding this endeavor dives into extensive technical intricacies, including data preprocessing methodologies, model architectures, and the thorough evaluation of the system's performance. Its ultimate goal is to illustrate how this innovation could enhance efficiency and accuracy in the crucial task of medical prescription transcription, potentially reshaping the landscape of healthcare documentation practices.

Keywords: Automated transcription, Data preprocessing, Technology, Healthcare, Medical prescriptions, Machine learning, Neural network architectures, Sequence-to-sequence model, Transcription errors.

* **Corresponding author Asmita Yadav:** Department of CSE & IT, Jaypee Institute of Information Technology (JIIT), Noida, India; E-mail: asmita.yadav85@gmail.com

Pancham Singh, Avinash Kumar Sharma, Mrignainy Kansal, & Amarjeet Prajapati (Eds.)

INTRODUCTION

This topic combines advanced technology and healthcare, aiming to automate and enhance the transcription process in the medical field [1, 2]. This innovative project focuses on leveraging machine learning techniques to accurately and efficiently transcribe prescription text. By employing neural networks and sequence-to-sequence models, the system translates medical prescriptions into readable and comprehensive transcriptions.

The primary objective of this project is to develop a sophisticated model capable of understanding and processing prescription data, then generating detailed transcriptions that accurately reflect the intended medical information [3 - 5]. This automated transcription system not only aims to streamline documentation tasks but also seeks to improve accuracy, reducing the potential for errors commonly associated with manual transcription processes [6]. The main script encapsulates the implementation of this project, leveraging libraries such as numpy, pandas, and Keras to preprocess data, build models, and perform inference. It incorporates sequential neural network architectures, Gated Recurrent Unit (GRU) for both encoder and decoder components, essential for understanding prescription context and generating transcriptions, respectively [7]. The script loads preprocessed data, trains a sequence-to-sequence model, and implements an inference mechanism to generate transcriptions from prescription texts. Moreover, it includes functions for model evaluation, such as displaying machine-generated transcriptions and comparing them with original transcriptions, enhancing the system's transparency and usability [8]. This project addresses the critical intersection of healthcare and machine learning, aiming to revolutionize medical transcription by harnessing the power of machine learning models. The report will delve into the technical details, model architecture, data preprocessing steps, and the performance evaluation of this innovative system, showcasing its potential impact on improving efficiency and accuracy in medical documentation workflows [9].

The paper presents the critical need for an automated transcription system that can accurately interpret prescription data, convert it into readable transcriptions, and alleviate the burdens associated with manual transcription. This project aims to bridge this gap by developing a sophisticated machine learning-based solution to revolutionize and optimize the transcription process within the healthcare domain [10]. It encapsulates the challenges and shortcomings prevalent in traditional manual transcription processes within the healthcare sector. In the solution approach, the main script is the foundation. It outlines the step-by-step process to implement a machine-generated transcription system based on prescriptions using a sequence-to-sequence model.

- Load prescription and transcription data from the CSV file "updateddf.csv". Split the data into training, validation, and testing sets using train_test_split.
- Utilize functions like "load_encoder_inputs" and "load_decoder_inputs" to load and preprocess the prescription and transcription data into numerical vectors suitable for model training.
- Construct a sequence-to-sequence model using an encoder-decoder architecture with GRU layers.
- Train the model using the prescription and transcription data, optimizing it to minimize the sparse categorical cross-entropy loss. Implement the Nadam optimizer with a learning rate of 0.001 for training.
- Load the best weights achieved during training using "seq2seq_Model.load_weights". Implement an inference mechanism "Seq2Seq_Inference class" for generating transcriptions from raw prescription texts using the trained model.
- Demonstrate the model's performance by generating machine-generated transcriptions from a subset of test prescription texts. Evaluate the quality and accuracy of the generated transcriptions against the original transcriptions from the test set.
- Extract encoder and decoder models for further analysis or potential deployment. Analyze the model's behavior, identify any limitations or biases, and explore potential improvements or fine-tuning methods.

Implementing this approach involves a systematic approach to data handling, model creation, training, evaluation, and analysis, culminating in a comprehensive understanding of the model's performance and its potential to address transcription challenges in the healthcare domain.

LITERATURE SURVEY

The existing research has introduced a prescription transcription system, yet it has also identified notable limitations and gaps in its approach. These shortcomings offer opportunities for refinement [11]. Hence, our project endeavors to build upon this foundation, addressing the identified gaps to enhance the overall efficacy and resilience of the transcription system. One notable limitation observed in prior work, as highlighted in a paper [12], stemmed from a restricted dataset, resulting in diminished accuracy in deciphering handwritten medicine names. To mitigate this issue, our project seeks to explore techniques aimed at enhancing accuracy and scalability. Furthermore, previous studies [13], used only a selected few writers' datasets, disregarding others. In contrast, our project aims to capitalize on a more diverse dataset to improve the model's adaptability across various handwriting styles. Moreover, challenges related to model size and processing efficiency [14], prompted our investigation into methods to optimize model size without compromising accuracy. Additionally, discrepancies between the dataset and domain [15] underscore the importance of meticulous dataset curation and preprocessing to ensure alignment with the medical prescription recognition domain. Furthermore, limitations regarding system generalization, as highlighted in a study paper, serve as a focal point for our project's objectives [16]. We aspire to develop a system capable of robustly recognizing medical terms across both trained and unseen prescription data, thereby advancing its utility and applicability in real-world scenarios.

Comparison of Existing Approaches to the Problem Framed

In the field of medical prescription recognition and transcription, several notable research papers have addressed the challenges of prescription texts. The list below outlines a survey of papers related to the topic in brief, with possible gaps/limitations within the proposed system as shown in Tables **1** and **2**:

Table 1. Comparison of existing approaches to the problem.

Papers	Title	Authors	Year Of Publication	Proposed System	Gaps
[1]	Medical Prescription Recognition using Machine Learning	Esraa Hassan, Habiba Tarek, Mai Hazem, Shaza Bahnacy, Lobna Shaheen, Walaa H. Elashmwai	2021	The proposed system uses a combination of image processing techniques and machine learning algorithms to recognize handwritten medicine names from images of prescription notes.	This system works on a very small dataset and has low accuracy.
[2]	Doctor's Handwritten Prescription Recognition System In Multi-Language Using Deep Learning	Pavithiran G, Sharan Padmanabhan, Nuvvuru Divya, Aswathy V, Irene Jerusha P, Chandar B	2022	The system uses machine learning techniques, including convolutional neural networks (CNNs), recurrent neural networks (RNNs), and long short-term memory (LSTM) networks, to recognize and translate handwritten prescription notes written in various languages.	This system cannot be used on all platforms.

(Table 1) cont.....

Papers	Title	Authors	Year Of Publication	Proposed System	Gaps
[3]	Doctor's prescription recognition using deep learning	Dr E Kamalanaban, M Gopinath, S Premkumar	2018	The proposed Medicine Box system is a mobile application that uses a convolutional neural network (CNN) to recognize and translate handwritten medicine names from prescription notes.	Only the top few writers' dataset is used and the others are discarded.
[4]	Recognition of Handwritten Medical Prescription Using Signature Verification Techniques	Seerat Rani, Abd Ur Rehman, Beenish Yousaf, Hafiz Tayyab Rauf, Emad Abouel Nasr, and Seifedine Kadry	2022	The recognition of handwritten Medical Prescription is done using Signature Verification. Machine learning models like SVM, Naive bayes classifiers are used.	The size of the model is huge and takes time to give out results.

Our project amalgamates insights from these studies to create a comprehensive solution. Leveraging larger, more diverse datasets, optimizing model efficiency, ensuring dataset consistency, and enhancing the model's generalizability, our solution aims to overcome these identified limitations and advance the accuracy and adaptability of machine-generated transcription of medical prescriptions.

Table 2. Comparison of existing approaches to the problem.

Papers	Title	Authors	Year Of Publication	Proposed System	Gaps
[5]	Medical Prescription Identification Solution	WRAD Wijewardena, N D Kodikara	2021	This system uses a neural network approach for the character recognition process and a knowledge based matching to accurately output the result.	This system can read only a line at once and not the whole prescription.
[6]	Handwritten Recognition using Transformer for Medical Prescription Application	Zobeir Raisi, Mohamed A. Naiel, Steven Wardell, Paul Fieguth and John Zelek	2019	Transformer-based architecture is used for handwritten text recognition since it preserves the spatial information within 2D images.	Dataset used is not consistent with their domain.

(Table 2) cont.....

Papers	Title	Authors	Year Of Publication	Proposed System	Gaps
[7]	Comparison Of Various Machine Learning Algorithms For Recognizing Text On The Medical Prescriptions	Sandhya P, Rama Prabha K.P, Jayanthi.R, V. Sujatha, Asha N, M B Benjula anbu malar	2022	A proposed approach for recognizing handwritten Medical prescriptions involves several steps, including image scanning, pre-processing, and training a convolutional neural network (CNN) for feature extraction. The results are then compared to a database of drug names using optical character recognition (OCR) to identify low-accuracy medicinal names.	Limited exploration of algorithms.
[8]	An online cursive handwritten medical words recognition system	Shaira Tabassum, Nuren Abedin, Md Mahmudur Rahman, Md Moshiur Rahman, Mostafa Taufiq Ahmed, Rafiqul Islam, Ashir Ahmed	2022	A bidirectional long short-term memory (LSTM) network is used to recognize the handwriting. It uses data augmentation techniques to improve the recognition efficiency.	This system only gives output for the trained data and cannot give output for any new data.

SOLUTION APPROACH AND METHODOLOGY

Overall Description of the Project

The primary objective is to create a robust, adaptable machine-generated transcription system specifically tailored for medical prescriptions. This system aims to automate transcription, ensuring accuracy, efficiency, and scalability while addressing key challenges identified in existing methodologies [17].

Approach and Methodology

- Curating a diverse and comprehensive dataset of medical prescriptions, ensuring consistency and relevance to the transcription domain.
- Employing advanced neural network architectures, an LSTM-based sequence-to-sequence model, to understand and generate transcriptions from prescription data.
- Optimizing model parameters, leveraging larger and diverse datasets, and implementing techniques to reduce model complexity while maintaining high accuracy.
- Focusing on enhancing the model's adaptability to diverse handwriting styles,

medical terminologies, and its capability to transcribe new, unseen prescriptions effectively.

The project aims to revolutionize the transcription process within healthcare, providing a scalable, accurate, and efficient solution for transcribing medical prescriptions. It seeks to reduce manual transcription efforts, enhance accuracy, and improve overall workflow efficiency in healthcare institutions.

Gather a diverse dataset of medical prescriptions, ensuring representation of various prescription formats, handwriting styles, and medical terminologies. Preprocess the dataset by removing noise, standardizing formats, tokenizing words, and encoding prescription-transcription pairs.

- Choose an appropriate sequence-to-sequence (GRU) model for the transcription task, considering its ability to capture contextual information.
- Customize the model architecture to handle diverse prescription formats and variations in handwriting styles effectively.
- Divide the dataset into training, validation, and testing sets.
- Optimize model hyperparameters to enhance accuracy and reduce overfitting.
- Train the model iteratively using prescription-transcription pairs, utilizing techniques like teacher forcing and attention mechanisms to improve learning.
- Evaluate model performance using metrics such as BLEU scores, word error rates, and precision-recall measures to assess accuracy.
- Implement strategies to reduce model complexity, enhance processing speed, and optimize resource utilization without compromising accuracy.
- Validate the model's ability to transcribe unseen prescriptions accurately and effectively handle new data.
- Create a user-friendly interface facilitating easy input of prescription data and displaying machine-generated transcriptions.
- Ensure the system can process and provide transcriptions swiftly to accommodate real-time requirements.
- Validate the model's accuracy, adaptability, and efficiency using separate validation datasets.

This solution approach outlines the systematic steps involved in developing a robust, accurate, and adaptable machine-generated transcription system for medical prescriptions, aiming to address the identified requirements and challenges in transcription accuracy, efficiency, and usability within healthcare contexts.

MODELING AND IMPLEMENTATION DETAILS

Design Diagram:

The detailed design diagram for this model is shown in Fig. (**1**).

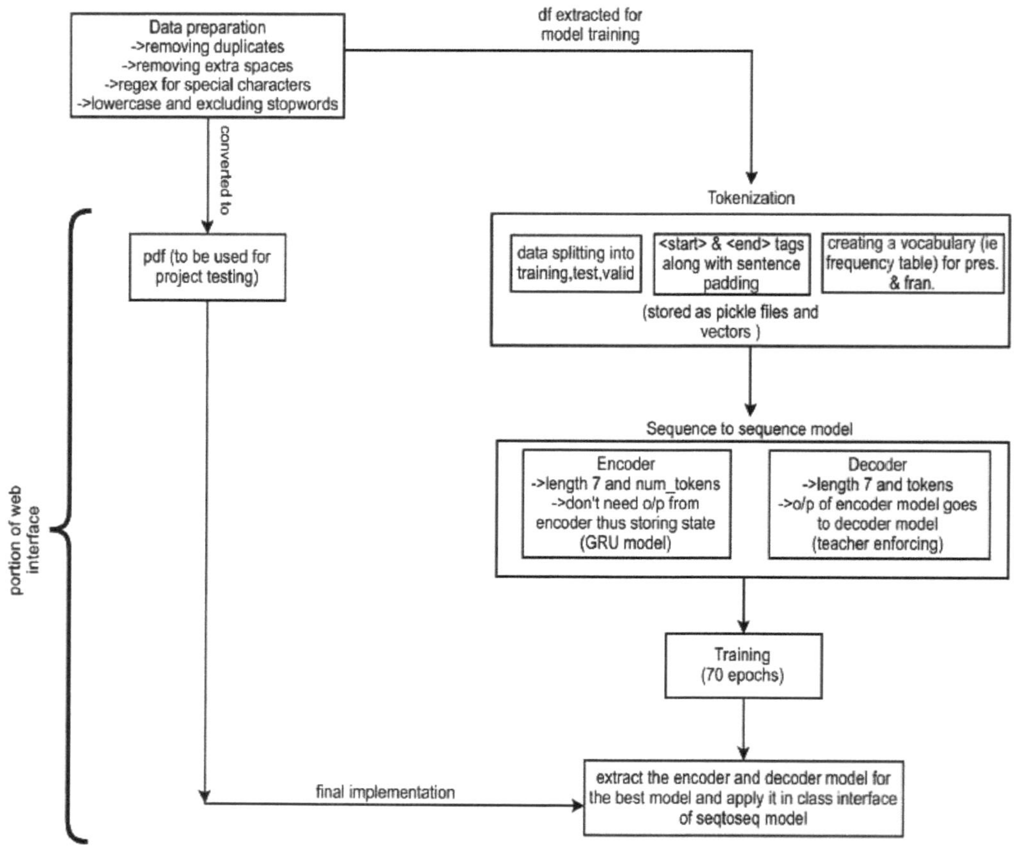

Fig. (1). Machine-generated transcription system flow chart.

Control Flow:

Fig. **2** is the approach to control flow from one process to another.

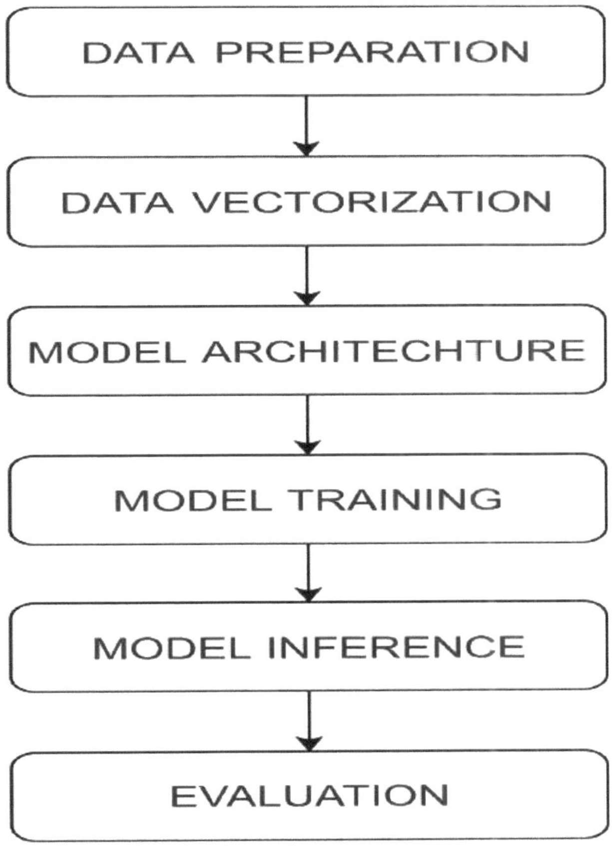

Fig. (2). machine-generated transcription system control flow.

Implementation details and issues

In preparing for the development of a machine-generated transcription system for medical prescriptions, the initial focus lies on data preparation, encompassing the collection of a diverse dataset covering various handwriting styles, formats, and medical terminologies, followed by meticulous preprocessing steps such as tokenization and encoding [18]. The subsequent design of the model architecture entails implementing a Seq2Seq framework utilizing GRU cells, incorporating embedding layers for word representations, and optionally integrating attention mechanisms to enhance focus on relevant input sequences. The training and optimization phases involve fine-tuning hyperparameters and selecting appropriate loss functions and optimization algorithms to improve model performance. Evaluation strategies include implementing metrics such as BLEU scores and cross-validation, to ensure robustness and generalizability.

In the inference and deployment phase, an inference pipeline and a user-friendly interface are developed for transcribing unseen prescriptions and presenting machine-generated transcriptions, respectively. Potential challenges such as limited and inconsistent data, model complexity, overfitting, hyperparameter tuning, and real-world applicability necessitate careful consideration and iterative refinement to ensure the system's reliability, accuracy, and practicality, emphasizing the importance of user feedback and continuous improvement.

Risk Analysis and Mitigation

In the development of a machine-generated transcription system for medical prescriptions, several risks and challenges must be addressed to ensure its reliability and effectiveness. The risk of insufficient or biased data can be mitigated by prioritizing data diversity through the collection of a comprehensive dataset that covers various prescription formats, handwriting styles, and medical terminologies [19].

Techniques like data augmentation and bias handling can further enhance dataset robustness and fairness. To mitigate the risk associated with model complexity and training time, efficient model architectures should be selected, and techniques such as model pruning and parallel processing can be employed. Risks of overfitting and underfitting can be addressed by implementing regularization techniques, cross-validation, and early stopping during training. Challenges in hyperparameter tuning can be mitigated by leveraging automated optimization tools and ensemble methods to effectively explore the parameter space.

Robust evaluation metrics and expert validation ensure comprehensive performance assessment and alignment with real-world medical practices. Continuous user feedback collection, and iterative enhancements based on evolving requirements ensure user acceptance and system improvement. Security and privacy concerns can be mitigated through data encryption, adherence to compliance requirements, and robust error-handling mechanisms. By adopting a proactive approach to risk identification and implementing appropriate mitigation strategies, a reliable and effective transcription system can be developed.

Results

This machine-generated transcript results are shown in Figs. (**3** and **4**).

```
==============================================
Prescription Text : proximal anastomosis used for vein
Transcription (original) Text : reverse saphenous vein graft circumflex
1/1 [==============================] - 0s 19ms/step
1/1 [==============================] - 0s 20ms/step
1/1 [==============================] - 0s 26ms/step
1/1 [==============================] - 0s 22ms/step
1/1 [==============================] - 0s 21ms/step
1/1 [==============================] - 0s 20ms/step
1/1 [==============================] - 0s 22ms/step
1/1 [==============================] - 0s 20ms/step
1/1 [==============================] - 0s 20ms/step
Machine generated Transcription : start reverse saphenous vein graft circumflex obtuse
343/343 [==============================] - 9s 25ms/step - loss: 0.8384
Loss on test data: 0.8384312391281128
```

Fig. (3). Result 1.

```
==============================================
Prescription Text : subluxation wedge withoutcontrast contrast spine
Transcription (original) Text : masses wedgecompression deformity intervertebral disk
1/1 [==============================] - 0s 25ms/step
1/1 [==============================] - 0s 21ms/step
1/1 [==============================] - 0s 20ms/step
1/1 [==============================] - 0s 21ms/step
1/1 [==============================] - 0s 24ms/step
1/1 [==============================] - 0s 23ms/step
1/1 [==============================] - 0s 20ms/step
1/1 [==============================] - 0s 20ms/step
1/1 [==============================] - 0s 26ms/step
Machine generated Transcription : start masses wedgecompression deformity intervertebral disk severe
==============================================
Prescription Text : examination under anesthesia diagnostic laparoscopy
Transcription (original) Text : preoperative diagnosis nonpalpable right undescended
1/1 [==============================] - 0s 19ms/step
1/1 [==============================] - 0s 20ms/step
1/1 [==============================] - 0s 20ms/step
1/1 [==============================] - 0s 25ms/step
1/1 [==============================] - 0s 22ms/step
1/1 [==============================] - 0s 22ms/step
1/1 [==============================] - 0s 20ms/step
1/1 [==============================] - 0s 24ms/step
1/1 [==============================] - 0s 20ms/step
Machine generated Transcription : start preoperative diagnosis nonpalpable right undescended testis
postoperative
```

Fig. (4). Result 2.

TESTING PLAN

Ensuring the reliability, accuracy, and functionality of the machine-generated transcription system for medical prescriptions necessitates a comprehensive test plan. The outlined plan encompasses various key aspects: defining the primary goal of validating accuracy, robustness, and usability; specifying test scope including components, functionalities, and scenarios; categorizing testing types such as unit, integration, and system testing to ensure individual components and overall system integrity; detailing testing scenarios focusing on data coverage, accuracy evaluation, edge case handling, and scalability assessment; executing tests with defined environments, documenting outcomes, and conducting user acceptance testing with domain experts; maintaining detailed documentation and reporting of test cases, logs, and results; and conducting regression testing to ensure continued functionality post-fixes or updates.

This systematic approach aims to address potential issues comprehensively and ensure the system's efficacy in real-world applications.

Error and Exception Handling

In practice, the machine-generated transcription system demonstrates functionality, but enhancements to error handling are warranted to improve reliability and the user experience. Specifically, data loading and processing procedures could benefit from additional error checks to handle missing or inconsistent data effectively. During model training, implementing try-except blocks around training procedures would aid in capturing and managing training-related errors gracefully [20]. Similarly, in model inference, incorporating exception handling mechanisms within the transcription generation process could enhance error resilience. Moreover, to enhance user interaction and reporting, integrating informative error messages or feedback mechanisms would improve usability. Theoretical approaches have identified potential error sources such as data biases, model complexities, and scalability issues, suggesting mitigation strategies including data bias handling, model optimization, and user feedback integration. Additionally, comprehensive testing scenarios and evaluation metrics are proposed to validate system accuracy, robustness, and usability. By addressing these practical and theoretical considerations, the transcription system can achieve greater reliability and usability, align with user expectations, and enhance overall system performance.

Limitations

While the machine-generated transcription system for medical prescriptions holds promise, it faces several limitations that may affect its efficacy and practicality.

Firstly, model complexity and performance issues, such as demanding computational resources and slower processing speeds with larger models, may restrict deployment in resource-constrained environments or hinder real-time transcription capabilities. Secondly, challenges in robustness include difficulties with ambiguous prescriptions or with accurately capturing domain-specific vocabulary, potentially leading to transcription errors. Additionally, limitations in generalization and adaptability may arise from the system's struggle to accommodate various handwriting styles or adapt to prescription variations across different medical specialties or regions. In terms of error handling and resilience, inadequate mechanisms to address unforeseen scenarios or system-level failures could impact reliability and user trust. Lastly, ensuring continuous improvement and maintenance is crucial to counter model degradation over time and address evolving medical terminology or prescription formats. Addressing these limitations through ongoing research, data refinement, and advancements in machine learning techniques is essential for enhancing accuracy and practical usability in healthcare settings.

Findings

Data Quality and Diversity: Identified the importance of diverse and high-quality datasets encompassing various prescription formats and handwriting styles for effective model training. Found that data inconsistencies and biases impact the model's ability to generalize across diverse prescription types, affecting transcription accuracy.

Model Complexity and Performance: Acknowledged that complex models contribute to accurate transcriptions but demand substantial computational resources and might hinder real-time processing. Discovered the trade-off between model complexity and inference speed, highlighting the need for optimized architectures for practical deployment.

Accuracy and Adaptability: Found the system's accuracy to be affected by ambiguous prescriptions or rare medical terminologies, highlighting the challenges in capturing domain-specific vocabulary. Noted limitations in the system's adaptability to unseen prescription styles or specialty-specific variations, impacting its overall robustness.

User Interaction: Emphasized the significance of user-friendly interfaces and user feedback mechanisms for enhancing usability and user acceptance within healthcare environments.

Discovered potential complexities in user-system interaction and the importance of intuitive interfaces for healthcare professionals.

Ethical and Regulatory Considerations: Identified the criticality of stringent data privacy measures and ethical considerations in handling sensitive patient information within prescriptions. Recognized the necessity of complying with healthcare data protection regulations to ensure ethical use and patient confidentiality.

Error Handling and System Resilience: Highlighted the need for robust error handling mechanisms and resilient systems capable of managing unforeseen scenarios for enhanced reliability. Acknowledged challenges in system resilience and the significance of addressing potential failure points for uninterrupted system operation.

Continuous Improvement and Maintenance: Recognized the importance of continuous model updates, maintenance, and adherence to evolving medical terminologies and prescription formats. Identified the risk of model degradation over time without regular retraining on updated data or advancements in machine learning techniques.

These findings collectively underscore the multifaceted nature of developing a machine-generated transcription system for medical prescriptions, emphasizing the need for comprehensive approaches to address challenges and improve system efficacy, accuracy, and usability within healthcare settings.

CONCLUSION AND FUTURE SCOPE

The development of a machine-generated transcription system tailored to medical prescriptions has revealed critical insights into the complexities, challenges, and opportunities inherent in automating transcription tasks in healthcare. This project delved into the intricate interplay between data, models, usability, and ethical considerations, shedding light on pivotal factors influencing system efficacy and practical deployment.

Data Quality and Model Performance: The cornerstone of transcription accuracy resides in the dataset's diversity and quality. Our findings underscore the indispensable role of comprehensive, diverse datasets in training models capable of handling varied prescription formats and handwriting styles. However, while complex models yield heightened accuracy, their computational demands pose trade-offs, necessitating optimization for practical real-time use.

Adaptability and Usability Challenges: The system's adaptability proved crucial, highlighting limitations in handling prescription variations outside the training dataset. Ambiguities in handwritten prescriptions and specialized medical terminology posed challenges, underscoring the need for robustness enhancements to accommodate diverse prescription styles effectively. Furthermore, the project emphasized the pivotal role of user-centric design, advocating for intuitive interfaces to facilitate seamless interaction within healthcare environments.

Ethical Compliance and System Resilience: Navigating ethical considerations and regulatory compliance emerged as paramount. Striking a balance between data privacy, patient confidentiality, and healthcare regulations became imperative, underlining the ethical responsibility inherent in handling sensitive patient information. Additionally, fortifying the system with robust error-handling mechanisms and resilience strategies emerged as foundational pillars for maintaining system reliability amid unforeseen challenges.

Continuous Improvement and Maintenance Strategies: The project highlighted the need for continuous learning and adaptation. The system's longevity hinges on regular updates, alignment with evolving medical terminologies, and vigilant maintenance to prevent model degradation over time. This highlights the iterative nature of development, emphasizing the perpetual need for enhancements and adaptations to sustain relevance within the dynamic healthcare landscape. Looking ahead, the insights gleaned from this endeavor pave the path for future advancements. Addressing identified limitations requires a concerted effort to refine datasets, optimize models for efficiency, enhance adaptability to diverse prescribing styles, and advance user-centric design for seamless integration into healthcare workflows. Moreover, continuous vigilance on ethical compliance and resilience strategies remains pivotal.

REFERENCES

[1] E. Hassan, H. Tarek, M. Hazem, S. Bahnacy, L. Shaheen, and W. H. Elashmwai, "Medical prescription recognition using machine learning", *Proc. IEEE 11th Annu. Comput. Commun. Workshop Conf. (CCWC),* pp. 973-979, 2021.

[2] P. Sandhya, and K. P. R. Prabha, "Comparison of various machine learning algorithms for recognizing text on the medical prescriptions", *J. Pharm. Negative Results,* pp. 2083-2091, 2022.

[3] E. Kamalanaban, M. Gopinath, and S. Premkumar, "Medicine box: Doctor's prescription recognition using deep machine learning", *Int. J. Eng. Technol. (UAE),* vol. 7, pp. 114-117, 2018.

[4] W. R. A. D. Wijewardena, "Medical prescription identification solution", PhD diss., 2021.

[5] P. Singh, M. Kansal, A. P. Singh, A. Verma, S. Tyagi, and A. V. Singh, "Real-time symptomatic disease predictor using multi-layer perceptron", In: *Future of AI in Medical Imaging* IGI Global, 2024, pp. 155-167.

[6] S. Padmanabhan, and N. Divya, "Doctors handwritten prescription recognition system in multi language using deep learning", *arXiv,* 2022.

[7] A. Khan, "Automatic medical prescription recognition using machine learning techniques", *Proc. Int. Conf. Artif. Intell. Big Data (ICAIBD),* pp. 23-28, 2020.

[8] R. Dhanasekaran, and V. Jeyalakshmi, "Prescription recognition system using convolutional neural

network", *Proc. Int. Conf. Smart Electron. Commun. (ICOSEC),* pp. 330-334, 2020.

[9] A. Agrawal, and A. Saha, "Automatic medicine prescription recognition system using machine learning", *Proc. Int. Conf. Signal Process. Integr. Netw. (SPIN),* pp. 524-529, 2021.

[10] P. Singh, M. Kansal, A. P. Singh, A. Verma, S. Tyagi, and A. V. Singh, "Real-time symptomatic disease predictor using multi-layer perceptron", In: *Future of AI in Medical Imaging* IGI Global, 2024, pp. 155-167.

[11] P. Kumar, and R. Kumar, "Deep learning based system for medical prescription recognition", *Proc. Int. Conf. Comput. Commun. Netw. Technol. (ICCCNT),* pp. 1-5, 2021.

[12] D. Verma, "A novel approach for recognition of handwritten medical prescriptions using deep learning", *Proc. Int. Conf. Artif. Intell. Inf. Commun. (ICAIIC),* pp. 1-6, 2021.

[13] A. Singh, "Recognition of handwritten medical prescriptions using deep convolutional neural network", *Proc. Int. Conf. Adv. Comput. Intell. Eng. (ICACIE),* pp. 1-6, 2021. [http://dx.doi.org/10.1109/ICACIE53806.2021.9614381]

[14] R. Jain, "Enhanced medical prescription recognition using deep neural networks", *Proc. IEEE Int. Conf. Comput. Intell. Knowl. Econ. (ICCIKE),* pp. 1-5, 2022. [http://dx.doi.org/10.1109/ICCIKE.2022.9754211]

[15] M. Kansal, P. Singh, P. Srivastava, R. Singhal, N. Deep, and A. Singh, "Mental health monitoring in the digital age: A comprehensive analysis", In: *Future of AI in Medical Imaging* IGI Global, 2024, pp. 168-183.

[16] A. Srivastava, "Analysis of machine learning algorithms for medical prescription recognition", *Proc. Int. Conf. Adv. Comput. Commun. Control Netw. (ICACCCN),* pp. 1-5, 2023. [http://dx.doi.org/10.1109/ICACCCN.2023.9758621]

[17] P. Singh, M. Kansal, M. K. Singh, S. Kumar, and A. Dwivedi, "Crop disease prediction using deep learning algorithms", In: *Convergence of Cloud Computing, AI, and Agricultural Science* IGI Global, 2023, pp. 290-305.

[18] R. Rathore, "Machine learning approach for automatic recognition of medical prescriptions", *Proc. Int. Conf. Adv. Technol. Control Comput. Commun. (ATCCC),* pp. 1-6, 2021. [http://dx.doi.org/10.1109/ATCCC52612.2021.9796941]

[19] P. Singh, A. Asthana, B. Solanki, S. Tomar, M. Kansal, and G. Tyagi, "A comprehensive analysis and sensitivity model for emotion detection in text", In: *Applications of Artificial Intelligence in 5G and Internet of Things* CRC Press, 2025, pp. 332-337.

[20] A. Agarwal, "A comparative study of machine learning techniques for medical prescription recognition", *Proc. Int. Conf. Artif. Intell. Big Data (ICAIBD),* pp. 1-6, 2022. [http://dx.doi.org/10.1109/ICAIBD.2022.9757521]

CHAPTER 8

Enhancing Education using AI

Saurabh Singhal[1,*], **Asheesh Tiwari**[2], **Ajeet Kumar Sharma**[1], **Rakesh Kumar**[2] and **Avinash Kumar Sharma**[1]

[1] *Department of Computer Science & Engineering (CSE), Sharda School of Computing Science & Engineering (SSCSE), Sharda University, Greater Noida, Uttar Pradesh, India*

[2] *Department of Computer Science & Applications, GLA University, Mathura, India*

Abstract: Artificial Intelligence (AI) has emerged as a transformative technology benefiting various industries, including education. AI has revolutionized learning by personalizing education, automating administrative tasks, and providing real-time feedback to both teachers and students. With advances in AI, both teachers and students need to understand its capabilities and limitations to effectively integrate it into their learning practices. This study investigates the use of AI in educational contexts, concentrating on its effects on teaching, learning, and administrative operations. The purpose of this study is to provide insights into the prospects and challenges of integrating AI technologies in education by reviewing current research and practical applications. Personalised learning, intelligent tutoring systems, adaptive assessments, administrative automation, and ethical considerations are all important topics to examine. The study concludes with recommendations for educators and policymakers on how to effectively leverage AI's capabilities while addressing concerns about privacy, equity, and the future role of human educators in a rapidly changing educational landscape. Overall, this study aims to contribute to the ongoing discussion regarding AI's capabilities while addressing concerns related to privacy, equity, and the future role of human educators.

Keywords: Artificial Intelligence (AI), Education, Evaluation, Learning, Teaching.

INTRODUCTION

Artificial Intelligence (AI) is a branch of computer science that aims to create machines capable of performing tasks that typically require human intelligence [1]. AI systems can learn from data, adapt to new inputs, and perform tasks autonomously. Artificial Intelligence, including natural language processing, machine learning, and computer vision, is a rapidly evolving field in education

* **Corresponding author Saurabh Singhal:** Department of Computer Science & Engineering (CSE), Sharda School of Computing Science & Engineering (SSCSE), Sharda University, Greater Noida, Uttar Pradesh, India; E-mail: me.ssaurabh@gmail.com

Pancham Singh, Avinash Kumar Sharma, Mrignainy Kansal, & Amarjeet Prajapati (Eds.)

[2]. It uses data analytics, cloud computing, and algorithmic development to analyse vast amounts of educational data, recognize patterns, and make informed predictions, thereby enhancing human decision-making in the field. It is transforming a variety of industries, including education, by emulating human intellect in robots capable of learning, reasoning, and problem-solving. AI in education has the ability to personalise learning experiences for students, provide real-time feedback, and even help create customised study programmes [3]. As technology advances, AI is likely to play a greater role in determining the future of education. This integration constitutes a paradigm shift, addressing long-standing issues and opening up new possibilities in teaching and learning. AI in education has the potential to narrow the access gap to excellent education, particularly for students living in distant or underdeveloped locations. Using AI technology, educators may build more inclusive and engaging learning environments for all students, regardless of background or learning style [4].

Education is critical for both societal development and personal improvement [5]. Traditional models struggle to accommodate various needs, keep up with technology changes, and optimise resource allocation (Fig. **1**). AI provides a promising solution by personalising learning experiences, reducing administrative procedures, and enabling data-driven decision-making. Machine learning and natural language processing enable educational institutions to adapt training, identify areas for improvement, and improve overall student performance. AI can also help instructors understand students' performance patterns, resulting in more effective teaching tactics and better learning outcomes [6].

AI is transforming personalised learning by adapting to individual requirements using different profiles and historical and real-time data [7]. Thus, optimizing learning paths, increasing engagement, and outcomes across different learner demographics. Traditional educational systems frequently use a one-size-fits-all model thatmay not adequately address individual learning preferences. To facilitate this, new AI-powered adaptive learning systems are making great progress. Intelligent Teaching Systems (ITS) use AI techniques, like Machine Learning (ML), to deliver personalized guidance and feedback to students [8]. These systems combine interactive simulations, virtual mentors, and adaptive evaluations to help students understand complex subjects at their own pace.

AI is also transforming educational evaluation techniques by automating processes such as grading and scoring. Natural language processing algorithms enable AI systems to analyse and evaluate student-generated content with high accuracy and consistency [9]. Automated grading systems save educators' time and enhance the reliability and objectivity of assessment outcomes, ensuring a fair and equitable evaluation of student performance. AI is revolutionizing educational institutions by enhancing teaching and learning processes and reshaping administrative functions. AI-driven enrollment management systems use predictive analytics to forecast enrollment trends, optimize recruitment strategies, and allocate resources more effectively [10]. These systems help anticipate course demand, allocate faculty and facilities efficiently, and enhance student retention. Collaboration between educators, policymakers, and stakeholders is crucial to harnessing AI's potential while mitigating risks.

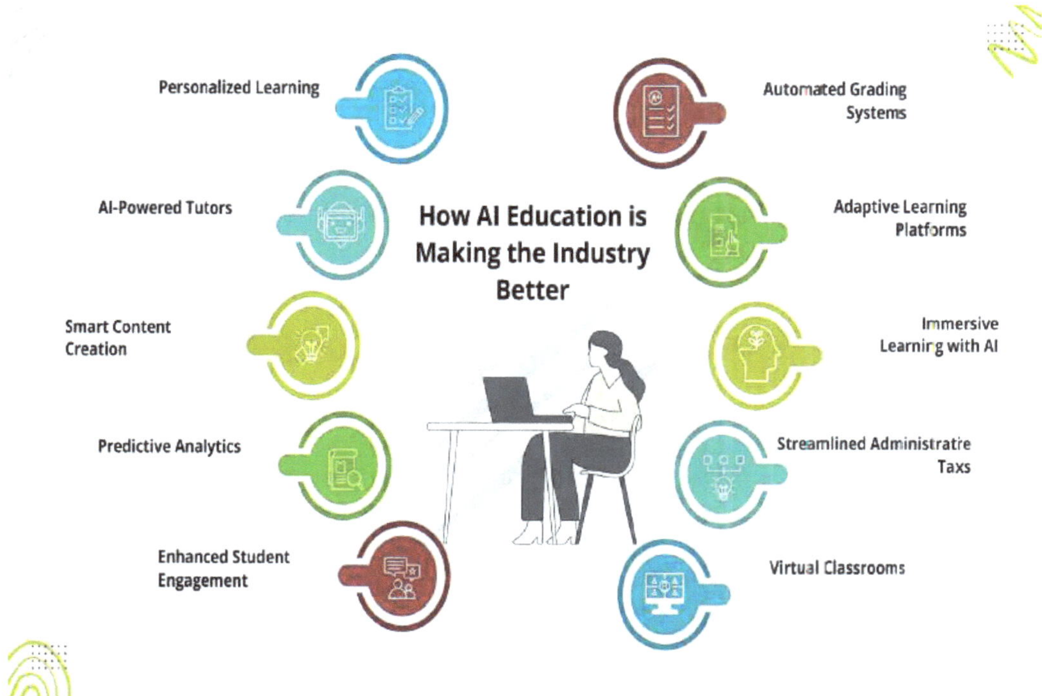

Fig. (1). How AI education is making the industry better.

This study investigates the varied functions of AI in educational contexts, focusing on its applications, benefits, problems, and ethical implications. The study seeks to provide a thorough picture of how AI is revolutionising education and determining the future of learning environments around the world by exploring current research and practical implementations. AI has the potential to personalise learning experiences, provide real-time feedback, and help identify areas where students may want further support. The study also addresses how AI might assist educators in streamlining administrative work, allowing them to focus more on individualised instruction and better student engagement.

AI in Teaching and Learning

Artificial Intelligence (AI) is revolutionizing teaching and learning practices by offering personalized, adaptive, and innovative solutions that cater to diverse learner needs and enhance educational outcomes. This section explores the applications of AI in education, its benefits, challenges, and the evolving role of educators in AI-enhanced classrooms.

Applications of AI in Teaching and Learning

AI technologies are now being used in a variety of educational settings, such as customised learning platforms, intelligent tutoring systems, and automated grading tools [11]. Personalised learning materials are used and the pace is tailoredto specific student needs, utilising computers to assess performance data. Adaptive learning platforms modify difficulty levels and sequences in real time based on student feedback, improving learning paths and engagement. These AI-enabled devices provide quick feedback, allowing students to track their progress and make adjustments in real time. AI assists educators in identifying struggling students and providing focused interventions to help them learn.

Intelligent Teaching Systems (ITS) are AI-powered educational programmes that replicate human teaching by offering personalised advice, feedback, and assistance [12]. These systems incorporate machine learning algorithms to recognise knowledge gaps, customise instructional tactics, and track progress (Fig. **2**). ITS improves student learning outcomes by providing interactive simulations, virtual mentors, and adaptive assessments. Natural Language Processing (NLP) is transforming language learning and communication abilities by using AI-powered tools to analyse and interpret linguistic data [13]. NLP-based tools allow students to practise and develop their language skills through interactive activities, automatic translations, and speech recognition technology, promoting fluency and communication in both native and foreign languages. Furthermore, smart content-generating tools and virtual reality simulations are revolutionising the creation and delivery of educational materials using AI. AI algorithms generate instructional resources, including textbooks, quizzes, and multimedia tools, depending on curricular needs and learning objectives. VR and Augmented Reality (AR) technologies improve experiential learning by immersing students in virtual worlds that replicate real-world scenarios, historical events, or scientific concepts, thereby enhancing conceptual understanding and practical skill development [14, 15].

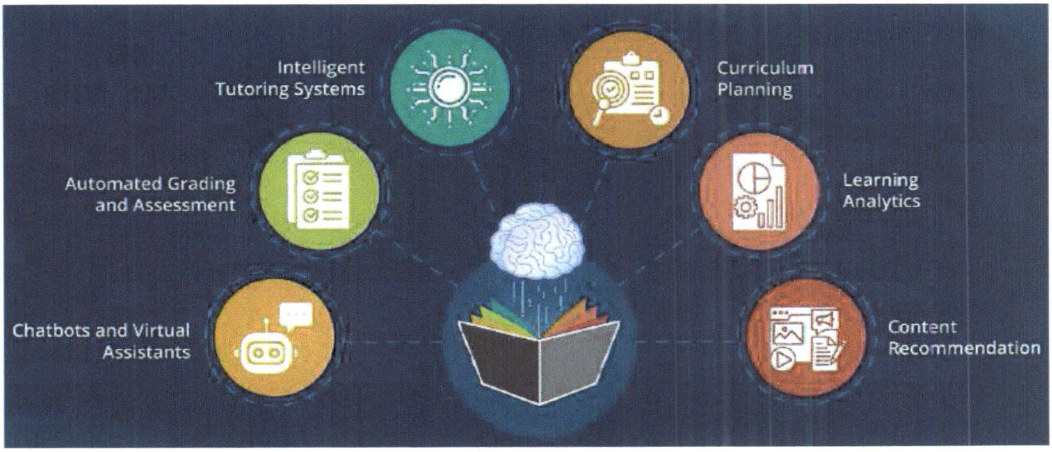

Fig. (2). AI in education: Use cases, solution, and implementation.

Benefits of AI in Teaching and Learning

AI integration in teaching and learning offers various benefits. One of the benefits is personalization, which caters to individual learning styles and paces. Based on individual needs, AI-powered adaptive learning systems customize instructional content in real-time, providing targeted support. This approach promotes student engagement, motivation, and academic success by addressing learning gaps and mastering subject matter. AI also enhances educational equity and accessibility by providing inclusive learning experiences for diverse student populations. Adaptive technologies, such as text-to-speech and speech-to-text converters, assistive technologies, and personalized learning interfaces, empower students with disabilities to participate actively in educational activities and achieve their academic potential. AI aids in data-driven decision-making in education by analysing vast amounts of data on student performance, trends, and instructional effectiveness [16]. It uses learning analytics and predictive analytics tools to provide valuable insights into student performance, learning habits, and growth opportunities. AI helps educators detect at-risk children early, improve curriculum design, and enhance teaching practices, enabling tailored interventions and techniques. Teachers can also customize lessons for each student, resulting in higher student commitment and academic performance.

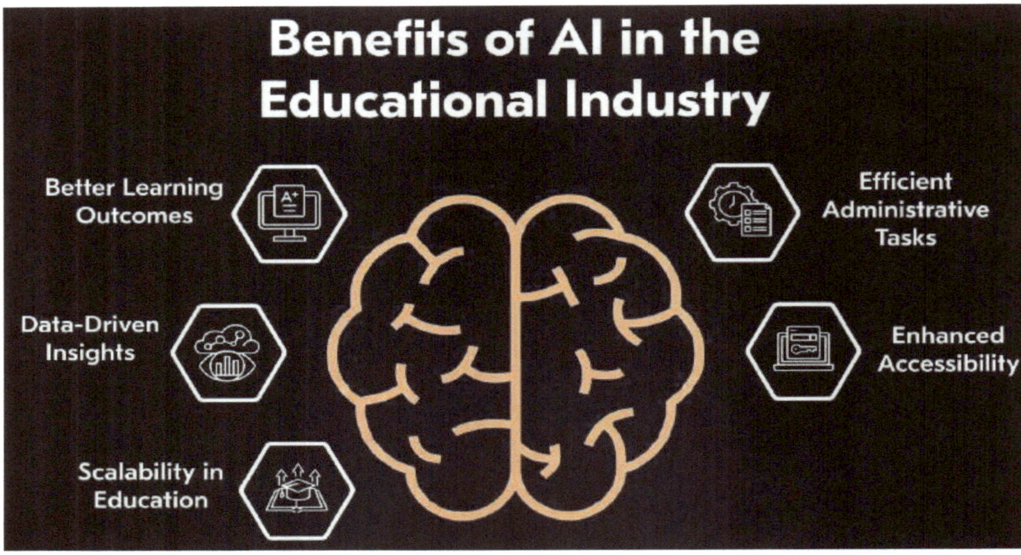

Fig. (3). Benefits of using AI in the education.

Challenges

AI has enormous potential in teaching and learning, but it also raises concerns about data privacy and security. AI technologies exploit sensitive student data to tailor learning experiences and evaluate performance. To ensure ethical use and confidence in AI-powered educational systems, educators and policymakers must adopt strong data protection measures, follow privacy legislation, and practise transparent data usage [17]. Equity and accessibility are critical for the deployment of AI-powered technologies, which may not be available to all students and educational institutions due to differences in technology infrastructure, digital literacy abilities, and financial resources. To promote fair access, policymakers and educators must engage in digital inclusion efforts, offer AI adoption training, and make AI-enhanced educational resources available to marginalised populations [18]. The incorporation of AI into education requires educators to adapt and learn new abilities. While AI can automate jobs and enhance efficiency, it cannot replace the role of human educators in encouraging critical thinking, creativity, and social-emotional skills. Educators must embrace lifelong learning, professional development opportunities, and collaborative teaching strategies.

AI in Assessment and Evaluation

Artificial Intelligence (AI) is revolutionizing assessment and evaluation practices in education by offering automated, adaptive, and data-driven solutions that enhance the accuracy, efficiency, and fairness of educational assessments. This section explores the applications of AI in assessment and evaluation, its benefits, challenges, and ethical considerations, as well as the evolving role of educators in leveraging AI for effective educational outcomes.

Applications of AI in Assessment and Evaluation

AI technology has transformed traditional evaluation methods by automating tasks, delivering customised feedback, and allowing for real-time data analysis [19]. One important application is automated grading and scoring, which employs machine learning algorithms to assess student replies in a variety of disciplines and formats. Natural Language Processing (NLP) algorithms examine written essays, open-ended inquiries, and structured responses to assess content relevancy, grammar, coherence, and compliance with scoring rubrics [20]. Automated grading systems help educators save time and reduce their workload. Adaptive assessments, a prominent use of AI in educational evaluation, dynamically adjust question difficulty and sequencing based on individual student responses, improving the testing experience and providing accurate insights into students' knowledge, skills, and learning progress. These evaluations personalise the testing process, uncover learning gaps, and provide tailored treatments. AI-powered learning analytics systems analyze student performance data to provide educators with insights into learning habits, academic progress, and instructional efficacy. These predictive algorithms forecast trends, identify at-risk students, and suggest adaptive actions. Using data-driven decision-making, educators can optimise curriculum design, customise instructional techniques, and improve educational outcomes for a wide range of student demographics.

Benefits of AI-based Assessment and Evaluation

Artificial intelligence integration in assessment and evaluation improves educational experiences, instructional efficacy, and student performance by automating duties such as grading, scoring, and data analysis. This minimises the workload of educators, allowing them to focus on tailored instruction, curriculum development, and student engagement activities. This efficiency enables rapid and constructive feedback, promoting continued progress and mastery of the subject. AI increases assessment accuracy and reliability by standardising scoring standards, reducing human bias, and ensuring consistent evaluation of student responses [21]. Machine learning algorithms use massive datasets to refine scoring models, increasing predicted accuracy and validity. Automated scoring methods reduce the subjectivity and unpredictability of human grading, resulting in trustworthy, objective evaluations of student performance across diverse populations and educational environments. AI-powered adaptive exams provide tailored learning experiences by adjusting test material and difficulty levels to each student's talents and progress. These algorithms adjust question difficulty based on prior responses, providing a suitable challenge and tailored support for future learning. This method increases student involvement, motivation, and achievement by fostering a supportive learning environment.

Challenges in AI based Assessment and Evaluation

The application of AI in assessment and evaluation poses problems, including data privacy and security. AI technologies leverage confidential student information to tailor examinations and evaluate performance. To ensure ethical use, educators and institutions must develop strong data protection mechanisms, follow privacy legislation, and maintain open data usage standards [22]. This will protect student data and foster trust in AI-powered assessment systems. Equity and accessibility are critical considerations in the implementation of AI-powered evaluation technology. Disparities in technology infrastructure, digital literacy skills, and financial resources can worsen existing educational inequities and limit opportunities for underserved student groups. To achieve fair access, authorities should invest in digital inclusion efforts, provide AI adoption training and assistance, and guarantee that AI-enhanced evaluation tools are usable and inclusive. AI-generated evaluation data mandates that educators create new skills and tactics. While AI algorithms can provide useful insights, human judgment is required to assess results, recognise learning trends, and make informed judgments. Professional development and training are required to integrate AI-powered assessment technologies into teaching practices, promote data literacy, and use data for personalised learning and academic achievement.

AI IN ADMINISTRATIVE PROCESSES

Artificial Intelligence (AI) is revolutionizing administrative processes in educational institutions by offering automated, data-driven, and predictive solutions that streamline operations, enhance efficiency, and improve decision-making. This section explores the applications of AI in administrative tasks, its benefits, challenges, ethical considerations, and the evolving role of AI in shaping the future of educational administration.

Applications of AI in Educational Administration

AI technologies are used in educational administration for various purposes, including student enrolment management, financial forecasting, and resource allocation. Predictive analytics, a primary application, uses machine learning algorithms to analyse historical data and predict future trends in student enrolment, retention rates, and academic performance [23]. This helps institutions anticipate course demand, allocate resources effectively, and implement targeted interventions for student success. AI is being utilised in student enrolment and admissions management, enhancing the application process, optimising recruitment strategies, and enhancing decision-making through data-driven insights and predictive analytics. Natural Language Processing (NLP) algorithms analyse application essays, recommendation letters, and other documents, enabling efficient and effective decision-making by admissions committees.

AI-powered administrative automation technologies automate chores like scheduling, correspondence management, and document processing, allowing administrative staff to focus on strategic projects and student support services. Chatbots and virtual assistants offer personalised support to students, faculty, and staff by answering questions, organising appointments, and delivering real-time information about institutional policies and processes. AI technologies improve educational institutions' financial management and budget forecasts by analysing spending patterns, revenue streams, and funding allocations. This aids in producing accurate projections, optimising budget planning, and identifying cost-cutting options. Administrators can use predictive models to make more informed decisions, reduce risks, and ensure long-term resource management.

Benefits of AI in Educational Administration

The use of AI in school administration improves operational efficiency, strategic decision-making, and institutional effectiveness. It automates time-consuming administrative procedures, decreases human effort, speeds up data processing, improves information accuracy, and increases workflow efficiency. This enables administrative staff to concentrate on higher-value activities, which contribute to institutional growth and student achievement. AI enhances data-driven decision-making by delivering real-time information about student demographics, enrolment trends, and academic performance. Predictive analytics models assist administrators in identifying at-risk students, implementing support interventions, and allocating resources effectively, resulting in higher student retention and success rates. This optimises operational tactics, improves service delivery, and elevates the student experience. AI-powered administrative automation improves service delivery and stakeholder satisfaction through personalised interactions. Students and professors can use chatbots and virtual assistants to quickly access information, settle inquiries, and obtain support. Automated systems promote uniformity, decrease errors, and adhere to policies, resulting in a positive institutional reputation and stakeholder trust.

Challenges

The application of AI in school administration has the potential to transform the profession, but it also brings new issues such as data privacy and security. AI systems rely on sensitive student and institutional data, necessitating strong data protection mechanisms, strict adherence to privacy legislation, and transparent data usage policies to safeguard personal information and retain stakeholder trust. Equity and accessibility are critical to the implementation of AI-powered administrative systems in educational institutions. Disparities in technology infrastructure, digital literacy skills, and financial resources might all work against AI's ability to improve efficiency and service delivery. To enhance fair access, authorities should prioritise digital inclusion measures, train and assist administrators, and guarantee that AI-powered solutions are available and helpful to all educational communities [24]. The incorporation of AI into administrative procedures mandates that educators and administrators acquire new skills and adapt to shifting technology landscapes. While artificial intelligence automates processes and improves productivity, human judgment and expertise are required for interpreting data insights, making strategic decisions, and promoting cross-functional collaboration. Educational leaders must invest in professional development and interdisciplinary collaborations to empower their employees.

ETHICAL CONSIDERATIONS IN AI EDUCATION

Artificial Intelligence (AI) is transforming education by offering personalized learning experiences, enhancing administrative efficiency, and improving educational outcomes. However, the integration of AI in educational settings raises significant ethical considerations that must be addressed to ensure responsible development, deployment, and use of AI technologies. This section examines key ethical issues related to AI in education, explores their implications, and discusses strategies for promoting ethical practices and policies.

Data Privacy and Security

AI education raises ethical concerns about data privacy and security, as AI systems use massive volumes of student data to customise learning experiences, measure performance, and aid decision-making [25]. To protect sensitive information from unauthorised access, breaches, and misuse, educational institutions and technology suppliers must establish strong data protection measures, follow privacy legislation, and maintain clear data collection, storage, and usage procedures. Stakeholders must examine the consequences of data anonymization and aggregation strategies in order to ensure individual privacy while maintaining data utility for AI-powered educational applications. Educators, administrators, and politicians must encourage data literacy in students and stakeholders.

Bias and Fairness

AI education presents a serious ethical dilemma in algorithmic decision-making, as AI systems can perpetuate biases based on race, gender, socioeconomic background, or learning difficulties [26]. This can result in unfair outcomes and uneven treatment. To reduce bias and promote fairness, educators and developers should use inclusive design practices, conduct regular audits of AI algorithms to detect and mitigate bias, and include various perspectives in AI development teams. Transparent documentation of decision-making procedures, accountability methods, and recourse options for affected individuals is critical for building trust, ensuring equity, and resolving ethical concerns about bias in AI education.

Transparency and Explainability

Transparency and explainability are important ethical considerations in education because they allow educators, students, and stakeholders to understand how AI algorithms make decisions, generate recommendations, and personalise learning experiences [27, 28]. Lack of transparency can damage trust, reduce participation, and limit users' ability to question algorithmic conclusions. Explainable AI (XAI) approaches assist in interpreting algorithmic outputs, comprehending the reasoning behind findings, and identifying potential biases or limitations in AI-powered educational applications. Promoting transparency enables stakeholders to make informed decisions, critically evaluate AI recommendations, and reduce the ethical hazards associated with algorithmic opacity.

Accountability and Responsibility

Accountability and responsibility are critical in AI education, as stakeholders must define roles, obligations, and accountability frameworks to ensure ethical AI deployment and governance [29]. Educational institutions, legislators, and technology suppliers must ensure that AI technologies follow ethical norms, respect student rights, and promote beneficial educational outcomes. Clear lines of responsibility include data management, algorithmic oversight, and decision-making procedures. Educators and administrators must have the necessary knowledge, training, and support to ethically integrate AI technologies into educational processes.

Human-centred Design and Ethical Use

Human-centred design concepts are essential for promoting the ethical use of AI in education by prioritising students' and educators' well-being, autonomy, and agency [30]. AI should supplement human expertise and judgement in educational decision-making processes. Educators should help students develop critical thinking, digital literacy, and ethical reasoning abilities, allowing them to engage responsibly with AI-powered products. Promoting ethical AI use necessitates ongoing examination, reflection, and adaptation of AI policies in response to technological breakthroughs, societal expectations, and ethical principles. Collaboration among educators, academics, policymakers, and industry stakeholders is critical to defining ethical frameworks and recommendations.

CHALLENGES AND LIMITATIONS

Artificial Intelligence (AI) holds immense promise to revolutionize industries, enhance productivity, and improve decision-making processes across various domains. However, the widespread adoption and implementation of AI technologies also present significant challenges and limitations that need to be addressed to realize their full potential effectively. This section explores key challenges and limitations associated with AI, their implications, and strategies for overcoming these obstacles.

Data Quality and Accessibility

The quality and accessibility of data pose important challenges for AI development. Large datasets are required for training machine learning models; however, biases and inaccuracies might result in biased AI models and incorrect results. Accessing high-quality, diversified datasets is challenging, particularly in industries with proprietary, sensitive, or sparse data. Limited data access stifles powerful AI applications and innovation in industries such as healthcare, finance, and the social sciences. Addressing data quality challenges necessitates better data gathering processes, data cleaning techniques, and measures to encourage data sharing while protecting privacy and confidentiality.

Ethical and Societal Implications

AI development and implementation provide substantial ethical challenges, such as privacy violations, algorithmic prejudice, accountability, and the influence on employment and societal norms [31]. Data privacy, security, fairness, openness, and ethical usage of AI in decision-making processes are all issues that must be carefully considered and regulated. To address bias in AI algorithms, fair procedures must be followed, data sources diversified, and bias detection and mitigation strategies implemented. Establishing ethical principles, regulatory frameworks, and accountability systems is critical for responsible AI development and deployment that is consistent with societal values and benefits all stakeholders.

Limited Generalization and Adaptability

AI systems, which are frequently taught for specialised tasks, may suffer from generalisation and adaptability to novel settings. These systems, which are intended for specific applications such as image recognition or natural language processing, may be inflexible in dealing with various settings or unexpected events. For example, historical data-based models may fail to generalise to new data distributions or changing conditions, resulting in performance degradation or inaccuracies in real-world applications. To improve AI robustness and adaptability, continuous learning algorithms and research in transfer learning, meta-learning, and reinforcement learning are required [32].

Technical Limitations and Computational Resources

Technical restrictions in AI development include computer resources, algorithmic complexity, and energy efficiency. Training complex models requires substantial processing power and storage, which can be costly and resource-intensive. Scaling AI programmes to process big datasets in real time creates issues in terms of processor speed, memory needs, and power consumption. For long-term AI adoption, AI algorithms must be optimised for efficiency while also lowering environmental impact. The goal of hardware acceleration, parallel computing, and algorithmic optimisation research is to improve the performance and scalability of AI systems [33].

Interpretability and Trustworthiness

AI systems' interpretability and trustworthiness are vital in critical applications such as healthcare and self-driving automobiles [34, 35]. Complex models, such as deep neural networks, can be difficult to understand, resulting in a lack of openness and confidence. This may impede regulatory compliance and limit AI use in safety-critical fields. Researchers are looking into explainable AI techniques to improve interpretability, provide insight into AI decisions, and help stakeholders understand and trust AI-driven outcomes.

Regulatory and Legal Challenges

AI technologies raise regulatory and legal concerns, such as data privacy, intellectual property rights, liability, and compliance with existing laws. The rapid rate of AI development frequently outpaces regulatory frameworks, creating uncertainty and gaps in legal standards. International efforts are underway to establish ethical principles, standards, and regulatory frameworks for AI, with the goal of promoting responsible AI development and use. This includes collaboration among policymakers, industry executives, and legal experts.

Strategies for Overcoming Challenges

The challenges and limitations of AI necessitate a multifaceted approach from researchers, developers, policymakers, and stakeholders across various sectors. Enhancing Data Quality: The initiative aims to improve data quality and accessibility by promoting data sharing, enhancing data collection practices, and implementing standardized protocols for data annotation and curation. Ethical AI Development: Ethical AI development involves incorporating ethical considerations into AI design and development processes, promoting diversity in AI teams, and implementing bias detection and mitigation strategies.

Advancing AI Research: The initiative aims to enhance the robustness, adaptability, and interpretability of AI by investing in fundamental research in AI algorithms, machine learning techniques, and computational methods. Regulatory Frameworks: They are crucial for establishing clear guidelines and ethical standards for AI development, deployment, and use, ensuring legal compliance and promoting responsible AI practices.

Education and Awareness: The initiative aims to enhance digital literacy, AI education, and ethical training among developers, educators, policymakers, and the general public to promote responsible AI technology use.

CONCLUSION

In conclusion, while AI offers transformative potential across various industries and domains, it also presents significant challenges and limitations that must be addressed to realize its full benefits effectively. From data quality and ethical considerations to technical limitations and regulatory challenges, overcoming these obstacles requires collaborative efforts, ethical guidelines, technological advancements, and regulatory frameworks that promote responsible AI development, deployment, and use. By addressing these challenges proactively and adopting strategies for responsible AI innovation, stakeholders can harness the transformative power of AI while ensuring ethical standards, societal benefits, and sustainable development in the AI era.

REFERENCES

[1] D. S. Grewal, "A critical conceptual analysis of definitions of artificial intelligence as applicable to computer engineering", *IOSR J. Comput. Eng.,* vol. 16, no. 2, pp. 9-13, 2014.

[2] P. Malak, and A. Ogurek, "Including natural language processing and machine learning into information retrieval", *Proc. Int. Conf. Nat. Lang. Process.,* 2019.

[3] L. Chen, P. Chen, and Z. Lin, "Artificial intelligence in education: A review", *IEEE Access,* vol. 8, pp. 75264-75278, 2020.

[4] M. Anis, "Leveraging artificial intelligence for inclusive English language teaching", *J. Multidiscip. Educ. Res.,* vol. 12, no. 6, pp. 54-70, 2023.

[5] A. K. Sharma, N. Chanderwal, A. Prajapati, P. Singh, M. Kansal, Ed., *Advancing Software Engineering Through AI, Federated Learning, and Large Language Models* IGI Global: Hershey (PA), 2024.

[6] X. Zhai, "A review of Artificial Intelligence (AI) in education from 2010 to 2020", *Complexity,* vol. 2021, p. 8812542, 2021.

[7] O. Tapalova, and N. Zhiyenbayeva, "Artificial intelligence in education: AIEd for personalised learning pathways", *Electron. J. e-Learning,* vol. 20, no. 5, pp. 639-653, 2022.

[8] F. AlShaikh, and N. Hewahi, "AI and machine learning techniques in intelligent tutoring systems", *Proc. 3ICT,* 2021.

[9] A. V. Y. Lee, "Supporting students' generation of feedback in large-scale online courses", *Stud. Educ. Eval.,* vol. 77, p. 101250, 2023.

[10] M. Kansal, and P. Singh, "A brief survey on metaverse", *Proc. AECE,* pp. 470-475, 2023.

[11] M. L. Owoc, A. Sawicka, and P. Weichbroth, "Artificial intelligence technologies in education", *IFIP AIKM,* 2019.

[12] A. Alam, "Intelligence unleashed: AI-enabled learning ecologies", *AIP Conf. Proc.,* vol. 2717, 2023.

[13] K. Kuddus, "Artificial intelligence in language learning", In: *Advanced Analytics and Deep Learning Models*, 2022, pp. 1-17.

[14] F. Salvetti, and B. Bertagni, "Virtual worlds and augmented reality", *Form@re,* vol. 19, no. 1, pp. 242-255, 2019.

[15] P. Singh, "A comprehensive analysis of emotion detection in text", In: *Applications of AI in 5G and IoT* CRC Press, 2025, pp. 332-337.

[16] Y. Teng, J. Zhang, and T. Sun, "Data-driven decision-making model in higher education", *Expert Syst.,* vol. 40, no. 4, p. e12820, 2023.

[17] F. Shwedeh, "AI adoption and educational sustainability in UAE", In: *Artificial Intelligence in Education* Springer, 2024, pp. 201-229.

[18] Milad Farahani, and Ghazal Ghasemi, "Artificial intelligence and inequality: challenges and opportunities", *Journal of Cultural Marketing Strategy,* vol. 8, no. 2, pp. 131-137, 2024.

[19] J. Wan, "AI-driven customized manufacturing factory", *Proc. IEEE,* vol. 109, no. 4, pp. 377-398, 2020.

[20] M. Kansal, "Enhancing real estate price prediction in smart cities", *Proc. ICDML,* pp. 71-84, 2024.

[21] D. R. P. Marín, "Automatic evaluation of users' short essays using statistical and shallow natural language processing techniques", *University of Madrid,* 2004.

[22] M. Richardson, and R. Clesham, "Rise of the machines? The evolving role of artificial intelligence technologies in high-stakes assessment", *Lond. Rev. Educ.,* vol. 19, no. 1, pp. 1-13, 2021.

[23] A. Namoun, and A. Alshanqiti, "Predicting student performance using data mining and learning analytics techniques: A systematic literature review", *Appl. Sci.,* vol. 11, no. 1, p. 237, 2020.

[24] F. Pedro, "Artificial intelligence in education: Challenges and opportunities for sustainable development", 2019.

[25] M. Kansal, "Enhancing real estate price prediction in smart cities: A comparative analysis of machine learning techniques", *Proc. Int. Conf. Adv. Distrib. Comput. Mach. Learn.,* Springer, pp. 71-84, 2024.

[26] R. S. Baker, and A. Hawn, "Algorithmic bias in education", *Int. J. Artif. Intell. Educ.,* pp. 1-41, 2022.

[27] K. Holstein, and S. Doroudi, "Equity and artificial intelligence in education", In: *The Ethics of Artificial Intelligence in Education* Routledge, 2022, pp. 151-173.

[28] H. Khosravi, "Explainable artificial intelligence in education", *Comput. Educ.: Artif. Intell.,* vol. 3, p. 100074, 2022.

[29] B. Memarian, and T. Doleck, "Fairness, accountability, transparency, and ethics (FATE) in artificial intelligence and higher education", *Comput. Educ.: Artif. Intell.,* p. 100152, 2023.

[30] P. Singh, and M. Kansal, "An online platform for timely access to medical care using real-time data analysis", In: *Wellness Management Powered by AI Technologies*, 2025, pp. 103-131.

[31] W. Holmes, and K. Porayska-Pomsta, "The ethics of artificial intelligence in education: Preactices, Challenges and Debates.", 2023.

[32] G. B. Mensah, "Artificial Intelligence and Ethics: A Comprehensive Review of Bias Mitigation, Transparency, and Accountability in AI Systems," 2023. [http://dx.doi.org/10.13140/RG.2.2.23381.19685/1]

[33] E. Chen, "Transfer learning strategies for AI applications", *J. Artif. Intell. Res.,* vol. 4, no. 1, pp. 91-101, 2024.

[34] M. A. Talib, "A systematic literature review on hardware implementation of artificial intelligence algorithms", *J. Supercomput.,* vol. 77, no. 2, pp. 1897-1938, 2021.

[35] V. Chamola, "A review of trustworthy and explainable artificial intelligence (XAI)", *IEEE Access,* 2023.

[36] V. Chamola, "Recent advances in trustworthy and explainable artificial intelligence", *IEEE Access,* 2023.

CHAPTER 9

Prediction of Air Quality Parameters (NO_2 and SO_2) in Smart Cities Using Seasonal Data: A Comprehensive Analysis

Pancham Singh[1,*], **Mrignainy Kansal**[2] and **Gagan Tyagi**[3]

[1] *Department of Computer Science, Engineering and Information Technology, Ajay Kumar Garg Engineering College, Ghaziabad, Uttar Pradesh, India*

[2] *Department of Computer Science and Engineering, Netaji Subhas University of Technology (NSUT), New Delhi, India*

[3] *Department of Development, Technical Architect, Tech Mahindra, Noida, Uttar Pradesh, India*

Abstract: Air pollution poses a substantial worldwide environmental dilemma that can lead to health issues impacting everyone across the globe, regardless of geographical location. It has a significant influence, both directly and indirectly, not only on human health but also on social and economic activity. Scientists globally are conducting research to assess and forecast the air quality index utilising sophisticated computational models. These algorithms have significantly transformed our understanding and methodology for predicting the API (Air Pollution Index). This study presents a machine learning method to forecast concentrations of Nitrogen Dioxide (NO_2) and Sulfur Dioxide (SO_2) using publicly available data from air quality monitoring stations across a large urban area. By preprocessing and extracting features from time-series data, the study employs various machine learning models to predict the levels of these pollutants. The models were rigorously evaluated through cross-validation to ensure their reliability and accuracy. The results confirm that the approach can effectively predict NO_2 and SO_2 levels, offering a robust tool for air quality management in urban environments. The use of linear and Lasso Regression, along with other machine learning algorithms, highlights the adaptability and precision of the predictive models developed in this research. This approach not only enhances our understanding of air quality dynamics but also aids in the proactive management of environmental health risks associated with air pollution.

Keywords: Air quality concentration station, Central pollution control board, Lasso regression, Linear regression, Machine learning algorithm, NO_2 concentration, SO_2 concentration.

* **Corresponding author Pancham Singh:** Department of Computer Science, Engineering and Information Technology, Ajay Kumar Garg Engineering College, Ghaziabad, Uttar Pradesh, India;
E-mail: pancham.akg@gmail.com

INTRODUCTION

Air pollution in metropolitan areas poses a significant threat to air quality due to emissions of pollutants like Nitrogen Dioxide (NO_2) and Sulphur Dioxide (SO_2). It is crucial to forecast pollutant levels to implement efficient pollution control measures. We utilise a machine-learning method to predict NO_2 and SO_2 levels using publicly accessible air quality data from multiple monitoring stations over a large urban area. Increased urbanisation has led to a rise in human activities that contribute to air pollution. Monitoring and predicting pollutant concentrations are crucial for public health and environmental management. Our research is centred on NO_2 and SO_2, pollutants originating from various sources such as vehicle emissions and industrial operations [1]. Nitrogen Dioxide (NO_2) and Sulphur Dioxide (SO_2) are major air pollutants that degrade air quality. NO_2, mostly originating from vehicle emissions and industrial operations, has a role in the formation of smog and respiratory problems. Sulphur Dioxide (SO_2) from burning fossil fuels and volcanic eruptions can cause acid rain and respiratory irritation. Collectively, these gases have detrimental effects on both human health and ecosystems, as well as the environment. The primary objective is to utilise machine learning to develop precise prediction models for NO_2 and SO_2 levels. Our goal is to create a device capable of predicting pollution levels for any day of any month, differentiating between summer and winter seasons. We incorporate a comprehensive system design into our procedure. We trained our models on data from 2021, split into two sets: summer (April to June) and winter (October to December). We employed machine learning techniques, starting with fundamental Linear Regression. This technique is used to establish the relationship between pollutant concentrations and independent factors. We also explored Lasso Regression and ElasticNet Regression to enhance forecast accuracy.

The data gathered from 40 monitoring stations in Delhi in 2021 was carefully organised. After calculating the average concentrations of NO_2 and SO_2, we separated the data into summer and winter groups. The models were subsequently trained in Python with libraries such as Pandas and NumPy. Linear Regression was used on both summer and winter datasets, showcasing a systematic approach including data import, cleaning, and model implementation. The previous work in this area is shown in Table **1**.

Table 1. Previous work in this area.

Author	Overview	Key Findings
Safeer, S., *et al.* [2]	This study examines recent advances in air quality prediction, with a particular emphasis on machine learning techniques.	Discusses numerous algorithms used in recent studies, emphasising their merits and drawbacks.

(Table 1) cont.....

Author	Overview	Key Findings
Zhang, W., *et al.* [3]	This study looks at the usefulness of linear regression in forecasting NOx and SO_2 levels.	Examines the linear relationship between dependent and independent variables, emphasising the simplicity and interpretability of linear regression.
Amin, F., *et al.* [4]	This paper investigates the use of Lasso and ElasticNet regression in predicting air quality metrics.	Examines how different regularisation strategies help model simplicity and handle multicollinearity.
Zaini, N., *et al.* [5]	Provides a thorough examination of deep learning approaches used to predict air quality.	This paper discusses the benefits of deep learning architectures, such as neural networks, in collecting complicated patterns in air quality data.
Bot, K., *et al.* [6]	Evaluates the predictive ability of several machine learning models for NOx and SO_2 concentrations.	Models such as Random Forest, Support Vector Machines, and Gradient Boosting are highlighted for their benefits and weaknesses.
Sokhi, R.S., *et al.* [7]	Examines the significance of considering temporal and spatial factors in air quality prediction.	Examines ensemble models that combine temporal and geographical data to improve prediction accuracy.
Ghoroghi, A., *et al.* [8]	This overview highlights the importance of feature engineering in improving the performance of air quality prediction models.	Discusses specific time series data properties that contribute considerably to correct forecasts.
Mukundan, A., *et al.* [9].	Investigates the effects of external factors, such as meteorological data, on the performance of machine learning models for air quality predictions.	Methods for using external variables to improve forecast accuracy are discussed.

RELATED WORK

Our research coincides with recent studies highlighting the significance of machine learning in predicting air quality. Significant articles explore the use of linear regression and sophisticated methods such as Lasso and ElasticNet in comparable situations [10]. Our study enhances forecasts by integrating different methods to increase their reliability. The proposed methodology of this paper is depicted in Fig. (**1**).

METHODOLOGY

Dataset Collection

The data was gathered from the Central Pollution Control Board (CPCB) website in Fig. (**1**). The data was downloaded in the form of Excel sheets for all 40 monitoring stations in Delhi for the period of one year, from January 1, 2021, to December 31, 2021, as depicted in Fig. (**2**).

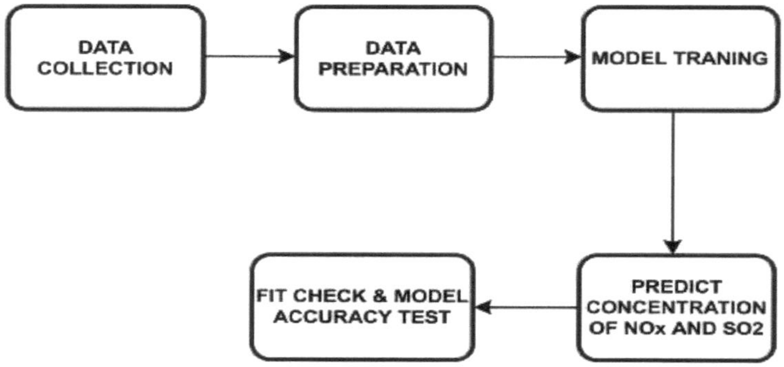

Fig. (1). Proposed Methodology.

1	From Date	To Date	Nox	SO2
2	01-04-2021 00:00	02-04-2021 00:00	22.0216	19.10735
3	02-04-2021 00:00	03-04-2021 00:00	33.8352	23.13265
4	03-04-2021 00:00	04-04-2021 00:00	51.3396	22.49882
5	04-04-2021 00:00	05-04-2021 00:00	47.2296	25.47735
6	05-04-2021 00:00	06-04-2021 00:00	55.6128	27.14
7	07-04-2021 00:00	07-04-2021 00:00	51.9428	26.34676
8	07-04-2021 00:00	08-04-2021 00:00	39.7508	15.92853
9	09-04-2021 00:00	09-04-2021 00:00	48.0108	18.67294
10	09-04-2021 00:00	10-04-2021 00:00	60.5004	20.55471
11	10-04-2021 00:00	11-04-2021 00:00	58.696	20.81206
12	11-04-2021 00:00	12-04-2021 00:00	65.21	25.07882
13	12-04-2021 00:00	13-04-2021 00:00	70.1292	25.54029
14	13-04-2021 00:00	14-04-2021 00:00	61.3188	25.60588
15	14-04-2021 00:00	15-04-2021 00:00	41.2752	20.48147
16	15-04-2021 00:00	16-04-2021 00:00	47.3004	21.86941
17	16-04-2021 00:00	17-04-2021 00:00	40.7272	20.28029
18	17-04-2021 00:00	18-04-2021 00:00	23.61	12.36382
19	18-04-2021 00:00	19-04-2021 00:00	29.6004	17.45382
20	19-04-2021 00:00	20-04-2021 00:00	36.7268	19.71794
21	20-04-2021 00:00	21-04-2021 00:00	22.6152	21.70265
22	21-04-2021 00:00	22-04-2021 00:00	15.1404	14.55529
23	22-04-2021 00:00	23-04-2021 00:00	15.2008	13.59324

Fig. (2). Summer Dataset.

Data Pre-processing

This step involved calculating the average concentration of NOx and SO_2 data and then categorising it into summer and winter data. Since the data was collected from 40 different stations, there were 40 Excel sheets. We need to calculate the average data for each day [11]. A snapshot of the data for IHBAS, Dilshad Garden, Delhi, CPCB, depicted in Fig. (**3**), illustrates how the data for each station appeared when it was downloaded [12]. The data for each station was in the same format as in the provided screenshot.

CENTRAL POLLUTION CONTROL BOARD

CONTINUOUS AMBIENT AIR QUALITY

Date: Saturday, May 21 2022
Time: 06:19:45 PM

State	Delhi
City	Delhi
Station	IHBAS, Dilshad Garden, Delhi - CPCB
Parameter	NOx,SO2
AvgPeriod	24 Hours
From	01-01-2021T00:00:00Z 00:00
To	31-12-2021T18:17:59Z 00:00

IHBAS, Dilshad Garden, Delhi - CPCB

Prescribed Standards		0-200	0-80
Exceeding Standards		NA	NA
Remarks			
From Date	To Date	NOx	SO2
01-01-2021 00:00	02-01-2021 00:00	97.33	12.41
02-01-2021 00:00	03-01-2021 00:00	69.08	18.1
03-01-2021 00:00	04-01-2021 00:00	37.3	12.68
04-01-2021 00:00	05-01-2021 00:00	39.02	15.63
05-01-2021 00:00	06-01-2021 00:00	27.16	11.35
06-01-2021 00:00	07-01-2021 00:00	38.94	12.24
07-01-2021 00:00	08-01-2021 00:00	22.05	9.76
08-01-2021 00:00	09-01-2021 00:00	36.74	16.58
09-01-2021 00:00	10-01-2021 00:00	32.97	13.44

Sheet1

Fig. (3). Data at IhBas, Dilshad Garden, Delhi.

Model Training

The coding was done in Python using Jupyter Notebook. The screenshot of the notebook is included below. The screenshot displays a step-by-step procedure for implementing the model. The model is first implemented using summer data for NOx concentration, followed by the implementation of SO_2 for summer [13]. Secondly, the model implementation for NOx concentration using winter data is presented, followed by the implementation of SO_2 for winter. The Snapshot of importing python libraries and reading data for summaryis depicted in Figs. (**4** and **5**).

```
In [1]: import pandas as pd     #importing libraries that will be used
        import numpy

In [2]: df  = pd.read_excel("summerData.xlsx")  # Reading the data for summer

In [3]: df.head()    # How the top 5 entries of trainning data looks like

Out[3]:
```

	From Date	To Date	Unnamed: 2	Unnamed: 3	Nox	SO2
0	01-04-2021 00:00	02-04-2021 00:00	NaN	NaN	22.0216	19.107353
1	02-04-2021 00:00	03-04-2021 00:00	NaN	NaN	33.8352	23.132647
2	03-04-2021 00:00	04-04-2021 00:00	NaN	NaN	51.3396	22.498824
3	04-04-2021 00:00	05-04-2021 00:00	NaN	NaN	47.2296	25.477353
4	05-04-2021 00:00	06-04-2021 00:00	NaN	NaN	55.6128	27.140000

Fig. (4). Snapshot of importing python libraries and reading data for summer.

```
In [4]: df=df.drop(['Unnamed: 2','Unnamed: 3'],axis='columns')

In [5]: df.head()  # checking top 5 entries

Out[5]:
```

	From Date	To Date	Nox	SO2
0	01-04-2021 00:00	02-04-2021 00:00	22.0216	19.107353
1	02-04-2021 00:00	03-04-2021 00:00	33.8352	23.132647
2	03-04-2021 00:00	04-04-2021 00:00	51.3396	22.498824
3	04-04-2021 00:00	05-04-2021 00:00	47.2296	25.477353
4	05-04-2021 00:00	06-04-2021 00:00	55.6128	27.140000

```
In [6]: df.isnull().sum()     #count null values column wise

Out[6]: From Date    0
        To Date      0
        Nox          0
        SO2          0
        dtype: int64
```

Fig. (5). Snapshot of checking for null values.

The Python libraries pandas and numpy are imported for use in Fig. (**4**). In cell 2 of Fig. (**4**), the data for summer is read. To examine the appearance of the data, the top 5 entries of the dataset are displayed using the head() function. In two unnamed columns (Fig. **4**) are removed [14]. To remove certain columns, the drop () function is used, which can be seen in cell 4 of Fig. (**5**). By examining the top 5 entries of the data, it is confirmed that the removal of the Not a Number (NaN) columns is successfully done [15]. To determine whether any null values are present in the data, the isnull() function is used. We must ensure that there are no null values in the dataset to prevent errors and maintain the accuracy of predictions. If there are any null values in the dataset, we must remove or replace them with appropriate values.

Splitting Training and Testing Dataset:

The forecast for the concentration of NOx is displayed. A method is created to receive user input for the month and day, and then calculate the concentration of NOx. This is an example provided below. The user can input their desired data and receive the corresponding output. The output of cell 21 indicates that on day 2 of the 5th month, the concentration of the NOx may be 30 [16].

Accuracy Test

Accuracy refers to the degree of correspondence between our model and the data. We divide our original dataset into train data and test data in the model. The train data is used to train the model, and once trained, we calculate the accuracy by providing test data as input to the model, which predicts the target variable (concentration of NOx and SO_2 in our case) [17]. Accuracy is determined by comparing expected and actual data in the test data set after making predictions. High accuracy occurs when anticipated values exceed actual values, whereas low accuracy occurs when projected values are lower than actual values. The model is trained with Lasso Regression, and ElasticNet regression is used to do accuracy testing of the model by employing several regression methods, such as Linear Regression, Lasso Regression, and Elastic Net Regression. The highest accuracy of 20.99% is attained in the Linear Regression scenario. The accuracy is 20.73% for Lasso regression and 19.74% for Elasticnet regression, both lower than for Linear Regression.

PROPOSED ALGORITHM

When data processing is done, insert it in the model. Based on these processed data [14], the Model is ready for predictions by using different techniques. The Machine learning algorithms used in this research paper are:

1. Linear Regression
2. Lasso Regression
3. ElasticNet Regression

Linear Regression

Linear regression is a fundamental and commonly used machine learning algorithm. The statistical formula is utilised for predictive analysis in linear regression to foresee continuous or hypothetical fluctuations [18]. The linear regression algorithm demonstrates a linear correlation between a dependent variable (y) and one or more independent variables (x), as suggested by its name. Linear regression shows a linear relationship and calculates how the dependent variable varies with respect to the independent variable. The linear regression model creates a straight line that illustrates the relationship between variables.

Mathematically, Linear Regression can be represented as: -

$y = \alpha 0 + \alpha 1x + €$

where,

y = Dependent Variable (Target Variable)

x = Independent Variable (predicator Variable)

$\alpha 0$ = Intercept of the line

$\alpha 1$= Linear Regression Coefficient

€ = Random error

Types of Linear Regression

- Simple Linear Regression - Simple Linear Regression is an application of Linear Regression that uses a single independent variable to predict the value of a numerical dependent variable [19].

It can be represented as: -

$y = \alpha 0 + \alpha 1x + €$

- Multiple Linear Regression refers to the use of more than one independent variable to predict the value of a numerical dependent variable [20]. Multiple Linear Regression refers to the use of more than one independent variable to predict the value of a numerical dependent variable.

It can be represented as:

y = α0 + α1x1 + α2x2+.......... + αmxm+ €

Lasso Regression

A type of linear regulation is Lasso regulation, sometimes referred to as the Last Absolute Selection and Drinking Operator. By limiting the sum of the absolute values of the model coefficients, the lower function in LASS is changed to reduce model complexity, as shown in Fig. (**6**) [21].

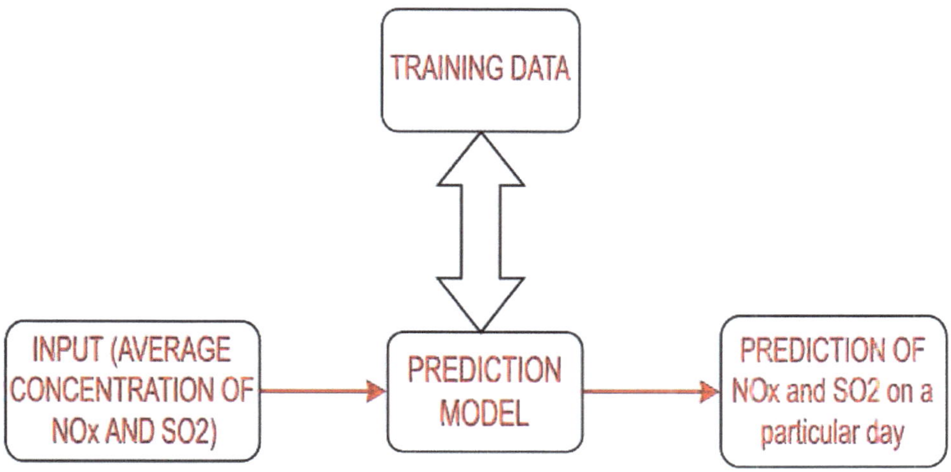

Fig. (6). Linear Regression.

The loss function for Lasso Regression is as follows: Loss function = oLS (ordinary Least Squares) + alpha * summation (absolute values of the magnitude of the coefficients)

In the aforementioned loss function, alpha is the penalty parameter that must be chosen. When applying an L1 norm constraint, certain weight values are compelled to become zero to allow other coefficients to have non-zero values. The Lasso class in scikit-learn is utilised for creating a Lasso regression model [22].

ElasticNet Regression

ElasticNet is a regression method that combines aspects of Ridge and Lasso regression, as well as absolute-value and squared-penalization. The model is analysed using the L2-norm and the L1-norm, with regularisation controlled by the parameter l1_ratio [23]. Ridge regression is a form of linear regression that modifies the loss function to minimise model complexity. This is achieved by utilising a penalty parameter equal to the square of the size of the coefficient.

Loss function = oLS + alpha * summation (squared coefficient values)

The parameter alpha in the loss function above must be selected [24]. A low alpha value may lead to overfitting, whereas a high alpha value may lead to underfitting. The Ridge class in scikit-learn is utilised to construct a ridge regression model [25]. The ElasticNet class in scikit-learn is utilised to construct an ElasticNet regression model.

RESULTS

Two models have been trained for predicting the NO_2 and SO_2 concentrations. One is for summer, and the other is for winter in Delhi. The model's accuracy has been evaluated using three regression techniques: linear regression, Lasso Regression, and Elastic Net Regression. Linear regression had the highest accuracy in summer, whereas elastic net regression had the highest accuracy in winter.

Data preparation involves calculating the average concentrations of NO_2 and SO_2 from all monitoring sites, and then dividing the data into separate datasets for summer and winter, as shown in Tables **2** and **3**. The data from CPCB for IHBAS in Dilshad Garden, Delhi, is displayed, featuring both the raw data and the final dataset post-averaging. Summer data covers the period from April 1, 2021, to June 30, 2021, while winter data covers the period from October 1, 2021, to December 31, 2021. The model is trained using Python in Jupyter Notebook, demonstrating step-by-step implementation for NO_2 and SO_2 concentrations in both summer and winter. Data integrity checks verify the absence of null values, which is essential for precise model predictions.

Table 2. Model evaluation metrics in winter.

Concentration	Technique	Accuracy
SO_2	Linear	37.91%
SO_2	Lasso	38.16%
SO_2	ElasticNet	89.34%
NO_2	Linear	43.93%
NO_2	Lasso	41.37%
NO_2	ElasticNet	91.24%

Table 3. Model evaluation metrics in summer.

Concentration	Technique	Accuracy
SO_2	Linear	88.92%
SO_2	Lasso	40.26%
SO_2	ElasticNet	45.25%
NO_2	Linear	93.52%
NO_2	Lasso	44.46%
NO_2	ElasticNet	34.15%

CONCLUSION

The research introduces a novel machine-learning framework to predict the levels of NO_2 and SO_2 in urban areas, utilizing data from air quality monitoring stations. The study effectively demonstrates the application of various regression models, including Linear, Lasso, and ElasticNet Regression, to predict pollutant levels across different seasons. Through rigorous testing and validation, the models exhibited significant predictive accuracy, making them valuable tools for environmental monitoring and urban planning. Our methodology involved a detailed process of data collection, pre-processing, and model training using machine learning algorithms. The data, segmented into seasonal sets, allowed for tailored predictions that reflect seasonal variations in pollutant levels. The models' performance was evaluated using cross-validation, highlighting the robustness of our approach in handling real-world data. This work not only contributes to the scientific community by providing a reliable method for air quality prediction but also offers practical implications for policymakers and urban planners. By integrating our predictive models into urban air quality management strategies, cities can better anticipate pollution levels and implement timely interventions. This proactive approach is crucial for safeguarding public health and ensuring compliance with environmental regulations.

REFERENCES

[1] P. Ma, F. Tao, L. Gao, S. Leng, K. Yang, and T. Zhou, "Retrieval of fine-grained PM2.5 spatiotemporal resolution based on multiple machine learning models", *Remote Sens.*, vol. 14, p. 599, 2022.

[2] S. Safeer, R.P. Pandey, B. Rehman, T. Safdar, I. Ahmad, S.W. Hasan, and A. Ullah, "A review of artificial intelligence in water purification and wastewater treatment: Recent advancements", *J. Water Process Eng.*, vol. 49, p. 102974, 2022.

[3] W. Zhang, Y. Wu, and J.K. Calautit, "A review on occupancy prediction through machine learning for enhancing energy efficiency, air quality and thermal comfort in the built environment", *Renew. Sustain. Energy Rev.*, vol. 167, p. 112704, 2022.

[4] F. Amin, R. Abbasi, A. Mateen, M.A. Abid, and S. Khan, "A step toward next-generation advancements in the internet of things technologies", *Sensors,* vol. 22, p. 8072, 2022.

[5] N. Zaini, L.W. Ean, A.N. Ahmed, and M.A. Malek, "A systematic literature review of deep learning neural network for time series air quality forecasting", *Environ. Sci. Pollut. Res.,* vol. 29, pp. 4958-4990, 2022.
[http://dx.doi.org/10.1007/s11356-021-17442-1]

[6] K. Bot, and J.G. Borges, "A systematic review of applications of machine learning techniques for wildfire management decision support", *Inventions,* vol. 7, p. 15, 2022.

[7] R.S. Sokhi, N. Moussiopoulos, and A. Baklanov, "Advances in air quality research—current and emerging challenges", *Atmos. Chem. Phys.,* vol. 22, pp. 4615-4703, 2022.

[8] A. Ghoroghi, Y. Rezgui, I. Petri, and T. Beach, "Advances in application of machine learning to life cycle assessment: A literature review", *Int. J. Life Cycle Assess.,* vol. 27, pp. 433-456, 2022.
[http://dx.doi.org/10.1007/s11367-022-02030-3]

[9] A. Mukundan, C.-C. Huang, T.-C. Men, F.-C. Lin, and H.-C. Wang, "Air pollution detection using a novel snap-shot hyperspectral imaging technique", *Sensors,* vol. 22, p. 6231, 2022.

[10] A. Singh, G. Vaidya, and V. Jagota, "Recent advancement in postharvest loss mitigation and quality management of fruits and vegetables using machine learning frameworks", *J. Food Qual.,* pp. 1-9, 2022.

[11] P. Singh, M. Kansal, R. Singh, S. Kumar, and C. Sen, "A hybrid approach based on Haar cascade, softmax, and CNN for human face recognition", *J. Sci. Ind. Res.,* vol. 83, pp. 414-423, 2024.

[12] M. Kansal, P. Singh, S. Kumar, and R. Sibal, "Predicting stock market price over the years by utilizing machine learning algorithms", *CRC Press,* pp. 72-78, 2023.

[13] N. Bacanin, M. Sarac, N. Budimirovic, M. Zivkovic, A.A. AlZubi, and A.K. Bashir, "Smart wireless health care system using graph LSTM pollution prediction and dragonfly node localization", *Sustain. Comput.,* vol. 35, p. 100711, 2022.

[14] P. Singh, M. Kansal, S. Singh, S. Gupta, and S. Maheshwari, "A conceptual prototype for transparent and traceable supply chain using blockchain", *Springer Nature,* pp. 207-217, 2023.

[15] J. Hofman, T.H. Do, X. Qin, E.R. Bonet, W. Philips, N. Deligiannis, and V.P. La Manna, "Spatiotemporal air quality inference of low-cost sensor data: Evidence from multiple sensor testbeds", *Environ. Model. Softw.,* vol. 149, p. 105306, 2022.

[16] P. William, Y.V.U. Kiran, A. Rana, D. Gangodkar, I. Khan, and K. Ashutosh, "Design and implementation of IoT based framework for air quality sensing and monitoring", *IEEE,* pp. 197-200.

[17] S.T. Hassan, P. Wang, I. Khan, and B. Zhu, "The impact of economic complexity, technology advancements, and nuclear energy consumption on the ecological footprint of the USA: Towards circular economy initiatives", *Gondwana Res.,* vol. 113, pp. 237-246, 2023.

[18] P. Singh, M. Kansal, M.K. Singh, S. Kumar, and A. Dwivedi, "Crop disease prediction using deep learning algorithms", *IGI Global,* pp. 290-305, 2023.

[19] P.W. Tien, S. Wei, J. Darkwa, C. Wood, and J.K. Calautit, "Machine learning and deep learning methods for enhancing building energy efficiency and indoor environmental quality", *Energy AI,* p. 100198, 2022.

[20] N.U. Khan, M.A. Shah, C. Maple, E. Ahmed, and N. Asghar, "Traffic flow prediction: An intelligent scheme for forecasting traffic flow using air pollution data in smart cities with bagging ensemble", *Sustainability,* vol. 14, p. 4164, 2022.

[21] A. Hasnain, Y. Sheng, M.Z. Hashmi, U.A. Bhatti, A. Hussain, and M. Hameed, "Time series analysis and forecasting of air pollutants based on prophet forecasting model in Jiangsu province, China", *Front. Environ. Sci.,* vol. 10, p. 945628, 2022.

[22] X.-B. Jin, Z.-Y. Wang, W.-T. Gong, J.-L. Kong, Y.-T. Bai, T.-L. Su, H.-J. Ma, and P. Chakrabarti, "Variational bayesian network with information interpretability filtering for air quality forecasting", *Mathematics,* vol. 11, p. 837, 2023.

[23] K.M. Pandey, M. Singh, Y.N. Prajapati, S.K. Sonkar, P. Singh, and M. Kumar, "Charitable trust management system to establish connections between charitable trust and the donors/adoptee", *J. Pharm. Negat. Results,* vol. 14, no. 2, 2023.

[24] K. Alnowaiser, A.A. Alarfaj, E.A. Alabdulqader, M. Umer, L. Cascone, and B. Alankar, "IoT based smart framework to predict air quality in congested traffic areas using SV-CNN ensemble and KNN imputation model", *Comput. Electr. Eng.,* vol. 118, p. 109311, 2024.

[25] S. Al-Eidi, F. Amsaad, O. Darwish, Y. Tashtoush, A. Alqahtani, and N. Niveshitha, "Comparative analysis study for air quality prediction in smart cities using regression techniques", *IEEE Access,* vol. 11, pp. 115140-115149, 2023.

CHAPTER 10

Producing Optimized Test Suites in Software Testing Using a Many-Objective Feedback-Based Model and Differential Evolution Algorithm

Updesh Kumar Jaiswal[1,*], **Pawan Kumar**[1], **Jaishree Jain**[1], **Ruchira Goel**[2], **Mradul Kumar Jain**[1] and **Deepika Yadav**[3]

[1] *Department of Computer Science and Engineering, Ajay Kumar Garg Engineering College, Ghaziabad, Uttar Pradesh, India*

[2] *Department of Applied Science, Ajay Kumar Garg Engineering College, Ghaziabad, Uttar Pradesh, India*

[3] *Department of Computer Science, Bharati Vidyapeeth's College of Engineering, New Delhi, India*

Abstract: In software project development, Artificial Intelligence (AI) may play a crucial role in enhancing Software Testing (ST) processes through automation. By leveraging AI techniques, testers can enhance the effectiveness of their testing processes, thereby improving overall software system quality. Recently, researchers introduced many-objective optimization approaches to address performance issues in Automated Software Testing (AST) within Search-based Software Testing (SBST). Decreased convergence speed to the local optimum and increased time complexity were two main problems identified with Evolutionary Algorithms (EAs) in SBST. These challenges are addressed by our proposed approach, which integrates a Many-objectives Feedback-based model with the Differential Evolution (DE) algorithm, enabling the production of optimized test suites to simultaneously address multiple testing objectives. Our work in this chapter represents a significant advancement in the ST field, enhancing intelligent evolutionary computation for producing optimized test suites for software applications. The control parameters in our proposed algorithm are self-adapted and learned from prior feedback of evolutionary searches. Considerations such as fitness function calculation and multi-criteria coverage were taken into account during AST. To validate our proposed approach, numerous real-time application-based experiments have been conducted. It was recognized that by applying our sophisticated AI-driven proposed approach to ST, testers can streamline their testing workflows, identify defects more comprehensively, and ultimately deliver software products of higher quality to end-users.

[*] **Corresponding author Updesh Kumar Jaiswal:** Department of Computer Science and Engineering, Ajay Kumar Garg Engineering College, Ghaziabad, Uttar Pradesh, India; E-mail: updesh1984@gmail.com

Pancham Singh, Avinash Kumar Sharma, Mrignainy Kansal, & Amarjeet Prajapati (Eds.)

Keywords: AI, AST, Heuristic search algorithms, Many-objective optimization problems, SBST, Test data.

INTRODUCTION

Traditional Software Testing (ST) employs manual methods to verify and validate software products. This approach depends heavily on the expertise and effort of testers who manually input data, execute test cases, and observe outputs to ensure that the software operates as expected [1]. This method is inherently subjective and prone to inaccuracies and inconsistencies. The manual nature of this testing results in lengthy cycles and high costs. Consequently, AST becomes indispensable, as it can dramatically shorten the development cycle and reduce costs. Recently, AI has emerged as a pivotal force in enhancing ST processes through automation. AI is used in SBST to increase testing coverage, efficacy, and efficiency by utilizing cutting-edge computational approaches [2].

To automate the production of a test suite based on predetermined standards like coverage, size, and execution cost, SBST uses search algorithms. The search procedure is guided by AI-driven heuristics, which aid in the prioritization and selection of test cases that are most likely to reveal flaws [3]. These heuristics may be derived from measures for code complexity, historical data, or other pertinent variables. AI systems optimize test cases to meet several coverage requirements, including branch, path, mutant, and statement coverage. This guarantees thorough testing of the program in various contexts. SBST optimizes the testing process by utilizing a variety of AI approaches and algorithms.

Nowadays, bio-inspired heuristic search algorithms are used in resolving the test case production challenge because they automate the testing process, improve test coverage, adapt to changing requirements, and ultimately result in more efficient and effective testing of software products [4]. By leveraging AI techniques, testers can improve the effectiveness of their testing processes, thereby enhancing the overall quality of software systems. In the realm of SBST, many-objective optimization approaches have been introduced to address performance issues in AI-based ASTs. The EAs used in SBST have encountered challenges, including slower convergence and increased time complexity. Evolutionary strategies focus on the optimization of test cases through mutation and selection processes, similar to genetic algorithms but with different strategies for mutation and selection [5].

In AST using AI, heuristic search algorithms have gained prominence for their ability to automatically generate test cases. The integration of heuristic search algorithms with automatic test case production (generation) transforms this process into a many-objective optimization problem, aiming to maximize coverage of branches, statements, mutations, *etc.* within the code. Moreover, the continuous evolution of software necessitates frequent updates and maintenance, further complicating testing process. As software systems become more sophisticated, the importance of developing robust and efficient testing strategies increases. Therefore, ongoing research and advancements in AI and Metaheuristic Algorithms (MAs) are crucial for addressing these challenges and ensuring the production of high-quality software [6]. In an optimized test case production problem, some complexity arises because a comprehensive test suite must ensure extensive coverage of different software paths, conditions, and potential execution scenarios.

The Dynamic Many-Objective Sorting Algorithm (DynaMOSA) or other existing algorithms are integrated into the EvoSuite framework and serve as a prominent solution for this challenge. It operates by searching multiple objectives simultaneously. However, its efficacy diminishes significantly when the number of objectives becomes excessively high. This is particularly problematic as modern software systems grow in complexity and scale, resulting in an increased number of potential execution paths and branches. To produce optimized test suites for testing the developed software products, a "Many-objectives Feedback-based Model using the Differential Evolution algorithm" is proposed. Our proposed method of Many-objectives Feedback-based test data production is termed MOFMDE. In the ST problem, the MOFMDE is applied to achieve four objectives: branch coverage, line coverage, mutation coverage, and multi-criteria coverage. These are considered while designing the new fitness function. The proposed adaptive feedback model with the DE algorithm has been designed based on various individual selection techniques. The control parameters in our proposed algorithm are self-adapted and informed by feedback from previous evolutionary searches. Key considerations, such as fitness function calculation and multi-criteria coverage, are incorporated into AST. To validate our approach, extensive real-time application-based experiments have been conducted [7]. The experimental results indicate that our AI-driven approach can streamline testing workflows, identify defects more comprehensively, and ultimately deliver higher-quality software products and services to end-users. Therefore, our research presents a significant advancement in ST by enhancing intelligent evolutionary computation for optimized test suite production.

This chapter is structured as Section 2, which reviews work related to optimizing test suite production. Section 3 describes the test suit production as a many-objective based optimization problem. Section 4 details our proposed Feedback-based search model for optimized test suite production. Section 5 discusses the experimental environment used. The outcomes are identified and discussed in Section 6. Lastly, Section 7 provides conclusions with recommendations for future research.

LITERATURE REVIEW

Heuristic-based search methods are now being applied by researchers to produce test cases automatically. The test case production (generation) problem was converted to a many-objective-optimization problem by Fraser *et al.* [8] using a weighted-sum approach that sums the fitness values of each coverage objective to determine the overall fitness value. The entire suite approach was presented and developed by researchers using the EvoSuite framework [9]. Numerous issues with single-objective search-based test case creation were unveiled by this method, such as dependencies between objective branches, variations in branch finding challenges, and wasteful search resource usage from several test cases addressing the same objective. Our investigations and evaluations of the literature offer a thorough grasp of the integration of AI methods into SBST. We provide researchers and practitioners in AI-powered ST with insightful information by covering a wide range of techniques, applications, challenges, and opportunities.

Zhang and Li [9] gave an automatic test suite producing method based on a longicorn beetle search algorithm. The targeted path group of program code was built with overall path similarity in mind, taking into account various paths. Sahin *et al.* [10] generated a thorough test suite utilizing the archive-based multi-criteria ABC methodology. This strategy improves the performance of the algorithm for generating test cases. During many-objective optimization, a weighted-sum method, similar to the whole-suite method, was utilized to simultaneously maximize the covered objectives. While weighted-sum techniques, like the entire suite, can be more efficient than conventional methods for single-goal search [11].

A many-objective genetic algorithm known as MOSA was introduced by Panichella *et al.* [12]. Since the search algorithm's objective for test case production was not to achieve population diversity, it made sense to prioritize people with fitness values close to zero. Yao [13] generated test cases that minimize unnecessary test cases and guarantee adequate testing.

Panichella *et al.* [14] recommended DynaMOSA, which improves the performance of MOSA and other existing algorithms by dynamically picking targets to cover. The classes under test have a large number of interdependent covering objectives. Panichella *et al.* [15] favored a multi-criteria technique using DynaMOSA. Researchers employed incremental control dependence frontier exploration to generate many-criteria test cases. Search-based test case creation has recently received improvements in terms of non-functional aspects. Grano *et al.*, for example, devised aDynaMOSA [16], which optimizes memory and time consumption of the test suite.

AI uses multi-objective optimization approaches to balance different testing goals. Several multi-objective optimization strategies and tools have been presented [17]. NSGA-II and NSGA-III algorithms are commonly utilized in this area. The NSGA-III excels at addressing multi-objective optimization issues, but it struggles with large-scale optimization problems [18]. Similar to numerous other evolutionary algorithms, NSGA-III may experience premature convergence on occasion. This is especially true if the diversity maintenance mechanism is unable to sustain an adequate level of variance within the population. To address these issues, Gu and Wang [19] improved the capabilities of NSGA-III by including the Information Feedback Model (IFM).

A traditional decomposition-based Multi-Objective Evolutionary approach (MOEA or MOAE) is indicated by MOEA/D. The update procedure for individuals in the standard MOEA/D algorithm is a forward search that does not use data from earlier individuals. Still, the prior version contains a great deal of helpful information. Some studies employed IFM, which allows the updating process to include information from prior iterations. As a result, Zhang *et al.* [20] introduced MOEA/D-IFM, a MOEA/D algorithm based on an information feedback model. The researchers suggested six variants of MOEA/D based on various information feedback models. These algorithms were classified into two categories based on the method of individual selection: fixed or random. To further enhance MOEA/D-IFM's performance, a new selection approach was also implemented at the same time. They conducted their experiments in four different ways. Using the CEC 2018 challenges, MOEA/D-IFM was evaluated in two respects. Six improved EAs were selected, and the best was tested on an extensive many-objective problems. Additionally, multi-objective backpack issues were solved by the authors using MOEA/D-IFM [21].

Preliminarily, several large-scale many-objective optimization algorithms (LSMaOAs) were developed and suggested to resolve various types of large-scale many-objective optimization problems (LSMaOPs). Prajapati [22] introduced a PSO-based LSMaOA, and it is depicted by MOPSO. Li *et al.* [23] employed PCA-DynaMOSA to generate test cases with high coverage in a short time while addressing DynaMOSA's weaknesses. The concept of Principal Component Analysis (PCA) was used to reduce dimensionality in a test case creation problem with too many objectives. It was a large-scale, multi-objective optimization technique and was nicknamed LSMaOA. To conduct their studies, certain projects and classes were chosen from the SF110 dataset based on the cyclomatic complexity of classes being tested. According to their experimental results, PCA-DynaMOSA beats DynaMOSA for creating test suites. Although in some cases, PCA-DynaMOSA converges slowly to the local optimum, increasing the time complexity. This issue can be linked to the algorithm's tendency to get stuck in suboptimal regions of the solution space, particularly in very complex and challenging fitness environments.

AI makes it possible to create adaptive methods that modify the testing plan in response to immediate feedback. These methods ensure more efficient test space exploration by allowing the search to be refocused based on intermediate results. Potential areas for improvement include the use of advanced metaheuristic techniques, adaptive parameter control, and feedback-based systems that make greater use of exploration and exploitation. Using non-dominated sorting algorithms to find better solutions, incorporating convergence and divergence archives, and developing more effective fitness evaluation methods could all help to overcome the limitations of current approaches for producing optimized test cases. The four main methods discussed in the literature review are summarized in Table 1 and are relevant to our research. The results obtained from these four methods will be detailed in Section 6 of this chapter.

Table 1. Overview of existing algorithms pertinent to our research.

Algorithm and its Full Name	Month & Year of Publication	Description
NSGA-III [24] Non-dominated Sorting Genetic Algorithm III	(January 2020)	This method utilizes the IFM to increase its capacity to solve large-scale optimization issues. The performance of NSGA-III might be sensitive to parameter settings, necessitating careful adjustment to produce the best results.
MOEA [25] Multi-Objective Evolutionary Algorithm	(February, 2020)	It was a decomposition-based Multi-Objective Evolutionary Algorithm (MOEA/D), and without utilizing the data from earlier individuals, the updating process for each individual involved a forward search. Achieving convergence to the true Pareto front can be challenging using this method.
MOPSO [26] Many-Objective Particle Swarm Optimization	(January 2022)	This method was able to address the Large-Scale Many-Objective Software Package Restructuring Problem (LSMaOSPR) by developing a customized PSO. For the vast and difficult LSMaOSPR issues, this proposed algorithm has sufficient capacity to produce an evenly distributed and well-converged approximation of the Pareto front.
LSMaOA [27] Many-Objective Search and Principal Component Analysis	(July, 2022)	It is a large-scale many-objective optimization algorithm (LSMaOA). Test case creation challenge and dimensionality reduction for superfluous objectives were accomplished using Principal Component Analysis (PCA). A PCA-based Dynamic Many-Objective Sorting algorithm (PCA-DynaMOSA) was created in order to solve the drawbacks of the Dynamic Many-Objective Sorting Algorithm (DynaMOSA) and to provide multi-criteria-based test cases with great coverage in a short time.

BACKGROUND

The process of producing test cases involves assembling a collection of scenarios that are useful for assessing a software system's functionality and performance. This issue is crucial to ST since it guarantees that the program satisfies its specifications and functions properly across a range of scenarios. A critical objective of test suite production challenge is to create an extensive collection of test cases that are capable of identifying a large number of problems and verifying that the software functions as intended under various conditions [28].

Introduction to the Test Case Generation Problem Using AI

The production of test cases must meet two requirements. First, a test case should have a few test statements. Second, ensure that the objectives are well tested. By efficiently improving the test case production problem, ST becomes more thorough, efficient, and trustworthy, resulting in higher-quality software products [29]. Nowadays, to optimize the test case creation problem, AI techniques, including reinforcement learning, multi-objective optimization, PSO, GA, and SA, are used. ST becomes more effective and efficient because of these techniques, which also improve test coverage, automate the testing process, and adjust to changing needs. Test case generation using AI ensures comprehensive testing of software products, leading to more dependable, higher-quality software. One effective way to optimize multiple testing criteria simultaneously is to generate test cases using a many-objective search method. This guarantees that the test cases generated are efficient in terms of execution time and resource use, in addition to being successful in covering various software elements. Software testers can increase testing dependability and rigor by utilizing sophisticated evolutionary algorithms.

Test Suite and Test Cases

In ST, a test case is a predetermined sequence of steps and conditions intended to confirm a specific feature or functionality of the software system. Every test case defines what a successful or unsuccessful test is based on its inputs, execution phases, and expected outcomes. A test suite is an assembly of test cases used to evaluate the functionality or aspects of a software program. It guarantees that the program satisfies its specifications and performs as planned [30]. Optimizing multiple goals simultaneously is known as many-objective optimization. Many-objective search techniques can be used in the context of ST to create test cases that optimize different testing criteria. This strategy can guarantee thorough test coverage and reveal possible flaws that conventional testing techniques might miss. When test cases are created using a many-objective search technique, all objectives that need to be covered are simultaneously searched for, rather than just one, and the test case that is ultimately acquired may cover one or more objectives.

Objectives Addressed in Our Research

An essential tool for explaining how a program is executed is the Control Flow Graph (CFG). In doing so, it provides a thorough understanding of the program's structure and flow by visually representing every path that can be taken during execution. Understanding the possible execution paths and determining crucial locations for testing requires this thorough illustration. The CFG is used to carefully formulate the computations of multiple coverage targets, including line coverage, branch coverage, and path coverage. We can systematically assess the comprehensiveness of our test cases and make sure they sufficiently cover the program's execution landscape by utilizing this graph. In this chapter, we look at a variety of objectives to ensure thorough testing. By addressing numerous characteristics of coverage, we hope to establish a strong framework for evaluating the effectiveness of our test cases.

Branch Coverage

The term "branch" describes a program's decision statements, such as "if" and "while". Nodes in the CFG have two outbound edges. Branches are the branch nodes' outward edges. Consequently, a branch node could have more than one branch [31]. The following fitness formula can be used to express the coverage of a test case t to a branch:

$$fB(t) = al(bi, t) + d(bi, t) \quad \textbf{(1)}$$

Where al(bi, t) stands for the distance from the branch executed by t to the objective branch to be covered. Furthermore, d (bi, t) represents the branch distance:

$d(b, t) = 0$ if branch has been covered (2a)

$d(b, t) = Dmin(t \epsilon T, b) / \{Dmin(t \epsilon T, b) + 1\}$ if current branch has been executed twice (2b)

$d(b, t) = 1$ other (2c)

where Dmin(tϵT, b) represents the minimum non-normalized distance.

Line Coverage

The bytecode of a certain line (statement) is represented by each node in a program's CFG. The following fitness formula can be used to express the line coverage of test case t:

$$fL(t) = al(si, t) + d\,(b(si), t) \tag{3}$$

where al(si, t) is the distance between statements, and d(b(si), t) is the distance between the current branch run by test case t and the branch closest to the current statement. Developers can create more robust and dependable software by making sure their test cases thoroughly assess the program's operation by optimizing its fitness value [32].

Mutation Coverage

A mutated program is formed by altering the nodes in the source program's CFG with some specific mutation operators. The mutation operators employed in our work are ChangeVariable, ChangeConstant, and ChangeArithmeticOperator. By running this procedure, one can determine the quality of the test cases and their capacity to detect flaws. The following fitness formula represents the mutation coverage of a test case t:

$$fM(t) = al(mi, t) + d\,(b(mi), t) + di(mi, t) + dp(mi, t) \tag{4}$$

where al(mi, t) depicts the distance from the statement node executed by t to the mutated node; d(b(mi), t) denotes the normalized branch distance of the mutated node; di(mi, t) interprets infection-status distance; and dp(mi, t) represents transmission distance [33].

Multi-criteria Coverage Test Case Generation

Two important requirements are considered when creating test cases: the minimum number of statements and the maximum coverage of all testing objectives. Additionally, different coverage criteria can be applied to improve the overall adequacy of testing. To ensure thorough testing, each of these criteria includes specific optimization goals, including line coverage, branch coverage, and mutant coverage. These goals must be fulfilled, and it is possible to create an efficient test suite by using advanced optimization techniques. Multi-criteria coverage test case production is the combination of covering all branches, lines, and mutations [34].

If the program under test has m objectives to cover, which include sB objectives of branch coverage, sL objectives of line coverage, and sM objectives of mutation coverage, then $m = sB + sL + sM$.

The test cases included in a test suite T = {t1, t2, t3, t4, · · ·, tn} are variable. Minimizing the fitness value of each of the m objectives is the aim of this research:

$$\min f_{B,i}(t)(i = 1, 2, 3, \cdots, sB) \quad \textbf{(5a)}$$

$$\min f_{L,j}(t)(j = 1, 2, 3, \cdots, sL) \quad \textbf{(5b)}$$

$$\min f_{M,k}(t)(k = 1, 2, 3, \cdots, sM) \quad \textbf{(5c)}$$

A test case in a test suite generates a problem with many methods in a call sequence. These methods' call sequences may cover several coverage objectives. Reducing or deleting these kinds of objectives might not result in the loss of crucial optimization data.

Many-objectives Feedback-based Model

Most metaheuristic algorithms' update processes fail to leverage knowledge from prior iterations. In our approach, earlier beneficial knowledge was pushed back into the update process. Let us grasp the background to this.

Information Feedback Model (IFM)

IFM is a methodical technique that uses iterative modifications and ongoing feedback to increase a process's efficacy. In software testing, the IFM entails gathering information on test execution, evaluating outcomes, and applying the knowledge gained to improve test cases and testing strategies. This iterative procedure ensures that any flaws or inadequacies in the initial testing phase are detected and corrected in later versions. The IFM contributes to improved software quality by exploiting real-time input during testing. IFMs support a flexible and adaptable testing framework that can handle intricate and changing software systems with ease.

Improving Metaheuristic Algorithms (MAs) with IFMs

Continuous feedback loops must be incorporated into the optimization process to improve MAs with IFMs in terms of both solution quality and performance. Because of their ability to handle complex optimization problems, MAs can greatly benefit from IFMs' iterative and adaptive features. The algorithm can dynamically modify its parameters and strategies based on input from each iteration, including performance measurements and evaluations of solution quality. The algorithm can learn from prior iterations, steer clear of traps, and more successfully take advantage of good patterns thanks to its adaptive methodology. By using IFMs, metaheuristic algorithms become more robust and adaptive to a wider range of problem scenarios while also accelerating the convergence towards optimal solutions. The development of increasingly sophisticated and effective optimization strategies is facilitated by this synergistic combination.

Feedback Adaptation Model (FAM)

FAM is an active framework that improves algorithm and process performance by providing constant feedback and iterative modifications. This methodology collects and analyses real-time data and performance indicators consistently in order to deliver actionable insights. These insights are then utilized to fine-tune and change the algorithm or process's parameters and tactics, ensuring that it stays effective and efficient under various conditions. By including this adaptive feedback mechanism, the model promotes a responsive and flexible approach to optimization, allowing for the rectification of flaws, the exploitation of effective patterns, and overall performance improvement. In complicated and changing contexts, where static solutions may not be sufficient and constant improvement is necessary to get the best possible outcomes, this adaptive aptitude is very helpful.

Many-objective-based Feedback Evolutionary Algorithm

This algorithm is a sophisticated optimization approach used to solve problems with several conflicting objectives. In contrast to conventional evolutionary algorithms, which generally concentrate on maximizing a solitary goal, this method incorporates feedback mechanisms to proficiently manage a more extensive array of purposes. The feedback part keeps an eye on the algorithm's performance all the time, giving statistics on how each goal is doing in real time. The algorithm is therefore able to maintain its efficiency and balance in addressing all objectives by using this knowledge to constantly modify evolutionary parameters and tactics. The technique can adjust to the high dimensionality and complexity of many-objective optimization problems by utilizing feedback loops, which improves convergence rates and solution quality. This approach is especially useful in domains where achieving the best results requires balancing numerous objectives [35].

Integrating the IFM and FAM into AST

The integration of IFM and FAM into AST has transformed the field by utilizing AI and advanced optimization methods. These feedback models give continuous, real-time data that dynamically alter ST tactics, increasing process efficiency and effectiveness. AI improves this by offering extensive data analysis and prediction capabilities, which help to refine the feedback and adaptation process. Improving MAs with IFM ensures that optimization tactics are constantly fine-tuned depending on performance measurements, resulting in robust and adaptive testing frameworks. The many-objective-based feedback evolutionary algorithm excels at balancing numerous conflicting objectives while fully optimizing the testing process. This integrated method not only increases test coverage but also provides higher quality and more reliable software systems by producing intelligent, adaptive, automated, and optimized test suites.

Differential Evolution (DE) Algorithm

DE is a robust and efficient optimization technique to solve complex, multidimensional problems. Unlike traditional optimization methods, the classical DE leverages a population-based approach, wherein multiple candidate solutions evolve over iterations. Each candidate (individual) is subjected to mutation, crossover, and selection processes inspired by natural evolutionary principles. DE is a stochastic optimization technique used to minimize an objective function. It has the benefit of detecting true global minima and achieving quick convergence with only a few control settings. The algorithm's ability to balance exploration and exploitation, its simplicity in implementation, and its minimal reliance on problem-specific knowledge make it particularly suitable for tackling the non-linear, high-dimensional optimization challenges addressed in this study. Through the iterative refinement of candidate solutions, DE demonstrates its effectiveness in converging towards the global optimum with high precision and reliability.

The Phases of the Classical DE Algorithm

A classical DE executes four phases as mentioned in Fig. (**1**). After initialization, the mutation process introduces variations by combining the attributes of different individuals, enhancing diversity within the population. Then the crossover (recombination) mechanism allows the exchange of traits among individuals, promoting exploration. Finally, the selection process ensures the survival of the fittest candidates, progressively steering the population toward optimal solutions.

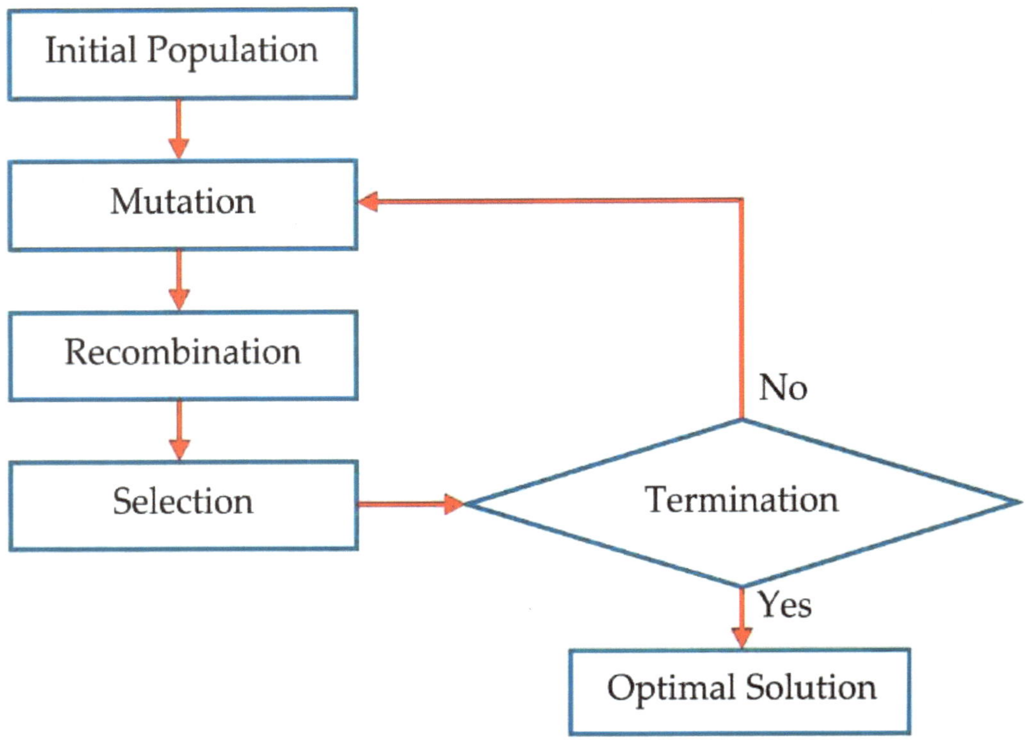

Fig. (1). Four Phases of the basic DE algorithm.

The Pseudocode of Classical DE

The goal of the DE algorithm is to resolve issues with continuous optimization. Every individual is portrayed as xi, G, where i = (1, 2, 3, . . ., NP), and G = (1, 2, 3, . . ., maxG) is the recent generation [22]. The viable zone can be defined using upper and lower bounds, *i.e.*, L = [L1, L2, L3,…., LD] and U = [U1, U2, U3,…., UD]. If randj lies between [0, 1] for the jth dimension, then the initialization phase is described as:

$$xji,G = Lj + randj * (Uj - Lj) \quad \textbf{(6)}$$

Following initialization, DE uses the mutation operator at each generation G to create a mutant vector vi, G for every unique xi, G. The mutation operator "DE/rand/1/bin" is used here [22].

$$vi,G = xr1,G + F * (xr2,G - xr3,G) \quad \textbf{(7)}$$

Three distinct randomly produced individuals are denoted by the indices r1, r2, and r3. The distinction between two individuals is adjusted using F, a predetermined control parameter. The pseudocode of the DE algorithm is mentioned in Fig. (**2**).

Algorithm 1: The DE algorithm with "DE/rand/1/bin"

Generate the initial population
Evaluate the fitness for each individual
while the stopping criterion is not satisfied **do**
  for i=1 to NP **do**
    Select three mutually different individuals $r1 \neq r2 \neq r3 \neq i$
    $j_{rand} = \text{int}(rand[1, D])$
    for j=1 to D **do**
      if $rand[0,1] < CR$ or $j = j_{rand}$ **then**
        $u_{i,G}^{j} = x_{r1,G}^{j} + F*(x_{r2,G}^{j} - x_{r3,G}^{j})$
      else
        $u_{i,G}^{j} = x_{i,G}^{j}$
      end if
    end for
end for
for i=1 to NP **do**
  Evaluate the offspring
  if the fitness function value of $u_{i,G}$ is no worse than $x_{i,G}$ **then**
    Replace $x_{i,G}$ with $u_{i,G}$
  end if
end for
end while

Fig. (2). The Pseudocode of basic DE.

Multi-criteria Many-objective Test Case Generation

Creating a sophisticated test suite that addresses several, frequently contradictory quality requirements in software testing is known as multi-criteria many-objective test case generation. This method seeks to simultaneously optimize a wide variety of objectives rather than concentrating on just one. One of these criteria could be to use a minimal test suite size to ensure thorough coverage of all branches, mutants, and statements of a program. Securing equilibrium among these varied objectives necessitates sophisticated algorithms and approaches capable of managing the many trade-offs present in multi-dimensional optimization issues.

This method effectively meets the requirements of various stakeholders while improving testing reliability and thoroughness and strengthening the overall quality and robustness of software systems by utilizing techniques like multi-objective optimization strategies and evolutionary algorithms [19, 23].

PROPOSED APPROACH

The many-objectives feedback-based Model utilizing the Differential Evolution (DE) algorithm represents a cutting-edge approach in optimization and decision-making processes. This model harnesses the power of DE, a robust and efficient evolutionary algorithm known for its effectiveness in solving complex multi-objective optimization problems. By integrating feedback mechanisms into the evolutionary process, the model iteratively refines solutions based on performance feedback, adapting dynamically to achieve multiple competing objectives simultaneously. This feedback-driven approach not only enhances convergence towards optimal solutions but also ensures adaptability in varying environments or problem landscapes.

In our proposed approach to designing a new framework capable of producing multi-criteria many-objective test suites, we combine the Many-Objectives Feedback-based Model with the DE algorithm. Our method is referred to as (MOFMDE). The overall working methodology (paradigm) of the MOFMDE technique is displayed in Fig. (**3**).

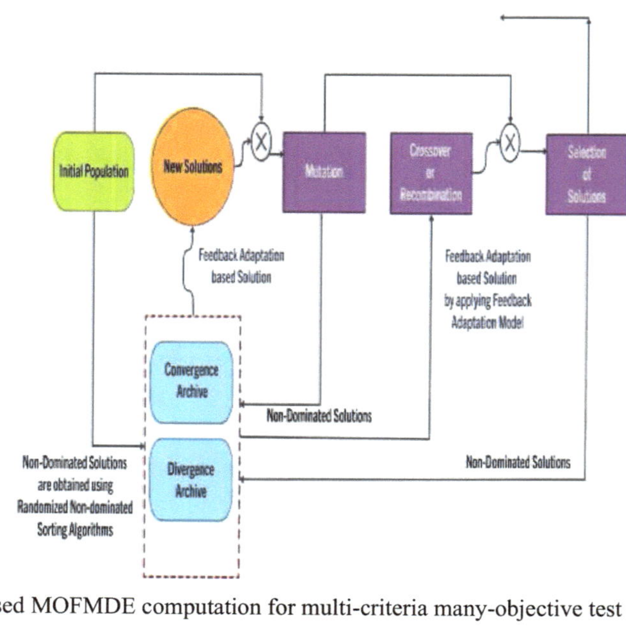

Fig. (3). The proposed MOFMDE computation for multi-criteria many-objective test suite production.

The Many-objectives Feedback-based Model incorporates various sophisticated elements, including the phases of the Differential Evolution algorithm, an adaptation feedback model, internal and external archives, and a randomized Non-Dominated Sorting Algorithm, all aimed at optimizing multi-criteria many-objective test case generation. This approach leverages Differential Evolution's mutation, crossover, and selection phases to iteratively refine test cases across multiple quality metrics simultaneously. The adaptation feedback model dynamically adjusts solutions based on performance feedback, ensuring adaptability and resilience in diverse testing scenarios. Internal and external archives manage solution diversity and historical knowledge, facilitating effective exploration and exploitation of promising test configurations. Meanwhile, the randomized Non-Dominated Sorting Algorithm efficiently categorizes solutions into Pareto fronts, balancing trade-offs among competing objectives. The fitness value derived from these processes guides adjustments to the search direction, enhancing the precision and effectiveness of the testing process in achieving maximum coverage using an optimized test suite. This comprehensive framework not only enhances the thoroughness of test coverage, including branch, line, and mutation coverage using an optimized test suite, but also advances the reliability and effectiveness of AST methodologies in diverse and complex environments.

Experimental Setup

Several tests were planned and carried out to assess the effectiveness of the proposed method. The experiment findings are examined and contrasted with the output of the other four working (existing) methods.

Required Hardware and Software

To perform the experiments and comparison, the following things are required:

Hardware- Intel Core i5-650 and 3.2 GHz Processor

Software- Windows 10, MATLAB, CKJM tool, and Python 3.12

Data Set

Using the CKJM tool, the code complexity of each class of the chosen projects was determined [25]. Subsequently, test classes were arranged based on complexity and objectives addressed. The final dataset contained projects with a higher number of objectives and more complicated classes. 14 projects are listed in Table 2. The tests were performed ten times to compare the performance of the proposed MOFMDE with NSGA-III, MOEA, MOPSO, and LSMaOA. Averaging of the running results was done for analysis and comparison.

Parameter Settings

To perform experiments, various control settings (parameters) of five methods (algorithms) are described in Table **2**.

Table 2. Parameter settings for five many-objective optimization methods.

Algorithm	Parameter	Feature of Algorithm
NSGA-III	Selection strategy	Survival of fitness
	Crossover probability	rand(0,1)
	Mutation probability	rand(0,1)
MOPSO	Inertia weight	1.3
	Acceleration constants c1 and c2	c1(1.25) and c2(2.2)
	Swarm size	100
LSMaOA Algo	Harmony Memory Consideration Rate	0.12
	Pitch Adjusting Rate	0.35
	Convergence Archive	100
MOAE Algo	Populization Size	100
	Scalrization Function	According to given algorithm
	Penalty Parameter	Random selection
Proposed Algorithm	Random value	rand(0,1)
	Mutation Factor	Random Probability(0, 1.3)
	Crossover Rate	Random Probabilty(0, 0.7)

Evaluation Criteria

The following concerns are taken for assessment measures with reference to the efficiency of five different methods:

Mean Coverage Value (MCV)

The MCV in the context of many objective fitness functions refers to a metric used to evaluate the overall coverage or extent to which a set of objectives or criteria is satisfied across multiple dimensions or goals within an optimization problem [26]. In other words, it measures how well a solution set covers the diverse objectives defined by various fitness functions. The MCV provides a numerical indication of how comprehensively conflicting objectives are met across the solutions generated by the optimization process [35]. A higher MCV indicates that a greater proportion of the objectives or criteria have been adequately addressed by the solutions, implying better overall performance in terms of objective coverage. Therefore, MCV serves as a quantitative measure of the effectiveness and completeness of the solutions obtained through the application of many objective fitness functions in achieving a balanced trade-off among multiple competing goals or requirements. In this chapter, MCV values of 14 different projects have been obtained using many-objective fitness functions.

The Fitness Functions

The fitness (objective) functions associated with multi-criteria coverage play pivotal roles in optimizing the test suites. By evaluating these metrics, software testers can systematically minimize redundancy and ensure comprehensive testing coverage across various dimensions.

RESULT AND DISCUSSION

Each test case is depicted as a multi-objective optimization tactic for line, branch, mutation, and multi-criteria coverage in order to maximize coverage and minimize test cases, as mentioned by the fitness functions provided in Section 3. Consequently, a range of tests was conducted, and a population size of 50 to 100 was selected. If the test suite success rate is considered in percentage (%) for 14

different projects, then the received results are examined using the four bases listed below.

Test Suite Line Coverage Analysis of MCV Value for Fourteen Projects

Table **3** demonstrates that the line coverage attained using the proposed approach MOFMDE, surpasses that of NSGA-III, MOEA, MOPSO, and LSMaOA. The MOFMDE achieves superior coverage across all 14 projects. When compared to these four existing methods, MOFMDE shows increased percentages for line coverage in terms of Mean Coverage Value (MCV) [28].

Table 3. Comparison analysis on line coverage using MCV (%).

Project Name	No of Class	NSGA-III	MOEA	MOPSO	LSMaOA	Proposed Approach (MOFMDE)
Jsecurity	3	78.19	80.64	78.18	79.44	82.65
Lavalamp	4	77.28	78.47	79.04	80.15	81.95
Firebird	5	81.21	82.35	83.40	84.31	87.14
Omjstate	3	79.14	79.65	77.98	77.81	85.99
Inspirento	1	78.02	78.31	79.17	80.20	84.78
Quickserver	3	77.09	78.90	78.92	79.05	83.08

(Table 3) cont.....

Project Name	No of Class	NSGA-III	MOEA	MOPSO	LSMaOA	Proposed Approach (MOFMDE)
geo-google	2	75.61	76.90	77.71	77.91	80.89
Bpmail	2	76.04	79.17	78.91	79.05	81.25
gangup	6	80.31	82.26	84.45	87.27	92.15
Javathena	5	85.97	85.65	86.98	86.81	95.29
Petsour	3	87.16	90.65	88.12	90.38	97.88
biblestudy	2	88.72	91.24	89.68	90.76	93.74
Glengineer	5	82.46	85.32	83.24	84.38	86.79
Schemaspy	3	81.59	84.81	82.87	83.72	86.58

Test Suite Branch Coverage Analysis of MCV Value For Fourteen Projects

Table **4** illustrates that the MOFMDE strategy achieves a higher branch coverage than NSGA-III, MOEA, MOPSO, and LSMaOA. MOFMDE consistently obtains higher branch coverage across all 14 projects that are analysed. MOFMDE shows higher branch coverage percentages in terms of MCV when compared to these four current approaches. This comparison demonstrates how well MOFMDE works to improve branch coverage in a wide variety of project scenarios and emphasizes its potential as a cutting-edge approach for multi-objective optimization in test suite production.

Table 4. Comparison analysis on branch coverage using MCV (%).

Project Name	No of Class	NSGA-III	MOEA	MOPSO	LSMaOA	Proposed Approach (MOFMDE)
Jsecurity	3	82.12	86.24	84.14	85.41	88.62
Lavalamp	4	81.28	84.68	83.34	84.65	87.26
Firebird	5	85.42	90.25	88.42	89.31	95.54
Omjstate	3	84.15	86.66	87.91	88.41	91.92
Inspirento	1	78.97	78.31	79.27	80.20	89.58
Quickserver	3	76.19	79.91	78.94	77.75	87.28
geo-google	2	79.32	80.24	78.21	78.97	86.89
Bpmail	2	75.04	78.27	76.44	76.85	90.25
Gangup	6	74.21	75.25	74.47	74.27	92.25
Javathena	5	84.97	86.68	85.95	85.11	97.49
Petsour	3	87.17	89.60	90.62	90.28	98.88
biblestudy	2	88.72	91.52	89.60	90.76	96.75

(Table 4) cont.....

Project Name	No of Class	NSGA-III	MOEA	MOPSO	LSMaOA	Proposed Approach (MOFMDE)
Glengineer	5	86.95	90.10	89.21	89.49	92.19
Schemaspy	3	85.59	90.19	88.89	89.71	92.47

Test Suite Mutation Coverage Analysis of MCV Success Rate for Fourteen Projects

Table **5** clearly shows that the mutation coverage attained using the MOFMDE approach exceeds that achieved by NSGA-III, MOEA, MOPSO, and LSMaOA. Across all 14 projects analyzed, MOFMDE consistently achieves superior mutation coverage. This comparison highlights MOFMDE's effectiveness in improving mutation coverage comprehensively across various project scenarios, emphasizing its role as a leading method in multi-objective optimization for enhancing software testing and quality assurance processes.

Table 5. Comparison analysis on mutation coverage using MCV (%).

Project Name	No of Class	NSGA-III	MOEA	MOPSO	LSMaOA	Proposed Approach (MOFMDE)
Jsecurity	3	80.12	84.49	82.33	84.49	86.91
Lavalamp	4	80.25	83.48	81.24	82.75	86.67
Firebird	5	84.87	85.95	83.42	84.41	91.61
Omjstate	3	82.92	89.24	87.88	88.01	88.37
Inspirento	1	76.94	79.33	78.27	80.78	82.68
Quickserver	3	85.97	88.91	87.23	89.75	91.13
geo-google	2	80.14	79.70	79.72	79.97	86.79
Bpmail	2	78.94	80.67	78.92	78.35	85.95
Gangup	6	82.41	82.16	86.85	86.23	88.32
Javathena	5	80.92	85.60	84.28	84.88	86.39
Petsour	3	91.76	93.61	92.14	91.48	97.92
biblestudy	2	92.34	95.44	93.18	94.86	98.99
Glengineer	5	85.49	90.30	87.29	89.18	95.73
Schemaspy	3	84.51	90.31	87.67	87.74	94.36

Test Suite Multi-criteria Coverage Analysis of MCV Success Rate for Fourteen Projects

The test suite multi-criteria coverage obtained with the MOFMDE technique is superior to that of NSGA-III, MOEA, MOPSO, and LSMaOA, as Table **6** demonstrates. MOFMDE consistently obtains higher multi-criteria coverage across all 14 of the analysed projects.

Table 6. Comparison analysis on multi-criteria coverage using MCV (%).

Project Name	No of Class	NSGA-III	MOEA	MOPSO	LSMaOA	Proposed Approach (MOFMDE)
Jsecurity	3	82.23	85.78	83.29	84.26	88.89
Lavalamp	4	83.76	83.76	86.58	87.28	89.12
Firebird	5	88.13	90.29	89.34	89.61	91.73
Omjstate	3	85.29	89.49	87.47	88.48	93.99
Inspirento	1	77.90	78.28	78.48	79.38	85.98
Quickserver	3	88.12	89.27	88.38	89.27	94.28
geo-google	2	82.83	86.58	86.11	86.67	88.87
bpmail	2	80.23	82.19	81.64	81.78	86.35
gangup	6	83.32	83.49	84.83	84.93	91.55
Javathena	5	84.96	85.25	86.74	86.51	90.99
Petsour	3	91.46	93.50	92.63	92.94	97.87
biblestudy	2	91.34	92.26	90.93	91.62	98.94
Glengineer	5	87.89	90.25	88.92	89.53	93.79
Schemaspy	3	88.65	91.48	89.83	90.62	95.58

Tables **3** - **6** provide clear evidence that the coverage achieved through the application of MOFMDE exceeds that of NSGA-III, MOEA, MOPSO, and LSMaOA. Across all 14 projects analysed, our proposed approach consistently demonstrates higher levels of coverage. In direct comparison with these existing methods, MOFMDE shows notable improvements in percentages for line coverage, branch coverage, mutation coverage, and multi-criteria coverage. Additionally, the success rate, represented as a percentage, is also considered in this evaluation. This comprehensive assessment underscores the efficacy of MOFMDE in enhancing testing comprehensiveness and effectiveness across a diverse set of project scenarios, establishing it as a promising advancement.

CONCLUSION AND FUTURE WORK

Conventional many-objective search-based algorithms often face challenges with inadequate selection pressure, especially when dealing with numerous objectives. To address this issue, it is crucial to employ algorithms with stronger search capabilities. In this chapter, we introduce the MOFMDE method for AST. Our proposed approach was validated through experiments conducted on selected open-source datasets and across 14 benchmark projects. The findings reveal that MOFMDE consistently outperforms NSGA-III, MOEA, MOPSO, and LSMaOA in terms of coverage achieved for the classes under test. When compared directly with these existing methods, MOFMDE demonstrates higher MCV across line coverage, branch coverage, mutation coverage, and multi-criteria coverage metrics. These results underscore the effectiveness of MOFMDE in improving the comprehensiveness and quality of test case generation for complex software systems, establishing it as a promising advancement in multi-objective optimization methodologies for software testing.

Creating more effective adaptive information feedback models represents a promising avenue for future research to enhance evolutionary computation in generating optimal test suites for large-scale, real-world complex software systems. These models could integrate a broad spectrum of nature-inspired algorithms and meta-heuristic methods, such as Teaching-Learning-Based Optimization (TLBO), Ant Colony Optimization (ACO), and others.

REFERENCES

[1] S. Anand, E.K. Burke, T.Y. Chen, J. Clark, M.B. Cohen, W. Grieskamp, M. Harman, M.J. Harrold, P. McMinn, A. Bertolino, and J.J. Li, "An orchestrated survey of methodologies for automated software test case generation", *J. Syst. Softw.,* vol. 86, pp. 1978-2001, Aug 2013. [http://dx.doi.org/10.1016/j.jss.2013.02.061]

[1] S. Anand, E.K. Burke, T.Y. Chen, J. Clark, M.B. Cohen, W. Grieskamp, M. Harman, M.J. Harrold, P. McMinn, A. Bertolino, and J.J. Li, "An orchestrated survey of methodologies for automated software test case generation", *J. Syst. Softw.,* vol. 86, pp. 1978-2001, Aug 2013. [http://dx.doi.org/10.1016/j.jss.2013.02.061]

[3] E.T. Barr, M. Harman, P. McMinn, M. Shahbaz, and S. Yoo, "The oracle problem in software testing: A survey", *IEEE Trans. Softw. Eng.,* vol. 41, no. 5, pp. 507-525, 2015. [http://dx.doi.org/10.1109/TSE.2014.2372785]

[4] C.H. Chen, C.Y. Huang, and C.C. Fang, "Applying slicing-based testability transformation to improve test data generation with symbolic execution", *Int. J. Performability Eng.,* vol. 17, no. 7, pp. 589-599, 2021.

[5] E. Dustin, J. Rashka, and J. Paul, "Automated software testing: Introduction, management, and performance", In: *Addison-Wesley*, 1999.

[6] B.W. Boehm, "Verifying and validating software requirements and design specifications", *IEEE Softw.,* vol. 1, no. 1, pp. 75-88, 2023.

[7] A.K. Kar, "Bio-inspired computing—A review of algorithms and scope of applications", *Expert Syst. Appl.,* vol. 59, pp. 20-32, 2016. [http://dx.doi.org/10.1016/j.eswa.2016.04.018]

[8] G. Fraser, A. Arcuri, and P. McMinn, "A memetic algorithm for whole test suite generation", *J. Syst. Softw.,* vol. 103, pp. 311-327, 2015. [http://dx.doi.org/10.1016/j.jss.2014.11.025]

[9] M. Zhang, and H. Li, "Research on automatic generation of test data for multi-path coverage", *Proc. AEMCSE,* pp. 1185-1188, 2021.

[10] O. Sahin, B. Akay, and D. Karaboga, "Archive-based multi-criteria artificial bee colony algorithm for whole test suite generation", *Eng. Sci. Technol.,* vol. 24, no. 3, pp. 806-817, 2021. [http://dx.doi.org/10.1016/j.jestch.2020.11.006]

[11] K. Deb, "Multi-objective optimization", In: *Springer*, 2014, pp. 403-449.

[12] M. Kansal, "Enhancing real estate price prediction in smart cities", *Springer,* 2024. [http://dx.doi.org/10.1007/978-981-99-8439-8_6]

[13] T. Yao, "Automatic generation of multi-path coverage test cases based on genetic algorithms", *M.S. Thesis, Univ. South China,* 2018.

[14] A. Panichella, F.M. Kifetew, and P. Tonella, "Automated test case generation as a many-objective optimisation problem", *IEEE Trans. Softw. Eng.,* vol. 44, no. 2, pp. 122-158, 2017. [http://dx.doi.org/10.1109/TSE.2017.2692386]

[15] A. Panichella, "Incremental control dependency frontier exploration", *SSBSE,* pp. 309-324, 2018.

[16] G. Grano, "Testing with fewer resources", *IEEE Trans. Softw. Eng.,* vol. 47, no. 11, pp. 2332-2347, 2021.

[17] A. Shamsu, "Software testing: Review on tools, techniques and challenges", *Int. J. Adv. Res. Technol. Innov.,* vol. 2, no. 2, pp. 11-18, 2020.

[18] H. Abdi, and L.J. Williams, "Principal component analysis", *WIREs Comput. Stat.,* vol. 2, no. 4, pp. 433-459, 2010. [http://dx.doi.org/10.1002/wics.101]

[19] Z. Gu, and G. Wang, "Improving NSGA-III algorithms with information feedback models for large-scale many-objective optimization", *Future Gener. Comput. Syst.,* vol. 107, pp. 49-69, 2020. [http://dx.doi.org/10.1016/j.future.2020.01.013]

[20] P. Singh, M. Kansal, R. Singh, S. Kumar, and C. Sen, "A hybrid approach based on Haar cascade, Softmax, and CNN for human face recognition", *J. Sci. Ind. Res.,* vol. 83, no. 4, pp. 414-423, 2024.

[21] G.G. Wang, and Y. Tan, "Improving metaheuristic algorithms with information feedback models", *IEEE Trans. Cybern.,* 2017. [http://dx.doi.org/10.1109/TCYB.2017.2780274]

[22] W. Yi, L. Gao, X. Li, and Y. Zhou, "A new differential evolution algorithm with a hybrid mutation operator and self-adapting control parameters for global optimization problems", *Appl. Intell.,* 2014. [http://dx.doi.org/10.1007/s10489-014-0620-3]

[23] P. Singh, "A transparency system for ICU using machine learning and AI", In: *IGI Global*, 2024, pp. 51-69.

[24] A.M. Dakhel, A. Nikanjam, V. Majdinasab, F. Khomh, and M.C. Desmarais, "Effective test generation using pre-trained large language models and mutation testing", *Inf. Softw. Technol.,* vol. 171, p. 107468, 2024. [http://dx.doi.org/10.1016/j.infsof.2024.107468]

[25] D. Li, W.E. Wong, S. Pan, L.S. Koh, S. Li, and M. Chau, "Automatic test case generation using many-objective search and principal component analysis", *IEEE Access,* vol. 10, pp. 85518-85529, 2022. [http://dx.doi.org/10.1109/ACCESS.2022.3198694]

[26] M. Kansal, "Mental health monitoring in the digital age: A comprehensive analysis", In: *IGI Global*, 2024, pp. 168-183.

[27] A. Panichella, F.M. Kifetew, and P. Tonella, "Reformulating branch coverage as a many-objective optimization problem", *Proc. ICST,* pp. 1-10, 2015.

[28] A. Prajapati, "A customized PSO model for large-scale many-objective software package restructuring problem", *Arab. J. Sci. Eng.,* 2022. [http://dx.doi.org/10.1007/s13369-021-06523]

[29] S. Huang, K. Yang, S. Qi, and R. Wang, "When large language model meets optimization", *Swarm Evol. Comput.,* vol. 90, p. 101663, 2024.

[30] B. Zhao, Z. Cui, J. Yang, X. Cai, and J. Chen, "A multi-task evolutionary algorithm for solving the problem of transfer targets", *Inf. Sci.,* vol. 681, p. 121214, 2024.

[31] "Advancing software engineering through AI, federated learning, and large language models", In: *IGI Global*, 2024.

[32] Y. Zhang, G. Wang, K. Li, and J. Dong, "Enhancing MOEA/D with information feedback models for large-scale many-objective optimization", *Inf. Sci.,* vol. 522, pp. 1-16, 2020.

[33] T. Guo, L. Huang, and H. Han, "An effective path planning method based on VDWF-MOIA for multi-robot patrolling in expo parks", *Electronics,* vol. 14, no. 6, p. 1222, 2025.

[34] P. Singh, U.K. Jaiswal, E. Jain, and V. Mishra, "A novel methodology utilizing modern CCTV cameras and software as a service model for crime detection and prediction", *Int. J. Performability Eng.,* vol. 21, no. 2, 2025.

[35] E. Ahmed, M. Oumer, and M. Hassan, "Diabetes-focused food recommender system to enabling digital health", *PLOS Digit. Health,* vol. 4, no. 2, 2025. [http://dx.doi.org/10.1371/journal.pdig.0000530]

CHAPTER 11

Revolutionizing Drug Discovery and Development through AI and IoT

Bharti Chugh[1,*], **Pankaj Bhatt**[2], **Kranthi Kumar K.**[2], **Anasuya Patil**[3], **Vema Kiran**[4] and **Jayasankar Narayanan**[5]

[1] *Department of CSE, Krishna Institute of Engineering & Technology (KIET), Ghaziabad, Uttar Pradesh, India*

[2] *Department of Pharmaceutics, Lloyd Institute of Management and Technology, Greater Noida, Uttar Pradesh, India*

[3] *Department of Pharmacy, KLE College of Pharmacy, KLE University- 590010, Bengaluru, Karnataka, India*

[4] *School of Pharmaceutical Sciences, Mohan Babu University (MBU), Tirupati, Andhra Pradesh, India*

[5] *Department of Pharmacy, SRM Institute of Science and Technology, Potheri, Tamil Nadu, India*

Abstract: AI and the IoT are revolutionizing drug development and discovery. By utilizing real-time data and sophisticated algorithms, researchers can rapidly identify potential drug candidates and assess their efficacy. In drug research, AI plays a vital role in predicting the pharmacological properties of lead compounds from their chemical structures, thereby improving the efficiency of medication discovery and development. It is possible to develop predictive models that estimate the key features of solubility, bioavailability, and toxicity by utilizing machine learning methods. These models provide a blueprint for designing new molecules with improved pharmacological attributes, thereby boosting the efficacy and safety of potential therapies. The integration of the IoT in the pharmaceutical industry accelerates the production of new drugs for conditions requiring treatment, reducing both time and costs. Utilizing cell-in-a-chip and organ-in-a-chip devices that replicate human physiological conditions, the early evaluation of potential formulations is significantly expedited. By analysing patient data and electronic medical records more effectively, AI enhances clinical trial design and speeds up patient recruitment. AI also helps optimise trial design by identifying which patient subgroups are more likely to respond to therapies. Real-time monitoring is enabled by AI-driven wearables, which ensure accurate data collection and the necessary modifications to trial protocols to improve patient safety. The chapter also examines how AI and IoT are used in drug research, including target identification, drug design, and clinical trials. Lastly, it addresses potential issues and constraints associated with these technologies, as well as future directions for this field's research and development. In conclusion, this chapter has

* **Corresponding author Bharti Chugh:** Department of CSE, Krishna Institute of Engineering & Technology (KIET), Ghaziabad, Uttar Pradesh, India; E-mail: bharti.kathpalia@gmail.com

Pancham Singh, Avinash Kumar Sharma, Mrignainy Kansal, & Amarjeet Prajapati (Eds.)

shown how AI and the Internet of Things could drastically improve the development and discovery processes, leading to better and more efficient treatments for a wide range of ailments.

Keywords: Connected and autonomous vehicles (CAVs), Cyber security, Federated learning, Predictive models, Vehicular Network.

INTRODUCTION

The term "drug discovery" refers to the process of identifying and evaluating compounds that can safely modify disease states, with the goal of developing medications that improve patients' quality of life [1]. This process is lengthy and resource-intensive, necessitating close collaboration across multiple academic disciplines [2]. The pharmaceutical industry places great emphasis on optimizing the drug discovery process because quickly identifying and selecting suitable drug candidates can significantly affect the cost and profitability of new medications [3]. The present state of the art estimates that the cost to bring a new drug to market is approximately $2.6 billion. Furthermore, despite promising results in lab testing, a novel medication may face challenges throughout the clinical trial stage [4]. 9.6% of these medication candidates successfully make it to market, according to phase I studies. A novel drug's market development and discovery are both difficult, drawn-out, and risky processes, but the profits can be enormous [5]. The process necessitates a significant financial investment, technological know-how, resources, and adherence to laws, standards, and regulations. All these elements add to the high cost of the R&D industry. Almost all the funding for the "pipeline" of drug discovery and development comes from the private sector, which must make enough money to pay for new treatments while also surviving and meeting its own expenses [6]. For a variety of reasons, the government will neither support nor nationalize drug development; instead, it will continue to take place in the private sector. To formally begin the drug discovery process, one must first choose a disease area and specify the therapeutic need to be addressed. Following this, the procedure identifies the physiological pathways that must be addressed and, ideally, identifies a particular molecular "drug target. In this stage, the main focus is on identifying a lead chemical structure, designing, testing, and optimizing it to ensure it meets all requirements for development into a pharmaceutical product [7]. After receiving approval, the medication can be sold and given to individuals who require it. Drug research and development are typically difficult, drawn-out procedures requiring a lot of resources and skills. AI and IoT have significantly transformed the pharmaceutical industry, accelerating drug discovery and improving patient care [8]. Health policy, medication development, precision medicine, clinical trials, and data-driven techniques are all made possible by the digitization of medical data [9]. The drug development process has been significantly altered by new analytical methods and computational advancements throughout the last ten years [10]. The use of AI techniques, such as structure-based drug design, *de novo* molecular design and optimization, and pre-clinical and clinical research, has grown in popularity as a result of recent technological advancements. Deep learning models and other analytical methods can be applied to biomedical datasets, such as genetic profiles, imaging data, and chemical and pharmacological databases, to streamline the discovery of effective medications and their therapeutic uses [11].

IoT-based smart gadgets are already becoming popular. One example is "Organ in a Chip," which enables businesses to do real-world diagnostics [12]. Combining the output from these devices with cognitive systems and big data analytics could present previously unheard-of opportunities, significantly increasing R&D productivity and hit rate [13]. "Chip in a pill" is a novel ingestible tablet that, upon ingestion, records health information, including pharmacological effects on important organs, and transmits it to a wearable device, contributing to the expanding influence of smart devices [14]. In addition to lowering the time it takes for medications to reach market, the use of smart devices in clinical development, supply chains, and patient interactions can also improve regulatory compliance by allowing real-time data streams to be proactively used to identify problems along the value chain [15]. Healthcare professionals (HCPs) can use data from wearable devices to administer Personalized Medicines (PM), which can shorten treatment times and increase drug efficacy. Moreover, by enabling targeted therapies, AI and IoT can enhance personalised medicine [16]. Researchers can create individualized therapy programmes that consider a patient's genetic, environmental, and lifestyle characteristics by evaluating patient data. Both patient outcomes and therapeutic efficacy may be enhanced by it. The difficulties encountered have drawn significant attention to AI systems' data-processing capabilities [17]. Experts believe AI can act as a catalyst for drug discovery, speeding up the process and cutting expenses. According to the market research company Bekryl, AI could save the drug discovery process more than $70 billion by 2028 [18].

Traditional Drug Discovery Method

Traditional drug discovery methods have historically followed a systematic process aimed at identifying and developing new medications (Fig. **1**) [19]. This approach typically begins with the identification of biological drug targets by determining the function of a protein or gene that defines its structure. The medicine will target or modify the protein that causes the disease or condition, thereby requiring a new treatment [20, 21]. After being identified and selected, molecular targets must show treatment effects on illness initiation or progression

[22]. Experimental models and tests are used to screen and evaluate the pharmacological relationship to the phenotype during target validation. Target identification and validation are iterative. HTS and knowledge-based screening are popular experimental screening strategies [23]. HTS uses automated robotics to swiftly execute millions of assays to match drug-like features with massive libraries of chemicals without previous knowledge. Focused screening narrows compounds to a smaller group that may have therapeutic target activity from literature or patent precedents [24]. Optimisation examines compound potency, selectivity, toxicity, safety, molecular mechanism, and distribution [25]. For lead compounds with poor activity intensity or specificity, incorrect pharmacokinetic properties, significant toxic side effects, or chemical or metabolic instability, developers modify the chemical structure to create a balanced development candidate. Pre-clinical testing is usually *in vitro* or *in vivo* [26]. Many years pass during preclinical testing. Pre-clinical trials gather efficacy, toxicological, pharmacokinetic, and pharmacodynamic data. The safe dose for human research is determined using this information. *In vitro* testing analyzes drug-molecule interactions in test tubes and labs. Drug compounds are tested *in vivo* using animal models and living cell cultures [27]. In clinical trials, how a medicine is absorbed and eliminated from the body, its side effects, and its efficacy are thoroughly examined [28]. After this, it involved a few dozen healthy volunteers for maximum performance and safety doses. The patient pool is expanded from a few dozen to 100+ to determine the dose when numerous doses were tested [29]. Drug developers will consider manufacturing increases if this phase of tests is successful. The most time-consuming and costly part of creating a new medicine. Drugs can fail clinical trials and be pulled from the process at any stage [30]. A pharmaceutical business may stop development for many reasons. Clinical and operational factors may cause failure. Ineffectiveness, safety, poor study design, and lack of financing are major reasons for trial failure [31].

Challenges and Limitations in Traditional Approaches

Traditional approaches in drug discovery, despite their historical significance, face several challenges and limitations that hinder their efficiency and efficacy [32]. Drug development represents a protracted, intricate, and expensive journey fraught with considerable uncertainty regarding the eventual success of a drug [33]. Identifying targets for many nervous system disorders is particularly challenging due to the unclear pathophysiology involved. Animal models often fall short in fully replicating the complexity of these disorders [34]. Addressing the heterogeneity among patient populations could potentially be mitigated through enhanced clinical phenotyping and genotyping [35]. Increased reliance on human data holds promise for enhancing the identification and validation of targets [36]. The absence of validated biomarkers for diagnosing and assessing biological states objectively remains a significant hurdle. Familiarity with current regulatory processes for Investigational New Drug (IND) applications can be facilitated through pre-IND meetings [37].

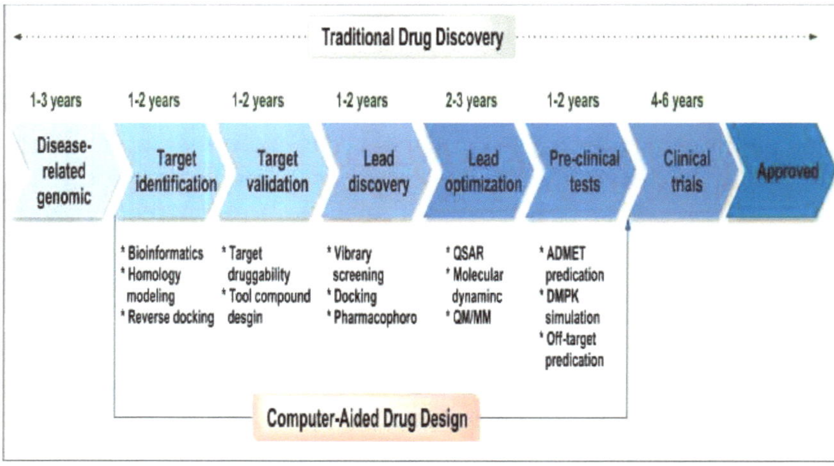

Fig. (1). Traditional drug discovery method with computer-aided drug design.

This approach typically begins with identifying biological drug targets defined by the function of a protein or gene, which dictates the structure of the protein. The drug is designed to target or modify the specific protein responsible for the disease or condition requiring treatment [38]. After being identified and selected, molecular targets must show treatment effects on illness initiation or progression [39]. Experimental models and tests are used to screen and evaluate the pharmacological relationship to the phenotype during target validation. Target identification and validation are iterative. HTS and knowledge-based screening are popular experimental screening strategies [40]. HTS uses automated robotics to swiftly execute millions of assays to match drug-like features with massive libraries of chemicals without previous knowledge. Focused screening narrows compounds to a smaller group that may have therapeutic target activity from literature or patent precedents [41]. Optimisation examines compound potency, selectivity, toxicity, safety, molecular mechanism, and distribution [42]. For lead compounds with poor activity intensity or specificity, incorrect pharmacokinetic properties, significant toxic side effects, or chemical or metabolic instability, developers modify the chemical structure to create a balanced development candidate. Pre-clinical testing is usually *in vitro* or *in vivo* [43]. Many years pass during preclinical testing. Pre-clinical trials gather efficacy, toxicological, pharmacokinetic, and pharmacodynamic data. The safe dose for human research is determined using this information. *In vitro* testing analyzes drug-molecule interactions in test tubes and labs.

Drug compounds are tested *in vivo* using animal models and living cell cultures [44]. How a medicine is absorbed and removed from the body, its side effects, and its efficacy are examined in clinical trials [45]. For this purpose, a few dozen healthy volunteers for maximum performance and safety doses are included. The patient pool is expanded from a few dozen to 100+ to determine the dose when numerous doses were tested [46]. Drug developers consider increasing manufacturing if this phase of testing is successful. It is the phase of drug research that lasts the longest and costs the most money. Drugs can fail clinical trials and be pulled from the process at any stage [47]. A pharmaceutical business may stop development for many reasons. Clinical and operational factors may cause failure. Ineffectiveness, safety, poor study design, and lack of financing are major reasons for trial failure [48].

AI has significantly revolutionized drug development and research, making profound impacts across various aspects of the field, as shown in Fig. (**2**). Some of AI's notable contributions include:

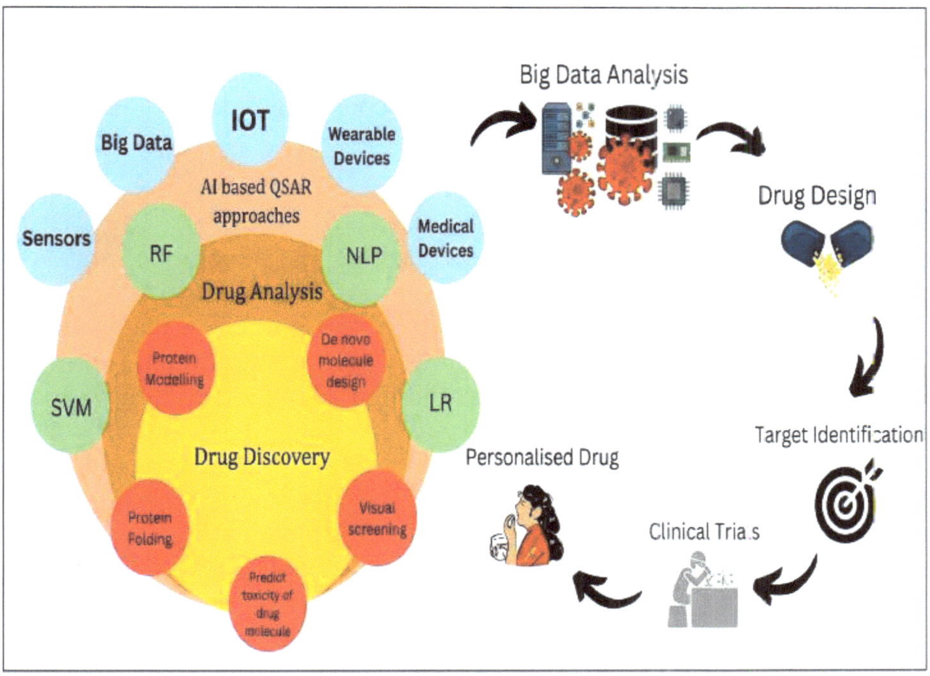

Fig. (2). Integration of AI and IoT in the drug development process.

IDENTIFICATION OF THE TARGET

To identify potential therapeutic targets, AI algorithms draw on a range of data sources, including genetic data, proteomic profiles, and clinical records. By identifying disease-related biological pathways and targets, these algorithms pave the way for more effective medication development [49].

The Use of Virtual Displays

It is now possible to efficiently screen extensive chemical libraries for potential therapeutic candidates likely to bind specific targets using AI [50]. AI helps to save time and costs by predicting binding strengths and modelling chemical interactions to prioritise compounds for experimental testing [51].

Relationship Between Structure and Activity (SAR)

AI modelling helps link a compound's chemical structure to its biological consequences. (Paul *et al.*, 2021). This capability empowers researchers to design compounds with specific characteristics such as potent efficacy, targeted selectivity, and favorable pharmacokinetic profiles, aiming to enhance therapeutic efficacy [52]. AI-driven QSAR methodologies, including LDA, SVMs, RF, and DT, have emerged as robust tools for accelerating QSAR investigations [53]. These techniques use machine learning algorithms to automate and streamline the discovery of relationships between chemical structures and biological activities. LDA is a statistical technique that is adept at separating data into discrete classes based on inherent patterns [54].

Design of Novo Drugs

AI, through techniques like reinforcement learning and generative models, offers powerful tools for suggesting novel chemical structures akin to pharmaceuticals [55]. AI broadens chemical space research by utilising massive chemical libraries and empirical data, helping uncover new potential treatment options [56]. Reinforcement learning enhances understanding of how a compound's biological effects correlate with its molecular structure [57], aiding the design of compounds with specific attributes, such as high potency, selectivity, and favorable pharmacokinetic profiles, to optimize therapeutic potential [58]. AI-driven QSAR methodologies, such as LDA, SVMs, RF, and DT, have emerged as robust tools for accelerating Quantitative Structure-Activity Relationship (QSAR) studies [59]. These methods harness the capabilities of machine learning algorithms to automate and streamline the process of uncovering connections between chemical structures and biological activities.LDA functions as a statistical technique adept at segregating data into discrete classes based on inherent patterns [60].

Drug Candidate Optimisation

AI algorithms have the capability to consider numerous variables such as pharmacokinetics, safety, and efficacy when evaluating and refining drug candidates [61]. This helps scientists optimise therapeutic molecules for better efficacy with fewer side effects [62].

Repurposing Drugs

Drug repurposing represents a promising avenue in drug discovery, aiming to repurpose existing medications for new therapeutic purposes, thereby minimizing time and economic expenditures [63]. Leveraging AI techniques to analyze vast biomedical datasets facilitates the identification of potential uses for medications already approved for other conditions. AI speeds up and lowers the cost of drug research by finding new uses for old medications [64].

Estimating Toxicity

By analysing the chemical and structural features of molecules, AI systems can predict which drugs are hazardous to the body [65]. Machine learning models trained on extensive toxicological databases can effectively identify potentially hazardous structural elements or anticipate adverse outcomes [66]. Researchers can use this predictive power to reduce the likelihood of adverse reactions in clinical trials and select safer chemicals for future development [67]. Toxtree, LimTox, pkCSM, and admetSAR are some of the web-based tools that are vital for reducing the costs of drug development and safety assessments (Table 1) [68]. These tools offer free or affordable access to predictive models and databases, minimizing the need for expensive experimental testing [69]. LimTox provides toxicity predictions for environmental chemicals, aiding in risk assessment and reducing the expenses associated with traditional testing methods [70]. pkCSM offers computational models to predict pharmacokinetic properties, assisting in optimizing drug development processes by minimizing costly experimental studies (Paul *et al.*, 2021). admetSAR specializes in forecasting ADMET characteristics of chemical compounds, providing valuable insights during initial screening phases and minimizing the costs associated with conducting *in vitro* and *in vivo* experiments [71].

Table 1. Examples of AI-based tools in drug discovery.

Tool	Description	References
AlphaFold2	Protein structure prediction using deep learning	[72]

(Table 1) cont.....

Tool	Description	References
DeepChem	Deep learning library for chemistry applications	[73]
DeepBind	Predicts sequence-specific RNA and DNA binding	[74]
DeepBar	A tool for analyzing protein binding sites	[75]
DeepScreen	Virtual screening tool for drug discovery	[76]
DeepConv-DTI	Deep learning for drug-target interaction	[77]
DeepPurpose	Framework for drug discovery with deep learning	[78]
DeepTox	Predicts the toxicity of a chemical compounds	[79]
AtomNet	Neural network for drug discovery and design	[80]
PathDSP	Pathway-based drug sensitivity prediction	[81]

IoT in Pharmaceutical Drug Development

IoT speeds up the process of finding successful solutions. Clinical trials, which typically consume 70% of the time required for FDA approval of a new drug, are expedited through IoT applications [82]. These tests must prove the remedy is safe and effective. The FDA usually allows the producer to create the medicine for the trial application alone. IoT can improve formulation selection and save development costs [83]. Cell-in-a-Chip or Organ-in-a-Chip are miniature laboratory trays made from tissue engineering that allow experiments and convey the chip's results after pharmaceutical component deposition [84]. Their live, tiny habitat duplicates essential physiological characteristics of the human body and reports parameters in real time *via* a smart interface. By administering the innovative medical formulation *via* the chip and then recording the material's reaction, we may learn about its absorption level, its interactions with other organs, and how it affects the sick [85]. IoT also simplifies clinical studies by tracking individuals' health outside research centres where the medicine is normally administered. It eliminates the need for regular check-ins and opens eligibility to those who cannot go far [86].

While people go about their everyday lives, smart health devices and wearable sensors record their physiological data in real-time and upload it to the cloud [87]. In February 2019, Current Health received FDA approval for an AI-powered arm-worn device that tracks vital signs from hospital settings to patients' homes. This device collaborates with pharmaceutical companies to monitor clinical trial participants remotely [88]. IoT sensors gather and upload production parameters to the cloud, providing comprehensive insights into the sequence of events and the origins of each ingredient in a recipe. Parameters such as temperature, humidity, gas exposure, and radiation are monitored. The cloud-based AI can detect minor degradation, predict trends, adjust the environment, or warn of potentially disastrous outcomes without intervention. It can also alert users to possible equipment failures or irregularities [89]. With IoT, pharmaceutical companies can monitor their medicines from the moment they are manufactured through to the patient's home, which is a huge boon. This capability ensures monitoring of conditions when a bottle of pills leaves a controlled environment, travels through shipping containers, trucks, and pharmacy storage rooms, and finally reaches the patient's care and home [90]. In a sector where precision is critical, understanding the supply chains and the specific conditions affecting each patient is essential. The Internet of Things (IoT) offers extensive tracking capabilities that significantly enhance drug monitoring and patient care. It monitors the journey of medication from the controlled environment of the manufacturing facility through shipment, storage in pharmacies, and finally to the patient's home. Additionally, IoT devices can verify the efficacy of treatments through physiological responses. Wearable sensors provide real-time data on cardiac health, mobility, and other health improvements [91]. For example, AliveCor's KardiaMobile is a medical-grade ECG device that captures cardiac data *via* a thin, metallic pad on the patient's fingertips, then transmits the information *via* Bluetooth to an iOS or Android device. Similarly, the Apple Watch can alert users aged 65 and older to abnormal heart rate and fall events, while the Motiv Ring connects to a smartphone to monitor heart rate and sleep patterns [92].

AI and IoT Integration in Pharmaceutical Manufacturing

The goal of modern manufacturing systems is to replace human knowledge with automated machinery in response to rising demands for more efficient operations and better quality products ("Adaptations of Pharma 4.0 from Industry 4.0. | Drug Invention Today | EBSCOhost," n.d.). The integration of AI in manufacturing holds substantial promise for the pharmaceutical industry. CFD thereby automates numerous pharmaceutical operations [93]. AI and IoT integration in pharmaceutical manufacturing offers significant advantages in enhancing operational efficiency, ensuring quality control, and meeting regulatory standards. By harnessing AI and IoT capabilities, pharmaceutical manufacturers can optimize production processes, monitor equipment performance in real-time, and streamline inventory management Table **2** [94]. DEM has found widespread application in pharmaceuticals, such as studying powder segregation in binary mixtures, predicting tablet paths during coating processes, and optimizing tablet production by analyzing factors like blade speed and shape [95]. ANNs and fuzzy models have been instrumental in understanding correlations between machine settings and tablet defects like capping on manufacturing lines [96]. Advanced AI tools such as Meta-classifiers and tablet-classifiers are employed to uphold stringent quality standards, identifying potential errors in tablet manufacturing processes [97]. Innovative systems, including patented technologies, are designed to customize medication regimens based on individual patient data, such as developing personalized transdermal patches tailored to specific therapeutic requirements [98].

Table 2. Examples of IoT tools used in drug discovery.

IoT Tool	Description	References
Proteus Discover	Digital medicine platform for medication adherence.	[99]
MC10 BioStamp	Wearable sensor for health data monitoring.	[100]
PhysIQ	Continuous monitoring for clinical trials.	[101]
Tactio Health	An IoT platform for remote patient monitoring.	[102]
VitalPatch	Wireless biosensor for vital signs monitoring.	[103]
ActiGraph	Activity monitors for remote patient monitoring.	[104]
Biovotion Everion	Wearable sensor for health and wellness tracking.	[105]
Empatica E4	Wearable device for physiological data collection.	[106]
Hexoskin	Smart garment for continuous health monitoring.	[107]
Current Health	Remote patient monitoring platform.	[108]
Zephyr BioPatch	Wearable biosensor for physiological monitoring.	[109]
Biostrap	Health tracking wearable for sleep and activity.	[110]
Garmin Health	Wearable devices for health and fitness tracking.	[111]
Apple Health	Health monitoring platform by Apple.	[112]

(Table 2) cont.....

IoT Tool	Description	References
Samsung Health	Health monitoring platform by Samsung.	[113]
Fitbit	Wearable devices for fitness and health tracking.	[114]
Omron Healthcare	Remote patient monitoring Devices.	[115]
Withings	Health-focused IoT devices for monitoring.	[116]
Moov	Wearable fitness tracker and coaching platform.	[117]
MySignals	eHealth IoT development platform.	[118]

ADVANTAGES OF AI AND IOT IN DRUG DEVELOPMENT

Robotics and the Internet of Things are reshaping numerous markets, including the pharmaceutical industry. When AI and IoT are integrated into the drug development process, several advantages occur:

- Integration and Analysis of Data:

AI systems can help researchers discover trends, patterns, and potential correlations by evaluating massive amounts of chemical, biological, and clinical data. IoT devices, such as smart instruments, sensors, and wearables, can generate data in real-time. Because of this, AI systems can process data continuously.

- Personalised Health Care: Artificial Intelligence (AI)

Facilitates the creation of customised treatment regimens by analysing clinical, molecular, and genetic data to identify drug reactions specific to each patient. IoT: Real-time patient data collection from connected devices enables ongoing monitoring and personalised treatment plan modifications.

- Drug Research and Development: AI

By forecasting potential therapeutic options, examining molecular interactions, proposing innovative combinations, and keeping tabs on clinical trials and providing real-time data, AI helps the drug discovery process move along more quickly. Additionally, sensors and gadgets can make drug testing and screening more effective. The application of AI and IoT in drug development is shown in Fig. (**3**).

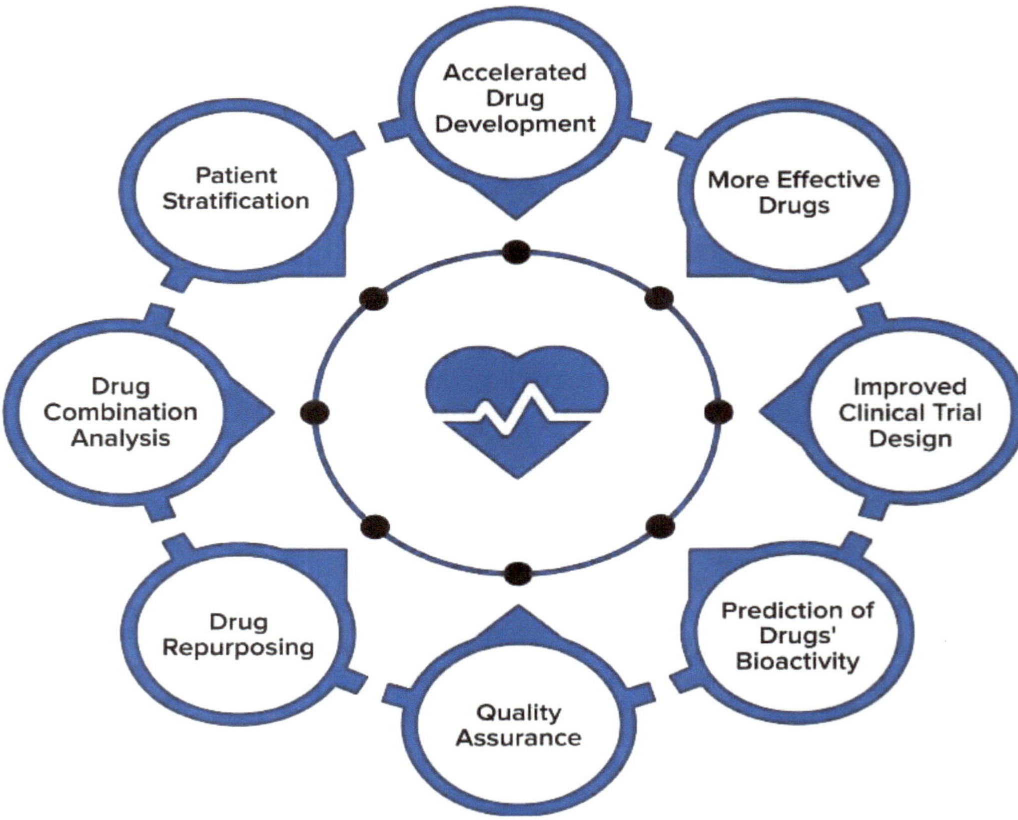

Fig. (3). Application of AI and IoT in drug development.

- Optimising Clinical Trials

When it comes to proving the efficacy and safety of medical treatments or interventions, clinical trials are the gold standard. The evidence they provide is crucial for informing medical practices and health policies. The purpose of these studies is to test the effectiveness and safety of new medications in human subjects for specific medical disorders. This process usually takes around six to seven years and a lot of money. However, leveraging vast digital medical data through AI implementation has the potential to mitigate these challenges. Artificial Intelligence (AI) can streamline clinical trials by facilitating the identification of suitable patient cohorts, predicting trial outcomes, and optimizing trial designs. By analyzing patient-specific genome and exposome profiles, AI can assist in selecting precise patient populations for enrollment in Phase II and III trials, thereby predicting drug efficacy early in the process. Liu *et al.* have introduced an open-source AI tool named Trial Pathfinder, which uses Electronic Health Records (EHRs) to simulate clinical trials. This tool analyzes various inclusion criteria and assesses overall survival risk ratios, revealing that some commonly used criteria have minimal impact on trial outcomes. Research using Trial Pathfinder has demonstrated that only 30% of treated patients met the inclusion criteria specified for each trial (Liu *et al.*, 2021). IoT and connected devices can improve clinical trials by increasing patient retention and reducing trial duration. To reap the benefits, life science companies need to collate, process, and transmit IoT data to healthcare providers in compliance. Today, pharmaceutical companies are keen to adopt effective drug development models to address key parameters, such as effective safety monitoring and retention management during trials. Using IoT devices for remote patient monitoring can improve data collection during clinical studies, producing more thorough and reliable results. Clinicians are now more aware of the immense potential of IoT-based devices in clinical research, and it is expected to grow rapidly. Clinicians are now more aware of the immense potential of IoT-based devices in clinical research, and it is expected to grow rapidly(Sato *et al.*, 2022With a valuation of USD 44.21 billion in 2023, the global market for healthcare IoT is expected to develop from 2024 to 2030 at a CAGR (compound annual growth rate) of 21.2%.

- Drug Safety Predictive Analytics

Artificial Intelligence: Assists in anticipating possible negative outcomes and safety issues by examining past data and spotting trends that conventional approaches might miss. IoT: By employing IoT devices to continuously monitor patients, early adverse event detection is facilitated, improving the evaluation of drug safety.

- Optimisation of the Supply Chain

Artificial Intelligence (AI): Boosts production efficiency by streamlining drug manufacturing procedures, anticipating equipment malfunctions, and guaranteeing quality control. IoT: Maintains the integrity of pharmaceutical items by tracking temperature, humidity, and other environmental factors in real-time throughout the supply chain.

- Remote Patient Observation: AI

Reviews patient records to provide insight into illness progression, therapy success, and potential medication adjustments. IoT provides constant remote patient monitoring, enabling medical professionals to act quickly by utilising real-time data.

- Privacy and Data Security

Advances in encryption, blockchain, and secure communication protocols assist in addressing these concerns and ensure the preservation of sensitive health information. AI and IoT: Present challenges relating to data security and privacy.

CONCLUSION

The convergence of AI and the IoT is propelling the ever-changing world of drug discovery and development. AI's predictive abilities and the IoT's capability to gather real-time data have fundamentally reshaped all aspects of innovation in pharmaceuticals, marking a transformative era in healthcare. AI's advancements and sophisticated tools are consistently aimed at tackling the challenges pharmaceutical firms face, profoundly influencing the process of drug development and product lifecycle, and contributing significantly to the rise of startups in this field. Integration of AI algorithms, including machine learning and deep learning models, enables swift analysis of vast biological datasets, accelerating tasks such as identifying novel compounds, forecasting molecular interactions, and advancing initiatives in personalized medicine. The fusion of IoT networks with drug delivery systems has revolutionized how medications are administered and monitored, empowering healthcare providers to deliver treatments with heightened accuracy, efficiency, and safety. Improved medication adherence, individualized dosages, and remote monitoring are just a few ways in which drug delivery systems enabled by the Internet of Things have the potential to revolutionise patient care. Wearable technology and smart tablets provide real-time monitoring of patients' vital signs and medication usage, enabling prompt adjustments to treatment strategies. With the help of implantable devices, patients can successfully manage their chronic illnesses. These devices provide continuous monitoring and customised medicine delivery. As we move forward, industry collaboration and innovation stand as catalysts for further advancements. To standardise methods, navigate regulatory complexity, and cultivate ethical practices, it is crucial for researchers, healthcare practitioners, lawmakers, and technology developers to collaborate. This unified approach will accelerate the integration of AI and IoT, ushering in a new era of drug discovery marked by efficiency, efficacy, and patient-centricity.

REFERENCES

[1] "Adaptations of Pharma 4.0 from Industry 4.0", *Drug Invention Today*. | EBSCOhost [WWW Document], n.d. URL https://openurl.ebsco.com/EPDB%3Agcd%3A9%3A7561705/detailv2?sid=ebsco%3Aplink%3Ascholarid=ebsco%3Agcd%3A142952419crl=c (accessed 1.16.24)

[2] S Ahmad, S Qazi, and K Raza, "Translational bioinformatics methods for drug discovery and drug repurposing", *Translational Bioinformatics in Healthcare and Medicine,* pp. 127-139, 2021. [http://dx.doi.org/10.1016/B978-0-323-89824-9.00010-0]

[3] L Ai, and H Yu, "Real-time intravascular shear stress in the rabbit abdominal aorta", *IEEE Trans Biomed Eng,* vol. 56, pp. 1755-1764, 2009. [http://dx.doi.org/10.1109/TBME.2009.2013455]

[4] "AI's potential to accelerate drug discovery needs a reality check", *Nature,* vol. 622, p. 217, 2023. [http://dx.doi.org/10.1038/D41586-023-03172-6]

[5] S Alagarsamy, "Applications of Internet of Things in Pharmaceutical Industry", *SSRN Electron J,* 2019. [http://dx.doi.org/10.2139/SSRN.3441099]

[6] M. D. Aleo, F. Shah, S. Allen, H. A. Barton, C. Costales, S. Lazzaro, L. Leung, A. Nilson, R. S. Obach, A. D. Rodrigues, and Y. Will, "Moving Beyond Binary Predictions of Human Drug-Induced Liver Injury (DILI) toward Contrasting Relative Risk Potential", *Chemical Research in Toxicology,* vol. 33, no. 1, pp. 223-238, 2020. [http://dx.doi.org/10.1021/acs.chemrestox.9b00262]

[7] A. Anbalagan, and C. F. Moreno-Garcia, "An IoT-based Industry 4.0 architecture for integration of design and manufacturing systems", *Materials Today: Proceedings,* vol. 46, pp. 7135-7142, 2021. [http://dx.doi.org/10.1016/j.matpr.2020.11.196]

[8] N. S. Arden, A. C. Fisher, K. Tyner, L. X. Yu, S. L. Lee, and M. Kopcha, "Industry 4.0 for pharmaceutical manufacturing: Preparing for the smart factories of the future", *International Journal of Pharmaceutics,* vol. 602, p. 120554, 2021. [http://dx.doi.org/10.1016/j.ijpharm.2021.120554]

[9] J. F. Arinez, Q. Chang, R. X. Gao, C. Xu, and J. Zhang, "Artificial Intelligence in Advanced Manufacturing: Current Status and Future Outlook", *Journal of Manufacturing Science and Engineering,* vol. 142, no. 11, p. 110804, 2020. [http://dx.doi.org/10.1115/1.4047855]

[10] J. Bajorath, "State-of-the-art of artificial intelligence in medicinal chemistry", *Future Science OA,* vol. 7, no. 8, p. FSOA702, 2021. [http://dx.doi.org/10.2144/fsoa-2021-0030]

[11] J. Bajwa, U. Munir, A. Nori, and B. Williams, "Artificial intelligence in healthcare: Transforming the practice of medicine", *Future Healthcare Journal,* vol. 8, no. 2, pp. e188-e194, 2021. [http://dx.doi.org/10.7861/fhj.2021-0095]

[12] A. Banerjee, C. Chakraborty, A. Kumar, and D. Biswas, "Emerging trends in IoT and big data analytics for biomedical and health care technologies", In: *Handbook of Data Science Approaches for Biomedical Engineering* Academic Press, 2020, pp. 121-152. [http://dx.doi.org/10.1016/B978-0-12-818318-2.00005-2]

[13] M. Basingab, "Distributed Simulation with Multi-Agents for IoT in a Retail Pharmacy Facility", *Information,* vol. 11, no. 11, p. 527, 2020. [http://dx.doi.org/10.3390/info11110527]

[14] M. Basingab, U. Balamesh, R. Bafaqih, O. Alamoudi, A. Hesiki, and A. Alghefari, *Agent-Based Modeling For Internet Of Things (IoT) Application In A Retail Pharmacy Industry,* vol. 11, pp. 1266-1275, 2020.

[15] T. J. Bateman, "Drug discovery", In: *Atkinson's Principles of Clinical Pharmacology* Academic Press, 2022, pp. 563-572.
[http://dx.doi.org/10.1016/B978-0-12-819869-8.00019-7]

[16] V. J. Beltrán-Carrillo, A. Jiménez-Loaisa, M. Alarcón-López, and J. L. L. Elvira, "Validity of the "Samsung Health" application to measure steps: A study with two different samsung smartphones", *Journal of Sports Sciences,* vol. 37, no. 7, pp. 788-794, 2019.
[http://dx.doi.org/10.1080/02640414.2018.1527199]

[17] A. Bender, and I. Cortés-Ciriano, "Artificial intelligence in drug discovery: what is realistic, what are illusions? Part 1: Ways to make an impact, and why we are not there yet", *Drug Discovery Today,* vol. 26, no. 2, pp. 511-524, 2021.
[http://dx.doi.org/10.1016/j.drudis.2020.12.009]

[18] P. Bhatt, S. Singh, V. Kumar, K. Nagarajan, S. K. Mishra, P. K. Dixit, V. Kumar, and S. Kumar, "Artificial intelligence in pharmaceutical industry: Revolutionizing drug development and delivery", *The Chinese Journal of Artificial Intelligence,* vol. 2, no. 3, 2023.
[http://dx.doi.org/10.2174/0129503752250813231124092946]

[19] A. Blanco-González, A. Cabezón, A. Seco-González, D. Conde-Torres, P. Antelo-Riveiro, Á. Piñeiro, and R. García-Fandiño, "The role of AI in drug discovery: Challenges, opportunities, and strategies", *Pharmaceuticals,* vol. 16, no. 6, p. 891, 2023.
[http://dx.doi.org/10.3390/ph16060891]

[20] P. Singh, M. Kansal, A. P. Singh, A. Verma, S. Tyagi, and A. V. Singh, "Real-time symptomatic disease predictor using multi-layer perceptron", In: *Future of AI in Medical Imaging* IGI Global: Hershey (PA), 2024, pp. 155-167.
[http://dx.doi.org/10.4018/979-8-3693-2173-7.ch009]

[21] S Brogi, and V Calderone, "Artificial intelligence in translational medicine", *International Journal of Translational Medicine,* vol. 1, pp. 223-285, 2021.
[http://dx.doi.org/10.3390/IJTM1030016]

[22] PM Chanal, MS Kakkasageri, and SKS Manvi, "Security and privacy in the internet of things: computational intelligent techniques-based approaches", *Recent Trends in Computational Intelligence Enabled Research,* pp. 111-127, 2021.
[http://dx.doi.org/10.1016/B978-0-12-822844-9.00009-8]

[23] H Chang, JY Choi, J Shim, M Kim, and M Choi, "Benefits of information technology in healthcare: Artificial intelligence, internet of things, and personal health records", *Healthcare Informatics Research,* vol. 29, p. 323, 2023.
[http://dx.doi.org/10.4258/HIR.2023.29.4.323]

[24] J Chen, X Luo, H Qiu, V Mackey, L Sun, and X Ouyang, "Drug discovery and drug marketing with the critical roles of modern administration", *American Journal of Translational Research,* vol. 10, p. 4302, 2018.

[25] Y Chen, O Yang, C Sampat, P Bhalode, R Ramachandran, and M Ierapetritou, "Digital twins in pharmaceutical and biopharmaceutical manufacturing: A literature review", *Processes,* vol. 8, p. 1088, 2020.
[http://dx.doi.org/10.3390/PR8091088]

[26] S Cho, and SH Lee, "Development of smart healthcare scheduling monitoring system for elderly health care", *International Journal of Internet, Broadcasting and Communication,* vol. 10, pp. 51-59, 2018.
[http://dx.doi.org/10.7236/IJIBC.2018.10.2.9]

[27] S Colombo, "Applications of artificial intelligence in drug delivery and pharmaceutical development", *Artificial Intelligence in Healthcare,* pp. 85-116, 2020.
[http://dx.doi.org/10.1016/B978-0-12-818438-7.00004-6]

[28] A.V. Creaser, *Wearable activity trackers for young people: usability, acceptability, feasibility, and behaviour change* Loughborough University: UK, 2022. [http://dx.doi.org/10.26174/THESIS.LBORO.22961723.V1]

[29] G Danan, and C Benichou, "Causality assessment of adverse reactions to drugs—I', *Journal of Clinical Epidemiology,* vol. 46, pp. 1323-1330, 1993. [http://dx.doi.org/10.1016/0895-4356(93)90101-6]

[30] M Kansal, P Singh, P Srivastava, R Singhal, N Deep, and A Singh, "Mental health monitoring in the digital age: a comprehensive analysis", *Future of AI in Medical Imaging,* IGI Global, pp. 168-183, 2024.

[31] M Dickson, and JP Gagnon, "Key factors in the rising cost of new drug discovery and development", *Nature Reviews Drug Discovery,* vol. 3, pp. 417-429, 2004. [http://dx.doi.org/10.1038/nrd1382]

[32] DV Dimitrov, "Medical Internet of Things and Big Data in Healthcare", *Healthcare Informatics Research,* vol. 22, pp. 156-163, 2016. [http://dx.doi.org/10.4258/HIR.2016.22.3.156]

[33] X Ding, and B Zhang, "DeepBAR: A Fast and Exact Method for Binding Free Energy Computation", *Journal of Physical Chemistry Letters,* vol. 12, p. 2509, 2021. [http://dx.doi.org/10.1021/ACS.JPCLETT.1C00189]

[34] "Target Validation; Drug Development Challenges", In: *Institute of Medicine* National Academies Press: Washington (DC), 2014.

[35] J Dulsat, B López-Nieto, R Estrada-Tejedor, and JI Borrell, "Evaluation of Free Online ADMET Tools for Academic or Small Biotech Environments", *Molecules,* vol. 28, 2023. [http://dx.doi.org/10.3390/MOLECULES28020776]

[36] N El-Rashidy, S El-Sappagh, SMR Islam, HM El-Bakry, and S Abdelrazek, "Mobile Health in Remote Patient Monitoring for Chronic Diseases: Principles, Trends, and Challenges", *Diagnostics,* vol. 11, p. 607, 2021. [http://dx.doi.org/10.3390/DIAGNOSTICS11040607]

[37] A Etzion-Fuchs, DA Todd, and M Singh, "dSPRINT: predicting DNA, RNA, ion, peptide and small molecule interaction sites within protein domains", *Nucleic Acids Research,* vol. 49, p. e78, 2021. [http://dx.doi.org/10.1093/NAR/GKAB356]

[38] X Fan, M Gong, Y Xie, F Jiang, and H Li, "Structured self-attention architecture for graph-level representation learning", *Pattern Recognition,* vol. 100, p. 107084, 2020. [http://dx.doi.org/10.1016/J.PATCOG.2019.107084]

[39] P Singh, M Kansal, S Lahiri, H Vishnoi, and L Mittal, "A Transparency System for ICU Using Machine Learning and AI", *Enhancing Medical Imaging with Emerging Technologies,* IGI Global, pp. 51-69, 2024.

[40] P. Singh, M. Kansal, S. Lahiri, H. Vishnoi, and L. Mittal, "A transparency system for ICU using machine learning and AI", *Enhancing Medical Imaging with Emerging Technologies,* IGI Global, pp. 51-69, 2024.

[41] C. Grebner, H. Matter, and G. Hessler, "Artificial intelligence in compound design", In: *Methods Mol. Biol.* vol. 2390. , 2022, pp. 349-382. [http://dx.doi.org/10.1007/978-1-0716-1787-8_15]

[42] "Healthcare IoT – worldwide", *Statista Market Forecast,* 2024.https://www.statista.com/outlook/tmo/internet-of-things/healthcare-iot/worldwide

[43] F. F. Hefti, "Requirements for a lead compound to become a clinical candidate", *BMC Neurosci.,* vol. 9, p. S7, 2008. [http://dx.doi.org/10.1186/1471-2202-9-S3-S7]

[44] O. D. Howes, and M. A. Mehta, "Challenges in CNS drug development and the role of imaging", *Psychopharmacology (Berl.),* vol. 238, pp. 1229-1230, 2021. [http://dx.doi.org/10.1007/S00213-021-05838-3]

[45] K. Huang, T. Fu, L. M. Glass, M. Zitnik, C. Xiao, and J. Sun, "DeepPurpose: a deep learning library for drug-target interaction prediction", *Bioinformatics,* vol. 36, pp. 5545-5547, 2021. [http://dx.doi.org/10.1093/bioinformatics/btaa1005]

[46] J. P. Hughes, S. S. Rees, S. B. Kalindjian, and K. L. Philpott, "Principles of early drug discovery", *Br. J. Pharmacol.,* vol. 162, p. 1239, 2011. [http://dx.doi.org/10.1111/j.1476-5381.2010.01127.x]

[47] J. P. Hughes, S. S. Rees, S. B. Kalindjian, and K. L. Philpott, "Principles of early drug discovery", *Br. J. Pharmacol.,* vol. 162, p. 1239, 2011. [http://dx.doi.org/10.1111/j.1476-5381.2010.01127.x]

[48] O. T. Inan, "Digitizing clinical trials", *npj Digit. Med.,* vol. 3, pp. 1-7, 2020. [http://dx.doi.org/10.1038/s41746-020-0302-y]

[49] M. Jamshidi, "Future of drug discovery: the synergy of edge computing, Internet of Medical Things, and deep learning", *Future Internet,* vol. 15, p. 142, 2023. [http://dx.doi.org/10.3390/fi15040142]

[50] P. Singh, A. Asthana, B. Solanki, S. Tomar, M. Kansal, and G. Tyagi, "A comprehensive analysis and sensitivity model for emotion detection in text", *Applications of Artificial Intelligence in 5G and Internet of Things,* CRC Press, pp. 332-337, 2025.

[51] K. B. Johnson, "Precision medicine, AI, and the future of personalized health care", *Clin. Transl. Sci.,* vol. 14, p. 86, 2021. [http://dx.doi.org/10.1111/cts.12884]

[52] A. Kishor, and C. Chakraborty, "Artificial intelligence and Internet of Things based healthcare 4.0 monitoring system", *Wirel. Pers. Commun.,* vol. 127, pp. 1615-1631, 2022. [http://dx.doi.org/10.1007/s11277-021-08708-5]

[53] G. Krikorian, and E. Torreele, "We cannot win the access to medicines struggle using the same thinking that causes the chronic access crisis", *Health Hum. Rights,* vol. 23, p. 119, 2021.

[54] N. F. Lahens, "Time-specific associations of wearable sensor-based cardiovascular and behavioral readouts with disease phenotypes in the outpatient setting of the chronic renal insufficiency cohort", *Digit. Health,* vol. 8, 2022. [http://dx.doi.org/10.1177/20552076221107903]

[55] J. H. Lam, "A deep learning framework to predict binding preference of RNA constituents on protein surface", *Nat. Commun.,* vol. 10, pp. 1-13, 2019. [http://dx.doi.org/10.1038/s41467-019-12920-0]

[56] G. Latif, "I-CARES: advancing health diagnosis and medication through IoT", *Wireless Netw.,* vol. 26, pp. 2375-2389, 2020. [http://dx.doi.org/10.1007/s11276-019-02165-6]

[57] I. Lee, J. Keum, and H. Nam, "DeepConv-DTI: prediction of drug-target interactions via deep learning with convolution on protein sequences", *PLoS Comput. Biol.,* vol. 15, 2019. [http://dx.doi.org/10.1371/journal.pcbi.1007129]

[58] G. S. Liu, "Performance evaluation for the IoT-based manufacturing system in pharmacy industry", *Int. J. Interact. Des. Manuf.,* 2023. [http://dx.doi.org/10.1007/s12008-023-01592-2]

[59] R. Liu, "Evaluating eligibility criteria of oncology trials using real-world data and AI", *Nature,* vol. 592, pp. 629-633, 2021. [http://dx.doi.org/10.1038/s41586-021-03430-5]

[60] P. Singh, and M. Kansal, "An online platform for timely access to medical care with the help of real-time data analysis", *Wellness Management Powered by AI Technologies,* pp. 103-131, 2025.

[61] M. K. Mahapatra, and M. Karuppasamy, "Fundamental considerations in drug design", *Computer Aided Drug Design (CADD): From Ligand-Based Methods to Structure-Based Approaches,* vol. 17, 2022.
[http://dx.doi.org/10.1016/B978-0-323-90608-1.00005-8]

[62] P. Manickam, S. A. Mariappan, and S. M. Murugesan, "Artificial intelligence (AI) and Internet of Medical Things (IoMT) assisted biomedical systems for intelligent healthcare", *Biosensors (Basel),* vol. 12, 2022.
[http://dx.doi.org/10.3390/bios12080562]

[63] M. M. Baig, H. Gholamhosseini, and M. J. Connolly, "Remote patient monitoring system: evaluation of medical devices from patients' perspective", *Health Care and Informatics Review Online,* 2014.

[64] J. Mao, "Comprehensive strategies of machine-learning-based quantitative structure–activity relationship models", *iScience,* vol. 24, p. 103052, 2021.
[http://dx.doi.org/10.1016/j.isci.2021.103052]

[65] J. L. Martin, and A. D. Hakim, "Wrist actigraphy", *Chest,* vol. 139, p. 1514, 2011.
[http://dx.doi.org/10.1378/chest.10-1872]

[66] A. Mayr, "DeepTox: toxicity prediction using deep learning", *Front. Environ. Sci.,* vol. 3, 2016.
[http://dx.doi.org/10.3389/fenvs.2015.00080]

[67] F. Miljković, R. Rodríguez-Pérez, and J. Bajorath, "Impact of artificial intelligence on compound discovery, design, and synthesis", *ACS Omega,* vol. 6, pp. 33293-33299, 2021.
[http://dx.doi.org/10.1021/acsomega.1c05512]

[68] G. Mitsi, "Implementing digital technologies in clinical trials: lessons learned", *Innov. Clin. Neurosci.,* vol. 19, p. 65, 2022.

[69] S. G. Morgan, H. S. Bathula, and S. Moon, "Pricing of pharmaceuticals is becoming a major challenge for health systems", *BMJ,* vol. 368, 2020.
[http://dx.doi.org/10.1136/bmj.l4627]

[70] H. Motahari-Nezhad, F. Zare, H. Akbari, and A. Sadeghdaghighi, "Health outcomes of Fitbit, Garmin or Apple Watch-based interventions: A systematic review of systematic reviews", *Journal of Biomedical Informatics,* vol. 133, p. 104165, 2022.

[71] R. Goel, U. K. Jaiswal, and P. Singh, "Deep learning for early brain tumor detection: a Keras-based approach using MRI and CT imaging", *Demystifying the Role of Natural Language Processing (NLP) in Mental Health,* IGI Global Scientific Publishing, pp. 145-180, 2025.

[72] B. Munos, "Lessons from 60 years of pharmaceutical innovation", *Nat. Rev. Drug Discov.,* vol. 8, pp. 959-968, 2009.
[http://dx.doi.org/10.1038/nrd2961]

[73] J. G. Nahr, H. Nozari, and M. E. Sadeghi, "Green supply chain based on artificial intelligence of things (AIoT)", *Int. J. Innov. Manag. Econ. Soc. Sci.,* vol. 1, pp. 56-63, 2021.
[http://dx.doi.org/10.52547/ijimes.1.2.56]

[74] S. Nandi, M. Mishra, and S. Majumder, "Usage of AI and wearable IoT devices for healthcare data: a study", *Machine Learning Algorithms for Signal and Image Processing,* pp. 315-337, 2022.
[http://dx.doi.org/10.1002/9781119861850.ch18]

[75] M. Nasseri, "Signal quality and patient experience with wearable devices for epilepsy management", *Epilepsia,* vol. 61, no. Suppl 1, pp. S25-S35, 2020.
[http://dx.doi.org/10.1111/epi.16527]

[76] National Academies of Sciences, Engineering, and Medicine, *Drug Development for Nervous System Disorders: Overview of Challenges and Potential Opportunities* National Academies Press:

Washington (DC), 2017.
[http://dx.doi.org/10.17226/24672]

[77] S. K. Niazi, and Z. Mariam, "Recent advances in machine-learning-based chemoinformatics: a comprehensive review", *Int. J. Mol. Sci.,* vol. 24, p. 11488, 2023.
[http://dx.doi.org/10.3390/ijms241411488]

[78] A. Nishikawa, "Remote vital signs data monitoring during home blood transfusion: a pilot study", *Health Sci. Rep.,* vol. 4, 2021.
[http://dx.doi.org/10.1002/hsr2.380]

[79] O. Obrezanova, "Artificial intelligence for compound pharmacokinetics prediction", *Curr. Opin. Struct. Biol.,* vol. 79, p. 102546, 2023.
[http://dx.doi.org/10.1016/j.sbi.2023.102546]

[80] O. Obrezanova, "Artificial intelligence for compound pharmacokinetics prediction", *Curr. Opin. Struct. Biol.,* vol. 79, p. 102546, 2023.
[http://dx.doi.org/10.1016/j.sbi.2023.102546]

[81] S. Oniani, G. Marques, S. Barnovi, I. M. Pires, and A. K. Bhoi, "Artificial intelligence for internet of things and enhanced medical systems", *Studies in Computational Intelligence,* vol. 903, pp. 43-59, 2021.
[http://dx.doi.org/10.1007/978-981-15-5495-7_3]

[82] D. Paul, "Artificial intelligence in drug discovery and development", *Drug Discov. Today,* vol. 26, p. 80, 2021.
[http://dx.doi.org/10.1016/j.drudis.2020.10.010]

[83] G. Pawar, "In silico toxicology data resources to support read-across and (Q)SAR", *Front. Pharmacol.,* vol. 10, p. 561, 2019.
[http://dx.doi.org/10.3389/fphar.2019.00561]

[84] J. M. Peake, G. Kerr, and J. P. Sullivan, "A critical review of consumer wearables, mobile applications, and equipment for providing biofeedback, monitoring stress, and sleep in physically active populations", *Front. Physiol.,* vol. 9, p. 743, 2018.
[http://dx.doi.org/10.3389/fphys.2018.00743]

[85] E. Pérez Santín, "Toxicity prediction based on artificial intelligence: a multidisciplinary overview", *Wiley Interdiscip. Rev. Comput. Mol. Sci.,* vol. 11, p. e1516, 2021.
[http://dx.doi.org/10.1002/wcms.1516]

[86] R. Qureshi, "AI in drug discovery and its clinical relevance", *Heliyon,* vol. 9, 2023.
[http://dx.doi.org/10.1016/j.heliyon.2023.e17575]

[87] R. Qureshi, "AI in drug discovery and its clinical relevance", *Heliyon,* vol. 9, 2023.
[http://dx.doi.org/10.1016/j.heliyon.2023.e17575]

[88] R. Qureshi, "AI in drug discovery and its clinical relevance", *Heliyon,* vol. 9, p. e17575, 2023.
[http://dx.doi.org/10.1016/j.heliyon.2023.e17575]

[89] A. Rajkomar, J. Dean, and I. Kohane, "Machine learning in medicine", *N. Engl. J. Med.,* vol. 380, pp. 1347-1358, 2019.
[http://dx.doi.org/10.1056/nejmra1814259]

[90] "Multi-centre randomized controlled trial of a smartphone-based event recorder alongside standard care versus standard care for patients presenting to the emergency department with palpitations and pre-syncope: the IPED study", *EClinicalMedicine,* vol. 8, pp. 37-46, 2019.
[http://dx.doi.org/10.1016/j.eclinm.2019.02.005]

[91] A. S. Rifaioglu, "DEEPScreen: high performance drug–target interaction prediction with convolutional neural networks using 2-D structural compound representations", *Chem. Sci.,* vol. 11, p. 2531, 2020.
[http://dx.doi.org/10.1039/c9sc03414e]

[92] F. Sabry, "Machine learning for healthcare wearable devices: the big picture", *J. Healthc. Eng.*, 2022. [http://dx.doi.org/10.1155/2022/4653923]

[93] J. Sarmiento-Rojas, "System for monitoring environmental variables in a pharmacy area using an alternative IoT architecture (a pilot study)", *IFMBE Proc.*, vol. 75, 2020pp. 1284-1291 [http://dx.doi.org/10.1007/978-3-030-30648-9_165]

[94] T. Sato, "Application of Internet of Medical/Health Things to decentralized clinical trials: development status and regulatory considerations", *Front. Med. (Lausanne)*, vol. 9, p. 903188, 2022. [http://dx.doi.org/10.3389/fmed.2022.903188]

[95] A. Sharma, J. Kaur, and I. Singh, "Internet of things (IoT) in pharmaceutical manufacturing, warehousing, and supply chain management", *SN Comput. Sci.*, vol. 1, pp. 1-10, 2020. [http://dx.doi.org/10.1007/s42979-020-00248-2]

[96] A. K. Sharma, "ToxiM: a toxicity prediction tool for small molecules developed using machine learning and chemoinformatics approaches", *Front. Pharmacol.*, vol. 8, p. 880, 2017. [http://dx.doi.org/10.3389/fphar.2017.00880]

[97] D. K. Sharma, S. Bhargava, and K. Singhal, "Internet of things applications in the pharmaceutical industry", *An Industrial IoT Approach for Pharmaceutical Industry Growth*, pp. 153-190, 2020. [http://dx.doi.org/10.1016/B978-0-12-821326-1.00006-1]

[98] N. Sharma, "A smart ontology-based IoT framework for remote patient monitoring", *Biomed. Signal Process. Control*, vol. 68, p. 102717, 2021. [http://dx.doi.org/10.1016/j.bspc.2021.102717]

[99] N. Sifuna, "African traditional medicine: Its potential, limitations and challenges", *African Traditional Medicine: Its Potential, Limitations and Challenges*, vol. 5, no. 4, p. 141, 2022. [http://dx.doi.org/10.36959/569/475]

[100] M. Singh, S. Sachan, A. Singh, and K. K. Singh, "Internet of things in pharma industry: possibilities and challenges", *Emergence of Pharmaceutical Industry Growth with Industrial IoT Approach*, pp. 195-216, 2020. [http://dx.doi.org/10.1016/B978-0-12-819593-2.00007-8]

[101] N Singh, P Vayer, S Tanwar, J-L Poyet, K Tsaioun, and BO Villoutreix, "Drug discovery and development: introduction to the general public and patient groups", *Frontiers in Drug Discovery*, vol. 3, p. 1201419, 2023. [http://dx.doi.org/10.3389/FDDSV.2023.1201419]

[102] C Smith, "Drug target validation: Hitting the target", *Nature*, vol. 422, pp. 342-345, 2003. [http://dx.doi.org/10.1038/422341a]

[103] P Singh, M Srivastava, M Kansal, AP Singh, A Chauhan, and A Gaur, "A comparative analysis of modern frontend frameworks for building large-scale web applications", *Proceedings of the International Conference on Disruptive Technologies (ICDT)*, IEEE, pp. 531-535, 2023.

[104] YC Tang, and A Gottlieb, "Explainable drug sensitivity prediction through cancer pathway enrichment", *Scientific Reports*, vol. 11, 2021. [http://dx.doi.org/10.1038/s41598-021-82612-7]

[105] V Thakare, G Khire, and M Kumbhar, "Artificial Intelligence (AI) and Internet of Things (IoT) in Healthcare: Opportunities and Challenges", *ECS Transactions*, vol. 107, pp. 7941-7951, 2022. [http://dx.doi.org/10.1149/10701.7941ECST]

[106] TS Toh, F Dondelinger, and D Wang, "Looking beyond the hype: Applied AI and machine learning in translational medicine", *EBioMedicine*, vol. 47, pp. 607-615, 2019. [http://dx.doi.org/10.1016/j.ebiom.2019.08.027]

[107] RPB Tonino, K Larimer, O Eissen, and MR Schipperus, "Remote Patient Monitoring in Adults Receiving Transfusion or Infusion for Hematological Disorders", *JMIR Human Factors*, vol. 6, 2019.

[http://dx.doi.org/10.2196/15103]

[108] TTV Tran, AS Wibowo, H Tayara, and KT Chong, "Artificial Intelligence in Drug Toxicity Prediction: Recent Advances, Challenges, and Future Perspectives", *Journal of Chemical Information and Modeling,* vol. 63, pp. 2628-2643, 2023.
[http://dx.doi.org/10.1021/ACS.JCIM.3C00200]

[109] LK Tsou, SH Yeh, SH Ueng, and CP Chang, "Comparative study between deep learning and QSAR classifications for TNBC inhibitors", *Scientific Reports,* vol. 10, 2020.
[http://dx.doi.org/10.1038/s41598-020-73681-1]

[110] R Villar, T Beltrame, and RL Hughson, "Validation of the Hexoskin wearable vest during lying, sitting, standing, and walking activities", *Applied Physiology, Nutrition, and Metabolism,* vol. 40, pp. 1019-1024, 2015.
[http://dx.doi.org/10.1139/APNM-2015-0140]

[111] N. S. Virdi, "Digital Medicines to Measure Drug Ingestion Adherence", *Adherence and Self-Management in Pediatric Populations,* Springer: Cham, pp. 87-97, 2018.
[http://dx.doi.org/10.1007/978-3-319-76593-8_7]

[112] LK Vora, AD Gholap, and K Jetha, "Artificial Intelligence in Pharmaceutical Technology and Drug Delivery Design", *Pharmaceutics,* vol. 15, 2023.
[http://dx.doi.org/10.3390/PHARMACEUTICS15071916]

[113] I Wallach, M Dzamba, and A Heifets, "AtomNet: A Deep Convolutional Neural Network for Bioactivity Prediction in Structure-based Drug Discovery", *arXiv,* .

[114] C Werner, N Hezel, and F Dongus, "Validity and reliability of the Apple Health app on iPhone", *Scientific Reports,* vol. 13, 2023.
[http://dx.doi.org/10.1038/s41598-023-32550-3]

[115] OJ Wouters, M McKee, and J Luyten, "Estimated Research and Development Investment Needed to Bring a New Medicine to Market", *JAMA,* vol. 323, pp. 844-853, 2020.
[http://dx.doi.org/10.1001/JAMA.2020.1166]

[116] N Zong, A Wen, and S Moon, "Computational drug repurposing based on electronic health records", *npj Digital Medicine,* vol. 5, 2022.
[http://dx.doi.org/10.1038/s41746-022-00617-6]

[117] P Singh, N Pahuja, M Kansal, and S Gurung, "Enhancing Tourism Experiences and Preserving Cultural Heritage with AR and VR", *International Conference on Disruptive Technologies (ICDT),* IEEE, 2024.

[118] P Szymański, M Markowicz, and E Mikiciuk-Olasik, "Adaptation of High-Throughput Screening in Drug Discovery—Toxicological Screening Tests", *International Journal of Molecular Sciences,* vol. 13, p. 427, 2012.
[http://dx.doi.org/10.3390/IJMS13010427]

CHAPTER 12

The Future of AI: Quantum Computing and Beyond

C. Chellaswamy[1,*], G. Gandhimathi[1], Uma Maheshwari K.[1] and C. Reginamary[2]

[1] *Department of Electronics and Communication Engineering, SRM TRP Engineering College, Tiruchirappalli 621105, Tamil Nadu, India*

[2] *Department of Electronics and Communication Engineering, MRK Institute of Technology, Kattumannarkoil 608301, Tamil Nadu, India*

Abstract: As Artificial Intelligence (AI) continues to revolutionize various industries, the integration of quantum computing promises to propel AI into unprecedented realms of capability and efficiency. This chapter explores the transformative potential of quantum computing in the future of AI, presenting a detailed overview of current advancements and future prospects. We begin by elucidating the fundamental principles of quantum computing, highlighting how quantum bits (qubits) and quantum entanglement differ fundamentally from classical computing paradigms. The discussion then moves to the synergistic relationship between AI and quantum computing, showcasing how quantum algorithms can enhance machine learning models, optimize complex problem-solving tasks, and enable real-time data processing at previously unattainable speeds. The chapter also delves into the potential of quantum computing in enhancing AI through quantum algorithms such as Grover's Algorithm and Shor's Algorithm. Simulation results for different cases have been studied, demonstrating the effectiveness of quantum computing in AI.

Keywords: Artificial intelligence, Grover's algorithm, Quantum computing, Quantum bits, Shor's algorithm.

INTRODUCTION

In recent years, Quantum computation (Qcom) has arisen as a revolutionary field at the forefront of scientific and technological advancement. Unlike conventional computing, which depends on bits that represent either 1 or 0, Qcom harnesses the principles of quantum mechanics to operate with quantum bits, or qubits. These qubits occur in a superposition of 1 and 0, aiding quantum computers to process vast amounts of information simultaneously and explore many solutions at once

* **Corresponding author C. Chellaswamy:** Department of Electronics and Communication Engineering, SRM TRP Engineering College, Tiruchirappalli 621105, Tamil Nadu, India; E-mail: drchellaswamy@gmail.com

Pancham Singh, Avinash Kumar Sharma, Mrignainy Kansal, & Amarjeet Prajapati (Eds.)

through quantum parallelism. This capability holds the potential to speed up computations for certain complex problems exponentially. At its core, Qcom relies on phenomena such as quantum entanglement and quantum interference, in which qubits can be correlated in ways that classical bits cannot, enabling transformative computational power [1]. While still in its infancy in terms of practical applications, Qcom research is rapidly advancing, driven by academic institutions, major corporations, and government initiatives worldwide. As we delve deeper into the capabilities and challenges of Qcom, its integration with AI promises to unlock new frontiers in fields ranging from cryptography and material science to machine learning and optimization. This chapter explores the fundamental principles, potential applications, and prospects of Qcom, highlighting its role in shaping the future landscape of artificial intelligence and beyond [2].

In the realm of artificial intelligence, the convergence of Qcom represents a transformative frontier, promising unprecedented capabilities that transcend the limits of classical computation. Qcom leverages the principles of quantum mechanics to manipulate information in ways that defy classical physics, offering exponential speedups for solving complex problems that are impractical for today's supercomputers [3]. This chapter explores the intersection of AI and Qcom, delving into foundational concepts such as quantum bits (qubits), quantum algorithms such as Grover's and Shor's, and the quest for quantum supremacy. As we stand on the brink of a new era in computing power, understanding these technologies not only unveils their potential applications across industries but also underscores the profound implications for the future of AI-driven innovation.

Artificial Intelligence (AI) has evolved over several decades, with substantial advances in methodology and techniques. AI has evolved in several periods, each distinguished by advances in techniques and technology. Beginning in the 1950s and 1960s, AI focused on symbolic reasoning, aiming to mimic human cognitive processes through rules and logical procedures, as evidenced by early systems such as the Logic Theorist. The 1970s and 1980s witnessed the growth of knowledge-based systems, notably expert systems, which employed knowledge representation and inference engines to simulate human skill in specialized fields such as medicine and finance [4]. The late twentieth century saw the machine learning revolution, in which statistical methodologies enabled computers to learn from data. Supervised learning permitted tasks such as classification and regression, whereas unsupervised learning found patterns in data without labelled instances. Reinforcement learning evolved as a method for decision-making through trial and error and has been used in domains such as robotics and gaming [5]. The 2010s saw a rise in deep learning, fuelled by huge data and advancements in processing capacity. Deep neural networks, with their capacity to autonomously learn hierarchical representations, have transformed Computer Vision (CV), Speech Processing (SP), and Natural Language/Linguistic Processing (NLP). Today, AI is advancing with applications in healthcare, finance, robotics, and beyond, propelled by advances in Quantum Computing, explainable AI, and ethical considerations to ensure responsible deployment and societal benefit.

Key methods for AI include a range of approaches that enable machines to emulate intelligent behavior and decision-making processes. These approaches have grown dramatically over decades of study and technology innovation, influencing AI capabilities and applications across several fields [6]. They include symbolic AI, which uses rules and logic to model human-like reasoning, machine learning, which includes supervised, unsupervised, and reinforcement learning techniques for learning from data; deep learning, Artificial Neural Networks (ANN) with several layers inevitably extract complex attributes from large datasets; NLP enables robots to interpret and produce human language; and computer vision, which focuses on algorithms for visual perception, where machines learn through trial and error by interacting with their environment [7]. These methodologies collectively form the foundation for developing AI systems capable of diverse tasks, from image recognition and language translation to autonomous decision-making and problem-solving in complex real-world scenarios.

Symbolic AI: Uses symbols, logic, and rules to model human-like reasoning and problem-solving.

Machine Learning: Includes supervised, unsupervised, and reinforcement learning techniques for learning patterns/attributes and making forecasts from data.

Deep Learning: Utilizes neural networks with several layers that inevitably learn the patterns/attributes from large datasets, particularly effective for tasks requiring complex data representations.

Natural Language Processing: Focuses on understanding and generating human language, enabling applications like machine translation, sentiment analysis, and chatbots.

Computer Vision: Involves algorithms and techniques for analysing and interpreting visual information from images and videos, used in object detection, recognition, and image generation.

Expert Systems: Knowledge-based systems that use rules and knowledge bases to provide expert-level decision support and problem-solving in specific domains.

Reinforcement Learning: Learning through trial and error by interacting with an environment, suitable for tasks requiring decision-making and optimization under uncertain conditions. AI has evolved dramatically over the past few decades, transforming from a theoretical concept into a pervasive technology influencing numerous aspects of modern life. The progression of AI can be traced through significant milestones and innovations across various domains, including machine learning, robotics, computer vision, deep learning, NLP, and more. Today, AI technologies are embedded in everyday applications and industries, driving efficiency, innovation, and new possibilities [8]. This chapter provides an overview of the current state of AI technologies, highlighting key developments and emerging trends that are shaping the future of this dynamic field. The timeline of the advancement of AI technologies is shown in Fig. (**1**).

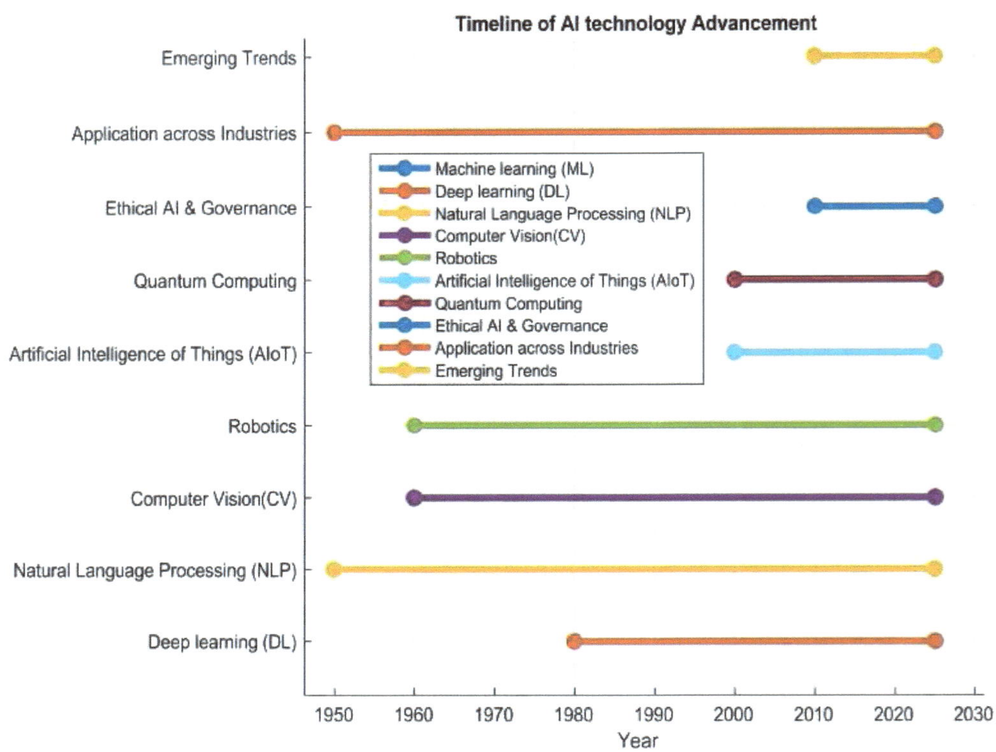

Fig. (1). Timeline of the advancement of AI technologies.

Machine Learning (ML): ML remains a fundamental aspect of AI, with supervised learning being extensively used for tasks such as object identification, speech processing, and NLP. Techniques like Convolutional Neural Networks (CNNs) are primarily used for image-related tasks, while Extended Memory Network (EMN) and Feedback Neural Networks (FNN) are common in sequence prediction and NLP. Gradient boosting machines, such as XGBoost and LightGBM, are particularly effective for structured or tabular data [9]. Unsupervised learning focuses on discovering patterns in data without explicit labels, using clustering algorithms such as K-means and DBSCAN, and dimensionality reduction techniques such as PCA and t-SNE. Generative models like variational autoencoders and Competitive Generative Networks (CGNs) have gained popularity to create new data points. Reinforcement Learning (RL) emphasizes training agents to make sequences of decisions, with deep reinforcement learning combining deep learning principles to enhance applications in autonomous driving and robotics [10].

Deep Learning: Deep learning continues to be pivotal, with neural networks featuring multiple layers being employed for complex tasks. Frameworks like TensorFlow and PyTorch facilitate the development and deployment of these models. Transformers have revolutionized NLP, with models like BTEM (Bidirectional Transformer Encoder Models) excelling at understanding text context, and PGT (Pre-trained Generative Transformer) models leading in text generation and comprehension [11].

Natural Language Processing: NLP has seen remarkable progress, with advanced models such as GPT-4 and BERT being used for text generation, summarization, translation, question-answering, and sentiment analysis. Conversational AI, including virtual assistants like Siri, Alexa, and ChatGPT, now offers more natural, context-aware interactions.

Computer Vision: In computer vision, significant advances have been made in image and video analysis, with algorithms excelling in object detection, image segmentation, and facial recognition. 3D vision techniques using 3D CNNs are enhancing applications in augmented and virtual reality, as well as in autonomous vehicles. AI is also transforming medical imaging by aiding in the diagnosis of diseases from radiology and pathology images.

Robotics: Robotics has benefited immensely from AI, with autonomous systems like AI-driven robots and drones being deployed in logistics, manufacturing, agriculture, and exploration. Human-robot interaction has improved, allowing for more intuitive and seamless collaboration.

AIoT (Artificial Intelligence of Things): The integration of AI with IoT has led to the emergence of AIoT, where smart devices are used in homes, cities, and industries for predictive maintenance, energy management, and personalized experiences. Edge AI, which involves processing AI algorithms locally on edge devices, reduces latency and bandwidth usage, making real-time applications more efficient.

Quantum Computing: Qcom is another frontier, with research focused on quantum algorithms that promise to solve problems more efficiently than classical computing. Quantum Machine Learning (QML) aims to leverage Qcom to enhance the speed and accuracy of ML models.

Ethical AI and Governance: Ethical AI and governance have become critical areas of focus. Efforts are underway to address biases in AI models to ensure fairness across different demographic groups and to develop methods that make AI decisions more transparent and explainable. Regulation is also being established to govern the responsible development and deployment of AI.

Applications Across Industries: AI applications are transforming various industries, including healthcare, where AI aids in medical imaging, personalized medicine, drug discovery, and patient care management. In finance, AI is used for personalized financial advice, credit scoring, algorithmic trading, and fraud detection. The transportation sector benefits from AI through autonomous vehicles, traffic management systems, and intelligent transportation infrastructure. Retail uses AI for customer service chatbots, personalized recommendations, inventory management, and demand forecasting.

Emerging Trends: Emerging trends in AI include generative AI, which creates realistic images, videos, and text using models like GANs and VAEs, and federated learning, which trains ML models across decentralized devices while keeping data localized. Explainable AI (XAI) is advancing efforts to make AI systems more transparent and understandable [12]. Overall, the current state of AI technologies is characterized by rapid advancements and extensive integration across sectors, driven by ongoing research, innovation, and the growing availability of data and computational resources.

Qcom intersects with AI by offering unprecedented computational power and efficiency through principles like quantum parallelism and entanglement. Quantum computers can accelerate complex AI algorithms, enhance machine learning tasks such as pattern recognition and optimization, and enable faster decision-making processes. However, challenges such as qubit coherence and algorithm development remain, necessitating ongoing research [13]. Ethical considerations, including data privacy and AI governance in the quantum era, also require careful attention. Despite these challenges, the synergy between Qcom and AI promises transformative impacts across industries, from healthcare to finance, by unlocking new capabilities and addressing current computational limitations.

Qcom applies quantum physics concepts to execute calculations in ways that traditional computers cannot. Understanding these foundational principles is key to appreciating how quantum computers work:

Superposition: In distinction to conventional bits, which can either be 1 or 0, superposition of both states can exist in a qubit or quantum bit. This means that a qubit can hold both 1 and 0 until it is measured. Two states (0 or 1) have been presented in a single-bit classical computer [14]. A quantum computer with one qubit can be simultaneously in two states. A two-bit computer can store only one of four potential combinations (2^2=4). A quantum computer with two qubits can store four potential values at once (Table **1**).

Table 1. Storage capacity of bits and qubits.

Bits or qubits	Traditional storage in bytes	Quantum storage in bits	Quantum storage in bytes
4	0.5	16 (2^4)	2 (16/8)
8	1	256 (2^8)	32 (256/8)
16	2	65536 (2^{16})	8192 (65536/8)
32	4	4294967296 (2^{32})	536870912 (4294967296/8)
64	8	18,446,744,073,709,551,616 (2^{64})	2,305,843,009,213,693,952 (18,446,744,073,709,551,616/8)

Quantum Entanglement: Qubits can become entangled, meaning that no matter how far apart they are, one qubit's state will instantly correlate with the other's state. This phenomenon permits quantum computers to process information in a massively parallel way.

Quantum Interference: Qubits can interfere with each other, a concept analogous to wave interference in classical physics. This interference enables quantum computers to increase the probability of obtaining correct answers while suppressing incorrect ones.

Measurement: When a qubit is measured, it collapses from a superposition of states (0 and 1) to a definite state (either 0 or 1). The measurement output is probabilistic, with the probabilities influenced by the quantum states before the measurement.

Parallelism: Superposition and entanglement enable quantum computers to run multiple calculations simultaneously, potentially completing some tasks far more quickly than traditional computers.

Exponential Speedup: Algorithms designed for quantum computers can exploit quantum parallelism and interference to achieve exponential speedup for particular tasks, such as searching unsorted databases or factoring large numbers. Complexity and Scalability: While these principles offer significant advantages, building practical quantum computers faces challenges such as maintaining qubit coherence (decoherence), minimizing errors, and scaling up the number of qubits and operations.

AI models and Qcom are related in several ways, primarily through the potential for Qcom to enhance the capabilities of AI models. Here are some key aspects of their relationship:

a. Computational Power: Quantum computers have the ability to exponentially expand processing power compared to classical computers for certain tasks. This can significantly accelerate the training and execution of complex AI models, particularly those involving large datasets and intricate algorithms.
b. Optimization: Quantum algorithms can be particularly effective in optimization problems, which are fundamental to many AI tasks such as parameter tuning in neural networks, resource allocation, and scheduling. Qcom's ability to explore multiple solutions simultaneously (quantum parallelism) and exploit quantum interference can lead to faster and more efficient optimization processes.
c. Algorithm Development: Researchers are exploring quantum algorithms specifically designed for enhancing AI tasks. For instance, QML algorithms aim to leverage quantum principles to improve pattern recognition, classification, and other AI capabilities beyond what is feasible with classical computing.
d. Simulation: Quantum computers could potentially simulate complex AI models and systems, which have greater efficiency and accuracy than classical computers. This capability is crucial for testing and refining AI algorithms in various scenarios, especially in fields like healthcare, where accurate simulations are critical.
e. Future Innovations: The intersection of Qcom and AI opens up new opportunities for innovation and discovery. It may lead to the development of entirely new types of AI models that harness quantum effects to solve problems in ways that classical models cannot.

Qcom offers several potential advantages over classical computing, primarily stemming from its ability to leverage the quantum principles of superposition, entanglement, and quantum interference. Here are detailed explanations of the advantages of Qcom:

Enhanced Computational Power: Compared with traditional computers, Quantum computers can solve some complex problems significantly faster. This is primarily due to their ability to leverage the quantum principles of superposition and entanglement, which allows them to process a vast number of possibilities concurrently [15]. For instance, tasks involving large-scale optimization, complex simulations, and cryptographic calculations could see significant speed improvements. Superior Problem-Solving Capabilities: Certain complex problems that are intractable for classical computers can be efficiently tackled by quantum computers. This includes complex tasks like factoring large numbers, which is fundamental to modern cryptography. Quantum algorithms, such as Shor's algorithm, can theoretically break widely used encryption methods much more efficiently than classical algorithms. Improved Machine Learning and AI: Quantum computing (Qcom) can improve machine learning (ML) algorithms by speeding up data processing and improving the efficiency of training models. Quantum Machine Learning (QML) has the ability to handle and analyze large datasets more effectively, leading to faster predictions. Techniques such as quantum annealing could optimize neural network training processes, providing new avenues for advancements in artificial intelligence. Potential for Breakthroughs in Cryptography: While Qcom poses a threat to present cryptographic techniques, it also offers the potential for developing new, more secure cryptographic methods [16]. Quantum Key Distribution (QKD), for example, uses the principles of quantum mechanics to create theoretically unbreakable encryption. This could lead to enhanced data security and privacy in the future. Energy Efficiency: Quantum computers, once fully developed and optimized, could perform complex computations with significantly less energy than classical supercomputers. This energy efficiency could be crucial in reducing the environmental impact of data centers and high-performance computing facilities. Solving Intractable Problems: Qcom can address problems that are currently unsolvable due to their complexity and size. This includes issues in various scientific fields, such as solving differential equations that model complex physical systems or understanding the behavior of large biological molecules, which are beyond the reach of classical computation

Despite these advantages, Qcom also faces significant challenges, such as qubit coherence (maintaining stable quantum states), error rates, and the complexity of developing scalable quantum algorithms.

QUANTUM COMPUTING: A NEW FRONTIER

Qcom promises a significant leap forward in computation, offering to address difficult glitches that are now beyond the capabilities of traditional processors. Leveraging the ideologies of quantum mechanics, quantum computers operate in ways basically dissimilar from their conventional counterparts [17]. This new frontier in computing has the potential to transform several fields, ranging from cryptography and materials science to artificial intelligence and beyond.

Quantum gates serve as the fundamental components of quantum circuits, akin to conventional logic gates in traditional computing. They deploy qubits using quantum operations, aiding in the implementation of quantum algorithms, unlike conventional gates, which operate on bits to produce deterministic outcomes, quantum gates that operate on qubits leverage superposition and predicament to perform multifaceted and reversible transformations [18]. Various gates with the corresponding matrix representation, number of qubits, functionality of the gate, and the effect on the qubit state are shown in Table **2**. The number of qubits specifies how many qubits the gate operates on. Single-qubit gates affect one qubit, while multi-qubit gates like the CNOT gate affect two or more qubits. The last column describes how the quantum gate transforms the qubit(s) state.

Table 2. Summary of key quantum gates: symbols, matrix representations, and functions.

Gate	Matrix Representation	Number of Qubits	Functionality	Effect on Qubit State
X gate	$\begin{pmatrix} 0 & 1 \\ 1 & 0 \end{pmatrix}$	1	Flips the state	0\rangle\leftrightarrow
Y gate	$\begin{pmatrix} 0 & -i \\ i & 0 \end{pmatrix}$	1	Combines bit flip and phase flip	0\rangle\leftrightarrow i
Z gate	$\begin{pmatrix} 1 & 0 \\ 0 & -1 \end{pmatrix}$	1	Flip the phase	0\rangle\rightarrow -
H state	$\frac{1}{\sqrt{2}}\begin{pmatrix} 0 & 1 \\ 1 & 0 \end{pmatrix}$	1	Create superposition	0\rangle\rightarrow\frac
S gate	$\begin{pmatrix} 1 & 0 \\ 0 & i \end{pmatrix}$	1	Applies a $\pi/2$ phas shift	1\rangle\rightarrow i
T gate	$\begin{pmatrix} 1 & 0 \\ 0 & e^{i\pi/4} \end{pmatrix}$	1	Applies a $\pi/4$ phas shift	1\rangle\rightarrow eiπ/4
CNOT gate	$\begin{pmatrix} 1 & 0 & 0 & 0 \\ 0 & 1 & 0 & 0 \\ 0 & 0 & 0 & 1 \\ 0 & 0 & 1 & 0 \end{pmatrix}$	2	Inverts the target qubit when the control qubit is in the state $\lvert 1 \rangle$ or $\lvert 0 \rangle$, the target qubit stays the same.	1\rangle)

Gate	Matrix Representation	Number of Qubits	Functionality	Effect on Qubit State
$R_x(\theta)$ Gate	$\begin{pmatrix} \cos(\theta/2) & -sin(\theta/2) \\ -isin(\theta/2 & \cos(\theta/2) \end{pmatrix}$	1	Rotates around the x-axis by angle θ	(\cos\theta/2)
$R_x(\theta)$ Gate	$\begin{pmatrix} \cos(\theta/2) & -isin(\theta/2) \\ -sin(\theta/2 & \cos(\theta/2) \end{pmatrix}$	1	Rotates around the y-axis by angle θ	(\cos\theta/2)
$R_x(\theta)$ Gate	$\begin{pmatrix} e^{-i\theta/2} & 0 \\ 0 & e^{i\theta/2} \end{pmatrix}$	1	Rotates around the z-axis by angle θ	e^{-i\theta/2}

Comparison between Conventional Computers and Quantum Computers While quantum computers leverage quantum-mechanical principles such as superposition and entanglement, to process information, classical computers rely on binary bits and sequential processing [19]. Understanding these distinctions is crucial for appreciating Qcom's potential and current limitations, as well as its impact on future technological advancements. A comparison between classical and quantum computers is listed in Table **3**.

Table 3. Comparison between quantum computers and traditional hardware.

Aspects	Quantum computers	Conventional computers
Basic Unit of Information	A qubit (quantum bit) which can represent 0, 1, or both simultaneously (superposition).	Bit (binary digit), which can represent either 0 or 1.
Processing Power	Can, in theory, solve certain critical problems exponentially quicker than conventional computers using quantum-mechanical algorithms.	Limited by Moore's law and the speed of electrons through silicon circuits.
Parallelism	Processes many possible outcomes simultaneously due to quantum superposition.	Generally performs operations sequentially, although parallel processing is possible to some extent.
Entanglement	Qubits can be entangled, leading to potential for highly correlated states and faster computations.	Not applicable; classical bits do not exhibit entanglement.
Error Correction	Requires sophisticated error correction methods (quantum error correction) due to sensitivity to noise and decoherence.	Error correction is well established using redundancy and algorithms such as ECC (Error-Correcting Codes).
Applications	Potential for breakthroughs in cryptography, drug discovery, optimization problems, and complex simulations.	A broad range of applications, including data processing, software development, gaming, and scientific computing.
Energy Efficiency	Quantum computers have theoretically been made energy-efficient for certain types of problems once scaled up.	Traditional hardware efficiency varies, but advancements in energy-efficient designs are ongoing.

Qcom represents a radical scheme in computation, harnessing the ideologies of quantum mechanics to potentially solve certain computational problems. These capabilities enable quantum algorithms to tackle complex tasks with unprecedented efficiency compared to classical algorithms, which rely on binary bits and operate through sequential processing [20].

In this comparison of time complexities, we explore several key computational tasks where quantum algorithms demonstrate significant advantages over classical counterparts. These tasks include integer factorization, database search, prime number verification, quantum system simulation, and solving systems of linear equations. Each task highlights how quantum algorithms leverage quantum parallelism and interference effects to achieve potentially dramatic speedups, fundamentally altering the landscape of computational possibilities. Understanding these differences in time complexities is essential for grasping the potential impact of Qcom across various fields, from cryptography and computational chemistry to optimization and artificial intelligence.

Qcom introduces algorithms that can potentially resolve certain critical problems exponentially faster than classical counterparts by leveraging quantum-mechanical principles such as superposition and entanglement. For instance, in integer factorization, classical algorithms such as trial division or Pollard's rho method typically run in sub-exponential time, with complexity growing significantly as the size of the number n increases. In contrast, Shor's algorithm can factor large integers in polynomial time, specifically $O\left(e^{\sqrt[3]{\left(\frac{64}{9}\right)}(\ln n)^{1/3}}\right)$, which is a significant improvement for applications in cryptography and number theory. Database search presents another stark contrast: classical linear search algorithms have a time complication of $O(N)$ where N denotes the number of items in the database. Quantum search algorithm (Ex, Grover's algorithm) offers a quadratic speedup with a time complication of $O(\sqrt{N})$. This quadratic speedup can revolutionize unstructured search tasks by drastically reducing the number of operations required compared to classical methods Table **4**.

Table 4. Comparative time complexities between quantum and classical algorithms.

Task	Classical algorithm	Quantum algorithm	Time Complexity
Integer Factorization	General algorithms (*e.g.*, Trial division, Pollard's rho)	Shor's algorithm	$O\left(e^{\left(\sqrt[3]{\left(\frac{64}{9}\right)}(\ln n)^{1/3}\right)}\right)$
Database Search (Unstructured)	Linear search	Grover's algorithm	$O(\sqrt{n})$

Task	Classical algorithm	Quantum algorithm	Time Complexity
Prime Number Verification	Primality testing (*e.g.*, AKS algorithm)	Quantum Fourier transform-based algorithms	$O((\log n)^2)$
Simulation of Quantum Systems	Classical simulations	Quantum phase estimation	$O((\log n)^2)$
Solving Systems of Linear Equations	Gaussian elimination	HHL algorithm	$O((\log^2 n)^2)$

Prime number verification, crucial for cryptography and security, traditionally relies on classical primality-testing algorithms such as the AKS algorithm, which runs in polynomial time. Quantum algorithms based on the quantum Fourier transform can verify prime numbers with a time complexity of $O((\log n)^2)$, showcasing a logarithmic improvement over classical methods. Simulation of quantum systems, a fundamental challenge in fields like material science and chemistry, is computationally intensive for classical computers [21]. Classical simulations typically scale exponentially with the number of quantum components involved. Quantum phase estimation algorithms offer efficient simulation capabilities with a time complexity of $O((\log n)^2)$ enabling faster insights into quantum behaviors that are impractical or impossible for classical computers to simulate accurately within reasonable timeframes. Lastly, solving systems of linear equations is essential across various scientific and engineering disciplines. Conventional Gaussian elimination approaches have polynomial time complexity, whereas the HHL algorithm on quantum computers achieves logarithmic complexity $O((\log^2 n)^2)$, which denotes the condition number. This logarithmic improvement highlights Qcom's potential to efficiently handle large-scale linear algebra problems.

Computational Power: Quantum supremacy demonstrates the ability of quantum computers to execute complex algorithms much faster than classical computers. Tasks that are currently infeasible or take an impractically long time for classical systems could be completed in a reasonable timeframe with quantum supremacy.

Technological Advancement: Achieving quantum supremacy signifies a breakthrough in quantum technology and engineering. It validates the progress in developing stable qubits, improving error correction techniques, and scaling quantum systems.

Scientific Discovery: Quantum supremacy opens doors to solving complex scientific problems that were previously computationally prohibitive. This includes simulations of quantum systems, optimization of complex processes, and advancement of fields such as materials science, drug discovery, and cryptography.

Economic Impact: Quantum supremacy could drive innovation across industries, boosting economic growth and creating new opportunities in finance, logistics, and healthcare through more efficient optimization and predictive modeling.

Ethical Considerations: Alongside technological advancement, quantum supremacy raises ethical concerns regarding data privacy, algorithmic fairness, and the societal implications of enhanced computational capabilities.

QUANTUM COMPUTING IN AI

Qcom is poised to revolutionize AI by offering unprecedented computational power and novel algorithms that could expressively improve AI abilities. This section explores the intersection of Qcom and AI, highlighting both theoretical potentials and practical applications.

Qcom holds immense promise for enhancing AI by addressing the inherent limitations of classical computers in processing large datasets and solving complex optimization problems. Unlike classical bits (0 or 1), Qcom introduces algorithms that can potentially resolve certain critical problems exponentially faster than their classical counterparts by leveraging quantum-mechanical principles such as superposition and entanglement. Quantum bits or qubits leverage superposition and entanglement to explore multiple states simultaneously. This capability enables quantum computers to process vast amounts of data more efficiently and to tackle computationally intensive AI tasks that classical systems struggle with (Fig. **2**).

For AI, tasks such as training complex models, which require significant computational resources, can be done more efficiently. For example, optimizing deep learning models, which typically involve large-scale matrix operations and iterative procedures, could yield significant speedups with quantum algorithms. QML is a burgeoning field that combines Qcom with classical ML techniques. Quantum algorithms have the potential to improve classical ML in several ways. Quantum Support Vector Machines (QSVMs) leverage quantum algorithms to enhance the performance of classical support vector machines. By operating in quantum feature spaces, QSVMs can perform classification tasks more efficiently, especially in high-dimensional spaces. This can be beneficial for applications such as medical diagnosis and financial forecasting, where accurate classification and prediction are crucial. Many AI problems can be formulated as optimization problems; the objective is to discover the best option from a set of available solutions. Qcom offers two powerful algorithms for optimization: the Algorithm for Quantum Approximate Optimization (QAOA). QAOA is intended for solving combinatorial optimization problems common in AI applications like resource allocation, scheduling, and logistics. Quantum computers can explore numerous potential solutions concurrently, increasing the likelihood of finding the optimal solution faster than classical methods. Grover's Algorithm: This algorithm can improve search tasks in AI, such as querying databases for specific accesses or optimizing neural network hyperparameters.

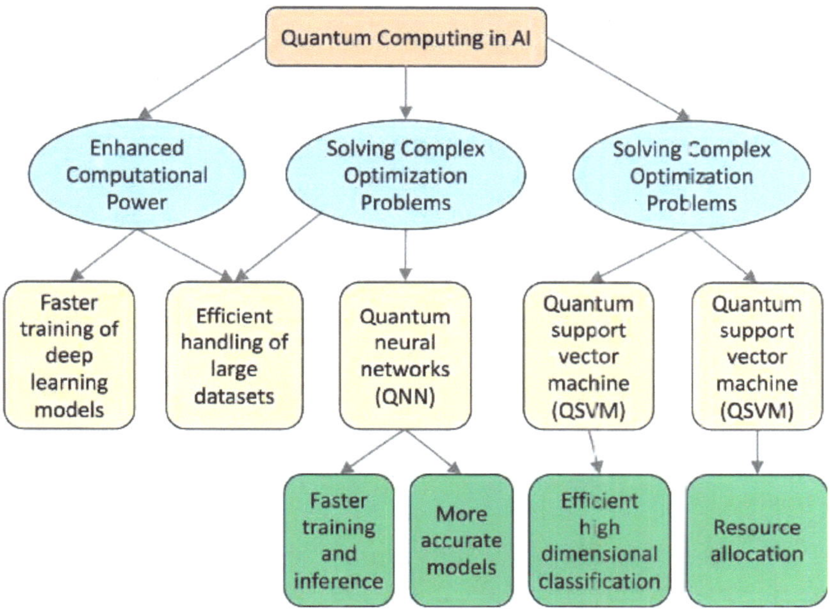

Fig. (2). Enhancing AI with quantum computing - key areas and potentials.

QUANTUM COMPUTING IN AI

Grover's Algorithm, a quantum technique, offers a quadratic speedup for unstructured search tasks. At the point of time complexity, classical computing requires $O(N)$ for searching N items in an unsorted database, but Grover's algorithm reduces this complexity to $O(\sqrt{N})$, offering a significant improvement for large datasets. Grover's method affords a quadratic speedup for unstructured search problems. Given a N size search space and a function $f(x)$ that maps the search space to $\{0,1\}$, where $f(x) = 1$ for the desired element and $f(x) = 0$ for all others, Grover's algorithm finds (x such that $f(x) = 1$. Start with a quantum system of (n qubits, where $= 2^n$, with the initial state $|0\rangle$: $|0\rangle = |0\rangle^{\otimes n}$. Apply Hadamard gate H to an individual qubit to generate an equivalent principle of superposition of all possible states:

$$|s\rangle = H^{\otimes n}|0\rangle = \frac{1}{\sqrt{N}}\sum_{x=0}^{N-1}|x\rangle \quad \textbf{(1)}$$

The oracle O_f be a quantum subroutine which flips the amplitude sign of the state consistent to the solution x:

$$O_f|x\rangle = (-1)^{f(x)}|x\rangle \quad \textbf{(2)}$$

The diffusion operator or Grover operator 'D' amplifies the correct state amplitude:

$$D = 2|s\rangle\langle s| - I \quad \textbf{(3)}$$

where I is the identity matrix and $|s\rangle$ is the equal superposition state. Each iteration of Grover's algorithm applies the oracle O_f followed by the diffusion operator D:

$$G = D.O_f \quad \textbf{(4)}$$

This sequence is repeated $O(\sqrt{N})$ times to amplify the correct state amplitude. The number of iterations k is approximately: $k \approx \lfloor \frac{\pi}{4} \rfloor \sqrt{N}$. After k iterations, the quantum state is measured. The probability of guessing the correct state x_O is significantly higher than any other state.

In 1994, Peter Shor created Shor's algorithm, which stands as a groundbreaking method in quantum computing. Its main job is to quickly break down large numbers into their prime factors. This is a big deal because factoring large numbers is really hard for regular computers; it can take a very long time. Classical methods, like the General Number Field Sieve, become slower as numbers get bigger. Shor's algorithm uses the unique abilities of quantum computers, like handling many calculations at once and using quantum properties to speed things up. It does this by finding patterns in numbers using quantum mechanics, which lets it figure out the factors of large numbers much faster than classical computers can. This algorithm is not only important for solving mathematical problems quickly but also has major implications for cryptography. For example, if it becomes easier to factor large numbers, it could affect the security of many encryption methods, such as RSA. Shor's algorithm is a big step forward in showing how Qcom could revolutionize computing power in the future.

Shor's algorithm leverages Qcom's ability to perform computations in parallel across a superposition of states. The algorithm consists of several key steps:

Initialization: Start with two registers: a quantum register $|x\rangle$ to hold the input for the function $f(x)$, and an auxiliary register $|y\rangle$ for storing intermediary values.

Superposition: Apply Hadamard gates to the $|x\rangle$ register to create a principle of superposition of all probable input values. This prepares all potential inputs simultaneously, exploiting quantum parallelism.

Function Evaluation: Use a quantum operation to compute $f(x)$ mod N in superposition. This step involves applying modular exponentiation $f(x) = a^x$ mod N, where a is chosen such that gcd $(a,N) = 1$. This operation is efficiently implemented using quantum circuits.

Quantum Fourier Transform: Implement a QFT on the $|x\rangle$ register. QFT enhances the amplitudes of states corresponding to the periods of $f(x)$ mod N. The e be the period of $f(x)$ mod N is as crucial as it relates directly to the factors of N.

Classical Post-processing: Use the measured value x to compute gcd $(a^{\frac{x}{2}} \pm 1, N)$, where r can be extracted from x. The factors of N can then be found using these results.

SIMULATION RESULTS

The simulation of Grover's algorithm is performed using an open-source Qcom software (Qiskit) development framework created by IBM, designed to make Qcom accessible to a wide range of users, from beginners to advanced researchers. It provides a comprehensive set of tools for creating, manipulating, and running Qcom programs on both simulators and real quantum hardware. Qiskit is structured into several key components, each serving a specific purpose in the Qcom workflow.

Qiskit Terra is the foundational layer that allows users to build quantum circuits at the level of quantum gates, providing tools for designing quantum algorithms, optimizing circuits, and managing their execution. Qiskit Aer is a high-performance simulator that enables the simulation of quantum circuits on classical computers, allowing for testing and debugging without the need for physical quantum hardware. Qiskit Ignis focuses on quantum error correction and mitigation, providing tools to characterize noise in quantum devices and implement techniques to mitigate its effects, thus improving the reliability of quantum computations. Qiskit Aqua is designed for applications of Qcom in several fields [22], offering high-level algorithms and tools to solve specific problems. Qiskit offers a range of features and capabilities, including circuit design *via* a simple, intuitive interface, quantum circuit simulation with Qiskit Aer, and access to state-of-the-art quantum processors *via* IBM Quantum. It also provides various visualization tools to help users understand and analyze their work, such as visualizing quantum circuits, state vectors, and the results of quantum computations. Additionally, Qiskit has a strong community of users and contributors, extensive documentation, tutorials, and educational resources to support users at all levels.

Getting started with Qiskit is straightforward. After installing it *via* pip, users can quickly create and simulate quantum circuits. For example, a simple quantum circuit can be created with two qubits, applying Hadamard gates, adding a CNOT gate, and measuring the qubits. This circuit can then be simulated using Qiskit's Aer simulator, and the measurement results can be visualized with a histogram. Based on the algorithm given in the above sub-section, three cases have been considered: 1) Number of qubits:3, Hidden bits:5, and No. of iterations: 1, 2) Number of qubits:4, Hidden bits:10, and No. of iterations: 3, and 3) Searching multiple target bits [23].

Case: 1 Initialize all qubits to the state |0⟩. A Designed Quantum circuit with Number of qubits:3, Hidden bit:5, for Grover's algorithm using Qiskit is shown in Fig. (**3**). The oracle, which knows the hidden bit, flips the amplitude of the target state |101⟩. Then, we apply 'D' (Grover diffusion operator), which amplifies the probability of the perceptible state (101) and drops the probabilities of all other states. After this single iteration, we measure the qubits. The response of the quantum state for case 1 is shown in Fig. (**4**). The percentage of probability distribution is shown in Fig. (**4a**). The exact probabilities depend on the number of qubits and iterations, but with one iteration and 3 qubits, the target state |101⟩ will have a much higher probability of being measured. For 3 qubits and two iterations, the target state |101⟩ typically has a probability close to around 50%, while the remaining 7 states share the rest of the probability distribution, roughly around 7-8% each. This means there is a high likelihood of measuring the state |101⟩, successfully identifying the hidden bit. The amplitude of the state vector for case 1 is shown in Fig. (**4b**). This results in the target state having a significantly higher probability of about 50% of being measured, while the probabilities of the other states are around 5.15% each. This demonstrates Grover's algorithm's ability to increase the probability of the target state, making it more likely to be found in a quantum search process.

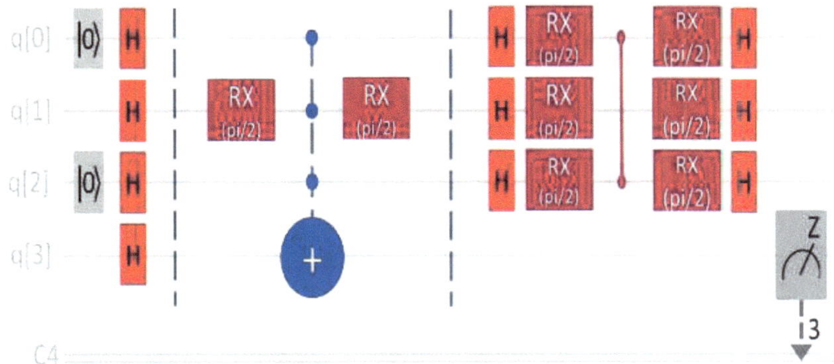

Fig. (3). Design of Quantum circuit with Number of qubits:3, Hidden bit:5 for Grover's algorithm (Case:1).

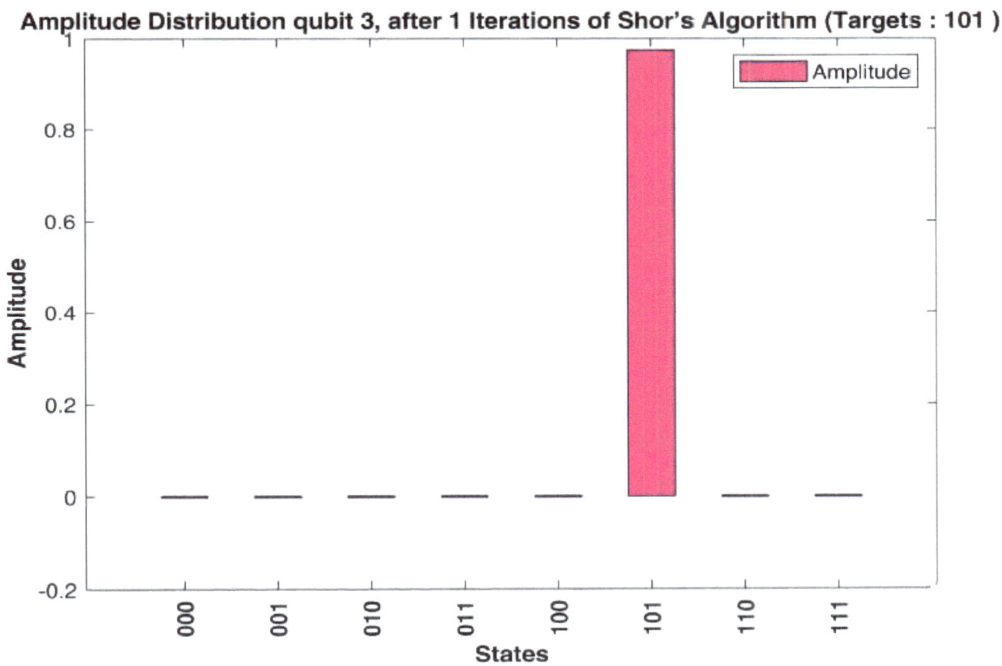

(Fig. 4) contd....

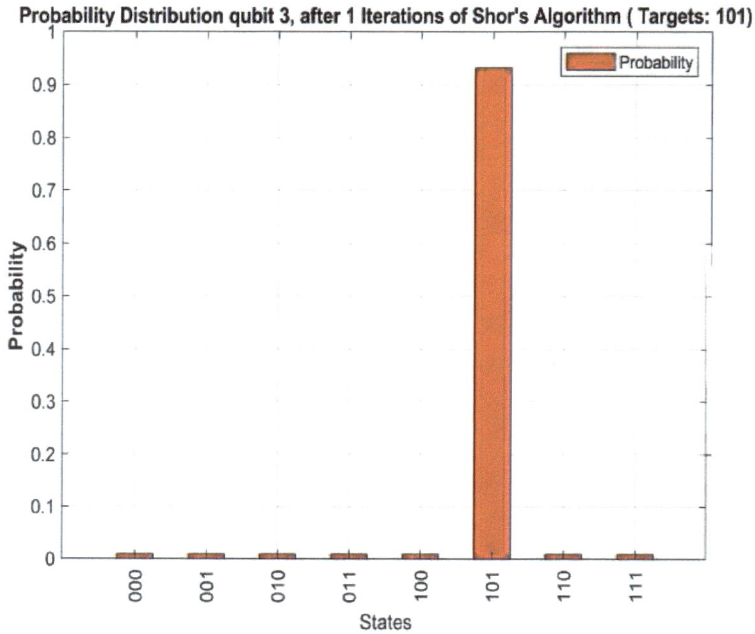

Fig. (4). Response of quantum state for case 1 under No. of iterations: 2 (a) percentage of probability distribution (b) Amplitude of state vector.

Case: 2 The Designed Quantum circuit with the Number of qubits: 4, Hidden bits:10, for Grover's algorithm using Qiskit is shown in Fig. (**5**). Several key operations drive the quantum circuit towards efficiently finding the marked state. Initially, all 4 qubits are initialized to |0000⟩. The Hadamard gates are then applied to create a principle of superposition of all 16 probable states, ensuring that each state has an equal probability amplitude. The oracle operation is crucial; it inverts the target state amplitude |1010⟩ sign, distinguishing it from the others. Following the oracle, 'Then, we apply 'D' (Grover diffusion operator), which amplifies the probability of the perceptible state (101) and drops the probabilities of all other states. This sequence of steps-Hadamard transformation, oracle application, and Grover diffusion - is repeated for 3 iterations to further enhance the likelihood of measuring |1010⟩. Finally, measurement collapses the superposition, yielding a high probability of observing the target state, as shown in Fig. (**6**). Probability measurement of a specific state is its amplitude squared. After 3 iterations, the probability amplitude of |1010⟩ is significantly higher compared to other states, resulting in a much higher probability of measuring |1010⟩.

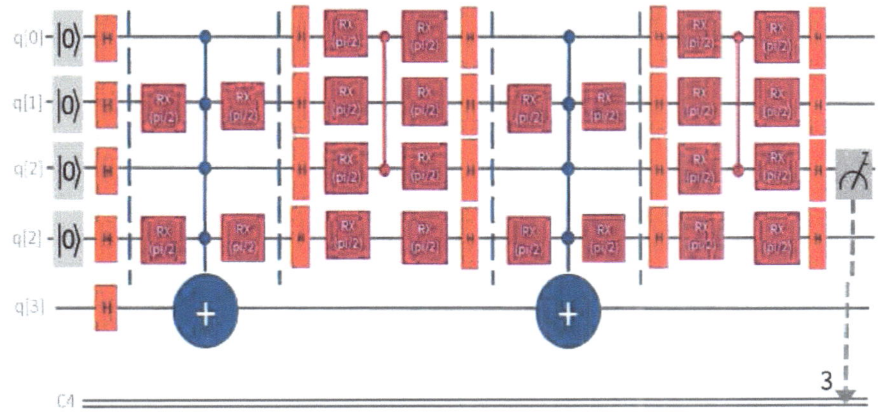

Fig. (5). Design of Quantum circuit with Number of qubits: 4, Hidden bit: 10, for Grover's algorithm (Case: 2).

Case: 3 Searching multiple target bits is also possible in Grover's algorithm. The simulation results of the Quantum circuit with the Number of qubits:5, multiple Hidden bit: 2,6,13,25 are shown in Figs. (**7a** to **7d**). Initially, all 5 qubits are initialized to |00000⟩. The Hadamard gates are then applied to create a principle of superposition of all 32 probable states, ensuring that each state has an equal probability amplitude. The oracle operation is crucial; it inverts the target state amplitude |00010⟩, |00110⟩, |01011⟩, |11001⟩ sign, distinguishing it from the others (Singh *et al.*, 2024)

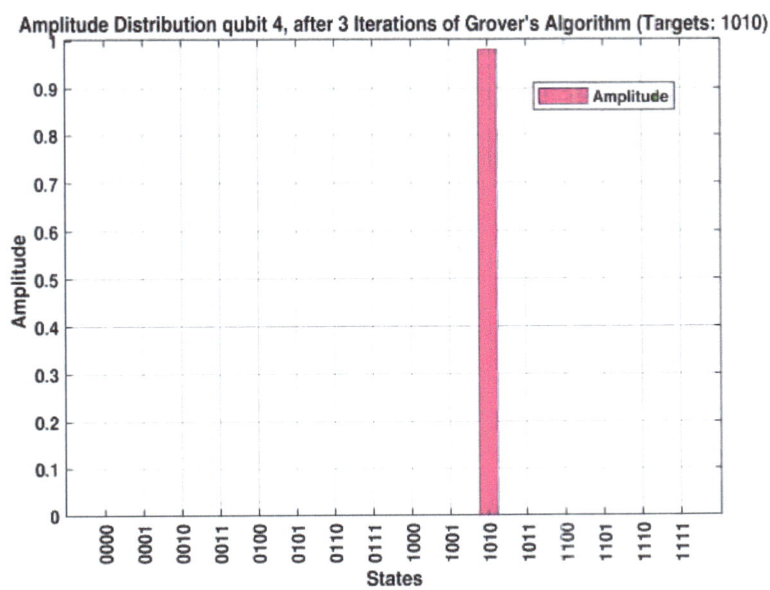

(Fig. 6) contd....

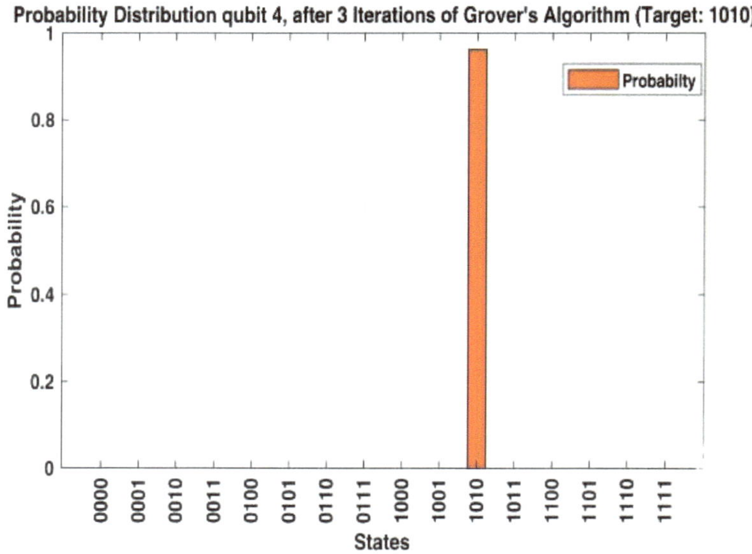

Fig. (6). Response of quantum state for case 2 under No. of iterations: 3 (a) percentage of probability distribution (b) Amplitude of state vector.

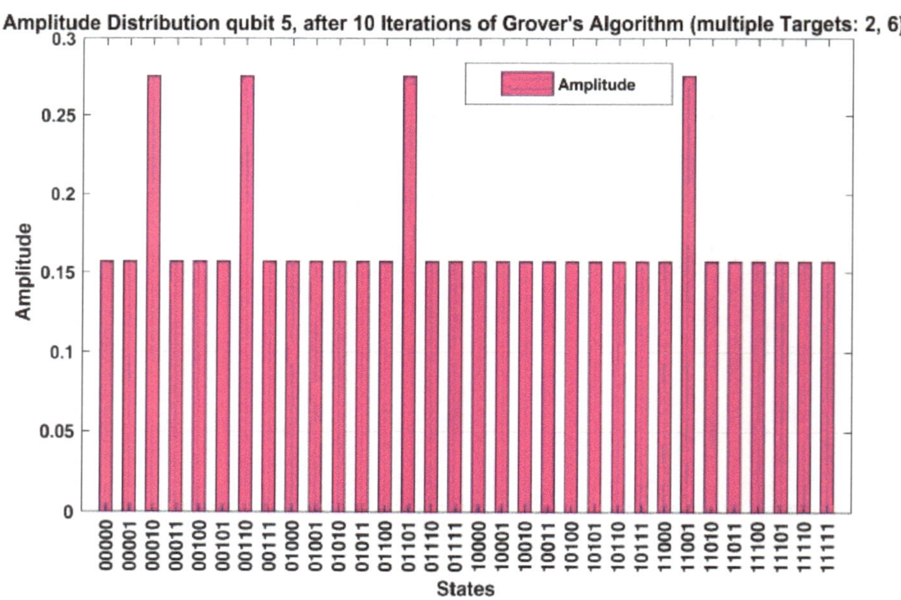

(Fig. 7) contd…

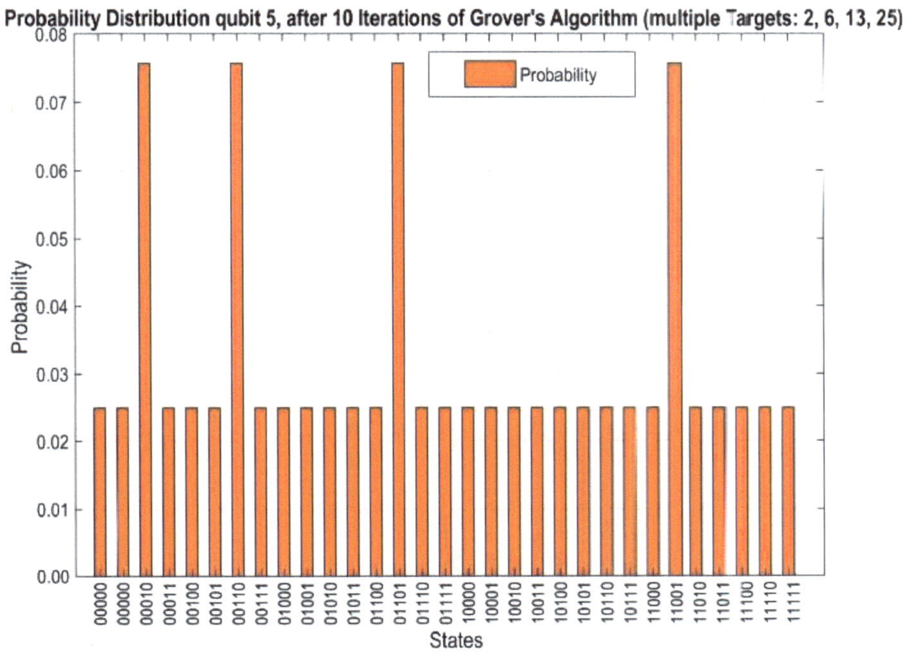
Probability Distribution qubit 5, after 10 Iterations of Grover's Algorithm (multiple Targets: 2, 6, 13, 25)
Probability
States

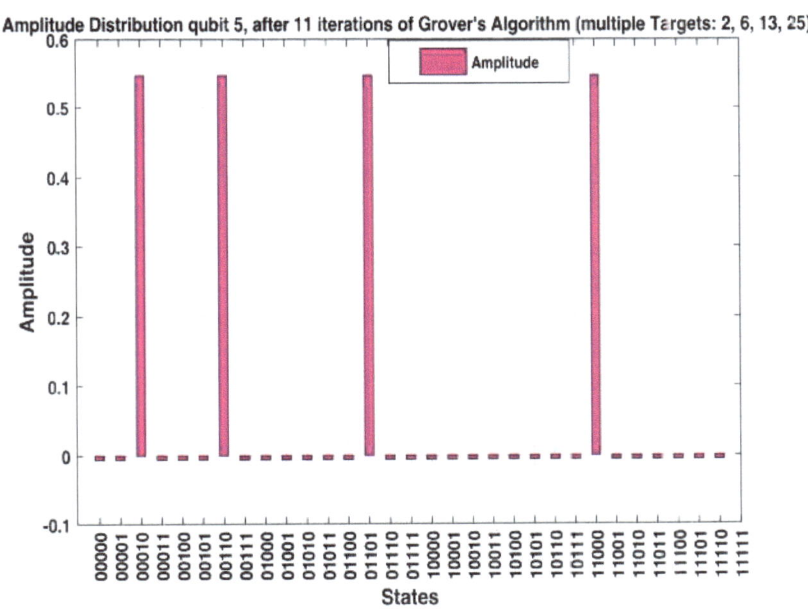
Amplitude Distribution qubit 5, after 11 iterations of Grover's Algorithm (multiple Targets: 2, 6, 13, 25)
Amplitude
States

(Fig. 7) contd…

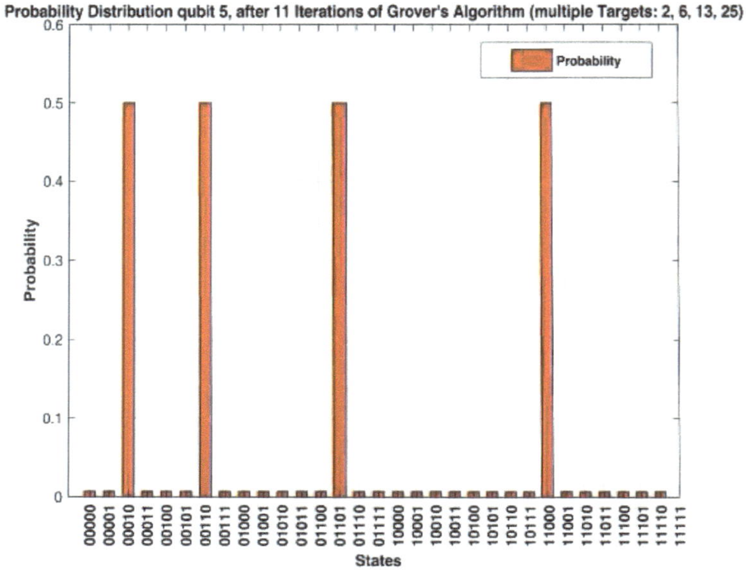

Fig. (7). Searching multiple target bits in Grover's algorithm (a) probability distribution of state vector after 10th iteration, (b) Amplitude of state vector after 10th iteration (c) probability distribution of state vector after 11th iteration, (d) Amplitude of state vector after 11th iteration.

Following the oracle, 'Then, we apply 'D' (Grover diffusion operator), which amplifies the probability of the perceptible states 00010, 00110, 01011, 11001, and drops the probabilities of all other states. This sequence of steps-Hadamard transformation, oracle application, and Grover diffusion- is repeated for 10 iterations to further enhance the likelihood of measuring |00010⟩, |00110⟩, |01011⟩, |11001⟩. Finally, measurement collapses the superposition, yielding a high probability (0.23281649) and amplitude (0.48251061*)* of observing the target states due to the constructive interference facilitated at iteration 10 by Grover's algorithm, as shown in Figs. (**7a** to **7d**). Grover's algorithm represents a powerful Qcom technique for unstructured search problems. It leverages quantum principles such as superposition and interference to achieve a quadratic speedup over classical search algorithms [24]. By iteratively applying transformations, the target state probability increases. Grover's algorithm provides a promising approach for accelerating tasks such as database search or optimization in Qcom applications [25].

For example, to find the factorization of the number 5, initialize a quantum circuit in Qiskit with 4 qubits and 2 classical bits. This setup is crucial as it defines the quantum register where operations will be performed and the classical bits where measurement results will be stored. The design of a quantum circuit for the factorization of number 5 under Shor's algorithm using Qiskit is shown in Fig.

(**8**). Hadamard gates are applied to all qubits in the quantum register. This step establishes a principle of superposition for all possible states, laying the foundation for quantum parallelism, where computations can be performed simultaneously across multiple states.

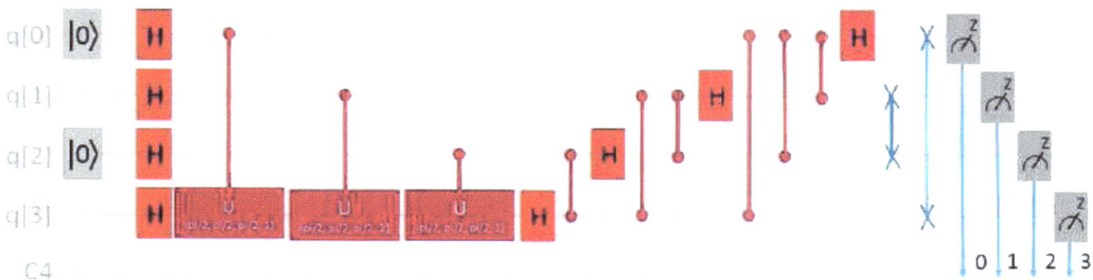

Fig. (8). Design of a Quantum circuit for factorizing number 5 using Shor's algorithm.

Implement modular exponentiation using controlled gates. For the chosen example with N=5 and a=2, this involves constructing a circuit that computes 2xmod 5. Modular exponentiation is a key component of Shor's algorithm, enabling efficient computation of powers modulo a modulus. The probability distribution is shown in Fig. (**9**). The quantum circuit is designed and measured, crumpling the quantum state onto classical bits.

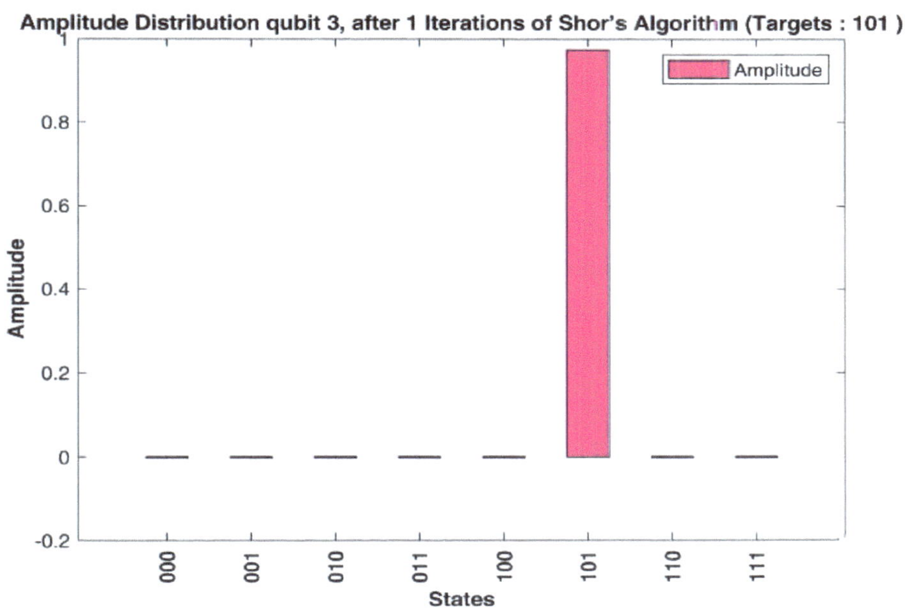

(Fig. 9) contd…

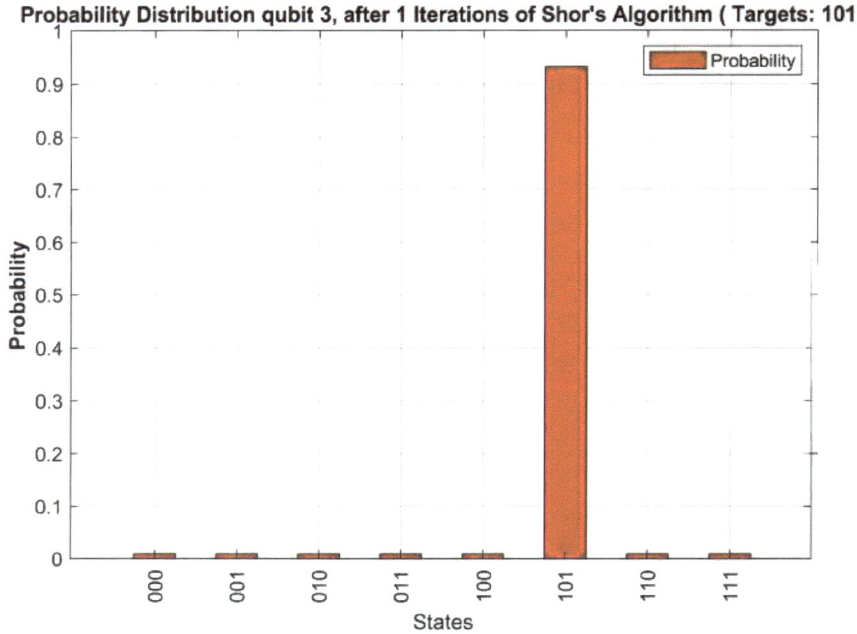

Fig. (9). Percentage of probability distribution for factorizing the number 5.

CONCLUSION

Qcom stands poised at the forefront of revolutionizing artificial intelligence and computing as we know it. From vastly accelerating complex calculations to unlocking new realms of machine learning and optimization, quantum technologies promise unparalleled advancements. Fundamental to this revolution are algorithms like Shor's, which promise to break current cryptographic standards by leveraging quantum parallelism to factor huge numbers exponentially faster than conventional computers. Similarly, Grover's algorithm offers unprecedented speedups in searching unstructured databases, revolutionizing optimization tasks central to AI. As we navigate towards harnessing quantum supremacy and expanding the quantum ecosystem, collaboration between researchers, industries, and governments will be pivotal. The future promises not just faster computers but a paradigm shift in problem-solving capabilities, ushering in an era where the once unimaginable becomes routine. As we venture into this uncharted territory, moreover, the fusion of AI and Qcom holds boundless potential to redefine what's possible in science, technology, and the human experience.

REFERENCES

[1] J. Ahn, "Toward quantum secured distributed energy resources: adoption of post-quantum cryptography (PQC) and quantum key distribution (QKD)", *Energies,* vol. 15, no. 3, p. 714, 2022.

[2] A. Ajagekar, and F. You, "Quantum computing based hybrid deep learning for fault diagnosis in electrical power systems", *Appl. Energy,* vol. 303, p. 117628, 2021.

[3] M. Kansal, "Enhancing real estate price prediction in smart cities: a comparative analysis of machine learning techniques", *International Conference on Advances in Distributed Computing and Machine Learning,* pp. 71-84, 2024.

[4] G. Benenti, G. Casati, and G. Strini, "Principles of quantum computation and information: volume I, basic concepts", *World Scientific,* 2004.

[5] G. Benenti, G. Casati, and G. Strini, "Principles of quantum computation and information: volume II, basic tools and special topics", *World Scientific,* 2007.

[6] A. Cowtan, "On the qubit routing problem", *Theory of Quantum Computation, Communication and Cryptography,* 2019.

[7] D. Deutsch, "Universality in quantum computation", *Proc. R. Soc. Lond. A,* vol. 449, pp. 669-677, 1995.

[8] M. H. Devoret, and R. J. Schoelkopf, "Superconducting circuits for quantum information: an outlook", *Science,* vol. 339, pp. 1169-1174, 2013.

[9] P. Krantz, "A quantum engineer's guide to superconducting qubits", *Appl. Phys. Rev.,* vol. 6, no. 2, p. 021318, 2019.

[10] P. Singh, "A transparency system for ICU using machine learning and AI", *Enhancing Medical Imaging with Emerging Technologies,* pp. 51-69, 2024.

[11] M. A. Nielsen, and I. L. Chuang, "Quantum computation and quantum information", *Cambridge University Press,* 2010.

[12] E. G. Rieffel, and W. H. Polak, "Quantum computing: a gentle introduction", *MIT Press,* 2011.

[13] C. Shao, "Reconsider HHL algorithm and its related quantum machine learning algorithms", *arXiv,* 2018.

[14] J. R. Shewchuk, "An introduction to the conjugate gradient method without the agonizing pain", *Carnegie Mellon University,* 1994.

[15] Z. Tang, "Quantum-secure microgrid", *IEEE Trans. Power Syst.,* vol. 36, no. 2, pp. 1250-1263, 2020.

[16] Z. Tang, "Quantum networks for resilient power grids: theory and simulated evaluation", *IEEE Trans. Power Syst.,* vol. 38, no. 2, pp. 1189-1204, 2022.

[17] P. Singh, "Real-time symptomatic disease predictor using multi-layer perceptron", *Future of AI in Medical Imaging,* pp. 155-167, 2024.

[18] A. Barenco, "Elementary gates for quantum computation", *Phys. Rev. A,* vol. 52, no. 5, p. 3457, 1995.

[19] N. D. Mermin, "Quantum computer science: an introduction", *Cambridge University Press,* 2007.

[20] M. Kansal, "A systematic study of services and security model in cloud computing: a brief overview", *Convergence of Cloud Computing, AI, and Agricultural Science,* pp. 1-16, 2023.

[21] A. Rayhan, and S. Rayhan, "Quantum computing and AI: a quantum leap in intelligence", *AI Odyssey,* p. 424, 2023.

[22] "Quantum computing: future of artificial intelligence and its applications", *Quantum Computing and Artificial Intelligence,* p. 163, 2023.

[23] Y. N. Prajapati, "A new approach of machine learning and deep learning algorithms based crop yield prediction", *IEEE International Conference on Quantum Technologies,* pp. 1-4, 2023.

[24] S. Kumar, "Quantum intelligence: merging AI and quantum computing for unprecedented power", *IEEE International Conference on Trends in Quantum Computing,* pp. 1-7, 2024.

[25] E. Hechler, "AI and quantum computing", *Deploying AI in the Enterprise,* pp. 273-295, 2020.

CHAPTER 13

Towards Safer Roads: Detecting Distracted Driver Behavior in Visual Media

Shweta Ran[1,*] and **Preeti Garg**[2]

[1] *Department of CSE & IT, Jaypee Institute of Information Technology, Noida, Uttar Pradesh, India*

[2] *Department of CSE, KIET Group of Institutions, Ghaziabad, Uttar Pradesh, India*

Abstract: Driving a car demands unwavering focus and attentiveness to ensure road safety. Failing to maintain alertness and concentration on the road and one's surroundings can lead to catastrophic consequences. Approximately 1.3 million people worldwide lose their lives in traffic accidents each year. In India, statistics from 2015-2019 reveal a staggering 23 lakh reported road accidents, averaging over 4.7 lakh annually. The objective of this research is to develop a robust system for detecting and categorizing a driver's activities while occupying the driver's seat. Leveraging various Machine Learning Models and Convolutional Neural Networks (CNNs), this system aims to discern whether the driver is operating the vehicle safely or engaging in activities that pose a risk of accidents or harm to others. Additionally, a comparative analysis of multiple machine learning models is performed to assess their individual accuracy in identifying distracted driver behaviors. This research contributes to the critical endeavour of reducing road accidents and saving lives by mitigating distracted driving behaviors.

Keywords: CNN, Distracted driver, Image classification, Machine learning, Video classification.

INTRODUCTION

A World Health Organization (WHO) survey finds that traffic accidents rank as the eighth most common cause of death globally, resulting in 1.3 million deaths yearly [1]. In addition, 20-50 million individuals are injured or disabled as a result of traffic accidents. The National Crime Research Bureau (NCRB) of the Government of India has determined that India has the highest number of road fatalities in the world, with a steady increase since 2006. In 2015, there were 1.46 lakh fatalities resulting from traffic accidents in India, and irresponsible driving

* **Corresponding author Shweta Ran:** Department of CSE & IT, Jaypee Institute of Information Technology, Noida, Uttar Pradesh, India; E-mail: shweta2610@gmail.com

Pancham Singh, Avinash Kumar Sharma, Mrignainy Kansal, & Amarjeet Prajapati (Eds.)

was identified as the leading cause [2]. In 2022, road accidents increased compared to 2021, according to an article published in the Times of India (Fig. **1**). Operating a vehicle is a responsibility that requires complex manipulations and the coordination of multiple senses. However, engaging in a variety of other distracting activities, such as using a cell phone, adjusting audio equipment, dining, or conversing with a passenger, can affect the driver. In its survey, WHO identified several risk factors, including human error, vehicle speed, intoxicated driver, non-use of seatbelts, child restraints, distracted driver, and hazardous road infrastructure, among others. In India, road safety is a major concern due to the country's large car population and complex traffic system. The nation has been implementing several regulations, programs, and awareness campaigns aimed at enhancing road safety. The main elements, difficulties, and resources pertaining to road safety in India include a high accident rate, diverse road users, driver behavior, vehicle safety, and infrastructure issues. Driver behavior is one of the primary reasons for road accidents [3]. A driver who is impaired or preoccupied is one of the leading causes of fatal road accidents. Typically, a drunk motorist loses control of the vehicle, resulting in an accident. To enhance road safety and reduce the number of accidents caused by driver error, identifying distracted drivers is the top priority. Detection systems can use various devices or technologies, such as cameras, sensors, or machine learning algorithms, to identify signs of distraction, including irregular or erratic driving behavior, inattention to the road, or failure to heed traffic signals.

1.68L: TOTAL DEATHS AT NEW HIGH

Traffic Rule Violation	Deaths In 2021	Deaths In 2022	% Of Total In 2022
Speeding	1,07,236	1,19,904	71.2
Driving drunk/on drugs	3,314	4,201	2.5
Driving wrong side/ violating lane rules	8,122	9,094	5.4
Using mobile phone	2,982	3,395	2.0
Jumping traffic signal	679	1,462	0.8
Others	31,639	30,435	18.1
Total deaths	1,53,972	1,68,491	

* Highest deaths among 2-wheeler riders (74,897), followed by pedestrians (32,825)
* UP registered most fatalities (22,595), followed by TN (17,884) & Maha (15,224)

Fig. (1). New article from Times of India showing total deaths [2].

Once a distracted driver has been identified, the system can alert the driver *via* visual, auditory, or haptic feedback, such as steering wheel vibration or alarm. In the event that law enforcement or emergency services are required, such as when a motorist becomes incapacitated or an accident occurs, the system can notify them. According to records from 2000-2024, researchers are actively working on driver behavior in road accidents (Fig. **2**).

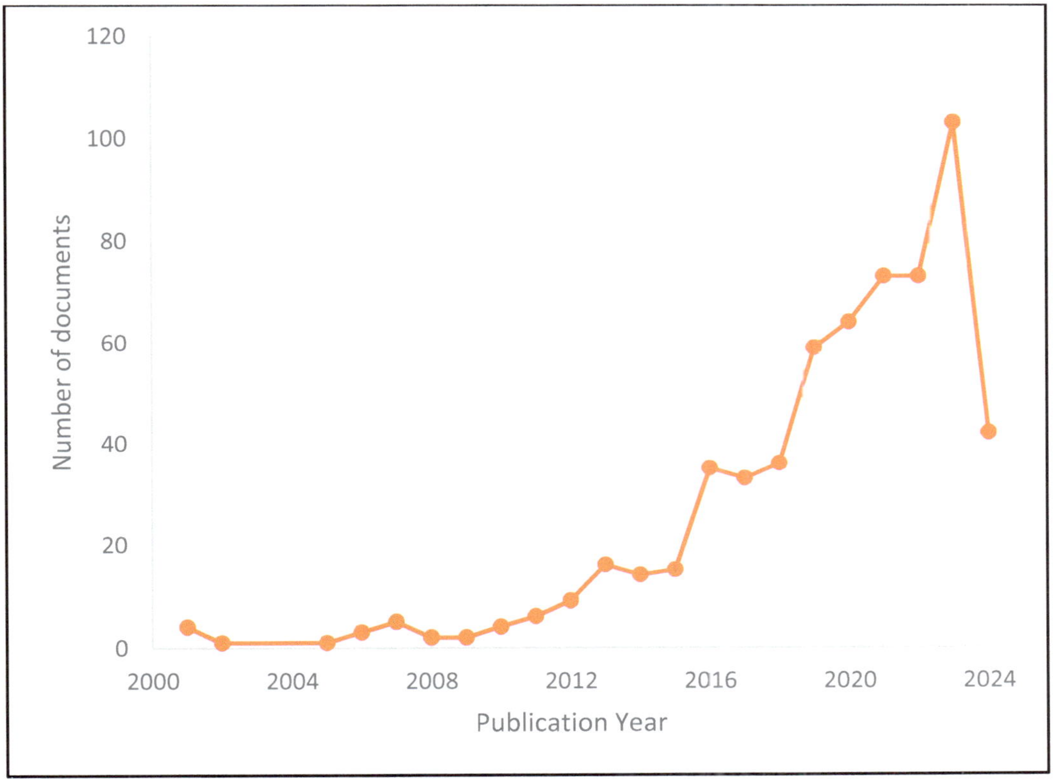

Fig. (2). Publication trend on driver behavior for road accidents.

Overall, distracted driver detection is essential for enhancing road safety, reducing accidents and fatalities, and encouraging responsible driving behavior. India is the second country actively working in this area, as shown in Fig. **3**, while the United States is the first.

LITERATURE SURVEY

This section compiles the work of researchers in the field of distracted driver detection.

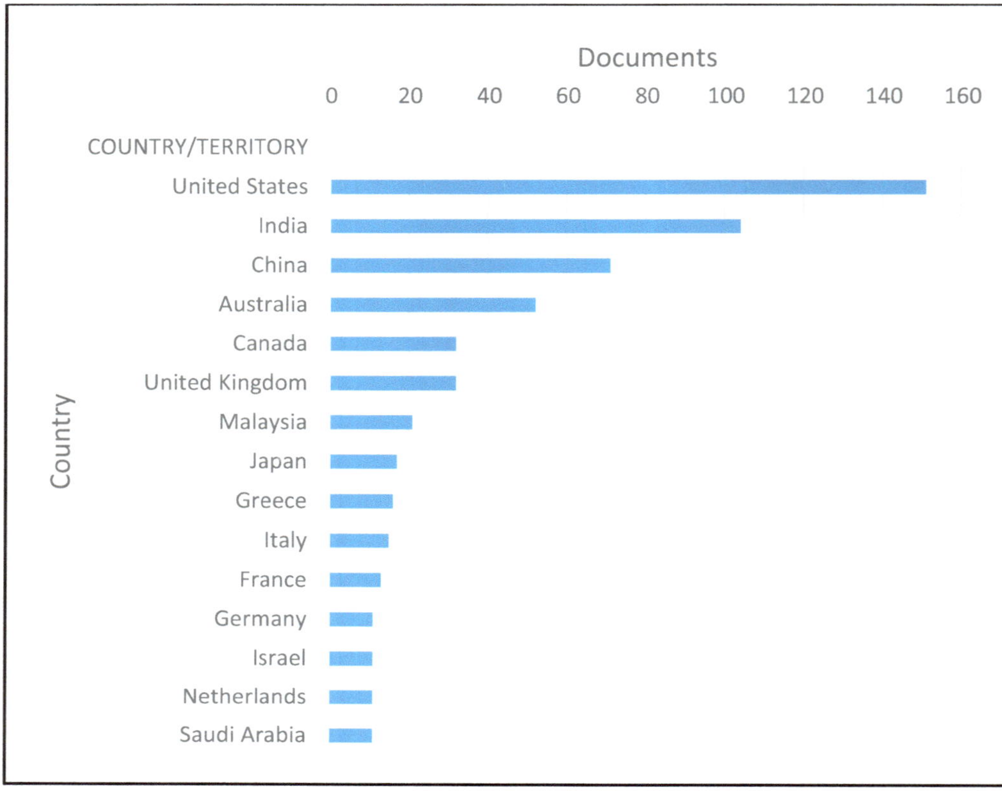

Fig. (3). Country-wise Publication on driver behavior for road accidents.

Alotalbi and Alotalbi conducted a literature review on the problem of detecting driver distractions using deep learning techniques. The authors emphasize the significance of detecting distracted driving in order to enhance road safety and provide an overview of the existing methods for driver distraction detection [4]. This paper provides a comprehensive discussion of deep learning techniques for driver distraction detection, including convolutional and recurrent neural networks, and contrasts their performance across different datasets (Fig. **3**).

Seshadri *et al.* [5] recorded the distinct positions of facial landmarks using a facial landmark tracking algorithm. Then, to assess whether a driver is using a cell phone, various characteristics are captured and categorized using previously trained classifiers. The authors also adopted a strategy to evaluate results from combining several classifiers, using pixel and other image characteristics to identify cell phone usage.

Choudhary *et al.* [6] accurately identified the driver's state utilizing OpenCV for object identification and feature-based image extraction. In addition to detecting drowsy driving, the proposed technology can operate in a variety of settings, including varying lighting, the use of eyeglasses, and facial hair, and focuses on CNN-based feature-extraction classification models. During training, the image features are extracted, transmitted to the classification layer, and fed into the SequeezeNet CNN architecture [7]. To classify the images, the accumulated features were fed into k-nearest neighbors, support vector machines, and random forests. The models were trained using 22,424 images of driver mistakes from a 10-class dataset. KNN, SVM, and RF models trained using images. The KNN model performed best in classification.

As a test scenario, Dalal and Triggs [8] employ linear SVM-based human detection. An experiment shows that feature sets currently available for human identification are significantly inferior to grids of Histograms of Oriented Gradient (HOG) descriptors, after analyzing various edge- and gradient-based descriptors.

The most effective Local Binary Pattern (LBP)-based method for characterizing a given texture was determined in a study [9]. After comparing a number of distinct approaches, the optimal fusion strategy is evaluated across multiple datasets and compared with numerous other approaches suggested in the literature. A random subspace ensemble of support vector machines and a separate support vector machine are evaluated. A comparison of various texture descriptors indicates that the performance of the suggested strategy in conjunction with the random subspace ensemble is preferable to that of other recent state-of-the-art approaches. This result is the result of in-depth research employing six benchmark databases spanning multiple disciplines.

Hossain *et al.* [10] conducted a literature review on the problem of detecting driver distractions utilizing deep learning techniques. The authors highlight distracted driving as a primary cause of road accidents and discuss the challenges of identifying it in real-world cases. The authors provide a detailed discussion of the deep learning methods used for a similar goal.

Darapaneni *et al.* [11] conducted a literature review on the issue of detecting driver fatigue using deep learning techniques. These are detailed, along with other techniques used for driver fatigue detection. The authors compare the efficacy of these methods on a variety of datasets and discuss their limitations and difficulties.

Feng and Yumeng [12] focused on identifying inattentive driving behaviors in images using multiple machine learning techniques. The model is fed images of the motorist captured while they are driving. Then, a vector is created by flattening and resizing these photographs. Each flattened vector is assigned a numeric designation in the range 0 to 9 based on the category to which it belongs.

In 2018, Baheti *et al.* [13] proposed a system that uses deep learning techniques to detect inattentive drivers. The paper emphasizes distracted driving as a leading cause of road accidents and describes their proposed system, which employs a deep convolutional neural network to classify drivers as distracted or not. The paper presents the results of their experiments, which demonstrate 96.44% accuracy in detecting inattentive driving, and compares their approach to other methods.

DATASET USED FOR DRIVER DETECTION

The dataset used for the current work, containing 22,424 images, is the State Farm Driver Detection dataset [14]. All images are coloured and have dimensions of 640 × 480 pixels. These pictures are broadly classified into 10 classes (Fig. **4**). In each picture, the driver is performing an activity in the car as indicated in the image.

The distribution of images per class is relatively balanced. Each of the total 10 classes is used to categorize the image dataset. Here, each category has approximately the same number of images. This is important because it prevents the model from being biased towards certain categories due to an uneven data distribution.

The image resolution is high enough to capture significant details of the driver's body, including the face and hands, which are important for identifying the driver's state. The JPEG file format for these images may make the images smaller in size, which can be beneficial for training models with limited computational resources.

The dataset, split into 2 parts, specifically training and test sets, is one of the standard practices in these models to evaluate the model's performance. The relatively smaller test set compared to the training set means the model's performance may be sensitive to the specific images chosen for the test set. Thus, it is preferred to validate the model's performance across multiple test sets to ensure consistent performance.

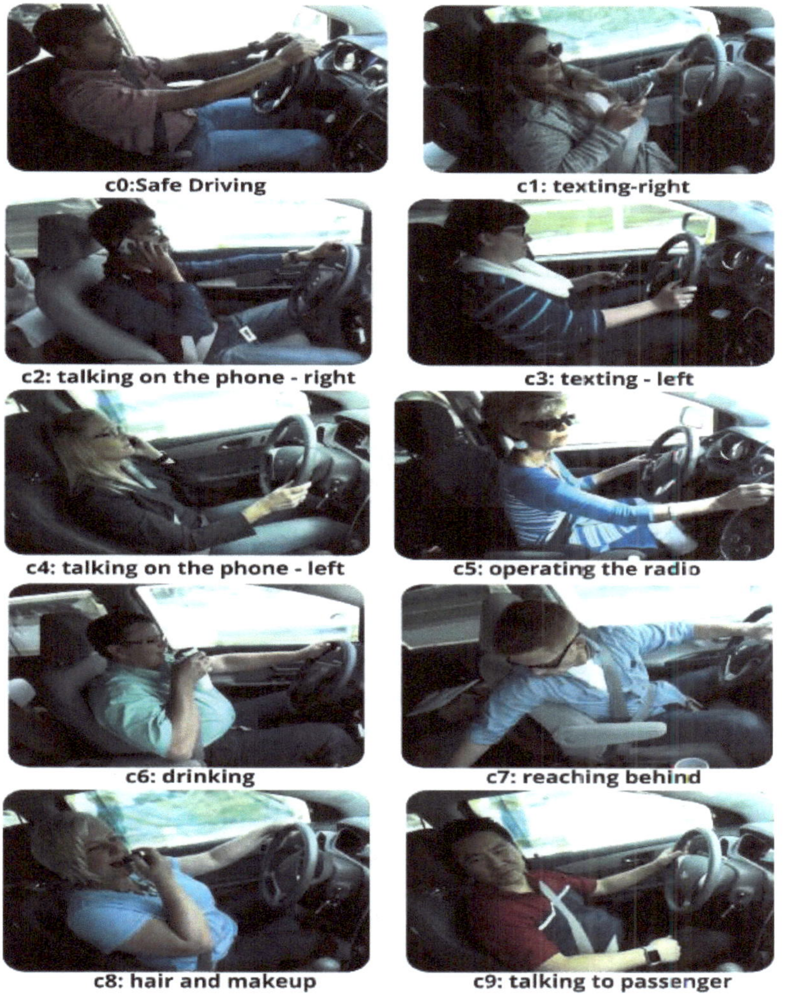

Fig. (4). Different classes of images based on the driver's behavior [14].

The dataset for models presents several challenges due to its high variability and complexity. The images used in this were collected under different lighting conditions, with different camera angles, and with varying amounts of motion blur. Additionally, the driver's appearance, clothing, and vehicles differ across images (Table **1**). Furthermore, some categories are visually similar to each other, making the classification task more difficult.

Table 1. Image dataset description.

Class	Description	No. of images
c0	Driving safely	2489
c1	Texting with the right hand	2267
c2	Talking on the phone with the right hand	2317
c3	Texting with the left hand	2346
c4	Talking on the phone with the left hand	2326
c5	Operating the radio	2312
c6	Drinking position	2325
c7	Reaching behind for something	2002
c8	Makeup or hair	1911
c9	Talking to a fellow passenger	2129

The high variability and complexity of the dataset make it harder for classification models to appropriately classify the driver's state. The differences in lighting conditions, camera angles, and motion blur may affect the quality and consistency of the images, making it difficult for the model to extract relevant features. The differences in the driver's appearances, clothing, and vehicles may also add additional noise to the images, making it more difficult to identify the driver's state.

Moreover, the fact that some categories are visually similar to one another poses a significant challenge for classification. For instance, the "talking on the phone" and "operating the radio or navigation system" categories may look similar, as both involve the driver using their hands to interact with a device. Therefore, the model must be able to distinguish between subtle differences in the images to classify them accurately.

Additionally, we have created a video dataset for distracted driver detection. Images were extracted from videos in real time, and driver activity was predicted. In the proposed work, various machine learning techniques, along with cnns, are implemented on both the image and the video datasets.

VARIOUS MODELS

In the past decade, machine learning and deep learning have marked their relevance in solving various issues in different sectors. Machine learning methods have been applied for distracted driver detection using decision trees [15], AdaBoost [16], K-nearest neighbors, and support vector machines [17]. Later, the benefits of Convolutional Neural Networks (CNNs) were also used for addressing the said issue.

AdaBoost trains weak classifiers repeatedly on training data, varying the weights of the training examples according to the performance of each classifier. The combined weak classifiers are weighted in the final model based on how well they performed on the training dataset. This method can handle complicated, non-linear interactions between the features and the output class and can be modified to accommodate various input feature types, making it useful for image detection.

Decision trees can handle a large number of input features, and their ability to handle nonlinear correlations between features and the output class makes them useful for image recognition tasks. In image recognition, features might include edge detection, texture, or color histogram features, all of which can be used to identify various objects or regions in an image. Decision trees can also handle noisy or missing data, which is frequently present in image recognition applications.

K-Nearest Neighbors (KNN) is a straightforward yet effective method for image detection. KNN works by finding the K-nearest neighbors of a given data point and using their weighted average or majority vote to determine the final label or prediction. This method can handle non-linear correlations between the features and the output class and is easily adaptable to various input feature types, making it useful for image detection.

Support Vector Machines (SVMs) are another effective method for image detection, based on the distances between the data points and the hyperplane. These models find the hyperplane that maximally separates the data into distinct classes. Since they can handle nonlinear interactions between the features and the output class, SVMs are effective for identifying intricate patterns and structures in the data, making them useful for image detection.

Convolutional Neural Networks (CNNs) [18], a type of deep learning model, are particularly effective for image detection. CNNs apply convolutional filters to the input image to extract important features such as corners, edges, and other relevant patterns useful for classification. These features are then passed through several fully connected layers, which perform the actual classification. This method is highly effective because it can automatically learn relevant features from raw input data without the need for manual feature extraction.

VARIOUS MACHINE LEARNING

Methods have been employed to classify distracted behaviors, with cnn-based models being the most commonly used [19]. used a convolutional two-stream network with multi-facial feature fusion to account for both static and dynamic information. a study [20] developed an ensemble of CNN models and observed that a genetic algorithm achieved a higher success rate in creating a weighted ensemble of classifiers. another widely used method is svms [21]; both linear and nonlinear svm classifiers can achieve a respectable level of accuracy. svm models are computationally less expensive and have the advantage of faster training, although cnn-based models typically achieve higher accuracy. another common strategy is semi-supervised learning, particularly when working with datasets that contain a large number of unlabeled images. semi-supervised approaches outperformed conventional supervised methods in terms of detection performance, according to [22]. shallow neural networks with feature extraction, random forests, and k-nearest neighbor are further strategies that have been investigated [23]. Proposed Model

The research aimed at identifying images, videos, and driver's activity and then classifying them into the appropriate class based on the identified features in the image [24]. The working flow of the model is illustrated in Fig. (**5**). The key steps taken in the work are as follows:

- Data gathering: Ten distinct classifications of driver activity, recorded by in-car cameras, are used in the State Farm Distracted Driver Detection Dataset.
- Data cleaning: The data may contain errors or irrelevant information that could negatively affect the model's performance. This stage entails purging the data of any extraneous details and mistakes.
- Image pre-processing: Image pre-processing is done to remove blur and noise from the photos. To eliminate any discrepancy, it is also crucial to make sure that all of the photographs have the same resolution.
- Image resizing: Consistency throughout the dataset is ensured by resizing all the images to a uniform size.
- Normalization: To make it simpler for the model to process, normalizing the picture pixels is crucial to make sure they fall within a specific range.
- Dataset split: Division of the dataset into training, validation, and testing sets. Training used 70% of the data, validation used 15%, and testing used 15%.
- Model definition: Python libraries such as 'sklearn' and PyTorch were imported to use the functionalities of different machine learning models and deep learning models.
- Model Training: The training dataset selected for this study was used to train the model. For CNN, backpropagation was used to optimize the loss function.

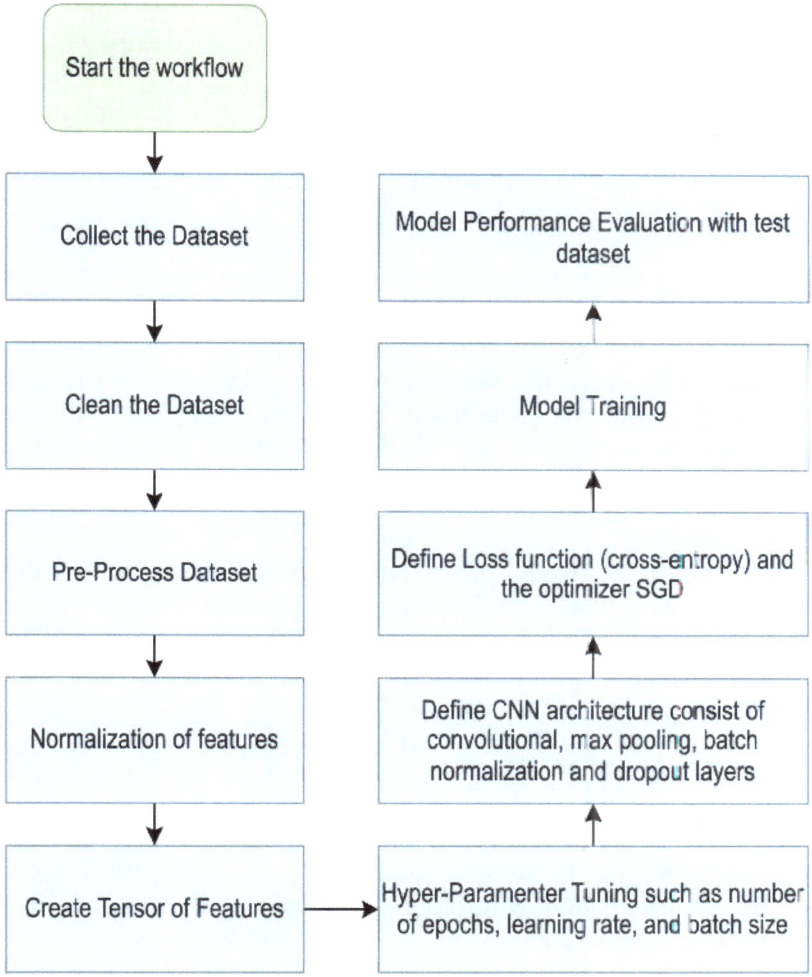

Fig. (5). Flowchart of the working model.

The images, or the array of pixels can be directly fed into this model and it yields some results, but the results are not as accurate and precise since this type of model training only takes into account the individual pixel intensities and does not account for the background colors, edge detection, and pixels around a particular pixel (utilizing a block of pixels together in training the model). These features are important for training the model, and hence there is a need for feature extraction techniques that yield the above-mentioned features for further processing and training [25]. There are several feature extraction techniques for extracting different kinds of features from images. In the proposed work, the feature extraction techniques, namely HOG and LBP, were used. Feature normalization was applied to scale the numerical values of the data to a common range. Then, dimensionality reduction techniques, specifically PCA and LDA, were applied to reduce the number of features and retain only the most important ones, thereby addressing overfitting and removing multicollinearity. Machine learning algorithms, including decision trees, AdaBoost, K-nearest neighbors, and support vector machines, were applied, and the results were gathered for classification.

A CNN model was subsequently trained using the images. The design of the model includes multiple convolutional and pooling layers, followed by fully connected layers and a final output layer. The number of convolutional and fully connected layers, as well as the number of filters per layer in the CNN, can be adjusted to tune the model's complexity [26]. The trained CNN is tested on a separate test dataset as part of the model assessment process. The accuracy statistic, which gauges the percentage of accurate classifications, is used to assess the model [26].

The CNN model learns to extract features from the pictures and map them to the appropriate class during the training phase. The model's output layer consists of 10 nodes, each representing a different class. The output layer generates a probability distribution over the 10 classes once a picture is run through the trained model.

For instance, the model determines the likelihood for each class (c0-c9) if the input picture shows a driver texting with their right hand. The motorist is probably texting with their right hand, according to the model's high likelihood for the class c9 outcome. For some other classes, such as c3, c4, or c5, the model may also assign a lower likelihood, suggesting that the driver is less likely to be involved in those activities.

The model's probability distribution can also be used to determine the classification's confidence level. The model is more confident in its forecast that the driver is texting with their right hand than it is in its prediction that the motorist is safely driving, for instance, if the model outputs a probability of 0.9 for c9 and a probability of 0.1 for c0. The model is less certain about its prediction and may need more testing if it assigns a probability of 0.5 to both c9 and c0.

Working Software for Driver Behavior Identification

An easy-to-use software is developed to identify the behavior of the driver (Fig. **6**). illustrates the outcome for an image.

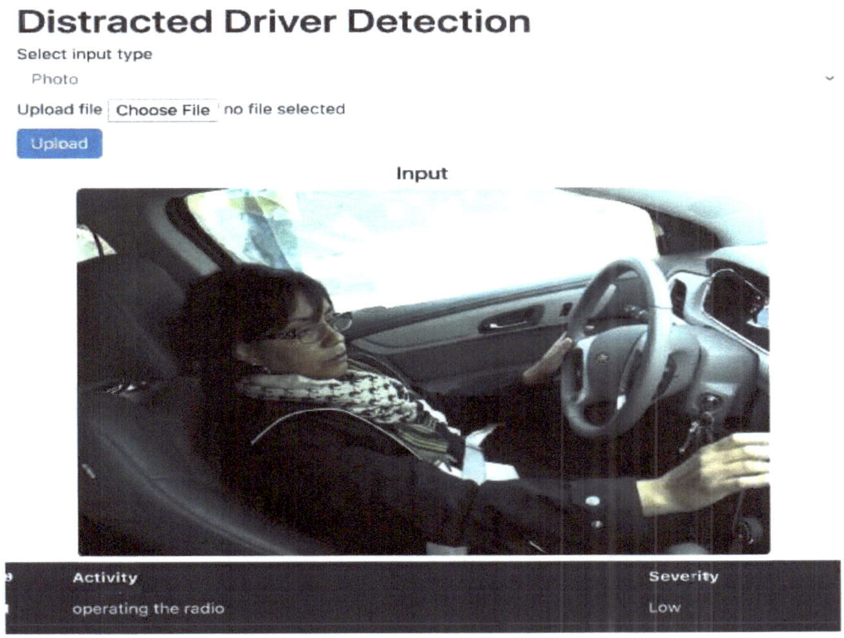

Fig. (6). Snapshot for driver behaviour based on image [14].

The system begins with the login process. After logging in, the system requests the user to upload an image of the driver. The image is uploaded and then pre-processed, including refinement and normalization for further processing. This normalized and refined image is passed through a CNN model containing several layers. Convolutional and pooling layers extract the most relevant features from the image, and the model predicts the output based on these features [30]. These features allow the system to identify the driver in various states, as depicted in Table **1**. Feedback is then provided to the user of the system.

Similarly, we have designed our system to process videos as well. For videos, we capture several frames and treat each frame as a separate image. These images are then processed using the CNN model, and the various states of the driver are returned as output. The videos are broken down into frames, and the activities in each frame are classified at regular intervals and displayed to the user. The user can also download a log of the activities.

RESULTS AND FINDINGS

The proposed classification technique is implemented and evaluated on the State Farm Driver Detection dataset. Here, the features from images and videos are extracted using HOG and LBP feature extraction algorithms. After this, the features are normalized, and dimensionality reduction techniques, namely PCA and LDA, are applied. Machine learning algorithms, namely decision trees, AdaBoost, K-nearest neighbors, and support vector machines, were applied.

Based on the accuracy metric, it is clear that each model's performance differs significantly from the others. AdaBoost attains the lowest accuracy for predicting driver behavior, while CNN outperforms the other models. The results indicate that, for our goal of identifying different classes of distracted drivers, a CNN outperformed conventional machine learning models. The accuracy of the CNN was 97.48%, which is greater than the accuracy of the KNN classifier, the top-performing machine learning model, which was 90.44%, as shown in Table **2**. The formula used for measuring accuracy is shown in Equation 1.

Table 2. Results based on different algorithms.

Classification Models	Success rate
AdaBoost	0.3946
Decision Tree	0.5588
K- Nearest Neighbor	0.9044
Support Vector Machine	0.9093
Convolution Neural Network	0.9748

Accuracy (Success rate) = TP + TNTP + FP + TN + FN (1)

The functioning of the proposed model was also evaluated across multiple images and videos. The model was also tested for videos. Each frame is treated as a single image and classified based on the activity. As illustrated in (Fig. **7**), the CNN model's confusion matrix depicts the predicted classification for each class. The effectiveness of the implemented model is generally assessed using a confusion matrix. There are a total of 10 classes in this work dataset, starting with C0 to C9. As per the matrix, for class C0, 639 instances are correctly classified, but 3 are misclassified as class 8.

Testing of the Software

We tested our developed software on various images. We created test cases for each class and found an image for each class. With our model, we predicted the class of the image. A few test cases that we have executed for our model are listed in Table **3**.

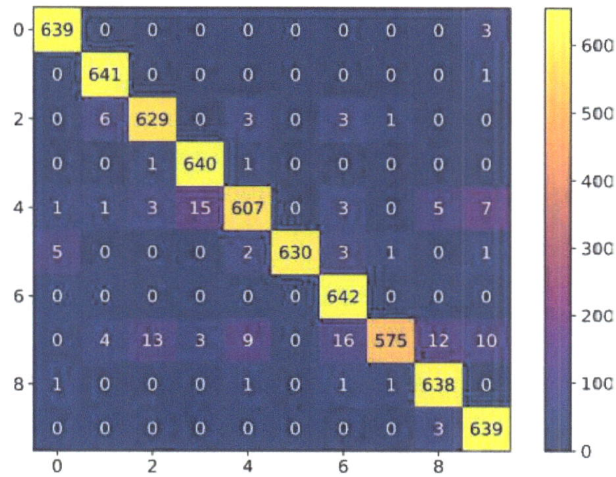

Fig. (7). Confusion matrix for the trained CNN model.

Table 3. List of a few test cases for testing the model.

Sample Test cases	Driver image for input	Outcome from our model	Expected Response	Status
1	**Image with resolution 1024x768 and good quality [14]**	Talking to a Passenger	Reaching Behind	Fail
2	**Image with resolution 640x480 and good quality [14]**	Operating the Radio	Operating the Radio	Pass
3	**Image with resolution 320x480 and low quality [14]**	Drinking	Drinking	Pass

CONCLUSION

The proposed and implemented algorithm offers a viable method for identifying and categorizing instances of driver distraction while driving, for both captured images and videos. The proposed work has implemented various machine learning techniques, such as decision trees, support vector machines, K-nearest neighbors, and AdaBoost. A CNN model is trained on the image and video dataset obtained from State Farm. Several test cases were executed to evaluate the efficacy of the approach. The accuracy of the CNN model was measured to determine the best-performing model for our objective. The results demonstrate the model's effectiveness in successfully detecting various forms of distracted driving behavior, such as texting, phone conversations, and eating, achieving commendable accuracy levels. The research concludes that behavior detection is performed best using the CNN model compared to traditional machine learning techniques.

Nevertheless, it is imperative to acknowledge certain limitations inherent to our solution. The model's performance is contingent on a single dataset, which may not encompass the full spectrum of real-world driving scenarios. To further advance the field of distracted driver behavior detection, future research should consider expanding the dataset to include a broader array of distracting situations, thus enhancing the model's versatility. By addressing these limitations, traffic safety can be further improved, and incidents related to distracted driving can be reduced.

CONSENT FOR PUBLICATION

The paper titled *"Towards Safer Roads: Detecting Distracted Driver Behavior in Visual Media"* utilizes a publicly available dataset from Kaggle, comprising 22,424 images. The dataset has been appropriately cited in the manuscript, both through a direct link and in Section 3 *via* a formal reference. Fig. (**4**) presents a representative collection of images sourced from this dataset. Fig. (**6**) and Table **3** illustrate the output generated by the implemented software; these are actual snapshots obtained during the execution of the system.

Dataset link: https://kaggle.com/competitions/state-farm-distracted-driver-detection

REFERENCES

[1] *Road traffic injuries*.https://www.who.int/news-room/fact-sheets/detail/road-traffic-injuries

[2] K. Annadurai, G. Mani, and R. Danasekaran, "Recurring tragedy of road traffic accidents in India: Challenges and opportunities", *Indian J. Crit. Care Med.,* vol. 19, no. 7, pp. 434-435, 2015. [http://dx.doi.org/10.4103/0972-5229.160303] [PMID: 26180444]

[3] C. Huff, "Vital stats", *Trustee: The Journal for Hospital Governing Boards,* vol. 68, no. 8, pp. 8-12, 2015.

[4] M. Alotaibi, and B. Alotaibi, "Distracted driver classification using deep learning", *Signal Image Video Process.,* vol. 14, no. 3, pp. 617-624, 2020. [http://dx.doi.org/10.1007/s11760-019-01589-z]

[5] K. Seshadri, F. Juefei-Xu, D.K. Pal, M. Savvides, and C.P. Thor, "Driver cell phone usage detection on Strategic Highway Research Program (SHRP2) face view videos", *2015 IEEE Conference on Computer Vision and Pattern Recognition Workshops (CVPRW),* 2015 [http://dx.doi.org/10.1109/CVPRW.2015.7301397]

[6] Y. Choudhary, A. Aggarwal, and A. Agarwal, "Detecting drivers' drowsiness using Haar cascade classifier", In: *2022 9th International Conference on Computing for Sustainable Global Development (INDIACom)*, 2022, pp. 318-322.

[7] S.K.S. Al-doorı, Y.S. Taspınar, and M. Koklu, "Distracted driving detection with machine learning methods by CNN based feature extraction", *International Journal of Applied Mathematics Electronics and Computers,* vol. 9, no. 4, pp. 116-121, 2021. [http://dx.doi.org/10.18100/ijamec.1035749]

[8] N. Dalal, and B. Triggs, "Histograms of oriented gradients for human detection", *2005 IEEE Computer Society Conference on Computer Vision and Pattern Recognition (CVPR 05),* 2005

[http://dx.doi.org/10.1109/CVPR.2005.177]

[9] L. Nanni, A. Lumini, and S. Brahnam, "Survey on LBP based texture descriptors for image classification", *Expert Syst. Appl.,* vol. 39, no. 3, pp. 3634-3641, 2012. [http://dx.doi.org/10.1016/j.eswa.2011.09.054]

[10] M.U. Hossain, M.A. Rahman, M.M. Islam, A. Akhter, M.A. Uddin, and B.K. Paul, "Automatic driver distraction detection using deep convolutional neural networks", *Intelligent Systems with Applications,* vol. 14, p. 200075, 2022. [http://dx.doi.org/10.1016/j.iswa.2022.200075]

[11] N. Darapaneni, J. Arora, M. Hazra, N. Vig, S.S. Gandhi, S. Gupta, and A.R. Paduri, "Detection of distracted driver using convolution neural network", *ArXiv,* 2022. [http://dx.doi.org/10.48550/arXiv.2204.03371]

[12] D. Feng, and Y. Yumeng, *Machine Learning Techniques for Distracted Driver Detection.*, 2019, pp. 1-6.

[13] B. Baheti, S. Gajre, and S. Talbar, "Detection of distracted driver using convolutional neural network", *2018 IEEE/CVF Conference on Computer Vision and Pattern Recognition Workshops (CVPRW),* 2018 [http://dx.doi.org/10.1109/CVPRW.2018.00150]

[14] A. Montoya, and D. Holman, https://kaggle.com/competitions/state-farm-distracted-driver-detection

[15] M.K. Wali, M. Murugappan, and B. Ahmmad, "Wavelet packet transform based driver distraction level classification using EEG", *Math. Probl. Eng.,* vol. 2013, pp. 1-10, 2013. [http://dx.doi.org/10.1155/2013/297587]

[16] F. Omerustaoglu, C.O. Sakar, and G. Kar, "Distracted driver detection by combining in-vehicle and image data using deep learning", *Appl. Soft Comput.,* vol. 96, p. 106657, 2020. [http://dx.doi.org/10.1016/j.asoc.2020.106657]

[17] C. Craye, and F. Karray, "Driver distraction detection and recognition using RGB-D sensor", *Proc.CVPR,* 2015pp. 1-11 Las Vegas, USA

[18] M. Çetinkaya, and T. Acarman, "Driver impairment detection using decision tree based feature selection and classification", *Results in Engineering,* vol. 18, p. 101025, 2023. [http://dx.doi.org/10.1016/j.rineng.2023.101025]

[19] W. Liu, J. Qian, Z. Yao, X. Jiao, and J. Pan, "Convolutional two-stream network using multi-facial feature fusion for driver fatigue detection", *Future Internet,* vol. 11, no. 5, p. 115, 2019. [http://dx.doi.org/10.3390/fi11050115]

[20] H.M. Eraqi, Y. Abouelnaga, M.H. Saad, and M.N. Moustafa, "Driver distraction identification with an ensemble of convolutional neural networks", *J. Adv. Transp.,* vol. 2019, pp. 1-12, 2019. [http://dx.doi.org/10.1155/2019/4125865]

[21] O.A. Osman, M. Hajij, S. Karbalaieali, and S. Ishak, "A hierarchical machine learning classification approach for secondary task identification from observed driving behavior data", *Accid. Anal. Prev.,* vol. 123, pp. 274-281, 2019. [http://dx.doi.org/10.1016/j.aap.2018.12.005] [PMID: 30554059]

[22] T. Liu, Y. Yang, G.B. Huang, Y.K. Yeo, and Z. Lin, "Driver distraction detection using semi-supervised machine learning", *IEEE Trans. Intell. Transp. Syst.,* vol. 17, no. 4, pp. 1108-1120, 2016. [http://dx.doi.org/10.1109/TITS.2015.2496157]

[23] Z. Li, Q. Zhang, and X. Zhao, "Performance analysis of K-nearest neighbor, support vector machine, and artificial neural network classifiers for driver drowsiness detection with different road geometries", *Int. J. Distrib. Sens. Netw.,* vol. 13, no. 9, 2017. [http://dx.doi.org/10.1177/1550147717733391]

[24] P. Singh, M. Kansal, R. Singh, S. Kumar, and C. Sen, "A hybrid approach based on haar cascade, softmax, and CNN for human face recognition: A hybrid approach for human face recognition", *J. Sci.*

Ind. Res. (India), vol. 83, no. 4, pp. 414-423, 2024. [JSIR].

[25] S. Kaplan, M.A. Guvensan, A.G. Yavuz, and Y. Karalurt, "Driver behavior analysis for safe driving: A survey", *IEEE Trans. Intell. Transp. Syst.,* vol. 16, no. 6, pp. 3017-3032, 2015. [http://dx.doi.org/10.1109/TITS.2015.2462084]

[26] M.H. Alkinani, W.Z. Khan, and Q. Arshad, "Detecting human driver inattentive and aggressive driving behavior using deep learning: Recent advances, requirements and open challenges", *IEEE Access,* vol. 8, pp. 105008-105030, 2020. [http://dx.doi.org/10.1109/ACCESS.2020.2999829]

SUBJECT INDEX

Pancham Singh, Avinash Kumar Sharma, Mrignainy Kansal, & Amarjeet Prajapati (Eds.)

P

Q

R

S

T

U

V

W

Y